Bridging Worlds

The Power of Heritage Languages in Social Cohesion

Edited by

Fabrice Jaumont and Jane F. Ross

CALEC – TBR Books
New York – Paris

Copyright © 2026 by Fabrice Jaumont and Jane F. Ross

All rights reserved. No part of this publication may be reproduced, distributed, or transmitted in any form or by any means without prior written permission.

TBR Books is a program of the Center for the Advancement of Languages, Education, and Communities. We publish researchers and practitioners who seek to engage diverse communities in education, languages, cultural history, and social initiatives.

CALEC – TBR Books
750 Lexington Avenue, 9th floor
New York, NY 10022
USA
www.calec.org | contact@calec.org

Cover illustration © Raymond Verdaguer
Cover design © Toscane Landréa

ISBN 978-1-63607-562-4 (Hardcover)
ISBN 978-1-63607-901-1 (Paperback)
ISBN 978-1-63607-561-7 (eBook)

Library of Congress Control Number: 2026931185

Table of Contents

Acknowledgements 9

Introduction:
Mapping Heritage Languages, Identity, and Social Cohesion
Fabrice Jaumont and Jane F. Ross 11

Part I – Foundations: Policies, Theory, Global Perspectives 15

Chapter 1 Sealing the Deal: The Role of Heritage Language Policies in Fostering National Cohesion and Preserving Diversity in the United States
Fabien Rivière Copa 17

Chapter 2 Advancing Social Cohesion Among Heritage Language Schools, Immigrant Populations, and Formal Language Education in the United States
Richard D. Brecht and Joy Kreeft Peyton 41

Chapter 3 Streamlining Heritage Language Education in Europe: From European Policies to State Support Measures
Renata Emilsson Peskova, Marie Boccou Kestřánková, Lenka Vaněčková, and Michaela Chlostová Munoz 69

Chapter 4 The Role of the French Heritage Language Program in Promoting Bilingualism and Cultural Integration for Francophone Students in the United States
Yann Gaboriau 95

Chapter 5 On How to Bridge Communication Between Multilingual Families and Schools: Tonga Schools Network
Isabelle Barth, Miglena Hristozova, and Antri Kanikli 117

Part II – Families, Identity, Intergenerational Transmission 131

Chapter 6 Teachers of Portuguese as a Heritage Language: Their Profiles, Contexts, and Perspectives
Felicia Jennings-Winterle 133

Chapter 7 Korean-American Parents' Efforts to Transmit the Korean Language to their Third-Generation Korean-American Children
Hanae Kim 153

Chapter 8 Portuguese in the Heart: Identity, Belonging, and Heritage Language from Adolescents' Perspectives
Ana Lucia Lico 173

Chapter 9 "Harmonizing Hyphens": Navigating Multiracial Identities in Mandarin-English Bilingual Classrooms
Jasmine Pham 199

Chapter 10 Between Two Worlds: The Arabic Language and Identity in Italy's Second Generation
Haifa Alsakkaf 221

Chapter 11 Bridging Worlds: Exploring the Dual Identities of Arabic Heritage Students
Issam Salameh Albdairat 233

Part III – Schools, Communities, Innovation 249

Chapter 12 Transformation of Heritage Language Schools during the Pandemic: Connectivity, Community, and Identity
Nina Paulovicova, Renata Emilsson Peskova, and Marta McCabe 251

Chapter 13 The Challenges of Albanian Heritage Language Schools in Canada
Marigona Morina 277

Chapter 14 Home is a Language : Building Diaspora Belonging Through Heritage Tongues
Djeneba Deby Bagayoko 295

Chapter 15 The Arabic Speaking Competition: A Tool for
Heritage Language Motivation and Identity Affirmation
Tony Calderbank, Janine Elya, and Chase Smithburg 307

Chapter 16 English as a Heritage Language: A Case Study in
Calabria, Southern Italy
Elizabeth Wardy, Jessica Salerno, and Steven J. Sacco 335

Chapter 17 Translanguaging in a Third Space: Enhancing
multilingualism and literacy through a bilingual buddy reading
program in South Africa.
Sibhekinkosi Anna Nkomo 357

Chapter 18 AI For Heritage Language Learning: Insights from
Mind Genomics
Angela Popovic 383

Conclusion:
Toward a Transformative Multilingual Future
Fabrice Jaumont and Jane F. Ross..399

About the Authors..403

About TBR Books 409

About CALEC 451

Acknowledgements

Our collaboration began in 2005 with the creation of the French Heritage Language Program in New York. Still thriving today, the program has served thousands of students and has expanded nationwide as part of the Embassy of France's French for All initiative, inaugurated by President Emmanuel Macron. What began as a shared project has become a lasting partnership, and this book—emerging nearly twenty years later—carries deep personal and professional significance for both of us.

Bridging Worlds has its roots in a 2011 conference on heritage languages and social cohesion that we organized and that was hosted by the Lycée Français de New York. That gathering of scholars, educators, and advocates sparked conversations and collaborations that have come to fruition in this volume.

We extend our heartfelt thanks to the authors of *Bridging Worlds*, whose research, insight, and dedication made this volume possible. Their contributions offer a rich and compelling exploration of heritage languages, deepening our collective understanding of identity, community, and multilingual education. We gratefully acknowledge the following contributors, listed in alphabetical order: Issam Salameh Albdairat, Haifa Alsakkaf, Djeneba Bagayoko, Isabelle Barth, Marie Boccou Kestřánková, Richard Brecht, Tony Calderbank, Michaela Chlostová Muñoz, Janine Elya, Renata Emilsson Peskova, Yann Gaboriau, Miglena Hristozova, Felicia Jennings-Winterle, Antri Kanikli, Hanae Kim, Ana Lucia Lico, Marta McCabe, Marigona Morina, Anna Nkomo, Nina Paulovicova, Joy Peyton, Jasmine Pham, Angela Popovic, Fabien Rivière Copa, Steven Sacco, Jessica Salerno, Chase Smithburg, Lenka Vaněčková, and Elizabeth Wardy.

We also thank the institutions and communities that supported each contributor's work and sustained the broader efforts reflected in this volume. Special thanks are due to French artist and illustrator Raymond Verdaguer for generously gifting us a magnificent cover illustration, and to graphic designer Toscane Landréa for transforming it into a beautiful cover design. We are especially grateful to CALEC (The Center for the Advancement of Languages, Education, and Communities) for supporting this project from its initial vision through publication.

Bridging Worlds reflects the shared commitment of a global community to honoring heritage languages and multilingual identities. We are grateful to all who helped build this bridge.

Fabrice Jaumont & Jane F. Ross

Introduction

Mapping Heritage Languages, Identity, and Social Cohesion

Fabrice Jaumont and Jane F. Ross

Heritage languages play a vital role in promoting social cohesion, shaping identity, and sustaining cultural diversity in today's interconnected and mobile world. More than mere vehicles for communication, they embody family histories, ancestral memory, and cultural heritage, anchoring individuals to communities that often stretch across continents. By maintaining linguistic ties to ancestral homelands, heritage languages foster intergenerational continuity and validate the identities of migrants and minority groups. They strengthen relationships within families, enhance mutual respect between cultural groups, and contribute to the development of inclusive civic societies. In doing so, heritage languages act as catalysts for social cohesion, civic participation, and intercultural dialogue, reinforcing the social fabric of increasingly multilingual societies.

This volume, *Bridging Worlds: The Power of Heritage Languages in Social Cohesion*, examines the complex relationships between heritage languages and societal integration. By bringing together contributions from scholars, educators, policymakers, and community activists, it highlights how heritage languages influence personal and group identity, community belonging, and intergenerational transmission. Spanning diverse regions—from European policy frameworks and North American bilingual classrooms to South African township schools and Calabrian villages shaped by reverse migration—the chapters reveal that heritage languages are not static cultural remnants. Instead, they are dynamic resources that evolve with each generation, enabling communities to negotiate hybrid identities, sustain cultural diversity, and build inclusive civic futures.

At a personal level, heritage languages allow individuals to construct and express hybrid identities. Adolescents often describe their heritage tongues as "languages of the heart," a phrase Ana Lucia Lico uses to characterize Brazilian teenagers' emotional connection to Portuguese as a bridge to family intimacy and the wider Brazilian diaspora. Jasmine Pham shows how multiracial students in Canadian Mandarin-English bilingual programs use their heritage languages to navigate cultural complexities, negotiate belonging, and resist marginalization. Hanae Kim examines Korean-American families, demonstrating the emotional labor and strategic decisions required to maintain Korean across three generations. Haifa Alsakkaf's research on Arabic-speaking youth in Italy and Issam Albdairat's work on Arabic heritage students in the United States further illustrate how heritage languages mediate between ancestral ties and host-society integration. Felicia Jennings-Winterle shifts the lens to educators, many of them immigrant women, whose work teaching Portuguese in diaspora contexts demonstrates how heritage languages are passed on not only through families but also through community institutions.

At the societal level, heritage languages function as bridges for integration and civic participation. Fabien Rivière Copa analyzes the U.S. Seal of Biliteracy, showing how the institutional recognition of multilingualism transforms it from a perceived obstacle to a civic asset that promotes national cohesion. Richard Brecht and Joy Kreeft Peyton examine community-based heritage language schools in the United States, arguing that these schools serve not only as language-maintenance hubs but also as crucial spaces of immigrant social cohesion by connecting families to mainstream education. Renata Emilsson Peskova, Marie Boccou Kestřánková, Lenka Vaněčková, and Michaela Chlostová Muñoz extend this discussion to Europe, exposing the discrepancy between multilingual ideals and practical policy support. Yann Gaboriau's study of the *French for All* initiative illustrates how institutional partnerships can frame heritage languages as cultural and economic resources. Similarly, Isabelle Barth, Miglena Hristozova, and Antri Kanikli's analysis of the Tonga Schools Network demonstrates how inclusive school policies in Europe can empower multilingual families and enhance educational equity.

The bridging function of heritage languages is particularly visible in grassroots initiatives and moments of disruption. Nina Paulovicova, Renata Emilsson Peskova, and Marta McCabe document how heritage schools in Alberta used the challenges of the COVID-19 pandemic to build virtual diasporic classrooms that sustained both language learning and community ties. Marigona Morina highlights the resilience of underfunded Albanian heritage schools in Canada, showing how committed educators and parents keep the language alive despite resource scarcity. Djeneba Bagayoko reframes heritage languages as forms of social capital, describing how they create informal networks of belonging and mutual support in migrant diasporas. Tony Calderbank, Janine Elya, and Chase Smithburg's chapter on Arabic-speaking competitions in the United Kingdom demonstrates how public performance can transform private language use into collective pride and motivation. Steven Sacco, Jessica Salerno, and Elizabeth Wardy expand the notion of heritage by exploring English as a heritage language in Calabria, where reverse migration has redefined linguistic belonging. Anna Nkomo presents a pedagogical innovation from South Africa, showing how translanguaging practices in buddy reading programs enhance literacy, self-esteem, and cultural pride among township students. Angela Popovic closes the volume by looking to the future, exploring how AI-driven learning platforms personalize heritage language acquisition, create global peer networks, and reshape intergenerational transmission in the digital age.

The book is organized into three thematic parts. Part I, Foundations: Policies, Theory, and Global Perspectives, outlines the conceptual and policy frameworks necessary for understanding heritage languages as public goods. Rivière Copa, Brecht and Peyton, Emilsson Peskova and colleagues, Gaboriau, and Barth, Hristozova, and Kanikli collectively argue that coherent policies and inclusive institutional practices are crucial for framing multilingualism as a civic strength and for embedding social cohesion into education systems. Part II, Families, Identity, and Intergenerational Transmission, shifts the focus to the intimate spaces of family and community. Kim, Lico, Pham, Alsakkaf, Albdairat, and Jennings-Winterle illustrate how heritage languages are central to identity formation, intergenerational solidarity, and emotional well-being, while also showing how families and educators negotiate the pressures of assimilation and language shift. Part III, Schools, Communities, and Innovation, emphasizes grassroots resilience and forward-looking strategies. Paulovicova and colleagues, Morina, Bagayoko, Calderbank and co-authors, Wardy, and co-authors, Nkomo, and Popovic show how communities, educators, and technological innovators sustain heritage languages in the face of migration, resource scarcity, and global crises, often turning challenges into opportunities for creativity and renewed engagement.

Taken together, these chapters show that heritage languages are not static relics but evolving practices shaped by agency, adaptation, and innovation. They strengthen cultural diversity, build bridges between communities, and foster inclusive civic futures. This volume calls for a shift in perspective: from viewing heritage languages as private family traditions to recognizing them as public goods that enrich education, nurture intercultural understanding, and reinforce social cohesion. Heritage languages are, quite literally, bridges between worlds—between past and future, between generations, and among culturally diverse communities. Supported through thoughtful policy, innovative pedagogy, and community engagement, they have the power to shape empathetic, inclusive, and culturally vibrant societies.

Part I – Foundations: Policies, Theory, and Global Perspectives

Chapter 1

Sealing the Deal: The Role of Heritage Language Policies in Fostering National Cohesion and Preserving Diversity in the United States

Fabien Rivière Copa

Language is more than just a tool for communication—it is a fundamental pillar of cultural identity, social cohesion, and national heritage. As UNESCO describes, language serves as a "vehicle of intangible cultural heritage,"[1] connecting individuals to their histories and communities. In multilingual societies, language policies play a crucial role in balancing linguistic diversity with national unity. Heritage language policies, in particular, provide a framework for preserving linguistic assets, empowering multilingual communities, and fostering social inclusion. These policies not only acknowledge the cultural and cognitive benefits of bilingualism but also challenge the prevailing monolingual paradigm that often dominates national discourse.[2]

The theoretical foundations of heritage language policies reveal their broader sociopolitical implications. Language maintenance and shift theory[3] explains how institutional support influences the survival of heritage languages and prevents linguistic erosion.[4] Language ideology theory[5] critiques monolingual biases that equate English

---

[1] UNESCO, 2003
[2] Seals & Shah, 2018
[3] Fishman, 1991
[4] Valdés, 2005
[5] Wiley & García, 2016

proficiency with patriotism and socioeconomic success while overlooking the advantages of multilingualism.[6] Additionally, critical language policy theory[7] exposes how policies that neglect heritage languages contribute to systemic inequalities, limiting opportunities for immigrant and indigenous communities.

The United States presents a unique linguistic landscape due to its rich heritage of multilingualism. Despite this diversity, the country has historically grappled with conflicting attitudes toward heritage languages. Assimilationist policies have long marginalized heritage speakers, reinforcing English as the sole language of civic and economic participation.[8] However, linguistic diversity remains an enduring feature of the nation. As of 2018, the U.S. Census Bureau (USCB) reported that 67.3 million residents—21.9% of the U.S. population—spoke a language other than English at home. The USCB's 2015 report further revealed that the country is home to at least 350 languages, including 150 indigenous languages. Despite this vibrant multilingual heritage, heritage language speakers often encounter limited institutional support, inadequate representation, and systemic barriers to maintaining their linguistic identities.

A central tension in language policy debates is the perceived trade-off between national unity and cultural inclusion. Critics argue that emphasizing heritage languages could undermine national cohesion by reinforcing linguistic divisions.[9] However, research suggests that well-implemented language policies can strengthen social cohesion by promoting bilingual proficiency, economic mobility, and intercultural understanding.[10] The Seal of Biliteracy, a nationwide initiative recognizing bilingual achievement among students, exemplifies how language policies can successfully integrate linguistic diversity with national identity.

---

[6] García & Kleifgen, 2018
[7] Tollefson, 2013; McCarty, 2011
[8] Gándara & Escamilla, 2017
[9] Portes & Rumbaut, 2014
[10] Flores & Schissel, 2014

This chapter explores the role of heritage language policies in fostering social cohesion while preserving linguistic diversity in the United States. It specifically examines the Seal of Biliteracy as a case study, demonstrating how localized initiatives can empower individuals and contribute to broader national unity. This chapter is structured into four key sections.

- Section 1 examines the historical evolution of heritage language policies in the United States, tracing their development from early assimilationist approaches to more recent efforts at promoting bilingual education. It explores how shifts in federal and state policies have shaped access to heritage language programs and multilingual education.
- Section 2 investigates the significant variations in bilingual education across different states, highlighting how policy decisions either support or hinder linguistic diversity. By comparing states with robust bilingual initiatives to those with restrictive English-only policies, this section underscores the disparities in access to language education.
- Section 3 focuses on the Seal of Biliteracy as a case study, analyzing its impact on education, employment, and social inclusion. This section evaluates the program's effectiveness in promoting biliteracy and its broader implications for national cohesion.
- Finally, Section 4 discusses policy recommendations for expanding and standardizing bilingual initiatives at the federal level. It considers how a cohesive national policy could address existing disparities, enhance access to heritage language programs, and integrate multilingualism as a national asset. Together, these sections build a comprehensive argument for the role of heritage language policies in fostering both linguistic diversity and national unity.

Ultimately, this chapter argues that a federally guided heritage language policy—centered on the principles of inclusion and multilingualism—can enhance both national identity and social cohesion. By recognizing bilingualism as a national asset rather than a divisive factor, policymakers can foster a more inclusive, globally competitive society.

Heritage Language Policies in the United States: Balancing Diversity and Unity

Overview of Existing Policies.

Unlike some countries that have formal national language policies—such as Canada, which recognizes both English and French as official languages, or France, where French is constitutionally enshrined as the national language—the United States has historically operated without a federally declared official language. While English has long been the dominant language in practice, it was not formally codified at the federal level – until 2025, when President Donald J. Trump signed Executive Order 14224, declaring English the official language of the United States. The order also rescinded prior federal requirements to provide language assistance to individuals with limited English proficiency, effectively shifting discretion over language access back to individual agencies.

In fact, language policy in the United States has historically been shaped by tensions between linguistic diversity and national cohesion. Even before this recent shift, federal efforts to support multilingualism have been sporadic and uneven, often influenced more by political ideology than by consistent national planning. Federal policies addressing linguistic diversity have largely focused on educational equity and civil rights, yet implementation has been inconsistent. The Bilingual Education Act of 1968, passed as Title VII of the Elementary and Secondary Education Act (ESEA), was the first major federal acknowledgment of the needs of non-English-speaking students. It provided funding for bilingual education programs aimed at students with limited English proficiency (LEP), emphasizing the importance of preserving students' heritage languages while they acquired English.[11] However, the Act faced

---

[11] Crawford, 2004

significant challenges over the years, including fluctuating political support and modifications that weakened its bilingual focus. In 2001, it was effectively replaced by Title III of the No Child Left Behind Act (NCLB), which shifted emphasis toward English language acquisition and away from sustained bilingual development.[12]

Another critical policy, Title VI of the Civil Rights Act of 1964, prohibits discrimination based on national origin in federally funded programs, which has been interpreted to include language discrimination.[13] This provision led to the landmark Lau v. Nichols Supreme Court case,[14] which ruled that schools must take affirmative steps to ensure that non-English-speaking students receive meaningful education. Although the decision reinforced bilingual support, it left instructional implementation to state discretion, resulting in widely variable application.[15]

In summa, these early federal policies laid the groundwork for bilingual education rights but failed to establish a unified national vision – leaving much of the decision-making power to individual states.

State-Level Initiatives: How States Shape Heritage Language Policies.

At the state level, support for heritage languages varies widely, reflecting broader political and ideological divides. Some states, such as California, New York, and Texas, have implemented robust bilingual education and heritage language programs, often in response to high linguistic diversity within their populations. California's Proposition 58[16] repealed the earlier Proposition 227,[17] which had mandated English-only instruction, and reaffirmed the state's commitment to dual-language programs.[18] In New York, the 2014 Blueprint for English Language Learner (ELL) Success set forth

---

[12] Gándara & Escamilla, 2017
[13] Wiley & Wright, 2004
[14] Lau v. Nichols, 1974
[15] Ovando, 2003
[16] Proposition 58, 2016
[17] Proposition 227, 1998
[18] Gándara & Mordechay, 2017

a framework for expanding bilingual and dual-language programs, recognizing the benefits of multilingualism in fostering cultural inclusion and economic opportunity.[19] Additionally, New York State Education Law §3204(2) mandates that schools provide bilingual education when there are at least 20 English language learners (ELLs) of the same home language at a single grade level.[20]

By contrast, other states have imposed restrictions on bilingual education. Arizona's Proposition 203,[21] Massachusetts' Question 2,[22] and California's former Proposition 227[23] were all driven by the English-only movement, which aimed to replace bilingual instruction with English immersion.[24] While California later reversed its stance with Proposition 58, Arizona and Massachusetts maintained English-only mandates for years, with Massachusetts modifying its approach in 2017 through the LOOK Act (Language Opportunity for Our Kids Act), which gave school districts greater flexibility in offering bilingual programs.[25] This patchwork of policies highlights a key tension: while some states move toward embracing multilingualism, others maintain restrictive stances, contributing to deep disparities in access to heritage language support.

These policies reflect the enduring debate over linguistic unity versus multilingualism, even in the face of extensive research confirming the cognitive, academic, and social advantages of bilingualism.[26]

---

[19] Menken & Solorza, 2014
[20] New York State Education Department, 2019
[21] Proposition 203, 2000
[22] Question 2, 2002
[23] Proposition 227, 1998
[24] Wiley & Wright, 2004
[25] Fu, 2024
[26] Cummins, 2000; García & Lin, 2016

The Debate on Heritage Language Policies: National Unity vs. Linguistic Diversity.

Amid these policy discrepancies, a central question remains: Does multilingualism strengthen or weaken national identity? Critics of heritage language policies contend that promoting bilingualism may fragment national unity by fostering linguistic enclaves rather than integration.[27] However, research from Canada and Switzerland—both nations with strong multilingual policies—demonstrates that linguistic diversity can enhance social cohesion rather than undermine it.[28]

The linguistic capital framework developed by Bourdieu suggests that proficiency in multiple languages provides social and economic advantages.[29] Countries that embrace multilingual policies tend to benefit from greater workforce mobility and global economic competitiveness. In contrast, nations that enforce strict monolingual policies often limit opportunities for both native-born citizens and immigrant populations.[30]

A growing body of research additionally supports the idea that maintaining skills in one's heritage language contributes to stronger cognitive development, higher academic achievement, and increased career opportunities.[31] Rather than weakening national identity, multilingual policies have been shown to foster intercultural competence and civic engagement, preparing students for success in a globalized society.[32] In essence, the evidence increasingly favors an inclusive model of national identity – one that views linguistic diversity as foundational to national cohesion rather than a challenge to it.

Thus, the historical and theoretical frameworks pinpoint that the challenge for policymakers in the United States is not whether

---

[27] Portes & Rumbaut, 2014
[28] May, 2013
[29] Bourdieu, 1991
[30] Ruiz, 1984
[31] García & Lin, 2021
[32] Lindholm-Leary, 2016

linguistic diversity should be supported, but how to balance national cohesion with inclusive language policies. The Seal of Biliteracy, introduced in California in 2008 and now adopted by all U.S. states and the District of Columbia, exemplifies a policy that successfully balances linguistic diversity with national identity by recognizing bilingual proficiency as an asset rather than a divisive factor.[33] By officially acknowledging students who demonstrate proficiency in both English and another language, the Seal of Biliteracy promotes heritage language maintenance while reinforcing a shared sense of national identity. As this chapter will continue to explore, the Seal of Biliteracy offers a compelling example of how localized language policy can generate national-level impact – providing a roadmap for future federal action.

The Seal of Biliteracy: A Case Study

Background, Implementation, and Objectives.

From Grassroots Advocacy to National Recognition: The Seal of Biliteracy is a national initiative that formally acknowledges high school students who have attained proficiency in two or more languages. First introduced in California in 2008 by Californians Together and then passed into legislation in 2011, creating the California State Seal of Biliteracy, the program was developed in response to increasing demand for recognition of bilingualism as an academic, cultural, and professional asset. This initiative emerged from a local grassroots movement, with coalition advocacy groups such as Californians Together and the California Association for Bilingual Education (CABE) playing a central role in its development by advocating for policies that affirm linguistic diversity and promote multilingualism as an asset rather than a barrier.[34] The initiative aligns with a broader national movement recognizing the cognitive, economic, and social benefits of bilingualism.[35]

---

[33] Heineke & Davin, 2018
[34] Heineke & Davin, 2018
[35] García & Lin, 2021

The program was established with the following key objectives:

1. Encouraging Bilingual Proficiency
2. Promoting Linguistic Diversity
3. Enhancing Workforce Readiness
4. Fostering Inclusive National Identity

By incentivizing heritage speakers to develop and maintain fluency in more than one language, the initiative fosters greater academic engagement in language learning. The program supports heritage language speakers and recognizes the value of multilingual communities in the United States. The Seal highlights multilingual skills as an advantage in a competitive job market, particularly in sectors such as healthcare, education, diplomacy, and international business.[36] By acknowledging bilingualism as a valuable resource, the Seal helps shift societal perceptions about multilingualism, reinforcing language as a bridge rather than a barrier.

Since its introduction, the Seal of Biliteracy has gained widespread acceptance across the nation. By 2024, all 50 states and Washington, D.C. had adopted the Seal, South Dakota being the last state to implement the initiative in January of 2024. The following two figures illustrate the policy's national momentum and broad legislative support within four years.

---

[36] García & Lin, 2021

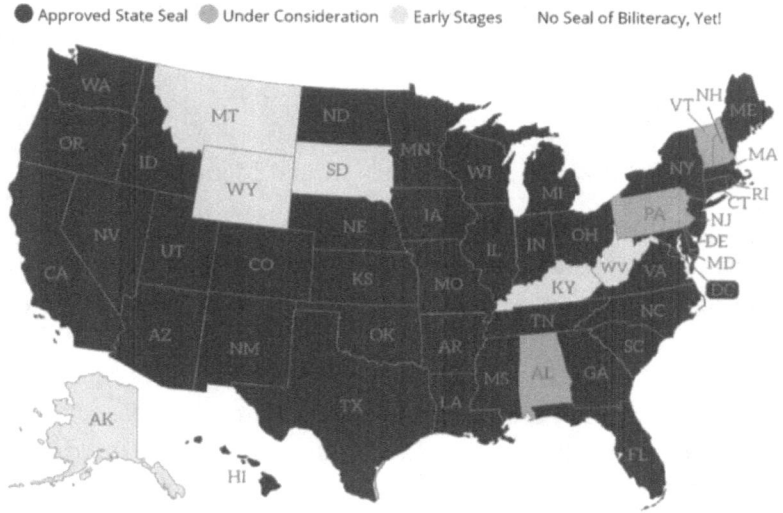

Figure 1. U.S. State Laws Regarding the Seal of Biliteracy (2020).[37]

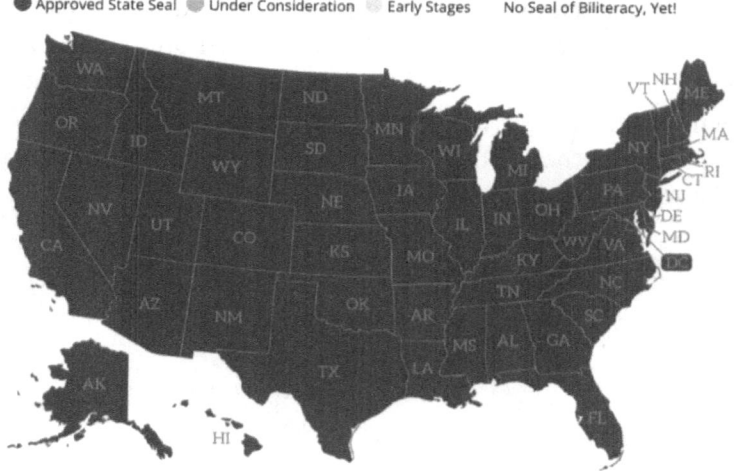

Figure 2. U.S. State Laws Regarding the Seal of Biliteracy (2024). [38]

---

[37] This figure illustrates the nationwide spread of the Seal of Biliteracy as of November 2020, highlighting the impetus with early adopters and states in progress. Source: sealofbiliteracy.org downloaded November 6, 2020.
[38] This figure shows the most recent adoption status as of November 2024, with all 50 states and Washington D.C. having implemented the Seal,

Challenges in Implementation - Unequal Access and Policy Barriers: Despite broad adoption, disparities remain in how states implement the program, leading to significant variations in student access and qualification criteria.[39]

While most states follow a similar framework, the requirements to earn the Seal may vary. In many states, students must demonstrate proficiency in English and at least one other language through a combination of assessments, including:

- Advanced Placement (AP) and International Baccalaureate (IB) language exams.
- State-administered language proficiency assessments.
- Portfolio-based language proficiency evaluations.[40]

Some states, such as California and New York, have well-established, structured assessment pathways, ensuring that students across diverse language backgrounds have multiple ways to qualify for the Seal.[41] Conversely, states with more restrictive bilingual education policies, including some in the South and Midwest, often provide limited support for language learning, making it harder for students to meet the required proficiency benchmarks.[42]

Toward a Federal Language Policy: The Role of the Seal of Biliteracy.

Given the fast-growing recognition of the Seal of Biliteracy across the United States, the Biliteracy Education Seal and Teaching (BEST) Act was introduced in the Senate on January 17, 2024, by Senator Brian Schatz (D-HI) and co-sponsored by a coalition of lawmakers. This represents a pivotal step toward solidifying multilingual proficiency at the federal level. The bill seeks to provide federal grants to states for the establishment and enhancement of Seal of Biliteracy programs. These programs recognize students who achieve

---

reinforcing the policy's national momentum and broad legislative support. Source: sealofbiliteracy.org downloaded November 30, 2024.

[39] Menken & Solorza, 2014
[40] Lindholm-Leary, 2016
[41] Gándara & Mordechay, 2017
[42] Menken & Solorza, 2014

proficiency in speaking, reading, and writing in both English and a second language, promoting linguistic diversity as an asset rather than a barrier.

In the House of Representatives, Congresswoman Julia Brownley (D-CA) has introduced a companion bill, emphasizing the importance of multilingualism and ensuring that Seal of Biliteracy programs remain accessible, particularly for heritage speakers, notably of Native American languages. The legislation has garnered support from major advocacy organizations, including the Joint National Committee for Languages and the National Council for Languages and International Studies (JNCL-NCLIS), whose Executive Director, Amanda Seewald, highlights its role in promoting equitable access to language recognition.

As of February 2025, the BEST Act remains under consideration in Congress. The bill was referred to the Senate Committee on Health, Education, Labor, and Pensions on January 17, 2024, and has not yet progressed to a floor vote. Despite this hiatus, the BEST Act is a testament to how the Seal of Biliteracy remains a significant policy milestone, underscoring a shift in U.S. language education priorities. By addressing accessibility barriers and expanding opportunities, policymakers can ensure that the benefits of biliteracy recognition reach a broader, more diverse student population.

Research Outcomes.

Research on the Seal of Biliteracy, though still emerging, highlights its role as both a symbol of linguistic achievement and a valuable credential for higher education and the workforce.[43] Studies consistently link the Seal to higher academic achievement, increased college enrollment, and greater professional opportunities. Bilingual students outperform monolingual peers in literacy, problem-solving, and cognitive flexibility, with those earning the Seal demonstrating stronger academic outcomes.[44]

---

[43] Gándara & Escamilla, 2017
[44] Thomas & Collier, 2012

Empirical data from multiple states show that Seal recipients have higher high school graduation rates, are more likely to attend four-year universities, and persist longer in higher education.[45] A California study found that bilingual students with the Seal were 12% more likely to enroll in college than their monolingual counterparts.[46] Similarly, research from Texas indicates Seal recipients are 10-15% more likely to meet college-readiness benchmarks on standardized tests like the SAT and ACT.[47]

Beyond academics, the Seal enhances college access and scholarships, as universities increasingly recognize it as a mark of academic rigor and global competency.[48] Some institutions offer bilingual students merit-based scholarships, language proficiency exemptions, and advanced placement credits.[49]

In the job market, the Seal provides tangible economic advantages. Employers in education, healthcare, international business, and government favor candidates with formal biliteracy credentials. A workforce study in California, Texas, and Florida found that Seal holders were 30% more likely to secure bilingual-designated positions and often received higher starting salaries.[50] Additionally, Seal recipients report greater self-confidence, cultural awareness, and adaptability—critical assets in today's global economy.[51]

From the Seal to Inclusive National Identity.

The Seal of Biliteracy plays a critical role in bridging the gap between language proficiency and real-world opportunities, providing multilingual students with academic, professional, and societal advantages. By recognizing bilingualism as an asset, the Seal

---

[45] Menken & Solorza, 2014; Callahan & Humphries, 2016; Heineke & Davin, 2018
[46] Gándara & Escamilla, 2017
[47] Sikes & Piñón, 2024
[48] Heineke & Davin, 2018
[49] Chen, 2020
[50] Gándara, 2015
[51] García & Lin, 2021

enhances job market competitiveness, facilitates higher education access, and fosters a more inclusive national identity. The six-step diagram below visually represents the multifaceted benefits of the Seal, demonstrating how it strengthens individual success while contributing to broader social cohesion.

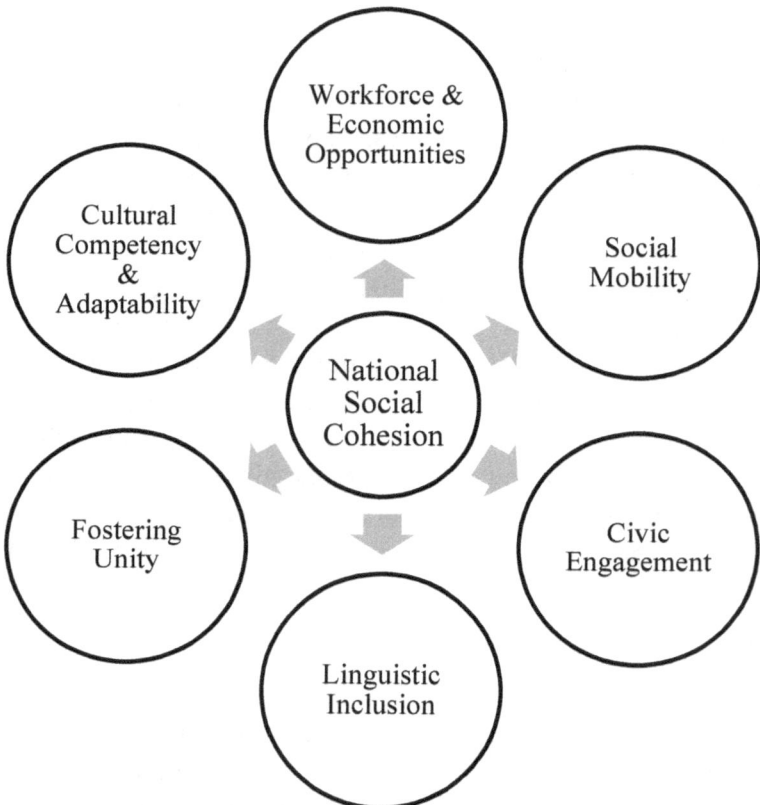

Figure 3. The multifaceted and interrelated benefits of the Seal contribute to broader social cohesion at the national level.

This diagram summarizes how the Seal of Biliteracy supports various components: economic empowerment, higher education access, civic engagement, national unity, and global competency – demonstrating its role in fostering and contributing to a shared core value: national social cohesion.

While the following benefits outline key ways in which the Seal of Biliteracy contributes to national social cohesion, these factors are not dependent on one another, nor are they listed in order of importance. Each element functions independently yet collectively reinforces the broader goal of fostering an inclusive and unified society:

1. The Seal of Biliteracy enhances workforce and economy opportunities by validating bilingual proficiency, a skill increasingly valued across industries such as healthcare, education, international business, and government services.[52] Research shows that bilingual employees earn 5% to 20% more than monolingual peers due to heightened demand for multilingual professionals, particularly in immigrant-rich states like California, Texas, and New York.[53] Additionally, multinational corporations and the U.S. government prioritize bilingual candidates for leadership roles, diplomacy, and national security, recognizing linguistic proficiency as essential for global market expansion and public service.[54] By increasing job market competitiveness and career advancement opportunities, the Seal of Biliteracy fosters economic empowerment and workforce integration.

2. By expanding academic opportunities and fostering social mobility, the Seal strengthens national cohesion by ensuring equitable access to higher education. The Seal of Biliteracy serves as a critical bridge between multilingual students—particularly first-generation immigrants and heritage language speakers—and higher education by mitigating systemic barriers to academic achievement.[55] Studies show that Seal recipients are significantly more likely to enroll in and complete college degrees, with research from California indicating a 12% higher enrollment rate

---

[52] García & Lin, 2021
[53] Carreira & Kagan, 2018; Lindholm-Leary, 2016
[54] Gándara & Mordechay, 2017; Menken & Solorza, 2014
[55] Gándara & Escamilla, 2017

in four-year universities among certified students.[56] Additionally, many postsecondary institutions recognize the Seal by offering academic credit, advanced placement, and scholarship opportunities, reducing tuition costs, and improving educational accessibility for low-income students.[57]

3. The Seal of Biliteracy promotes civic engagement by empowering bilingual individuals to serve as cultural and linguistic mediators in their communities, particularly in healthcare, legal services, and social work.[58] Research highlights the essential role of bilingual professionals in bridging language barriers and improving access to public services, especially in diverse and immigrant-rich areas.[59] Furthermore, multilingual individuals with strong cultural ties are more likely to engage in civic activities such as voting, volunteering, and community leadership, reinforcing democratic participation and social cohesion.[60] By fostering cross-cultural communication and active civic involvement, the Seal of Biliteracy strengthens community integration and contributes to a more inclusive society.

4. The Seal of Biliteracy plays a pivotal role in redefining national identity by promoting linguistic inclusion and valuing multilingualism as a national strength rather than a division.[61] By recognizing diverse linguistic communities, the Seal aligns with successful multilingual policies in countries like Canada and Switzerland, where linguistic diversity fosters social cohesion rather than fragmentation.[62] Additionally, schools that implement Seal programs report increased student participation in cultural exchange initiatives and global studies, reinforcing a more interconnected and globally aware generation.[63] By

---

[56] Gándara & Escamilla, 2017; Heineke & Davin, 2018
[57] Menken & Solorza, 2014
[58] Carreira & Kagan, 2018
[59] Lindholm-Leary, 2016
[60] García & Lin, 2021
[61] Gándara & Escamilla, 2017; Ruiz, 1984
[62] May, 2013
[63] García & Lin, 2021

embracing linguistic diversity and shared civic values, the Seal contributes to national unity and social cohesion.

5. The Seal of Biliteracy strengthens national unity by integrating multilingual communities into mainstream society while preserving linguistic diversity as a cultural asset.[64] By promoting inclusive language policies, the Seal aligns with global models, such as those in Canada and Switzerland, where multilingualism aims at fostering unity rather than weakening national cohesion.[65] Additionally, educational institutions that adopt Seal programs report increased student engagement in international relations, cultural exchange, and global studies, fostering cross-cultural understanding and social harmony.[66] Through its recognition of multilingualism as a unifying force, the Seal helps cultivate a more inclusive, cohesive, and globally connected society.

6. The Seal of Biliteracy fosters cross-cultural understanding by encouraging students to engage with diverse linguistic and cultural perspectives, both nationally and globally.[67] Research indicates that students who earn the Seal are more likely to participate in international exchange programs, global studies coursework, and multicultural initiatives, enhancing their cultural competency and adaptability.[68] By promoting bilingualism as a tool for global engagement, the Seal helps cultivate a generation of individuals who can navigate and contribute to an increasingly interconnected world. Through this emphasis on global awareness, the Seal not only benefits individual students but also strengthens societal cohesion by bridging cultural divides.

---

[64] Menken & Solorza, 2014
[65] May, 2013
[66] García & Lin, 2021
[67] García & Lin, 2021
[68] Menken & Solorza, 2014

Findings and Recommendations: Strengthening Multilingual Education for the Future.

Despite its widespread adoption, the Seal of Biliteracy still faces significant challenges in funding, access, and equity. While some states invest heavily in bilingual education, others allocate minimal resources, leaving underfunded school districts with limited access to quality language instruction.[69] Wealthier districts also have a clear advantage in language proficiency assessments, offering a range of testing options that many rural and low-income students struggle to access.[70] Additionally, heritage language speakers—whom the Seal aims to support—often face structural barriers. Many immigrant and indigenous communities lack formal education in their heritage languages, making it difficult for them to meet the necessary proficiency requirements.[71]

Yet, the Seal of Biliteracy is more than just a recognition of multilingual achievement—it is a powerful tool for economic mobility, social integration, and national cohesion. By bridging bilingual education with workforce development, the Seal opens doors to career opportunities, financial stability, and civic engagement. Some states have turned the Seal into a model for success, demonstrating how localized initiatives can drive national change. California, New York, and Illinois, for example, have built strong programs that prioritize accessibility, comprehensive assessments, and policy backing. Their success offers a blueprint for broader adoption:

- Flexible Assessment Options: Offering multiple ways to demonstrate proficiency, such as AP/IB exams, state assessments, and portfolio evaluations, ensures that diverse learners have a fair shot at earning the Seal.[72]

---

[69] Lindholm-Leary, 2016
[70] Gándara & Mordechay, 2017
[71] Carreira & Kagan, 2018
[72] Gándara & Mordechay, 2017

- Early Language Education Investment: States that introduce bilingual education from elementary school see significantly higher participation in Seal programs.[73]
- Financial and Institutional Support: Dedicated funding for teacher training, curriculum development, and language testing expands program reach and effectiveness.[74]

The success of the Seal of Biliteracy at the state level underscores its potential for federal integration. By incorporating Seal certifications into college admissions, workforce training, and national education policies, the United States can solidify bilingualism as a national priority.[75] Standardizing the Seal across all states will help eliminate disparities, ensuring that every student—regardless of geography or socioeconomic status—can unlock the lifelong advantages of biliteracy.

Toward a Federal Policy on Multilingualism?

As linguistic diversity in the United States continues to expand—over 67 million residents now speak a language other than English at home[76]—the need for a cohesive federal policy on multilingualism has never been more pressing. Without national coordination, disparities in bilingual education, access to multilingual resources, and economic opportunities persist. While state-led initiatives like the Seal of Biliteracy have made progress in recognizing and promoting bilingualism, the absence of a unified federal framework has resulted in uneven implementation, with systemic inequalities in funding, policy enforcement, and educational access.[77] A federally guided approach is essential to ensure that multilingualism is recognized as an asset available to all students, regardless of geography or socioeconomic background.[78]

---

[73] Lindholm-Leary, 2016
[74] Menken & Solorza, 2014
[75] García & Lin, 2021
[76] U.S. Census Bureau, 2021
[77] Gándara & Mordechay, 2017
[78] García & Lin, 2021

The Limitations of a Patchwork Approach.

Currently, language education policies vary significantly from state to state, creating a landscape of opportunity for some students while leaving others at a disadvantage. In states like California and New York, dual-language immersion (DLI) programs and state-supported bilingual assessments provide structured pathways for students to achieve biliteracy.[79] In contrast, restrictive policies in states such as Arizona and Tennessee limit bilingual instruction, making it difficult for heritage language speakers to maintain proficiency in their native languages.[80]

This uneven distribution of resources and opportunities disproportionately affects low-income and immigrant communities, many of whom lack access to community-based heritage language programs outside the school system.[81] Moreover, while the Seal of Biliteracy represents a crucial step forward, its implementation is inconsistent across states, with varying levels of accessibility and support for students seeking certification.[82] Without a national policy ensuring equal recognition and access, multilingual students remain subject to the inconsistencies of their state's education system rather than benefiting from a standardized, equitable framework.

The Case for Expanding Heritage Language Education Nationwide.

A national multilingual policy would provide a structured, equitable approach to language education, ensuring that all students—regardless of their state of residence—have the opportunity to develop bilingual proficiency. Such a framework would include:

- Equitable Access to Multilingual Education and Funding: Expand bilingual and dual-language programs across public schools, ensuring equitable resource allocation.[83] Provide dedicated funding for heritage language programs, curriculum

---

[79] Menken & Solorza, 2014
[80] Lindholm-Leary, 2016
[81] Carreira & Kagan, 2018
[82] Gándara & Escamilla, 2017
[83] Lindholm-Leary, 2016

development, teacher training, and student scholarships, particularly in low-income and rural areas.[84]
- Strengthening Bilingual Teacher Training and Educational Standards: Invest in comprehensive bilingual teacher preparation programs, addressing shortages through professional development, tuition reimbursement, and credentialing pathways.[85] Establish federally defined proficiency benchmarks, standardized assessments, and integrate bilingual education into national curricula.[86]
- Recognition and Integration of Multilingualism in National Policy: Standardize the Seal of Biliteracy to ensure national recognition and accessibility in education and the workforce.[87] Promote dual-language immersion (DLI) programs, integrate heritage languages into school curricula, and expand early childhood language education to enhance cognitive development and cultural identity.[88]
- Multilingualism as an Economic and Workforce Asset: Establish incentives for bilingual workforce development through federal tax credits and grants for businesses in key sectors.[89] Expand federal language access services in public institutions, create a National Multilingual Task Force to oversee implementation, and integrate bilingualism into STEM and vocational training initiatives to meet labor market demands.[90]

Implications for Policymakers and Society.

A federal multilingual policy presents an opportunity to strengthen national cohesion while embracing linguistic diversity. Policymakers must recognize that heritage language maintenance and bilingual

---

[84] Carreira & Kagan, 2018; Gándara & Mordechay, 2017
[85] Menken & Solorza, 2014
[86] García & Lin, 2021
[87] Heineke & Davin, 2018
[88] Gándara & Escamilla, 2017; Lindholm-Leary, 2016
[89] Gándara & Escamilla, 2017
[90] Ruiz, 1984; May, 2013; Heineke & Davin, 2018

education are not simply educational concerns but critical factors in social integration and economic competitiveness.[91]

A national Seal of Biliteracy framework, coupled with increased funding for heritage language programs, would ensure that all students, regardless of background, have access to bilingual education. Moreover, embedding multilingual policies within the federal workforce and economic development strategies would bolster the nation's global competitiveness.[92]

For society at large, recognizing and supporting linguistic diversity can foster intercultural understanding and civic participation. In the United States, a federal language policy would help shift public perception of bilingualism from a barrier to an advantage, leading to greater community engagement and inclusivity.[93] Incorporating language education into broader national policy discussions will not only benefit heritage language speakers but also reinforce the importance of cultural inclusivity and economic resilience. Federal policymakers should, therefore, view multilingualism as a cornerstone of modern education and workforce development.

A federal policy on multilingualism is essential to bridge gaps in bilingual education, expand economic opportunities, and ensure that linguistic diversity remains a national strength rather than a localized advantage. Standardizing bilingual education, supporting heritage language maintenance, and investing in workforce development will allow the United States to harness its linguistic diversity as both an educational and economic asset. By recognizing multilingualism as an integral component of national policy, the nation can foster a more equitable, globally competitive society—one that embraces its rich linguistic heritage and prepares future generations for success in an increasingly interconnected world.

---

[91] Menken & Solorza, 2014
[92] Gándara & Mordechay, 2017
[93] Ruiz, 1984

Areas for Further Research.

While existing research highlights the benefits of multilingual policies, further studies are needed to examine the long-term impact of localized language policies on national cohesion. Investigating how state-level bilingual education programs influence student achievement, economic mobility, and civic engagement would provide deeper insights into effective language policy design.[94]

Furthermore, more extensive research on the Seal of Biliteracy's broader implications is necessary. A potential avenue of research is to analyze how Seal-certified students perform in higher education and the job market, evaluating whether biliteracy credentials contribute to long-term career advantages.[95] Understanding the factors that enhance or hinder Seal of Biliteracy implementation across states would be invaluable in crafting a standardized national approach.

Finally, more research is needed on the intersection of multilingual policies, national identity, and social integration. As the United States continues to diversify, understanding how language policies shape social cohesion will be crucial in developing equitable and effective educational frameworks.[96]

Concluding Comments: Heritage Language Policies for a More Inclusive Society

Heritage language policies are not just about preserving linguistic traditions—they are about shaping inclusive, cohesive societies that embrace diversity as a national strength. The Seal of Biliteracy stands as a powerful testament to this vision, proving that language policies can both celebrate multilingualism and reinforce national unity. By formally recognizing bilingual proficiency, the Seal provides students with tangible academic and economic advantages, fostering a more inclusive workforce and a globally competitive society.

---

[94] Carreira & Kagan, 2018
[95] Heineke & Davin, 2018
[96] García & Lin, 2021

However, the disparities in state-level implementation reveal the limitations of a fragmented approach. While some states have embraced bilingual education as a cornerstone of educational and social equity, others continue to uphold restrictive policies that hinder access to heritage language programs. This inconsistency underscores the need for a federally coordinated policy—one that standardizes bilingual education, ensures equitable access to language certification, and integrates multilingualism into national economic and educational strategies.

A federal framework inspired by the Seal of Biliteracy could catalyze national cohesion, reinforcing the idea that multilingualism is an asset rather than a liability. By bridging linguistic diversity with policy-driven inclusion, the United States can position itself as a leader in global competency, social integration, and economic innovation. The conversation around language policies must, therefore, shift from whether multilingualism should be supported to how it can be systematically and equitably implemented for the benefit of all.

Heritage languages are more than tools of communication—they are, as UNESCO powerfully reminds us, "a vehicle of intangible cultural heritage"[97] linking individuals to their histories, communities, and shared values. As of 2021, 67 million residents in the United States – more than one in five – spoke a language other than English at home,[98] an undeniable testament to the nation's rich and ever-expanding linguistic landscape. Ensuring that every student, regardless of their background, has the opportunity to develop and maintain bilingual proficiency is not just an educational priority but a societal imperative. In embracing a multilingual future, the United States can truly "seal the deal" on fostering a more inclusive, dynamic, and globally engaged nation.

---

[97] UNESCO, 2003
[98] U.S. Census Bureau, 2021

Chapter 2

Advancing Social Cohesion Among Heritage Language Schools, Immigrant Populations, and Formal Language Education

Richard D. Brecht and Joy Kreeft Peyton

Language learning in the United States is robust. While stagnant or declining language enrollments in our schools, colleges, and universities are vexing,[99] these numbers should not be taken as indicative of decreasing interest in bilingualism and language learning across the country. Two distinct data sources support this assertion: First, heritage language schools, which enroll tens of thousands of speakers of the language learned every year, are a thriving enterprise. When students become parents, they often bring their children to school. Many of these schools are visible on a school map,[100] and some of them, like the following, are profiled in the Coalition of Community-Based Heritage Language Schools profiles database.[101]

Founded in 1935, the German School of San Francisco (GSSF) is the oldest German-language school in the San Francisco Bay Area. The GSSF is a Saturday school, a non-profit organization with the goal of teaching the language and culture of German-speaking countries. The school offers classes for all ages, with 108 students, 19 teachers, and assistants. Learning takes place through various

---

[99] MLA, 2021. See also American Councils for International Education, 2017
[100] CCBHLS, Map of Community-Based Schools, 2025
[101] CCBHLS, Profiles of Community-Based Heritage Language Schools, 2025

media—by reading books, completing projects and art, singing songs, watching movies, and playing vocabulary-enriching games. A wide range of exams, both from Germany and the U.S., are completed at various levels by students each year, with the ultimate goal being that students obtain the German Language Diploma Level II (DSD II).

These schools are an inspiration across heritage communities nationwide. Additionally, relevant language learning apps are attracting more and more learners, although the numbers are difficult to specify.[102]

Here we argue that language educators and policy makers should view language learning within a much broader perspective than has been the practice in the past, embracing all of these systems: formal education, comprising PreK-12 public, private, and charter schools as well as college and university programs; community-based heritage language schools; home schooling; and online language applications. Each of these sectors deserves the attention that the K-16 system has enjoyed, as is evident from the paucity of data across the online and home schooling sectors.

The exception to this data deficit is heritage language learning, our focus here. Heritage languages constitute a significant but neglected component of language learning in this country. This assertion is based on the documented heritage language education enrollments, which deserve national attention, particularly as they relate to potential outreach to immigrant communities and partnerships with the K-16 system. Heritage weekend and after-school programs support a constant and growing cadre of emergent bilinguals because of America's abiding role as the go-to destination for immigrants around the world. Given the overall number of 'foreign-born' in the United States, now at 42.6 million according to the latest U.S. Census

---

[102] For example, Duolingo, Transparent Language, 7000 Languages, Rosetta Stone, and other successful companies are serving a growing number of language learners now and into the future, some in formal education programs, some in community-based heritage language programs, some learning at home, and others learning on their own.

data,[103] reaching out to them and connecting them with heritage language schools could significantly strengthen the home language maintenance of these populations and also continue to enhance the existing Community-Based Heritage Language Schools (CBHLS). This outreach would benefit the new immigrant communities, as it has the previous generations of arrivals to our shores, both ensuring and broadening the country's multilingual heritage.

This focus on heritage languages is critical to understanding the purpose of language learning, adding an important goal to the traditional ones of language development and usage, by enabling strong personal and community identity and social cohesion among families and local and regional residents.[104] In towns and cities across the U.S., rural, urban, and suburban, emergent bilingualism among traditional heritage language and recent immigrant learners can directly influence greater respect for diversity among parents, neighbors, and influencers, while also providing educational and employment benefits for their children. The resulting broadening awareness of, and respect for, multilingualism can also raise the consciousness of state and local leaders to see more clearly the need to provide equal access to social, health, and legal services in the languages of their communities in pursuit of a more just society. Heritage communities themselves must recognize their power and influence in language learning and the nation's multilingualism. Specifically, we argue here that they must broaden and strengthen outreach to immigrant communities and organizations, and they should work to develop stronger partnerships with K-16 language programs.

This chapter is written primarily for educators in all of the language sectors listed above, but it is aimed as well at district and

---

[103] U.S. Census Bureau, 2024

[104] Social cohesion refers to the extent of connectedness and solidarity among groups in society. It identifies two main dimensions: the sense of belonging of a community and the relationships among members within the community itself. Accessed 10/28/24 from Social Cohesion – SpringerLink

federal policymakers, NGO leaders, and researchers working in the heritage language field. It has three goals: First, after describing the benefits and history of heritage languages and heritage language education in this country, we argue for the Coalition of Community-based Heritage Language Schools (CBHLS)[105] to be a galvanizing force in bringing cohesion among heritage, immigrant, and formal language education communities.

Second, we propose a broad framework of goals and objectives for integrating CBHLS into the burgeoning immigrant communities and the K-16 language education system, strengthening their sense of belonging within America's languages, and building stronger relationships among members of these three entities.

Third, we provide evidence from CBHLS for the integrative role that they are playing, including describing specific challenges and best practices of the ways that bilingual communities, and particularly these schools, are building social cohesion, identity, and cultural diversity through the contributions they make to the language learning landscape. Examples are provided of school projects now underway and some next steps that these schools might take to connect with other schools and start new ones, with new immigrant communities, and with the K-16 language education system. To a certain extent, these constituencies have been interacting, but a strong unified effort is called for now, given language education's new opportunities and existential challenges.

Benefits of Heritage Language Education

Heritage language education is as American as apple pie, a natural consequence of our history of immigration, past and present, individuals born abroad, and later generations born here. According to the American Community Survey, approximately 68 million people over the age of five in the United States speak a language other than English at home, representing roughly 21% of the population.[106] Over 14% of our population is 'foreign-born', totaling almost 46

---

[105] CCBHLS, About Us, 2025
[106] ACS, 2022

million.[107] These long-standing and recent immigrant populations are distributed across hundreds of heritage communities in the U.S., including Native American, Latino, Asian, African, Middle Eastern, European, Caribbean, and Pacific Islander, and their subdivisions. The benefits they bring to our society and the challenges they face need to be acknowledged, and more proactive measures need to be undertaken to recognize and integrate them into our education system.

There are abundant studies of heritage language education, regarding both its benefits and its implementation, among the latest being Cruickshank, Lo Bianco, and Wahlin's recent work.[108] The focus has been primarily on the learners, but the benefits to society could be better elaborated and appreciated, and an overall framework on how community-based heritage language education fits into language education in general in the U.S. could be developed.

Benefits to Society: Diversity and Social Cohesion

Immigrant families settle into monolingual communities, sometimes bringing discomfort but also appreciation of diversity, including 'different' cultures and languages. This heritage tradition, and the Community-based Heritage Language Schools (CBHLS) it creates, have for over 100 years demonstrated how new immigrant communities can successfully integrate into this English-dominant society.[109] A recent example is an Afghan migrant family that settles into a rural town. This might result in some initial aversion on the part of the residents. Still, it can build an understanding of and appreciation for 'difference' manifested by other cultures and languages. Other immigrant families might follow, and gradually a different, more diverse community rises and builds its own parent-run community-based heritage language schools. The children grow up and enter the K-12 schools. Their classmates experience first-hand the challenges and benefits of this country's natural bilingualism as

---

[107] U.S. Census Bureau, 2024
[108] Cruickshank et al, 2024
[109] See, for example, chapters in Peyton et al, 2001; Wiley et al, 2014

well as a sense of community well-being, increased civic engagement, and strong academic performance. This process can serve as a model for newer immigrant communities to this country from Asia, Africa, and Latin America on how to successfully integrate into and contribute to English-dominant societies.

These efforts to produce an appreciation of 'difference' between others' and one's own culture, through 'Third Place'[110] awareness, are especially welcome in these times of political, social, and racial division. Multilingualism, one of our richest and most productive characteristics, can bind us together as much as resistance to it, and even denial, can tear us apart. The U.S. is historically a multilingual country, which is one of our richest, most distinctive, and productive characteristics. Our multilingualism is a reality that our history justifies, a resource that our economy needs, a rationale that reinforces our foreign policy advocacy for liberal democracy, and a vital part of our national character that must be nurtured and expanded among all residents.

Benefits to Learners: Identity and Self-Efficacy

These schools, and the communities they serve, offer advantages to their children, their community, and the nation. Aberdeen found that they provide the following six benefits for heritage language learners (HLLs):[111]

- Provide additional exposure to the heritage language and literacy, with increased engagement and proficiency over time.
- Offer opportunities for same-language friendships and a sense of belonging.
- Offer opportunities to develop cultural pride and a strong sense of self-worth.
- Promote the value of learning multiple languages and the importance of lifelong learning.

---

[110] Lo Bianco, Liddicoat, and Crozet, 1999
[111] Aberdeen, 2016

- Promote holistic personal development and personal rewards while learning to do service work and community development.
- Provide support for newly arrived families and contribute to family stability.

These benefits may be viewed as constituting a new identity for heritage learners, a theme that attracted much attention over a decade ago.[112] The evidence for these assertions in the success of CBHLS is the building of over a thousand schools, now with increasing outreach to new immigrant communities. CBHLS's exemplary school projects and their 'next steps' are documented in recent CBHLS Webinars and Coalition Cafés. The speakers and these ACTFL resources[113] offer assurances that the CBHLS system is willing and able to take its place as an equal member of the language education system in the U.S. However, more concrete steps must be taken to unify the focus and document the results of working with new immigrant communities and integrating them within the formal education system.

History of Heritage Language Education in the U.S.

A country built on immigration, enslaved or voluntary, is naturally multiethnic and multilingual, which results in many communities across the nation accepting the responsibility of teaching English AND 'heritage' languages to their children. This history of centuries of immigration and schools supporting their languages continues today, reinforced by the current surge of foreign-born populations, strengthening the system of after-school and weekend schools, and attracting new learners from Asia, Africa, and Latin America. Currently, "There may be as many as 8,000 CBHLS teaching approximately 200 languages (including 91 indigenous languages) to

---

[112] e.g., Brinton et al., 2008; Brown, 2009; Carreira & Chik, 2014; Kim, 2009; Leeman, 2015; Mister, 2023; Showstack et al, 2024; Val & Vinogradova, 2010; Yu, 2015; Zhou & Liu, 2022

[113] ACTFL, Heritage Learners

more than 1.5 million students."[114] And their numbers continue to grow:

> The population among the 29 largest heritage language groups in the U.S increased at a higher rate than the total population between 1980 and 2019. The overall U.S. population grew by approximately 47 percent, while the heritage language population grew by 194 percent. Among the two largest heritage language groups, the Spanish-speaking community increased by about 31 million, and the Chinese-speaking community increased by about 3 million during this period.[115]

A quick query of ChatGPT provides hundreds of heritage/immigrant communities across the U.S. (See Appendix A). Perlin's 2024 study of the immigrant communities of New York City documents over 700 languages in that city alone.

These communities and their schools constitute a strong source of social cohesion among themselves and offer the promise of building strong multiethnic communities as immigrant families integrate into monolingual communities across the nation. This 'heritage' tradition and the Community-based Heritage Language Schools (CBHLS) system it creates demonstrate how new immigrant communities can successfully integrate into this English-dominant society. At the same time, Native American populations were decimated and enslaved, while voluntary immigration built this nation's multilingual population. The 'colonial' languages of English, French, and Spanish dominated early on. Still, centuries of arrivals speaking languages from around the world have resulted in many culturally unique communities, determined to learn English while also preserving their home languages.

As a result of these traditions, U.S. society is historically and inherently multilingual, the home of America's languages. We use the term "America's Languages" to mean the languages of our

---

[114] Heritage Language Programs Data from the Coalition Map of Community-Based Schools
[115] U.S. Census Report, 2019

indigenous peoples, the languages of our colonial period, the languages spoken by the generations of immigrants landing on our shores, and the languages taught in our schools as *foreign, world, ancient,* and *Sign* languages (ASL) used by people who are Deaf or hard of hearing. The term seeks to unify these traditional distinctions under one clear historical reality: multilingualism from different populations, regardless of origin. This term was proposed by Brecht[116] and adopted by the national commission of the American Academy of Arts and Sciences (AAAS) for the title of its groundbreaking study, *America's Languages: Investing in Language Education for the 21st Century*,[117] and it established the website "America's Languages Initiative: A Guide to Exemplary Programs and Practices in U.S. Language Education," supported by two grants from The Mellon Foundation, with the goal of supporting a national strategy to improve equitable access to language education in this country.[118] 'America's Languages' recognizes multilingualism as inherent in this society and heritage languages as a vital characteristic of our society.

Coalition of CBHLS as a Galvanizer of Integration

Community-based heritage language schools (CBHLs) are already playing a significant galvanizing role in this rich language landscape, and they can do more. There are thousands of these schools teaching hundreds of languages, as documented decades ago.[119] Some of them have been in existence for a long time. For example, German schools, many of which are still in operation, date from the 19th century; e.g., Boston (1874) and New York (1892).[120] The St. Casimir Lithuanian Saturday School of Los Angeles[121] (founded in 1949) celebrated its 75th anniversary in 2024. These schools are typically non-profit

---

[116] Brecht, 2016
[117] American Academy of Arts and Sciences, 2017
[118] COERLL, 2025
[119] Fishman, 1966; Fishman, 1985; CCBHLS, Map of Community-Based Schools, 2025
[120] Ludanyi, 2014
[121] Los Angeles Šv. Kazimiero Lituanistinė Mokykla St. Casimir Lithuanian Heritage School. About Us / School Introduction.

organizations, founded and operated by parents from the respective heritage language or immigrant community. Their goal is to maintain and teach the language and culture of their heritage. The language is usually (but not always) spoken in the home or the community. These schools might offer classes for learners from PreK to Grade 12 as well as for adults. In many schools, non-heritage language speakers are welcome as well. Classes take place on weekends or after school, and some run summer camps in addition to classes during the school year.

Although these schools often rent space on public or private school premises on weekends or after school during the week, they operate outside the public and private school systems. They supplement the education that students receive in their regular schools and are not subject to the regulations of the U.S. education system. To document students' proficiency levels, schools administer U.S. language assessments and, when available, appropriate assessments used in the students' home countries. Many also use the State Seal of Biliteracy[122] and the Global Seal of Biliteracy[123] to recognize students' language proficiency levels. In some states, they collaborate with public schools so that students receive credit for their language proficiency, even if they have not studied the language in public school. In these videos,[124] recent high school graduates of CBHLs describe the value of the school (Bulgarian, French, and Greek) they attended in developing their language, the value of the language in their lives, and the value of receiving the Global Seal.[125]

This brief characterization of CBHLs illustrates their potential as a driving force in unifying America's Languages through concerted efforts to reach out to immigrant communities and the formal education system, as illustrated here:

---

[122] Seal of Biliteracy, 2025
[123] The Global Seal of Biliteracy, What Is the Global Seal of Biliteracy
[124] CCBHLS, Student Voices: Global Seal of Biliteracy, 2023
[125] See the mission, vision, and goals of the Coalition. CCBHLS, Coalition Goals, 2018

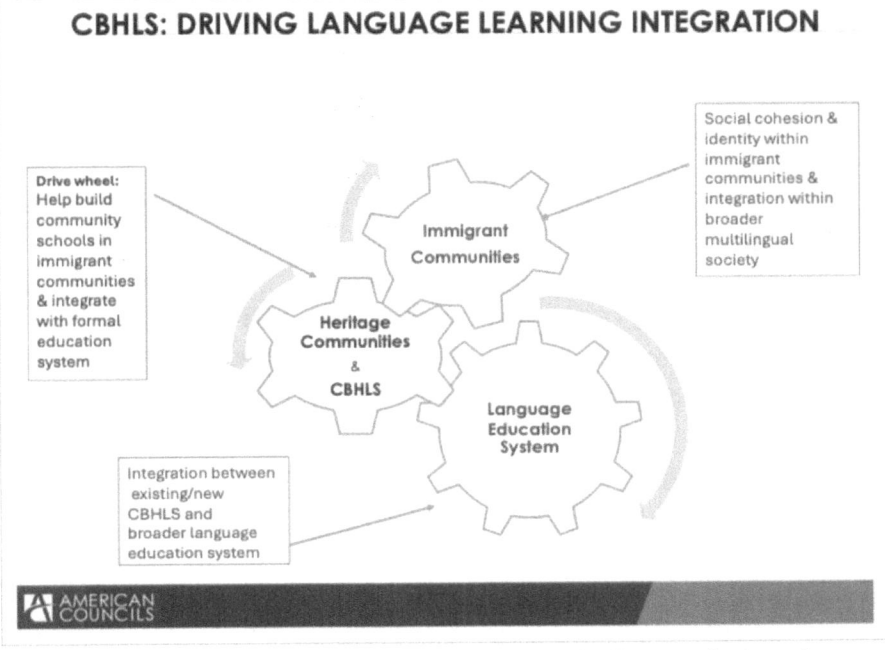

This potential is best illustrated by the challenges facing these schools and the successful practices they are implementing.

Challenges That These Schools Face

A review of the literature and the community-based programs in the Heritage Language Programs Database[126] points to the following challenges:

- Visibility: Many are not known at all by the public schools, or even the other CBHLs, in their area.
- Funding: In the United States, they do not receive funding from the federal, state, or district government, and most charge tuition; many struggle to have enough funding to be sustained. Potential funders might be those with a mission to support access to bilingual or language education, including the U.S. and State Departments of Education, Department of Defense Education Activity (DODEA), school systems with

---

[126] CCBHLS, Map of Community-Based Schools, 2025

local community connections, and private foundations like the Mellon and Ford Foundations with a longstanding commitment to underserved populations.
- Teachers: Recruitment and training. Many teachers in these schools speak the language taught, but do not have professional development or certification to teach at a top level in the formal language education system.
- Materials: Many school leaders do not have the materials they need, from their home country or from the United States, to sustain an effective curriculum and to have books for students' pleasure reading. Many are working to develop these materials.
- Recruiting and keeping students in the program over time: Often, when they reach middle and high school, students want to drop out of school. They have a lot going on during the weekends, and they might not see the value of knowing their language. Programs exist to nurture heritage learners and keep them in school. For example, Dual Language Immersion programs excel at accommodating heritage language learners, building programs from kindergarten through high school. Utah's BRIDGE program is the latest innovation that reinforces DLI through high school and as a successful transition to higher education language programming.
- Meeting space: They often rent and pay for meeting space in schools, churches, and organizational spaces.

Addressing the Challenges

CBHLS is implementing several practices to address these challenges; benefit students and parents; and build strong, engaging programs. Descriptions of these can be found in the Coalition's Heritage Briefs[127] and School Profiles.[128]

---

[127] Heritage Language Coalition. n.d.. *Heritage Briefs*
[128] Heritage Language Coalition. n.d. *School Profiles*

- Keeping students engaged in learning their language throughout their school years
- Helping students understand the value of their multilingualism
- Making it possible for students to gain credit and recognition (State and Global Seals of Biliteracy) for their language proficiency
- Collaborating with public schools and universities to accomplish these goals
- Holding strong, vital summer programs in addition to classes year-round
- Writing curriculum and lessons
- Writing pleasure reading books for students
- Working with art, music, drama, and film in the language
- Engaging and supporting parents and helping them to become advocates for the language and the schools
- Collaborating with public schools
- Receiving support from the home country

Shuhan Wang outlined successful practices that these schools can implement to address challenges such as teacher shortages, lack of motivation among students, the need for clearer goals, more relevant curriculum design and instruction, and recognition of learners' proficiency outcomes.[129] She proposes a new framework for language education that includes three pillars of learning: purpose, process, and product of learning. She suggested that we focus more on the learners' needs, goals, and the development of human intelligence instead of measuring their deficiencies in the heritage language. She also emphasized the importance of developing soft skills in the AI age, which robots cannot replace.

Building a Unifying Framework for CBHLS

The examples above form a basis for a broader action agenda within a unifying framework that includes integration with the broader

---

[129] Wang, 2024

language learning enterprise. This agenda contains a rationale, approach, goals and objectives, partnerships, advocacy, and funding.

Rationale: Building on CBHLS and the K-16 Sector

The rationale should now be clear for building a framework with the Coalition of CBHLs as the galvanizer for integrating immigrant communities, schools, and the K-16 sector. The power of CBHLs has never been specifically recognized and harnessed to this end. Better acknowledgement by, and inclusion in, the formal language education system can advantage both, on the one hand by providing more heritage language speakers in the K-16 realm and on the other by benefiting from the formal education system's resources, research, and practices. Furthermore, the Coalition enjoys the community backing that K-16 programs find difficult. It also has strong participation from students and parents, who can advocate for more equal access to language rights across the nation.

Approach

The framework here involves proactive partnerships with immigrant communities and language and educational organizations, and efforts. This bottom-up campaign calls for an 'emergent engagement strategy' at the grassroots level and more engagement with civil society organizations. The development of proactive partnerships is straightforward within language education efforts, but the 'emergent engagement strategy' requires some elaboration. 'Emergent strategy,' as defined by adrienne maree brown, following Obolensky, is based on "emergence" as "...the way complex systems and patterns arise out of a multiplicity of relatively simple interactions."[130] In this case, "emergent strategy"

> Evolved into strategies for organizers building movements for justice and liberation that leverage simple interactions to create complex patterns, systems, and transformations— including adaptation, interdependence and decentralization,

---

[130] brown, 2017, p. 3; Obolensky, 2014

fractal awareness, resilience and transformative justice, nonlinear and iterative change, creating more possibilities...and now it's like...ways for humans to practice being in right relationships to our home and each other, to practice complexity, and growing a compelling future together through relatively simple interactions (p. 23).

Regarding language learning, this involves understanding that we are in this together—heritage and immigrant communities and the K-16 language education system. Strengthening this system involves

- parents and their children understanding what benefits there are for their future health and wellbeing;
- parents engaging their broader family, friends, and acquaintances concerning these benefits and their decision to enroll their children in language programs, and taking this message to parent and teacher associations;
- extending this outreach consistently to local and state officials, as well as district school boards and university leadership.

Starting with parents does not mean that conversations necessarily begin with "language" *per se*. Still, they might revolve around their children's future well-being and success, followed by the benefits of education and specifically bilingualism and language learning to their children's self-efficacy, cognitive abilities, educational success, and employment opportunities, and only then to support language education across all of these sectors.

In this regard, civil society organizations should be approached to assist in the effort:

> Approximately 1.5 million non-government organizations (NGOs) operate in the United States. These NGOs undertake a wide array of activities, including political advocacy on issues such as foreign policy, elections, the environment, healthcare, women's rights, economic development, and many others. They often develop and address new approaches to social and economic problems

that governments cannot address alone. Many NGOs in the United States operate in fields that are not related to politics. These include volunteer organizations rooted in shared religious faith, labor unions, groups that help vulnerable people, such as the poor or disabled, and groups that seek to empower youth or marginalized populations. NGOs exist to represent virtually every cause imaginable.[131]

While the language field is well acquainted with the partnerships discussed in the following section, our endeavors in advocating for bilingualism for a healthy citizenship and productive society certainly fall within the missions of many of these civil society organizations and deserve our and their attention and collaboration.

Goals and Objectives

A.   Initial Organizing Efforts

In this regard, the U.K. effort on HHCL (Heritage, Home, Community Languages)[132] offers relevant and appropriate guidance, particularly in the initial stage.

- Identify priorities for the development of this effort.
- Create a resonance group of key stakeholders; e.g., those running regional networks supporting languages, heritage, and culture.
- Develop an 'emergent strategy' and reach out to 'civil society' organizations.
- Initiate a communication strategy for the dissemination of information and support, with effective messaging and advocacy.

B.   Internal Actions

1. Collaborate with existing heritage language and culture organizations. (See Appendix B.)

---

[131] U.S. Department of State, 2025
[132] Association for Language Learning, Home / Heritage / Community Languages ALL, "Language Zones."

2. Strengthen and expand CBHL schools: Provide them with information and resources on important topics, such as

- How to start a new community-based school and form a nonprofit organization.
- How to improve an existing program in a school – including teacher training, teacher retention, increased enrollment, student and parent engagement, effective instruction, school administration, and tax issues.
- How to grant students recognition for language proficiency – through tests, credits, State and Global Seals, and other ways.
- How to use technology in these schools.
- How to reach out to and work together with the local language community.
- How to collaborate with other schools and organizations focused on specific languages.
- How to form state, district, or regional groups of CBHLS.
- How to form a language umbrella organization for schools.
- How to incorporate project-based and inquiry-based learning in CBHL schools.
- How to develop official statistics on HL teaching and learning by collecting comprehensive data about community-based schools.

Partnerships

Strive for CBHL schools to become a full part of the national language education landscape through collaboration with immigrant and home-schooling communities and organizations, as well as K-16 programs and communities, for example:

1. Immigrant, refugee, and homeschooling communities and organizations
    - Immigrant communities. A quick query of ChatGPT on immigrant populations identifies hundreds of examples (See Appendix A.)

- Immigration and rescue organizations. (See Appendix C.)
2. Civil Society organizations focusing on social justice. (See Appendix D.)
3. Established language organizations and initiatives:
    - AATS (e.g., American Association of Teachers of Spanish) and other umbrella organizations (e.g., ACTFL, The Joint National Committee on Languages [JNCL/NCLIS], Modern Language Association [MLA], National Association of District Supervisors for Languages [NADSFL], National Council of State Supervisors for Languages [NCSSFL], etc.)
    - The "America's Languages" initiative. A recent project supported by the Mellon Foundation identifies exemplary programs across language education that are successful at reaching out to underserved learners in the U.S., including Black and People of Color, rural and urban poor, indigenous, heritage, immigrant, and deaf and hard-of-hearing communities.[133]
4. Home-schooling organizations
    - Home Schooling Legal Defense Association[134]
    - Coalition for Responsible Home Schooling[135]
5. K-12 programs and communities
    - Recognition of students' HL proficiency via
        - AP credit
        - State and Global Seals of Biliteracy

---

[133] COERLL & American Councils, America's Languages: Model Programs & Practices
[134] Home School Legal Defense Association, About Us / Advocates for Homeschooling
[135] Coalition for Responsible Home Education, "Joining a Homeschool Group"

- Language proficiency tests from home countries
- Other pathways
- Students receiving U.S. high school credit for their language skills (students should be able to substitute proficiency in their heritage language for classes offered)
- Support of CBHLS becoming accredited to provide testing results on the graduation documents of their students
- Support of CBHLS in finding ways to provide legitimization to their teachers (U.S. credit and certification for professional development and workshops from the home country)

6. Higher education institutions that accommodate heritage language speakers. For example, individual institutions (like American University) with a tradition of supporting heritage and indigenous languages, with

- Conferences and workshops
- Customized curriculum design
- Credit and/or Advanced Placement
- Higher levels of the language curriculum are needed to accommodate students entering their programs at more advanced levels.

7. Researchers
- Review existing data from established sources like the National Heritage Language Resource Center (NHLRC) and the National Less Commonly Taught Languages Resource Center (National LCTL Resource Center, NLRC) at Michigan State University.
- Include these data in official U.S. education statistics.

8. Global connections
    - Global Heritage Language Think Tank[136]
    - Professor Ken Cruickshank's newest study of heritage language schools in many countries[137]

Advocacy

Increase the visibility of CBHL schools to U.S. educators, politicians, researchers, and other stakeholders by

- Representing these schools to U.S. educators (school districts, U.S. Department of Education), politicians (State Boards of Education, state representatives), researchers, and other stakeholders
- Articulating the contributions of these schools to language education and to the well-being of communities
- Articulating the most pressing needs and challenges common to these schools (such as funding and recognition of proficiency) and advocating for the needs and challenges to be addressed
- Holding annual conferences, webinars, and online discussions
- Doing outreach via a website, Facebook page, and newsletter
- Doing outreach to and partnerships with different languages and schools
- Working with language representatives and umbrella organizations of different language groups to share experiences and best practices

Funding

Support CBHL schools to find opportunities to apply for funding from potential funders with a mission to support access to bilingualism and language education. These might include (depending on the status of these entities):

---

[136] Heritage Language Exchange Network. n.d.. *Global Heritage Language Think Tank*. Retrieved from hlenet.org/thinktank

[137] Cruickshank et al., 2024

- Public and private funding opportunities
- United States Department of Education -Titles 1, 3, 6
- Other U.S. government funding: Department of State, the Department of Defense Educational Activities (DODEA), and school systems with local community connections
- Individual states, like efforts in Utah, Virginia, and Washington
- Private foundations with a history of supporting heritage and indigenous communities and a longstanding commitment to underserved populations: e.g., Ford, Kellogg, and Mellon Foundations
- JNCL/NCLS-supported and other Congressional advocacy

However, under the current administration, many of these programs have experienced and are threatened with severe reductions that threaten their established missions.

These lists represent only a first approximation of the work that needs to be done. This work must be honed through local and national discussions for prioritization, additions, revisions, and deletions.

Conclusion

The times are challenging language education as perhaps never before: Overall enrollments in K-16 language programs are shrinking; immigrants are being demeaned or even threatened to be removed from their homes despite their economic benefit to the nation;[138] the spread of World English grows; Artificial Intelligence (AI), Large Language Models (LLMs), and translation and educational technology expand; half of the nation's population is turning inward, while 'liberal democracy' is being threatened around the world; and the lack of acceptance of diversity, human rights, and access to language services is a battle far from won. And, strong as ever, if not more so, is the need for language abilities and services in pursuit of social justice through recognition of diversity at home, as well as the

---

[138] See Pope, 2025

traditional and still relevant benefit of language and cultural understanding for national security and economic competitiveness abroad.

Simply put, *all* of America's Languages need to be mobilized *together* to confront these challenges while taking advantage of their immense advantages, starting from a much broader understanding of their history and current status among the American populace and recognition of their value to individuals, families, and communities. To be sure, calls by academics and legislators for support and expansion of language education will and should continue, but history shows that this is not enough. Community-based Heritage Language Schools stand out as a dynamic force to galvanize a broader 'emergent strategy' and outreach to 'civil society,' given that these schools are intricately connected with growing communities of foreign-born and potentially rural and urban minority populations, whose vital interests in their children's future can be served by language learning.

Appendix A. Heritage/Immigrant Communities in the U.S., From ChatGPT

1. Chinatown (SF, NYC)
2. Little Italy
3. Irish-American communities (Boston, New York, Chicago)
4. Mexican-American communities (California, Texas, Arizona)
5. Vietnamese-American communities (Orange County, California, and Houston, Texas)
6. Indian-American communities (Silicon Valley, California, and New Jersey)
7. Greek-American communities (New York City, Chicago, and Boston)
8. Polish-American communities (Chicago, New York City, and Detroit)
9. Arab-American communities (Dearborn, Michigan, Los Angeles)
10. Ukrainian-American communities (New York City, Chicago & Philadelphia)
11. German-Russian communities (North Dakota, Kansas, and Colorado)
12. Scottish-American communities (Appalachia and the Midwest)
13. Portuguese-American communities (New Bedford, MA & Newark, NJ)
14. Haitian-American communities (Miami, New York City, and Boston)
15. Armenian-American communities (Los Angeles, Glendale, and Fresno)
16. Iranian-American communities (Los Angeles, D.C., & New York City)
17. Nigerian-American communities (Houston, Dallas, and Atlanta)
18. Mauritanian-American communities (NYC, Houston, & Atlanta)

19. Maldivian-American communities (NYC, LA, & D.C.)
20. Tajik-American communities (NYC, LA, & D.C.)
21. Kyrgyz-American communities (NYC, LA, & D.C.)
22. Turkmen-American communities (NYC, LA, & D.C.)
23. Uzbek-American communities (NYC, LA, & D.C.)
24. Bahamian-American communities (Miami, NYC, & Atlanta)
25. Haitian-American communities (Miami, NYC, & Boston)
26. Barbadian-American communities (NYC, Miami, & Atlanta)
27. Jamaican-American communities (NYC, Miami, & Atlanta)

linguistic rights of children that relate to, among others, pupils' human rights, children's rights, linguistic rights to maintain and develop their HL, and the freedom from an involuntary language shift towards the majority language.[152]

Education is a human right, and it is seen as the key to improving the living conditions of people worldwide. Although all students should have equal access to quality education and equal opportunities,[153] it has been abundantly shown that language barriers pose a significant challenge for plurilingual students to study in mainstream educational settings with traditional focus on teaching the language of instruction and in the language of instruction.[154] Instruction in HL and learning through the medium of HL provide HL pupils with additional education and additional pathways to education.[155]

Community-based HL schools have a long tradition of providing HL education in all geographical locations.[156] They are language learning institutions that have unique organizational structures, funding models, curricula, community and cultural events, and locations. These schools are typically organized and operated by HL communities, religious institutions, or community members. A defining feature is that these schools are not organized by and funded through the local public school system. Still, they are influenced by the local system, which further increases the broader diversity of HL school types. For many HLs, these schools are the only way that HL learners have access to formal language instruction in their home language.[157]

Community-based HL schools often provide HL instruction. Yet, sometimes, states create other solutions for their HL learners, such as accredited primary schools, accredited HL schools and programs,

---

[152] Szoszkiewicz, 2017
[153] European Agency for Special Needs and Inclusive Education, 2017
[154] Cummins, 2000; OECD, 2023
[155] Cruickshank et al., 2023; Lamb, 2020
[156] Cruickshank et al., 2023
[157] Lamb, 2020

Appendix B. Examples of Heritage Language and Culture Organizations

See also heritagelanguageschools.org/coalition/organizations

- Pew Research Center Hispanic Trends Project (2015)
- Asian-American and Pacific Islander (AAPI) Data (2017)
- National Center for Education Statistics (NCES) (2019)
- Migration Policy Institute
- American Community Survey cultural events to help preserve the language
- Arab-American Institute
- South Asian-American Policy & Research Institute
- Korean-American Coalition
- Southeast Asia Resource Action Center
- U.S. Department of Education: Bilingual Education Programs
- University of Minnesota Hmong
- Ethiopian Community Center in Washington, D.C
- Brazilian-American Center in Framingham, Massachusetts
- Japanese-American Citizens League
- Ukrainian Congress Committee of America
- American-Turkish Association of New York
- South Asian-American Digital Archive Bengali
- Greek Orthodox Archdiocese of America
- Minnesota Department of Health Somali
- Armenian National Committee of America
- Iranian-American Community Center
- Punjabi Cultural Society of America
- Chinese for Affirmative Action
- Philippine-American Society of Greater Philadelphia Tagalog
- Florida International University Cuban community
- University of Texas at Dallas, Pakistani Urdu

- Gujarati Samaj of New Jersey
- Thai Community Development Center in Los Angeles
- Louisiana State University French-speaking immigrants, including those from Haiti and African countries, speak French or Haitian Creole at home.
- Cambodian Mutual Assistance Association of Greater Lowell, MA
- Persian Cultural Center in San Diego
- Nepali-American Foundation
- Ukrainian Educational and Cultural Center in Philadelphia
- Hungarian Cultural Association of Cleveland
- American Jewish Committee
- Tamil Cultural Association of Southern California
- Portuguese-American Leadership Council of the United States
- Lithuanian-American Community of Chicago
- Serbian-American Museum St. Sava in Chicago
- Ethiopian Community Development Council in Virginia

Appendix C. Examples of Immigration and Rescue Organizations

Immigration Organizations

- Immigration Advocates Network
- Immigration Policy Center
- Migration Policy Institute
- National Center for Law and Economic Justice
- National Council of La Raza
- National Immigration Forum
- National Network for Immigrant and Refugee Rights
- Urban Institute

Rescue Organizations

- International Rescue Committee (IRC)
- Lutheran Immigration and Refugee Service (LIRS)
- United States Committee for Refugees and Immigrants (USCRI)
- Catholic Charities USA
- World Relief: Upwardly Global
- Ethiopian Community Development Council (ECDC)
- Iraqi Mutual Aid Society (IMAS)
- Asian Pacific Development Center (APDC)
- Minnesota Council of Churches (MCC)
- The International Rescue Committee's local offices

Appendix D. Examples of Civil Society Organizations

- Asian & Pacific Islander-American Health Forum
- Center on Budget and Policy Priorities
- Center for Law and Social Policy
- Civil Rights Litigation Clearinghouse (Washington Univ., St. Louis, MO)
- Food Research Action Center
- Immigration Advocates Network
- Immigration Law Help
- Immigration Policy Center
- Interfaith Worker Justice
- Migration Policy Institute
- National Center for Law and Economic Justice
- National Center for Youth Law
- National Council of La Raza
- National Employment Law Project
- National Health Law Program
- National Immigration Forum
- National Lawyers Guild, National Immigration Project
- National Legal Aid and Defender Association
- National Network for Immigrant and Refugee Rights
- National Senior Citizens Law Center
- Sargent Shriver National Center on Poverty Law
- Transactional Records Access Clearinghouse
- Urban Institute

Chapter 3

Streamlining Heritage Language Education in Europe: From European Policies to State Support Measures

Renata Emilsson Peskova, Marie Boccou Kestřánková, Lenka Vaněčková, and Michaela Chlostová Munoz

Heritage Language Education in the Light of European Policies

Multilingualism is an integral part of democratic citizenship and social cohesion in Europe. According to the Universal Declaration of Human Rights, "(e)ducation shall be directed to the full development of the human personality and the strengthening of respect for human rights and fundamental freedoms."[139] All children have the right to have equitable access to education and to use and develop their mother tongues.[140] Educational equity is also closely related to equitable access to heritage language (HL) education. Education in and through an HL is the basis for education for active European citizenship and social cohesion, through creating links with the (parents') country of origin, as well as the country of residence.

HLs are languages that are not official languages of the community or country where the speaker is currently residing, and they are spoken by individuals and groups living in that community and country.[141] HL learners are children or adults who are in the process of learning an HL.[142] Some HL learners may be ancestrally

---

[139] United Nations, 1948
[140] UN General Assembly, 1989
[141] Cummins, 1992
[142] Valdés, 2005

affiliated with a language and culture but have lost the ability to use the language in personally meaningful ways. These learners often have intrinsic motivation and cultural knowledge that second language learners do not.[143] In contrast, some HL learners may appear "near-native" and can use the language for multiple purposes in multiple contexts. These learners may differ from monolingually-educated speakers in their knowledge of grammar, vocabulary, literacy, and popular culture. They have varied linguistic repertoires and plurilingual language systems due to an interruption in their language learning and use.[144] In this research, we use the term HL pupil when we speak about HL users who acquire their competencies in HL not only in the family environment but also in formal or non-formal educational institutions organized or supported by the country of origin, by the country of residence, or by grassroots organizations.

HL education contributes to the development of learners' plurilingual and intercultural competencies that are highly valued in educating European citizens in the 21st century.[145] The Council of Europe emphasizes that "(p)olicies which are not limited to managing language diversity but which adopt plurilingualism as a goal may also provide a more concrete basis for democratic citizenship in Europe."[146] According to Article 22 of the Charter of Fundamental Rights of the EU,[147] the provision of quality education in two or three languages is an obvious prerequisite for modern education in the European Union. Research and reports on the provisions for HL education in Europe are scarce, nor is there a comprehensive knowledge of existing HL coalitions and organizations in the European context. The struggle for recognition

---

[143] Lee & Shin, 2008
[144] Montrul, 2016
[145] Council of Europe, 2007
[146] Ibid., p. 10
[147] Charter of Fundamental Rights of the EU, 2000

of HL is similar to that of sign languages, official minority languages, and indigenous languages.[148]

There is little or no knowledge about the assistance that countries provide for their expatriates to maintain their children's HLs. Although the number of users of the HL of all nations continues to grow in Europe and worldwide, European countries do not yet pay sufficient attention to the issues of teaching HL to this specific group of young speakers, and neither are their competencies in HL formally acknowledged. Without formal education in HL, standard varieties and literacies are mostly not transmitted and developed. The development of formal structures of HL education, its formal recognition, as well as the field of heritage didactics, are needed to fulfill the human linguistic rights of plurilingual speakers in Europe.[149]

The 4EU+ project, *Educating heritage language learners and pupils learning a second language: Differences in approaches,*[150] was concerned with registrations of HL learners by countries of origin, linguistic support for the HL development that the countries of origin offer, and pedagogies that teachers from HL schools in countries of residence employ to support HL pupils. The premise was the need for the differentiation of pedagogical approaches to teaching HL speakers, some of whom are educated in two school systems simultaneously, the local educational system and some form of HL education, either community-based non-formal educational settings, or formalized HL schools. The participating countries were France, Switzerland, the Czech Republic, Poland, Italy, and Iceland. We explored the issues of respect for linguistic human rights in the light of weak or non-existent opportunities to develop and learn HL in educational settings, and the different pathways that European countries have developed to provide these opportunities. Additionally, the perspectives of primary classroom teachers, who educate HL users,

---

[148] Aberdeen et al., 2021
[149] Boccou Kestřánková & Hrdlička, 2024
[150] 4EU+ 2023

on the linguistic support that they can provide to their plurilingual pupils, were explored.

In this article, the main aim is to map if and how four European countries, the Czech Republic, France, Iceland, and Switzerland, register HL pupils in their national languages, and what educational solutions they offer to them. The national provisions for HL education are further discussed in view of children's educational and linguistic human rights, and the concept of social cohesion. Document analysis of available policy and academic documents in each respective country was conducted. Two research questions that this article aims to answer are:

1) How do four European countries support the learning of their language abroad among HL pupils?
2) How do current provisions for HL education for HL pupils respond to existing policies of the Council of Europe on linguistic human rights and access to education?

To answer these questions, we searched available information and documents in four countries, and we employed the document analysis method.[151] This research has a local and a European dimension. By collecting information from four different European countries, we showcase some functional examples of states supporting their HL pupils' HL learning, thus creating linguistic bridges between the countries of origin and the new generations of their diaspora. These examples may also be interesting in the international context, where circumstances and practices to support HL learning may be hugely different.

Links between HL Education, Children's Educational and Linguistic Rights, and the Concept of Social Cohesion

This research contributes to the state of the art in the field of HL education, which is growing, yet often overlooked and underestimated. The research is rooted in the field of educational and

---

[151] Bowen, 2009

online solutions, or state-run examinations. Other opportunities to learn HL and through HL may be in international schools, bilingual primary schools, immersion schools, content and language integrated learning (CLIL) models, HL classes organized by the local authorities,[158] and other educational settings. More models exist, for example, European schools.[159]

Educational contexts characterized by growing linguistic diversity require new understandings of the relations between language, education, and human rights.[160] These relations are expressed in children's linguistic human rights, a term that emphasizes the concept of equality for all languages enshrined in the Universal Declaration of Linguistic Rights.[161] Signatories to the United Nations Convention on the Rights of the Child[162] who incorporated it into their domestic policies have a legal obligation to respond to children's linguistic human rights. That can be done by addressing the increasing language diversity in domestic educational policies and practices, for example, by making provisions for HL education. HL pupils' right to learn their HL is further rooted in the Universal Declaration on Linguistic Rights[163] and the European Charter for Regional and Minority Languages.[164]

The discourse on linguistic human rights, and specifically on HL education, is also closely related to the concept of social cohesion. The idea of social cohesion is mostly associated with shared norms, values, and identification, relations between individuals, participation, trust towards institutions, and the unequal distribution of resources. Its multidimensionality makes it a complex term that can be controversial and interpreted even in opposing terms.[165]

---

[158] Gruntová, 2018; Schader, 2015
[159] Office of the Secretary-General of the European Schools, 2023
[160] Gollifer et al., 2024
[161] UNESCO, 1996
[162] UN General Assembly, 1989
[163] UNESCO, 1996
[164] Council of Europe, 1992
[165] Schiefer & van der Noll, 2017

HL education could be seen as disruptive or conducive to social cohesion, depending on stakeholders' perspectives. The negative views, often strengthened during the time of increased migration and refugee crises, highlight the risk of the disruption of social cohesion by creating compartments and parallel societies,[166] and little or no benefit of HL education for learning the societal majority language.[167] Arguments that positively link HL education and social cohesion focus on the development of feelings for one's community, a sense of belonging, understanding and respecting linguistic and cultural diversity,[168] developing positive plurilingual identities in safe educational spaces of HL schools,[169] the respect for human and linguistic rights, the respect for plurilingualism, personal, professional, and economic growth, harnessing cultural and linguistic diversity for identity creation, and civic participation.[170]

HL education responds to children's human, educational, and linguistic rights, and can also be seen as a way towards increased social cohesion of the receiving societies. HL education offers states a pathway to fulfill their obligations toward HL users, both within local contexts toward plurilingual students residing in the countries, and pupils speaking HL of the country with residence abroad. Although practical implementation of HL education poses challenges even in rich countries committed to values of social justice and inclusion,[171] the arguments rooted in European and international policies and declarations provide a clear message to the nations of the world about their obligations to protect and promote children's linguistic human rights and educational rights.

---

[166] Damanakis, 2017
[167] Ólafsdóttir et al., 2017
[168] Aberdeen et al., 2021
[169] Emilsson Peskova, 2021
[170] Arvanitis, 2017
[171] Emilsson Peskova et al., 2023

An Analysis of Provisions for the Support of HL Education in Four European Countries

Qualitative methodology was employed to gain insight into the provisions of four European countries. The research data was collected in two phases. The first phase involved identifying and collecting data about state support of HL learning abroad, and the other phase entailed pilot studies to understand pedagogies that teachers in countries of residence employed to support HL learners in their classrooms. This article reports on the data collected in the first phase in the Czech Republic, France, Iceland, and Switzerland, where the researchers systematically searched for accessible information online, in published documents, and by contacting local authorities and organizations. The researchers in each country followed the same protocol (see Table 1).

1) Find out about the registration of HL pupils (with or without citizenship) by countries of origin.	Sub-questions
	Does any registration of pupils with HL take place in your country?
	Does the state keep a register of these pupils?
	How many pupils are enrolled in HL schools with Czech, French, Icelandic, or Swiss languages as their HL? How many pupils are officially enrolled in schools?
	Where did you get this information? If you did not obtain it, where did you look for it?
	Is the information about registrations easily available to the public, i.e., parents, students, and educators?

2) What specific linguistic support for HL development does each country provide to its HL learners abroad?	Sub-questions: Does your country offer HL summer schools, courses, learning materials, or projects? Is the support free of charge or paid? How is the support (incl. linguistic support) advertised and made public (especially to parents)?
3) Are there any accredited HL schools?	Sub-questions: Are there accredited HL schools outside your country that provide HL instruction, not first/dominant language instruction, and whose school reports are recognized by your country's Ministry of Education as equivalent to school attendance in your country?

Table 1. The research protocol

The team analyzed the data with document analysis, which is a systematic method of extracting, organizing, and interpreting printed and/or online documents.[172] Table 2 shows the documents that we accessed and analyzed to answer our research questions.

---

[172] Bowen, 2009

Type of document	Document	Criteria for choosing
Czech Republic		
Website – government	Ministerstvo zahraničních věcí České republiky [Ministry of Foreign Affairs of the Czech Republic]	- Information about the Czech diaspora - Information about Czech schools abroad - The annual international conference of Czech schools abroad
Website – government	Ministerstvo školství, mládeže a tělovýchovy [Ministry of Education, Youth and Sports]	- Support of the Czech diaspora - Education Act, 561/2004, §38
Website – official statistics	Český statistický úřad [Czech Statistical Office]	- Official statistical data of the Czech Republic, i.e., the number of inhabitants, the number of foreign nationals
Website – official statistics	Statistický informační systém MŠMT [Statistical information system of the Ministry of Education, Youth and Sports]	- Official statistical data of the Czech Republic - A system for registering pupils who take differential exams at STEM schools

Website – research	Výzkumné projekty Čeští krajané [Research Projects Czech Compatriots]	Official results of academic research on the Czech diaspora
Law – Education Act	Školský zákon, 561/2004 Sb., §38 [Education Act, 561/2004, §38]	• Registrations of Czech HL pupils
Policy document – Education policy	Rámcový vzdělávací program pro základní vzdělávání [Framework curriculum for compulsory education]	• Information about educational and linguistic support for plurilingual students
Personal communication (E. Tučková, 02/06/23)	Ministry of Education, Youth and Sports of the Czech Republic, Department of Primary Education	• Number of Czech children educated abroad • Consultation about the Education Act, 561/2004, §38
France		
Document/recherche of the Court of Accounts	Cour des comptes: L'Enseignement français à l'étranger [Court of Account: French education abroad]	Resume of the situation of the French language abroad
Website – statistical data	Statista	Comparison of demographic data with other found numbers

Website of the Ministry of Europe and Foreign Affairs	France Diplomatie [French diplomacy]	General information about French citizens living abroad
Website of the French administration	Service Public [Public service]	Organization of compulsory school attendance in France
Iceland		
Website – official statistics	Hagstofa Íslands [Statistics Iceland]	Number of foreign nationals in Iceland, and the number of Icelandic minors living abroad, are not available
Website – registrations of inhabitants	Þjóðskrá [Registers Iceland]	Number of foreign nationals in Iceland and the number of Icelandic minors living abroad are not available
Personal communication (Á. M. Urbancic, 04/26/23)	Statistics Iceland	Information about registrations of Icelandic nationals (minors) living abroad
Policy document – Education policy	National Curriculum Guide for Compulsory Schools	Information about educational and linguistic support for plurilingual students in Iceland

Switzerland		
Website – Federal statistics	Office fédéral de la statistique - Effectif des Suisses de l'étranger selon le pays ou le territoire de résidence, circonscription consulaire, droit de cité, sexe et âge, 2016-2022 [Federal Statistical Office - abroad by country or territory of residence, consular district, citizenship, gender and age, 2016-2022]	Official statistical data of the Confederation
Website – research	Service de la recherche en éducation de Genève [Research on education service of Geneva]	Number of children from the canton of Geneva studying abroad, and the type of schools
Personal communication (E. Guilley, 04/06/23)	Service de la recherche en éducation de Genève [Research on education of Geneva]	Number of children from the canton of Geneva studying abroad, and the type of schools
Website – research	Écoles suisses à l'étranger [Swiss schools abroad]	Type of support for HL learners from Switzerland Information about Swiss schools abroad, linked to the official administrative website of the Confederation

Table 2. Overview of sources of information selected for analysis

We started the analysis in each country by identifying existing documents about HL education, institutional websites, and other accessible resources related to our research questions. After that, we compared and discussed the findings from all four countries, and we organized the information according to our sub-questions. Next, we searched for themes to elicit from our integrated data. The following step was to interpret the data and the themes and to place them in the context of the documents of the Council of Europe. The themes are presented in the section on findings, while contextualizing the findings within European policies takes place in the discussion section. The research study followed the standard ethical guidelines of the Charles University Code of Ethics.[173] Data on HL pupils and HL instruction are not publicly available and easily accessible in each country. Thus, the reliance on different documents and personal communications in each country is among the unescapable limitations in the data collection.

State Support of their Languages Abroad by Four European countries

In the following four short sections, findings from four countries are described, and the research question about registrations of HL pupils, including the sub-questions, is answered.

Czech Republic

The Czech Republic (CR) has a population of just under 11 million.[174] Since World War II, Czech society has been predominantly monolingual with one official language and a small number of national minorities. Approximately 250,000 Czechs currently live abroad,[175] but the Czech diaspora is significantly larger. Around 2.5 million compatriots, i.e., participants in migration from the Czech territory, claim Czech origin and maintain ties to the

---

[173] Charles University, 2018
[174] Český statistický úřad, 2022
[175] Ministerstvo zahraničních věcí ČR, 2023

CR.[176] The Czech school system is decentralized, which means that the responsibility for educational outcomes lies with individual schools, rather than with the state administration.[177]

The CR registers Czech pupils studying abroad, in accordance with Section 38 of the Education Act.[178] Legal representatives (parents and custodians) of Czech citizens receiving education abroad must register the child with the Ministry of Education, Youth and Sports (MŠMT ČR) or a STEM school (a school of parents'/custodians' choice in the CR) and prove to them that the child attends compulsory education abroad. The MŠMT ČR thus partially maintains the record of one important subgroup of pupils who have Czech as an HL and may also be educated in Czech. However, it cannot be deduced from this registration whether the pupils have developed Czech as an HL.

According to the provisions of Section 38(3) of the Education Act, it is possible for Czech pupils who have been enrolled in a primary school abroad for a long time to attend a primary school in the CR simultaneously. This means that these pupils can attend classes during their stays in the CR, e.g., during spring break in the country of residence, and they are obliged to take the mentioned differential exams regularly during the school year in the CR. Information on these pupils can be found in the Statistical Yearbooks of Education.[179] The data on HL pupils is inaccurate because these pupils are listed together with pupils with permanent residence in the CR, educated in a language other than Czech, e.g., pupils attending English medium schools in Prague. These pupils also take differential examinations in Czech STEM schools. This means that these two groups of children are included in one category.

The most important linguistic support for the maintenance and development of Czech abroad is undoubtedly the promotion of the growth of Czech HL schools. While these schools were established

---

[176] Výzkumné projekty Čeští krajané, 2023
[177] Müllner, 2021
[178] Školský zákon 561/2004
[179] Statistický informační systém MŠMT ČR, 2023

through the initiative of the Czech diaspora, the MŠMT ČR, and the Ministry of Foreign Affairs (MZV ČR) encourage the work of these schools by providing counseling and financial support. The support also includes activities of the Department for Compatriot Affairs of the MZV ČR. Additionally, the National Pedagogical Institute of the CR, the Faculty of Arts of Charles University, the Institute of Language and Preparatory Studies of Charles University, and others, offer methodological support for teachers of Czech HL pupils.

The MZV ČR recognizes the existence of two basic types of Czech schools abroad: contracted and non-contracted. Non-contracted schools are schools without a contract with the MŠMT ČR. The total number of these schools is not known. They are run mostly voluntarily by non-governmental local organizations. Their curricula depend on the size and activity of the community that runs the school; they have different organization and activities, and they adapt to local conditions. All over the world, new Czech schools are continuously being established and dissolved due to various circumstances.

Contracted schools are Czech schools abroad with which the MŠMT ČR has signed a contract, and which are listed as education providers contracted to provide education to Czech citizens during the period of compulsory school attendance. These schools provide primary education, sometimes only for the initial years of primary school. These institutions provide education following the requirements set out in the Framework curriculum for primary education. Their pupils can therefore receive a certificate that corresponds to the report card from the STEM school in the CR. There are currently fifteen Czech contracted schools, located in Austria, France, Germany, Italy, Spain, Switzerland, the UK, and the USA.[180] The CR financially supports all contracted schools, and most non-contracted schools also claim some financial support.

---

[180] MZV ČR, 2023

Education in Czech for pupils abroad is usually not free, and parents pay school fees.[181]

France

The total population of France is about 68 million.[182] The estimated number of French citizens living abroad is about 2.5 million.[183] In France, there is no register of French HL pupils living abroad, according to the information from the Ministry of Education.[184] However, the issue of maintaining the HL of French youth living abroad is important in France, and the state has made various provisions to promote it since 2012.[185]

Although there is a register relevant to our topic, it is unfortunately outdated: A register held by the Ministry of Foreign Affairs on French people living abroad, where they can voluntarily register. The latest update is from February 2021. The role of the register, to keep in contact in the case of danger, was probably taken over by a consular application, Fil d'Ariane.[186] Since then, the data has not been directly accessible to the public.

The educational organization National Centre for Distance Education (CNED) provides complementary online courses for pupils who live abroad and wish to continue in the French National Education system upon return to France. One of their programs is created specifically for the French pupils' needs.[187] However, information about their registration or the number of pupils involved in this special program was not available. CNED is only one of the organizations that provide this service. Still, it is widespread and, in partnership with the French Ministry of Foreign Affairs, mainly concerns teaching the French language abroad.[188]

---

[181] For more information, see Boccou Kestřánková & Hubáčková, 2023
[182] Statista, 2023
[183] France Diplomatie, 2023a
[184] J. Caillaudeau, personal communication, August 4, 2023
[185] Cour des comptes, 2016
[186] France Diplomatie, 2023b
[187] Cour des comptes, 2016
[188] Ibid.

The Ministry of Education maintains a list of organizations that provide French education abroad, mainly the same national education as in France. The list is not exhaustive, and it includes several types of organizations (accredited, not accredited, and partnership organizations). Currently, schools in 139 countries are listed. Approximately 370,000 pupils attend these schools; however, it is indicated that 60% of them are foreign nationals,[189] so it can be understood that these 60% are French HL pupils growing abroad without a French nationality, or they are French second language users with a high language competence level. However, the total number of French HL pupils is not available or publicly accessible.

The needs of French HL pupils are covered mainly by CNED's online courses, but also by local organizations, linked to various extents to French national education. The French government has aimed to support and collaborate with the French HL organizations since 2012,[190] but its tangible steps are unclear. It seems that various initiatives concerning HL French originate from the HL organizations rather than the government, even though both of them perceive mutual support and collaboration as critical. That may change with the new *Council of Interministerial Orientation in the Education of French Abroad*, established in July 2023. In its review, we can read that "French education abroad creates today the political priority of the government within the Ministry of Europe and Foreign Affairs."[191]

Iceland

Iceland has a population of 387,758,[192] with about twenty percent of the total population having international roots. In December 2022, 48,951 Icelanders lived outside the country, or 13.2% of the population. Traditionally, Icelandic communities living abroad preserved their language, in particular when a larger number of

---

[189] Ministère de l'Éducation nationale et de la jeunesse, 2023a
[190] Cour des comptes, 2016
[191] Ministère de l'Éducation nationale et de la jeunesse, 2023b
[192] Hagstofa Íslands, 2023

Icelanders resided in one locality. An example of this is Gimli, Manitoba, Canada, where over 100,000 people of Icelandic descent have lived since 1875 and preserved their language and culture until today. In modern history, Jónshúsið in Copenhagen, Denmark, is an example of an Icelandic community center, serving a population of about 4,000 residing in the former Icelandic capital.[193]

Statistics Iceland (Icel. Hagstofa Íslands) traces the number of children with Icelandic citizenship living abroad, through the applications for Icelandic citizenship of parents for newborn babies abroad (children of Icelandic citizens have an automatic right to Icelandic citizenship), and through compulsory registration of legal residence abroad of Icelandic citizens. Regarding information about pupils, Statistics Iceland collects information about students who attend schools in Iceland, and about undergraduate/graduate students who received a study loan in Iceland. The statistics offices of other countries could register general information about Icelandic students abroad.[194]

Registers Iceland (Icel. Þjóðskrá) registers Icelandic children who moved abroad.[195] If they attended a preschool or a compulsory school in Iceland, it would be possible to find out about their registered mother tongue. However, only one mother tongue can be registered per person, and therefore, the information is not complete. The Ministry of Education and Children does not keep a registry of Icelandic students studying abroad. No special Icelandic course for Icelandic HL speakers living abroad exists, nor are there special tests for Icelandic competence of Icelandic HL learners living abroad.[196]

Thus, to answer the research question about registrations, no official register of Icelandic HL pupils exists in Iceland. There is no list of existing community-based Icelandic HL schools, and the Icelandic government supports no such schools. These schools have existed temporarily in cities with Icelandic diaspora, but they

---

[193] Jónshús, 2023
[194] Á. M. Urbancic, personal communication, April 26, 2023
[195] Þjóðskrá, 2023
[196] D. Honkowicz-Bukowska, personal communication, April 26, 2023

received no official support, nor have authorities listed them. Icelandic authorities do not provide any specific linguistic support to Icelandic HL pupils in primary and secondary schools abroad. Icelandic children residing in the Nordic countries can learn Icelandic as a mother tongue as part of their compulsory schooling if certain conditions are fulfilled. These provisions are, however, offered by the local governments of the Nordic countries, not by the Icelandic authorities. Similarly, Iceland offers mother tongue instruction to Swedish and Norwegian pupils, and all school children learn Danish as a foreign language.[197] In its policy documents, Iceland confirms plurilingual children's rights to develop and learn their mother tongues.[198] Therefore, it is possible to say that although Iceland fails to support Icelandic HL teaching abroad, it has taken some measures to support HL teaching of some languages locally.

Switzerland

Switzerland is a Confederation consisting of 26 cantons, and each of them has its own school system and organization. According to the Federal Statistical Office, 168,753 children aged 0 to 17 live abroad,[199] yet no information is provided about their schooling, at the federal or cantonal level. Local authorities, for example, the Research on Education Services of Geneva, do not collect such information.[200] Hence, the places and types of schooling, as well as the number of children enrolled in them, are unknown. Three types of schools abroad are presented on the webpage of Education Suisse – Schweizerschulen im Ausland: Swiss schools abroad, international schools, and other schools or training projects.[201]

In this section, the focus is on the Swiss schools abroad. There are currently 17 Swiss schools based in 10 countries: Brazil, Chile, China, Italy, Colombia, Mexico, Peru, Singapore, Spain, and Thailand. Some

---

[197] Emilsson Peskova et al., 2023
[198] Ministry of Education, Science and Culture, 2014
[199] Office fédéral de la statistique, 2022
[200] Service de la recherche en éducation de Genève, 2023
[201] Education Suisse – Schweizerschulen im Ausland, 2023

of them, such as Italy and Mexico, host more than one school. The first Swiss school was founded in 1839 in Napoli. Since then, more than 20 schools have opened, some of which have closed. These schools mostly offer bilingual, even plurilingual education (mostly in German, one of the official Swiss languages, in the language of the host country, and/or in English) to children of Swiss citizenship as well as pupils of other nationalities. 7,500 pupils, of whom 1,800 have Swiss nationality, are currently enrolled in these schools.

Based on Swiss law from March 2014, Swiss schools are private schools accredited by the Confederation. Each of the 17 schools is supervised by one of the Swiss cantons.[202] In private schools, school fees are partly paid by the parents, with the Confederation contributing at a maximum of 50% to the costs. The cost to families was not readily available on the website, and thus, it is hard to estimate how accessible this type of schooling is to families abroad.

All Swiss schools abroad follow the Swiss educational system and offer a certification recognized by Swiss authorities. Thus, they provide primary education, sometimes also secondary education, therefore enabling their students to access studies and apprenticeships upon their return to Switzerland. All teachers in Swiss schools must have teacher certification from Switzerland, and Swiss citizenship is desirable. The teaching and learning support in Swiss schools abroad is the same as in Swiss local schools, according to the official curriculum for German-speaking cantons. Additionally, each Swiss school uses the specific pedagogical and didactic supports of its mentor canton, with adaptations made by teachers.[203]

In the above section, findings from four European countries were presented. Each section represented one country, and it answered the first research question: How do four European countries support the learning of their language abroad among HL pupils? Sub-questions

---

[202] Loi sur les écoles suisses à l'étranger, 2014
[203] For more information, see Education Suisse – Schweizerschulen im Ausland, 2023

about registrations of pupils and HL schools were also answered. The summary of the results is displayed in Table 3 below.

	Registration of HL pupils (with or without citizenship) by countries of origin	Linguistic support for HL pupils abroad is provided by the country of origin.	Existence of accredited HL schools outside of the country of origin
Czech Republic	Yes, by the Ministry of Foreign Affairs of the Czech Republic	Yes, mainly by the promotion of Czech HL schools	Yes, 15 HL schools contracted by the Ministry of Education, Youth, and Sports
France	No	No	Yes, schools in 139 countries are listed, with approximately 370,000 pupils
Iceland	No	No	No
Switzerland	No	Yes, by partial reimbursement of school fees, providing specific pedagogical and didactic support	Yes, 17 Swiss schools based in 10 countries, with 7,500 pupils

Table 3. Overview of provisions for the support of HL education provided by the four countries of origin

In short, the Czech Republic is the only one out of the four countries that imposes the duty on parents of children and youth with Czech citizenship to register their children either with the Ministry of Education, Science and Sports, or with STEM schools in the Czech

Republic. At the same time, the Czech Republic records whether Czech citizens abroad receive compulsory school education. However, the total group of pupils developing Czech as HL is not recorded according to the available sources. The Czech Republic, France, and Switzerland contract, establish, and support distinct types of schools that teach their languages either as HLs or as first languages abroad.

The countries support these schools with counseling, staff, finances, and other means. These countries also have lists, or registers, of these HL schools, available to their citizens abroad, although the lists may not be comprehensive and easily accessible. The number of pupils enrolled with HL schools is not publicly available, and based on personal communications of the researchers with ministries and national statistics offices, it is nonexistent. Iceland is the only country of the four that does not provide any support or financing to its expatriate communities to maintain and teach Icelandic to children abroad.

National Provisions for HL Education against the Backdrop of European Policies

The following section contains the discussion of the findings from four countries, and the answer to the second research question: How do current provisions for HL education for HL pupils respond to existing policies of the Council of Europe on linguistic human rights and access to education? We maintain that offering HL education to children corresponds to the policies of the Council of Europe,[204] as well as international policies,[205] as it gives pathways to education in pupils' HL, and through HL, while providing them with sociocultural settings in which children can enjoy, affirm, and develop their plurilingual identities in safe educational spaces.[206] European policies give a clear message to European countries about children's linguistic and educational rights and about the common

---

[204] Council of Europe, 1992, 2007
[205] United Nations, 1948; UNESCO, 1996; UN General Assembly, 1989
[206] Emilsson Peskova, 2021

goals of social cohesion in society. The implementation of children's rights and joint political goals rests upon individual countries that make vastly different provisions in HL education for their speakers.[207]

France and Switzerland support numerous educational institutions and arrangements abroad, and the Czech Republic builds to a considerable extent on existing grassroots educational organizations and supports them financially and professionally. Iceland, on the other hand, with a population of under half a million people and small compatriot communities dispersed across the globe, has not found other solutions than digital to support Icelandic teaching to children living abroad. France and Switzerland have the longest history of supporting their languages, while the Czech Republic has been developing its HL support only since the early 90s. Iceland was largely isolated and monolingual until the early 90s when it joined the Schengen economic area. While Czech and Icelandic are only spoken by the nationals of the two countries, German and French, taught by Swiss and French HL organizations, are in general spoken by much larger populations worldwide for historical and other reasons. Solutions adopted by individual countries seem to be systematic, based on their legal and political structures, yet also organic, built on current situations and needs. There may be several reasons why countries offer different solutions, such as the population and its language profile, the number of HL speakers abroad, economic and political situations, or indeed, the effort to fulfill their legal obligations to secure children's linguistic and educational rights.[208]

HL education in Europe has multiple shortcomings. Primarily, it is available only to a small number of plurilingual children. The accessibility of HL instruction is limited for distinct reasons, such as fees for schooling in HL schools, limited numbers of HL schools, and their locations only in some countries, in larger cities, and in larger expatriate communities. The countries' long-term perspectives are not clear from the national documents analyzed in this study.

---

[207] Emilsson Peskova et al., 2023
[208] Ibid.; Gollifer et al., 2024

Collaborations to provide HL education in Europe are bilateral at best, action plans regarding the provision of HL education are not readily available, and are probably nonexistent. Coordination of HL education on a European level would enhance the field, yet it is hard to foresee it soon because of the complexity and marginalization of the field. There are limited resources, few reports, and HL research in Europe is insufficient. Acknowledgment and testing of competencies in HL across Europe are also not coordinated and readily accessible. We envision that coordinated European policy would support the educational systems of European countries to improve the education of HL users systematically. Coordinated measures in HL assessment and international certifications, such as the Global Seal of Biliteracy,[209] could both promote positive attitudes of HL learners towards HL learning and provide measurable proof of language competence acquired within or outside of the formal educational system. Such steps would also promote European linguistic diversity, social cohesion, and lead the new generation towards active citizenship.

A Vision for a Coordinated European Framework in HL Education

Despite the growing number of HL speakers in Europe and of HL schools in non-formal and formal educational contexts, and the increasing interest of experts in research in the field of HL education, systemic measures (European policy, HL methodologies, assessment, teaching resources, etc.) that would ensure the functional connection of theory and practice are largely absent for the time being. An accessible, systematic, high-quality HL education for young HL speakers is needed to fulfill the European language policies and linguistic human rights and educational rights, anchored within them. That requires a series of interrelated and complementary steps on the part of states, primary and secondary schools, and universities. On the state level, we suggest that it is necessary to introduce a series of educational measures (e.g., adjusting curricula), ensure the

---

[209] Global Seal of Biliteracy, 2023

development of suitable teaching materials (e.g., the need for suitable textbooks according to the national educational policies), comprehensively encourage the maintenance of active citizenship of compatriots abroad (e.g., the issue of distance voting rights), and provide funding for research in the field of heritage linguistic and HL education.[210] That also entails collecting information about HL pupils and monitoring the needs of expatriate and multilingual families living abroad. Although each of the countries involved in this project, as well as other European countries, is implementing certain supporting steps, these appear to be little coordinated and not comprehensive, as the frameworks of human, children's, educational, and linguistic rights require.[211] Our recommendation is thus in agreement with the valid European and international policies that all countries should make a tangible effort to provide their citizens and their children abroad with access to HL education. We conclude this article with the recommendation that the systemic, educational, and individual perspectives of HL speakers in the European context be further explored, described, compared, coordinated, and improved. Through the recognition and systematic support of HL education, not only would the rights perspectives be addressed, but also the issues of European citizenship, democratic dialogue, internationalization, and social cohesion within and across communities and regions.

Acknowledgements

This publication is an outcome of the Charles University 4EU+ mini-grant project Educating heritage language learners and pupils learning a second language: Differences in approaches, Grant No. 4EU+/23/F2/07.

---

[210] Boccou Kestřánková & Hrdlička, 2024
[211] For the Czech perspective, see Boccou Kestřánková & Hrdlička, 2024

Chapter 4

The Role of the French Heritage Language Program in Promoting Bilingualism and Cultural Integration for Francophone Students in the United States

Yann Gaboriau

The French Heritage Language Program (FHLP), founded in 2005, is a collaborative initiative between Villa Albertine, the French Institute for Culture and Education, and the Albertine Foundation. It is part of the French for All initiative, launched by President Emmanuel Macron of France during his visit to the United States in December 2022. French for All is a new initiative to support bilingualism and access to French language instruction across the United States. French for All is a national program that advocates for equitable access to French language education through a comprehensive strategy that spans all levels of education – from K-12 to higher education. With the guiding principle that learning a language is a right rather than a privilege, French for All tackles all aspects of the language-learning continuum with a four-pronged approach: the FHLP, which helps immigrant high school students to view their home language as an asset for their academic and cultural lives; the French Dual Language Fund, which provides resources to strengthen bilingual K-12 education in over 30 states; the French in Higher Education Program, which encourages innovation and career opportunities in French departments at universities; and the Future Teachers Program, which recruits and prepares a new generation of diverse French teachers.

Through a coordinated effort to create a network of French language programs that are visible, inclusive, and sustainable, eventually, the French for All initiative envisions a world in which the benefits of bilingualism are made available to all students in today's interconnected world.

The FHLP promotes bilingualism and integration of French-speaking migrants in the US. In the heterogeneous society of the United States, the FHLP plays a significant role in maintaining language and culture-based diversity. The program helps Francophone learners to be fostered with their heritage language, while also integrating into the broader English-speaking environment. As such, it reflects the attempt to resolve the problem of cultural integration and identity maintenance. Language and culture-based programs are held to develop students' linguistic skills. However, they also make a significant contribution to the sense of belonging and self-identity. Consequently, the FHLP aims to promote the multicultural dimension of education, as well as to combine all the cultural fences and clusters through understanding and interaction.

Expansion of the FHLP through the French for All Initiative and National Call for Proposals

In an effort to strengthen and expand French heritage language education across the United States, the FHLP launched a national Call for Proposals in 2023 under the French for All initiative. This strategic expansion initiative aims to reach underserved Francophone communities and increase student access to culturally responsive, heritage-based French instruction in both school districts and community organizations.

For the 2024–2025 academic year, the FHLP made a landmark investment in French heritage education in the United States by funding six diverse projects across the country. The Cocomatl French Afterschool Program in Atlanta received $10,000 to educate students about Congolese culture and heritage, using music as a key instructional tool for French heritage speakers. The Bellevue School

District in Seattle was awarded $30,000 to develop a curriculum that supports teachers in effectively educating French heritage speakers while deepening their understanding of students' cultural backgrounds.

Evanston Township High School in Illinois also received $30,000 to promote multilingualism and mentorship through its French Heritage Student Action Group. In Minnesota, the Alliance Française of Minneapolis–St. Paul was granted $8,500 to offer workshops and explore cultural apprenticeship opportunities for Francophone students. Additional funding supported projects at Pierre Part Elementary School in Louisiana, which received $8,500, and the New York French-American Charter School in Harlem, New York, which was awarded $12,000.

Research consistently demonstrates that language and culture are deeply interconnected. Together, these projects advance culturally responsive education and provide students with meaningful opportunities to engage with diverse Francophone cultures and communities. In addition, the projects funded point out a broad thematic scope with regard to cultural heritage, tackling both educational and cultural challenges in Francophone communities. One such example is the Cocomatl French Afterschool Program, which offered the possibility for unique Congolese cultural education, depicting music as a means for education amongst students. This method corresponds with Culturally Responsive Education (CRE) theory, as it delivers a transformative methodology in order to support learners with cultural responsiveness. The second project of this type was presented by the Pierre Part Elementary in Louisiana, which focused on Acadian and Cajun heritage, offering both tutoring opportunities as well as genealogy education in order to tackle the pressure of heritage loss. Finally, the Alliance Française of Minneapolis/St. Paul engaged with Francophone youth by organizing workshops, allowing the participants to outline their cultural identity and traditions. Such educational projects fit the opinion of CRE theory supporters who believe that inspirational methods with regard to CRE are crucial for equal educational opportunities and cultural empowerment.[212] The variety of this project array stands as proof of the French for All scope in relation to furthering cultural diversity and educational equality.

2025–2026 Funded Projects

The FHLP continued its growth in 2025–2026, selecting seven new projects for funding to promote learning opportunities for the Francophone population in the United States. The Francophone Charter School of Oakland, CA, received $10,000 to run a workshop around literature that connects cultures. The Bellevue School District in WA received $8,500 to build on its heritage program with theatre works, focusing on literature and tying culture together. In New York, the KIPP NYC College Prep School will start a French heritage class with cultural field trips and intensive exam prep, engaged with the deep cultural immersion funded by $23,000. In New Hampshire, the Franco-American Center's $20,000 high-immersion afterschool program hopes to guide the early connection of the Francophone culture by games and activities that encourage engagement and building identities within the young community and strengthen ties.

The growth of the FHLP has significantly expanded access to culturally responsive French instruction for underserved Francophone communities. The *French for All* initiative breaks down barriers by addressing the specific cultural and linguistic needs of these communities. Each project embeds elements of heritage such as music, literature, and interactive activities to foster identity and belonging. By promoting multilingualism, the program supports both language development and cultural preservation.

FHLP Partnerships and Support

In the case of key partnerships such as Société Générale and Princeton University, the FHLP has a lot to gain from such alliances in supporting the program's goals in nurturing bilingualism and cultural integration. Being linked with Société Générale encourages

---

[212] D'Andrea Martínez et al., 2023

bilingualism to be used and practiced in the workplace. This is an important goal of the program, as most Francophone students hope to find success in their careers by using both languages. Princeton University's partnership with the FHLP implies the potential development of academic exchanges and research collaborations. Through this kind of collaboration that extends beyond language and into cultural studies, FHLP aims to create opportunities for cultural exchange.[213] As such, the benefits of key partnerships are apparent not only in the linguistic capabilities of students but in their understanding of cultural issues and American society as a whole. It addresses the challenge of staying true to one's heritage while learning to adapt in a new culture (e.g., for Francophone students, realizing they have a new cultural identity as Americans).[214]

Moreover, the FHLP plays a key role in supporting the linguistic growth of Francophone students, as it allows them to develop their language acquisition and proficiency further. During the implementation of the FHLP, students are allowed to develop further expertise in the French language, which is integral to their academic endeavors as well as to the preservation of their cultural background. The curriculum used for the FHLP specifically targets the heritage language learning processes, which provide students with the opportunity to further the development of their vocabulary and understanding in holistic ways.[215] As such, the attention placed on the students' linguistic competencies promotes their capacity to create strong connections to their cultural background while also allowing them to adapt and thrive in bilingual communities, one of the most important skills in a globalized and interconnected society. As such, the FHLP fosters a linguistic approach to education that recognizes the significance of language acquisition in maintaining one's cultural heritage, as this program inspires Francophone students to be more connected to their culture while allowing them to master the linguistic skills required by various contexts.

---

[213] Ghorayeb, 2022
[214] Porter et al., 2023
[215] Ibid.

The FHLP plays, on the other hand, a key role in culturally developing Francophone students. It has been established that this initiative contributes to the learning process through the increased understanding of cultural components, which are of vital importance for Francophone students. The FHLP places a large emphasis on the diversity of Francophone cultures. It is deeply embedded in the program with a variety of activities and curricula aiming to explore the cultures and celebrate them. This cultural component of language learning has a positive impact on students' holistic development because it helps them connect with their cultural symbols and develop a strong cultural identity. Teaching the importance of cultural components in students' holistic development can help them face the double challenge of leaving their heritage symbols behind in the process of integrating into a wider context.

In addition to this, the FHLP highlights significant educational benefits among Francophone students due to their improved performance and a greater level of involvement in the learning environment. With the implementation of immersive and specialized French language learning, students are able to fine-tune their oral and written language skills, which are integrated into a variety of academic subjects. Such language proficiency often results in greater educational involvement, noted by the increased level of confidence in their written and spoken communications, allowing students to contribute more to classroom discussions and group activities. The FHLP's programs support these elements by providing a context to address and close any academic gap that may have resulted from the switching of languages, thereby allowing students to keep up with their monolingual classmates.[216] Thus, apart from the FHLP's ability to help achieve the desirable academic results, the students' overall greater engagement in learning processes as a result of the language programs ultimately allows them to be provided with the necessary skills that will carry over to their future academic and career pursuits.[217]

---

[216] Wernicke, 2022
[217] Ghorayeb, 2022

Heritage Language Maintenance

One of the elements addressed by FHLP is the maintenance of the language, which is essential to Francophone students' identity and sense of belonging. This further reflects the role of heritage language in the achievement and retention of a connection to cultural aspects while balancing their place in American society as members of a bilingual community. The FHLP approach underlines the nature of French beyond a mere language and, instead, as a living part of the students' cultural identity, where their capabilities with the language are woven into their personal and cultural development.[218] Building on this ensures that students can maintain their language, allowing for an easier transition from their environment while in the program to their interactions with peers and family members, where the language is used as well. FHLP thus contributes to ensuring a sense of belonging, given that Francophone students have a cultural hallmark that serves as a means for them to define their presence in a predominantly English-speaking context.

Nevertheless, this seamless transition for Francophone students as they integrate into English-speaking society poses the challenge of reconciling their need to maintain their heritage language while adapting to its English counterpart. The integration is complicated by the potentially conflicting cultural aspects associated with the Francophone culture of the students. As such, students may be expected to simultaneously uphold their heritage language and culture while adapting and fully accepting these cultural aspects that are new to them. Bilingual programs in schools, such as those adopted by FHLP, play a critical part in facilitating this transition for students.[219] Schools with bilingual frameworks create an atmosphere where the continued usage of both the 'host' and 'heritage' languages is encouraged, thereby allowing the students to maintain and nurture their cultural identity while becoming effective members of English-using milieus. In this regard, the bilingual focus of the FHLP enables

---

[218] Driever & Bagheri, 2020
[219] Ibid.

students' successful transition into English-speaking programs while simultaneously allowing them to maintain their cultural and linguistic identity. This not only benefits the students' long-term integration and success in Canadian society but also supports the overall themes in transcending boundaries related to multilingual education policy.[220]

Alignment with the Seal of Biliteracy

In the scope of policy standards, the FHLP has deep connections to state and federal policy standards. One of the main initiatives in the United States that addresses language policy issues is the Seal of Biliteracy. It highlights the importance of being bilingual and having language skills.[221] Research shows that the Seal of Biliteracy recognizes students who are proficient in English and other languages, increasing their employability and cultural awareness. By establishing such connections, the program mentioned above promotes an inclusive language policy in the sense that heritage speakers are recognized and known within the education system. At the same time, the FHLP is part of the globalized human capital literatures that promote issues of language and enable students' language development and diversity that are important in the workforce.[222] Such a link empowers the heritage speakers to recognize academic qualifications while at the same time allowing policies and proposals to be created that aim to implement multilingual skills among scholars, addressing the issues of equality and accessibility for linguistic matters in education.

In addition, the contribution of the FHLP to language standards becomes evident with the goals established in the Seal of Biliteracy. Whereas state and federal efforts align with this program to help educational entities endorse multilingualism and promote legislation aiming at the promotion of linguistic proficiency.[223] This program's

---

[220] Porter et al., 2023
[221] Heineke & Davin, 2020
[222] Pshigusa, 2024
[223] Pshigusa, 2024

efforts drive the educational system to support the recognition of heritage languages by including them in linguistic opportunities for development. The integration of this program's efforts helps post-secondary institutions endorse recruitment and partnership pipelines that promote enrollment and biliteracy opportunities in community initiatives.[224] In this sense, the FHLP has a relevant role in encouraging educational policies based on the significance of the cultural and linguistic capital of heritage speakers.

Moreover, the FHLP's alignment with policy standards such as the Seal of Biliteracy further cements the program's significance in terms of practicality regarding educational improvements. Through this policy connection, students are afforded credentials such as the Seal of Biliteracy, which attests to their multilingual abilities.[225] The policy presented allows for acknowledgment of heritage speakers and entitlement to the educational benefits associated with the Seal of Biliteracy. The FHLP's link with policy standards reinforces commitments to creating and supporting a workforce that upholds linguistic diversity and cultural competency, which are crucial for global engagement.[226]

Mentoring Programs and Success

FHLP mentoring programs support academic and career success by enhancing students' experience in rare but key areas. The mentoring programs assist students with hands-on activities to develop resumes, network, and help them to prepare and be ready for upcoming career and college opportunities. Activities such as creating a winning résumé and cover letter guide students in building the skills needed to meet industry standards and expectations.[227] Networking through FHLP mentoring helps students to meet professionals who work in bilingual settings, giving them options to break through hired hands and what to expect one step ahead to support their career

---

[224] Davin & Heineke, 2024
[225] Davin & Heineke, 2024
[226] Heineke & Davin, 2020
[227] Wernicke, 2022

opportunities, possible expansion of career life, and what different industries have. All this mentoring influence gives Francophone students a realistic approach and active skills to walk through overcoming struggles related to dealing with unique educational and follow-up career development demands. All of these help them to assimilate into society at large and function, delivering good outcomes.[228]

Moreover, the mentoring support provided by the FHLP is essential for helping Francophone students develop application and academic confidence. The mentoring support usually involves conducting workshops focused on fine skills necessary for the application process.[229] This may include assisting students in writing their personal statements, understanding the complex college admission process, and other relevant pieces of information. Students are guided in a more personalized form. They may eventually feel the positive effects and outcomes in terms of how they can present and sometimes sell themselves to admissions panels. Students are able to use the guidance in getting used to the nature of the expectations in getting into and doing college, which may help students in terms of how confident they feel and being prepared for the experience. Therefore, mentoring support offered in FHLP may help Francophone students explore higher education access opportunities to be able to feel confident in terms of getting into and existing academic spaces.[230]

Benefits of Mentoring

Mentoring initiatives at the level of Société Générale and Princeton University provide specific benefits to French Heritage Speakers. First among them is the skill of creating LinkedIn accounts, which is among the most valuable tools when it comes to networking and career building. Mentoring programs are significant when it comes to enhancing an individual's skills, especially with regard to resume

---

[228] Ghorayeb, 2022
[229] Driever & Bagheri, 2020
[230] Wernicke, 2022

making.[231] In addition, due to the programs that provide structured mentoring, individuals are given the chance to learn about networking skills, which are crucial to building a strong network and connections in their careers. This is closely related to the last benefit, wherein the mentoring initiatives at the program-level that help mentees to learn and acquire the basic principles of learning the right resume and professional portfolio presentation skills would help make them employable in the future.

Just as important, mentors from Société Générale and Princeton University also play a role in helping the students decide what extracurricular activities to select that will positively affect their college applications. For French Heritage Speakers, their engagement in extracurricular activities should involve choosing activities based on what they are truly enthusiastic about and what they want to pursue in the future, while also enhancing the power of their college applications. For example, engagement in French cultural extracurricular activities would help strengthen the students' ties with their heritage and also positively affect their college applications since this can exhibit their passion for their culture as well as their leadership capabilities — aspects that the college admission personnel highly consider. Moreover, mentoring in particular engagement, such as volunteering and other community service activities, or taking part in international contests, can add significant value to the students' applications and can even influence their acceptance into their dream competitive programs.[232] Therefore, by continuously developing their extracurricular engagement, they can contribute to writing their stories positively, and this can help determine the potential that the application schools are looking for.

In addition, the mentoring programs provide students with the necessary writing skills that French Heritage Speakers need for a college essay and a letter of application. Through the guidance, students learn how to write their applications best, as many of them

---

[231] Roger & Vinot, 2019
[232] Perkins et al., 2023

have difficulty comprehensively putting their thoughts and accomplishments together since they struggle to express themselves in the written word.[233] By allowing mentor-mentee interactions that include constructive criticism and writing exercises, students learn to apply the necessary skills to describe how their experiences qualify them for admission. The programs also help students navigate the complicated process of applying for financial aid in undergraduate colleges by teaching them the basic principles of writing descriptions for their financial statements and assisting them in completing the required documents.[234] Overall, the efforts that mentoring programs make to assist students not only with their applications but also with their financial documentation help students prepare for the demands of their future academic goals.

Empowering Dreams: The FHLP Mentoring Program with Princeton University

In partnership with Princeton University, the FHLP launched a transformative mentoring initiative during the 2024–2025 school year. Designed to guide Francophone high school students as they navigate the path toward higher education, the program connected FHLP participants with undergraduate mentors from the Princeton course FRE 372 *Migration, Diversity, Diaspora: Francophone Perspectives*.

Over the course of several months, students engaged in meaningful one-on-one conversations, college prep workshops, and collaborative activities focused on building academic confidence and broadening access to postsecondary opportunities. A particular focus was placed on understanding the U.S. college admissions process, financial aid options, and the role that bilingualism and cultural identity can play in shaping a strong college application. The results were powerful and personal.

---

[233] Shor & Pariser, 2016
[234] Perkins et al., 2023

> The mentorship program with Princeton really helped me feel more confident about my future. I've always dreamed of studying medicine and going to a top school like Harvard, but I didn't know how to make that dream a reality. My mentor (Yassine) explained the college application process, how to apply for financial aid, and how to build a strong profile with extracurricular activities. He also talked to me about the option of transferring, which I didn't know much about before. He encouraged me to believe in myself and take each step one at a time. Now I feel like I have a plan—and that it's possible. *Oumou, FHLP student*

For many students, the program offered not only information, but motivation and clarity.

> Thanks to the mentorship program with Princeton, I now have a much better understanding of the steps to get into college. My mentor (Emilio) helped me think more clearly about my future. I want to go to medical school. He explained how I can start preparing now, which subjects to focus on, and how extracurricular activities, like volunteering or even helping out with family responsibilities, can make my application stronger. This program gave me confidence and made me believe that this dream is truly possible. *Abdoul, FHLP student*

The FHLP–Princeton mentoring program reflects the broader mission of the FHLP: to empower Francophone youth in the United States by leveraging their bilingualism as an asset and providing pathways to academic and professional success. Thanks to partnerships like this one, students are not only imagining brighter futures, but they are also learning how to build them.

Educational Credentials and Opportunities

As a result, credentialing programs like the AP French exam, Global Seal of Biliteracy, and New York State Seal of Biliteracy provide comprehensive opportunities for Francophone students in the U. S.

Firstly, credentialing programs offer a certificate for the students to prove his/her language proficiency. It reflects that the students possess adequate skills and are also committed to being biliterate. Credentialing programs are paramount in recognizing bilingualism and biliteracy. Also, credentialed students are at an advantage in higher education and employment.[235] The students can show proof of the linguistic skills they acquired and open wider doors for education and work. Therefore, credentialing programs have a significant impact on Francophone students as they can benefit from the opportunities presented with their biliteracy.[236] The students can use their language skills and biliteracy in different sectors where multilingualism is appreciated.

As such, the credentialing of the AP French exam and the Global Seal of Biliteracy as education credentials offer Francophones promising economic returns as their knowledge of the French language raises their employability and prospective careers. Credentialing indicates French language learners' bilingualism and allows students to be market-ready as they fulfill employers' growing need for multilingual workers across various industries and businesses. Studies suggest that credentialing in more than two languages yields favorable labor market results, as employers perceive bilingual individuals as suitable workers.[237] More than that, being bilingual suggests better salaries, as employers are able to communicate and establish networks more easily with the firm's clients, suppliers, especially those from the increasingly globalized societies.[238] Ultimately, credentialing through programs such as these found in the FHLP contributes greatly to equipping students with the tools needed to succeed in the future, not only in personal development but also in economic growth and sustainability.

The vast majority of students enrolled in the FHLP have been obtaining the Global Seal of Biliteracy over the past six years

---

[235] Heineke & Davin, 2021
[236] Porter et al., 2023
[237] Churkina et al., 2023
[238] Porter et al., 2023

(approximately 75% students obtain it each year), by scoring three or more on the AP French exam. This accomplishment reflects the increasing value attached to bilingualism as an asset for individuals and society at large. Also, on average, four FHLP graduates obtain the New York State Seal of Biliteracy each year. This is a particular milestone that we are striving to encourage and expand through more targeted support and curriculum alignment. As highlighted by García and Kleyn, "emergent bilinguals develop their full linguistic repertoire more effectively when their home languages are recognized and valued in academic settings."[239] The above recognitions provide our students not only with significant linguistic and cultural affirmations but also with concrete academic and economic benefits. Furthermore, Callahan and Gándara established that "biliteracy is strongly linked to increased academic achievement and long-term career opportunities."[240] This finding serves as a basis for improving access to and availability of the aforementioned biliteracy seals and certificates in heritage language programs.

Moreover, the implementation of bilingual and multilingual approaches in educational settings provides important benefits from an academic perspective, particularly in improving students' cognitive functions and school performances. These benefits enhance the students' executive functioning by improving their problem-solving skills and multitasking qualities, which are crucial in various academic fields.[241] In addition, being bilingual helps learners obtain better metalinguistic awareness that enables them to perceive and think about language systems, which results in improved competence regarding language use. According to Alvear, schools applying bilingual education frameworks have become associated with enhanced levels of student engagement and achievement, further emphasizing the significance of bilingual and multilingual policies in promoting factors related to student achievement.[242] Thus, by

---

[239] García & Kleyn, 2016
[240] Callahan & Gándara, 2014
[241] Heineke & Davin, 2021
[242] Alvear, 2019

nurturing educational institutions that encourage language diversity, bilingual and multilingual policies not only address students' individual linguistic needs but also facilitate the academic community's engagement in school performances that may contribute to the potential multilingualism in the broader society.

Economic and Academic Advantages of Bilingualism

To further understand the underlying economic implications of adopting bilingualism and multilingualism policies, it is essential to elaborate on their positive impacts on individual and societal levels. Individual-level economic opportunities of bilingual and multilingual policies arise from the fact that they increase the economic productivity of individuals able to speak more than one language through increased access to job markets and wage opportunities.[243] On the societal level, bilingual and multilingual policies promote the exchange of cultural experiences, resulting in the development of new and diverse markets and increased cultural dynamism, consequently promoting the overall thriving of the economy more stably.[244] The bilingual and multilingual educational frameworks also promote an enhanced ability for collective problem solving and increased cognitive flexibility, both of which are universal traits useful across professions and industries. The establishment of job market opportunities and the enhanced cognitive skills acquired through bilingualism and multilingualism in educational frameworks can be leveraged into a long-term economic growth trajectory for many nations and societies, where cultural diversity is embraced and promoted as a unique driver of opportunity and creativity.[245]

Likewise, a detailed analysis of bilingualism indicates that there are significant academic benefits related to cognitive growth as well as learning outcomes. Bilingual students retain higher executive functioning abilities, including better cognitive flexibility and

---

[243] Churkina et al., 2023
[244] Heineke & Davin, 2021
[245] Porter et al., 2023

attention control, among others.²⁴⁶ The cognitive advantages offered due to bilingualism have also been linked to better metalinguistic awareness and problem-solving skills, thereby providing an opportunity for students to accurately employ and assess language patterns in L1 and L2 domains. As noted by Porter and Umansky, bilingualism has the potential to improve students' enthusiasm and motivation levels that could lead to positive academic achievement across various subjects.²⁴⁷ Therefore, child bilingual policies promoting academic benefits not only facilitate the personal growth of a particular student but also help schooling systems improve due to cognitive development and the benefits associated with linguistic variety and diversity on a wider scale.

Following the approach of Joshua Fishman, the purpose of the FHLP is to preserve and promote the legacy of the French-speaking population. The goal mentioned above fits well with Fishman's emphasis on the idea that sustaining heritage language is the way to protect communities. According to him, doing so is crucial to maintaining distinguishing attributes, both cultural and social, of the unique communities.²⁴⁸ Therefore, this program is not just aimed at making students bilingual in their native language. Its target is to make students proud of their culture and their heritage and help them maintain those legacies. Massifying their use in society, the program not only pursues linguistic goals aimed at the preservation of the right of students to use their language. It also highlights the need for and importance of nurturing a supportive educational environment in which they are encouraged to build common ground in their cultural exchanges.²⁴⁹ By promoting these two objectives, the program is successful in ensuring that Francophone students do not forgo their linguistic and cultural ties, even if in the active building up of those new ties, students become part of a larger societal framework.

---

[246] Alvear, 2019, pp 477-513
[247] Porter et al., 2023
[248] Laleko, 2023
[249] Aravossitas et al., 2021

Additionally, Jim Cummins's view on bilingual education can further provide insights into the outcomes of the FHLP. Cummins highlights the cognitive and academic added value that derives when students' home languages are adopted as central to their education.[250] Incorporating students' multilingual codes as cognitive resources highlights the FHLP's core aim of empowering transformative education that promotes linguistically and culturally proficient students, as articulated by Cummins. Whereas FHLP also benefits their students in upholding their cultural identity, their students' literacy, and numeracy development, as per Cummins, also derives from utilizing their languages as resources in the production of knowledge.[251] Consequently, the FHLP's outcomes complement Cummins' outlook as demonstrated through the model's educational approach that upholds an inclusive model valuing language backgrounds, which enriches students' learning and academic experiences while maintaining their cultural background.

Challenges and Progress of the FHLP

The FHLP is an exemplary program that is designed to sustain and value the unique linguistic and cultural resources available to the French-speaking communities. The program has a focused commitment not only to enhance the language skills of heritage speakers but also to enhance linguistic self-esteem and cultural identification that supports a more multicultural ecosystem. FHLP has issues like any other program that are challenging to address, including funding, staffing, and teacher retention, but most of them are ongoing, definitely jeopardizing its implementation. Despite facing these challenges, FHLP continues to display worthy traits of resilience and creativity through collaboration and innovative programming. Addressing issues paired with the program's inherent characteristics and valuing its strengths creates a balance of

---

[250] Cummins, 2021
[251] Cummins, 2024

sustainability for FHLP, making it an important program in heritage language education.

Challenges Facing the FHLP

For the FHLP, funding challenges are structural. The program relies primarily on external sources of funding, which highlights a dilemma regarding the sustainability and growth of its initiatives. In other words, as long as projects are not funded consistently, it becomes difficult for the program to commit long-term efforts to maintain existing initiatives or develop new ones that address the evolving needs of vulnerable communities. While grants have led to considerable progress at the project level, the lack of stable funding remains a major obstacle to the program's long-term development and sustainability.[252] Consequently, these financial difficulties point to an urgent—if not essential—need for consistent funding to secure the future of the FHLP and its capacity to grow over time.

In addition, the FHLP also faces another major issue related to the recruitment and retention of qualified French teachers who are also proficient in culturally responsive teaching. The shortage of qualified teachers who not only hold linguistic competence but also culturally sensitive competence presents another major barrier to the implementation of the program.[253] Culturally responsive teaching is characterized by the competence of the teachers to customize the teaching materials based on the children's cultural and linguistic experiences. However, many teachers often feel unsure when practicing the culturally responsive principles in the classroom, although they feel confident in building strong relationships with the students.[254] In this case, developing training programs tailored specifically to increase teachers' self-efficacy in implementing culturally responsive strategies can eventually enable teachers to stay

---

[252] Montrul & Polinsky, 2021
[253] Howard, 2021
[254] Cruz et al., 2020

in the program. In order to maintain the educational goals of the program and the services to heritage learners, the FHLP should emphasize creating a long-lasting teacher training program that meets the diverse needs of its students.

Moreover, the FHLP has difficulties in outreach and curriculum development that require multilingual communication and adaptability. This means that engaging with immigrant and refugee communities calls for a sophisticated approach that is culturally sensitive and aware in order to gain their trust and develop rapport.[255] This complexity illustrates people's need to improve communicative outcomes and need to be open toward ideas while respecting cultural differences. In addition, the FHLP faces another issue with a standardized curriculum, especially the preparation for the AP French exam, since the lack of standardization in curriculum practices makes achieving defined results across sites challenging.[256] Through overcoming these challenges in curriculum and communication, the FHLP will continue its commitment to educating and empowering students with language and cultural knowledge by following its goal to preserve and protect French students' heritage language education.

Moreover, amidst present challenges, the FHLP has proven to be remarkably adaptive, strategically launching new initiatives and refining its approach over time. The program has maintained strong collaborative partnerships that expand access to authentic resources, most notably through a dedicated Google Classroom that houses a wide range of materials from *Enseigner le français avec TV5MONDE* and *Le français facile avec RFI*. These tools enrich instruction by offering culturally relevant and linguistically appropriate content tailored to heritage learners.

Additionally, the FHLP has developed its own curricular framework, which is structured around thematic units—such as identity, family, health, and the arts—and aligned with the 5 Cs of the ACTFL Standards (Communication, Cultures, Connections,

---

[255] Chang & Viesca, 2022
[256] Gist et al., 2019

Comparisons, and Communities). This framework, grounded in project-based pedagogy, ensures coherent instruction across different sites while allowing for flexibility and local adaptation.

In response to shifting demographics and funding constraints, the FHLP has continued to innovate in its programming and curriculum development. These efforts strengthen the program's resilience and affirm its role as a vital platform for sustaining linguistic and cultural heritage within the U.S. education system.

The coordinator of the FHLP has been instrumental in elevating teacher training tailored to heritage language education. From July 10 to 14, 2024, he successfully trained 13 educators from all across the United States during the inaugural professional development program BELC États-Unis, held at San Diego State University (SDSU). These participants included French as a Foreign Language (FLE) teachers, Alliance Française instructors, and educators from bilingual French programs in both public and charter schools, reflecting the diverse and growing community of heritage language educators nationwide. The training emphasized the use of authentic materials, the ACTFL 5 Cs framework (Communication, Cultures, Connections, Comparisons, and Communities), project-based pedagogy, and best practices for evaluating and assessing French heritage speakers. The BELC (Bureau d'études des langues et des cultures) training, conducted by France Éducation International (FEI), is renowned for its excellence in French language pedagogy and provides a vital platform for these teachers to refine their skills and deepen their expertise. Building on this momentum, the coordinator also led a similar session during the inaugural French for All Summer Institute in 2025 at the University of Wisconsin – Madison, which brought together K-12 and higher education educators from across the country, further strengthening the network of professionals dedicated to advancing French heritage language teaching.

Conclusion

The FHLP has demonstrated its effectiveness and continues to play a vital role in promoting bilingualism and the cultural integration of

Francophone students in the United States. Through strategically developed partnerships and carefully implemented projects, the FHLP addresses the essential components of students' linguistic, cultural, and academic trajectories. The program supports students not only in maintaining their heritage language and identity, but also in finding their place within an English-speaking society. In this respect, the mentoring initiatives and emphasis on credentials promoted by the FHLP provide students with significant academic and professional advantages, strengthening their bilingual experience and preparing them to meet the global challenges of an increasingly multicultural and multilingual world. Overall, the FHLP is a highly significant program that fosters the preservation of linguistic diversity and the cultural enrichment necessary for both individual and collective development within language communities.

Chapter 5

On How to Bridge Communication Between Multilingual Families and Schools: Tonga Schools Network

Isabelle Barth, Miglena Hristozova, and Antri Kanikli

In our Western world, which is very monolingual, the arrival of children who have lived in migration has changed the way schools have to operate. However, the school systems are not all ready and equipped to welcome this diversity of cultures and languages. Teachers in primary and elementary schools are not fully trained to embrace these diversities. They lack the training and mostly the tools to welcome those children and their families. However, as Maria Coady wrote in 2019: "High-quality education and equitable education for all students is more pressing today than ever before". She was at that time working with rural teachers welcoming migrant children in rural Florida. As we will demonstrate, for the well-being of the plurilingual students accepted in the school and for their academic success, it is vital to establish good relationships and efficient communication between their plurilingual parents, who have a migration background, and the school stakeholders –[i.e., not just the teachers, but also any person working within the school, from the principal to the person in charge of the canteen or cafeteria, as well as the secretaries and nurses].

When arriving in a new country, migrant families are confronted with numerous challenges, from getting a job and accessing health care for their families to understanding the local language and the way their host country is functioning. One of these challenges is the academic education of their children. It is all the more difficult when you do not know the system, nor speak the local or societal language, to try to understand how it works and what they should be doing.

Coming to a new country is often synonymous with giving the children an education that they would not get in their home country. It is of immense importance for the migrant families who know what they expect from formal education for their children. When families of migrant backgrounds register their children in local schools, they do not know what to expect from the school system. They are not necessarily aware of the requests from the schools. What are the schools expecting from them? What are the schools expecting from their children? What are they expecting from the school? There is a lot of information they need to know and understand, information that can be so obvious for the local school stakeholders. This can only be done through proper communication. Some parents have never been to school themselves, and they are sometimes not aware that school is compulsory. This can explain some of the absenteeism that is being noticed in some schools. The culture the family is coming from influences this absenteeism; for example, when in their country of origin, the girls stay at home when help is needed; parents may think they can do the same in their host country. Even if the parents have been to school themselves, it can be daunting and intimidating to send their children into another system that is completely unknown to them.

On the other hand, schools that welcome the children of those families could feel at a complete loss. They welcome children who come from many diverse cultures and many different languages. It can be difficult for school staff to have children within their walls who do not understand what they are saying. What can they do with those cultures and languages? Should they be used? How will they communicate with the parents and make themselves understood? It is not an easy task for them to communicate with families who speak very little or do not speak at all the school language. Even if modern technologies can be of immense help, they are not sufficient. This is making communication problematic and relationships with families difficult.

These home-school connections have rarely been looked at when families do not use the school language at home. Communication with parents who do not master the school language, who do not understand the school policies and rules, can become difficult. Parents often feel at a loss when trying to help their children. Targeting the importance of communication for the well-being of the children has been at the heart of our project, Tonga Schools. It is not aiming at giving new tools to teachers, but rather at providing teachers, administrators, school counsellors, and support staff [who play important roles in the education of the students[257]], the proper tools to communicate better with the parents of their students without having to ask the latter to serve as translators and thus help children be successful. As we mentioned in our framework [which can be found on our website]: "School is a place where people meet and where communication happens."

When we interviewed parents and school staff, we realized that there is a lack of understanding between the families and the school staff. Families seem to be lacking the information they need to help their children as best as possible. They do not always understand what is happening in schools. They feel at a loss when it comes to helping their children with homework. Very often, as they do not speak the school language properly, they do not dare go into the school and ask questions, for fear of being rejected and being laughed at. They feel anxious and unsure. There is an insecurity on their side, which school staff are not always aware of or may have never heard of. This is not linked to the fact that the school is not sharing, but because parents do not understand what is being shared. Schools do not always have the tools and the methods to share the information in all the languages present among their students. Parents do not always dare ask, feeling ashamed because they do not speak the societal language well. However, effective communication and relationships are important in the formal education of children.

Theoretical Framework

Scientific research encourages the establishment of a close collaboration between school and parents, as this has been proven to

---

[257] Coady, 2019

have a significant impact on the child's academic progress.[258] The foundation of this collaboration is effective communication between the two partners: the school staff and the parents. Viewing this collaboration as a partnership is crucial to being successful in supporting the child's academic advancement.[259] Parents who do not speak the school language are often not able to achieve this, which increases inequality for children from families speaking minority languages.

Communication initiated by the school often fails to address the fact that there are parents who do not know the school language, which undermines the desired partnership that is needed. Those parents feel excluded from this process; hence, they would not be able to pursue the role of the partner in this parent-school relationship. The lack of acknowledgement of the families' linguistic and cultural diversity impedes the achievement of an efficient partnership to the benefit of minority children. The Tonga School project addresses this problem by developing tools that educate school staff and parents on how to establish effective communication, which is the basis of the targeted partnership.

Apart from language, an important barrier to establishing the school partnership for those families is the fact that parents are not familiar with the school culture. There are specific roles that the school expects parents to undertake, which, if you come from another country, may not be known or obvious. The collaboration between the school and families adheres to cultural codes that those families do not know. The dynamics involved in this process, thus, disfavor parents from a migration background who often fail to respond to what is expected from them. The implementation of practices that do not follow the cultural codes of the school enhances the "otherness" approach towards minority families,[260] which further increases the gap between them and the school.

---

[258] See, among others, Hoover-Dempsey, & Sandler, 1995; Patrikakou et al., 2005; Wilder, 2014
[259] Epstein, 2011
[260] Hughes & MacNaughton, 2000

According to Conus and Fahrni, the type of communication that builds a partnership relationship between parents and school is informal and reciprocal.[261] Many scholars support bi-directional, reciprocal communication,[262] as it is considered to be a necessity for establishing a close collaboration between school staff and families and ensuring that families are actively involved in their child's schooling. Facilitating this type of informal, reciprocal communication that both partners initiate, the school and parents, is central to the design of the tools and the educational material of this project.

Erasmus+ Project: Tonga Schools

The Erasmus+ Tonga Schools Network project, launched in October 2023, is a collaboration between five partner organizations from five European countries (four NGOs from France, Germany, Spain, Sweden, and UCLan Cyprus University). It is committed to improving communication and fostering stronger connections between plurilingual families and primary schools. With a focus on boosting inclusive education and cultural integration, the main goal is to support the educational success of children from diverse linguistic and cultural backgrounds by fostering better relationships between schools and families.

To achieve this, we started by listening to both school staff and plurilingual families through semi-structured interviews. Based on a questionnaire implemented simultaneously in all partner countries, the interviews explored several key aspects:

From the Perspective of Schools/School Staff:

- Whether and how the school environment incorporates and values multiple languages through activities, posters, or curriculum.
- The policies surrounding the use of home languages within school boundaries, classrooms, and informal settings.

---

[261] Conus & Fahrni, 2019
[262] See, among others, Christenson & Sheridan 2001; Epstein, 2011; Bouffard, 2008; Dumoulin et al., 2013; Lueder, 2011

- How schools establish relationships with parents who do not speak the school's language.
- The level of parental participation in parent-teacher meetings, school activities, and their integration into the school community.
- Challenges staff face in engaging with linguistically diverse parents.
- Staff attitudes toward multilingualism, including their own language practices and views on using students' home languages.
- How language policies shape classroom practices and informal interactions.
- The use of students or external translators to bridge communication gaps.

From the Perspective of Plurilingual Families:

- Family strategies for passing on their languages and the challenges they face in ensuring their children maintain these languages.
- Parental perceptions of whether their languages are accepted or welcomed at school.
- Experiences of inclusivity or rejection, including how schools accommodate language differences in communication, events, and support services.
- Frequency of attendance at parent-teacher meetings and the underlying reasons.
- Reliance on children as translators during these interactions, and its impact on communication and understanding.

The interviews with both parents and school staff were thus a first step to identify specific challenges and communication barriers on both sides. Through an in-depth analysis, a cornerstone of our approach was to develop a comprehensive set of resources designed to address the challenges encountered by plurilingual families and schools.

A. Development of Resources for Parents and Schools

Central to this approach is the development of a robust collection of resources aimed at bridging the communication gap between plurilingual families and schools, as well as putting a focus on the impact of a strong partnership between parents and school staff. Therefore, a key focus was placed on creating resources that facilitate collaboration, foster mutual understanding, and support. These include:

- A Framework and a Toolkit for school staff: A practical resource offering frameworks, strategies, and templates to help school staff engage effectively with families, focusing on multilingualism, cultural understanding, and clear communication.
- An Online Training Platform: training for school staff providing skills to welcome cultural and linguistic diversity within the school boundaries, including strategies for effectively welcoming new families, exploring various levels and forms of integration, raising awareness about discrimination, and diverse cultural and language trajectories.
- A Booklet for Families: A document enabling families to reflect on their linguistic and cultural practices, fostering understanding and collaboration with the schools of their children during their educational journey.
- Family Portraits: Offering a deeper understanding of family perspectives and needs.
- Videos: Multilingual visuals on key themes of the project, empowering parents and school staff to understand and utilize opportunities and frames for fostering effective dialogue.
- A Guide on How to Establish Parents' Cafés: A step-by-step guide for creating dedicated spaces where parents and school stakeholders can engage in meaningful dialogue about education and how to be involved in the school community.

- Policy recommendations and a manifesto: Guidance for schools and policymakers to foster inclusive and effective educational practices.

The creation of the resources is an ongoing and collaborative process involving all project partners. Each partner is responsible for developing initial drafts of the resources in English. These drafts are brought to partner meetings, where they are discussed, refined, and further developed. During these meetings, partners address cultural and national differences in education systems to ensure the resources are tailored to the specific needs and expectations of each participating country. Additional documents are created to respond to unique challenges and requirements identified in the different countries.

Once the English versions of the resources are finalized, they are translated into the languages of all partner countries to ensure accessibility. The translated materials are uploaded to the project homepage, making them available for wider use.

Separate phases of testing are implemented throughout the project. School staff and parents are actively involved in testing the toolkit, online platform, and booklet for parents at various stages. Their feedback on the use and quality of the resources is continuously gathered and analyzed to guide further improvements and adaptations. This iterative approach ensures that the materials are effective and meet the needs of the diverse audiences they are designed to support.

B. Example: Toolkit for School Staff

A key component of the Tonga project is the Toolkit for school staff, which provides schools with strategies, templates, and frameworks to foster communication and inclusivity. It is tailored to help educators better understand the unique needs of families who may not be fluent in the local language, ensuring all voices are heard and valued. The toolkit includes:

- A Comprehensive Framework: This outlines the importance of multilingualism and plurilingualism, exploring how children can benefit from maintaining their heritage languages while mastering school languages. It introduces diverse strategies and explains the educational benefits of strong language planning as well as the impact of fostering "spoken dialogues" about language use in order to recognize parents' language choices and support both children's sense of belonging and their academic development.

- Grounded in research, the framework addresses the cognitive and social benefits of linguistic diversity, offering insights into overcoming monolingual biases. Additionally, it underscores the need for intercultural training for school staff and encourages proactive, family-centered approaches to build trust and engagement.
- Practical Tools and Templates, Communication Guidelines: The toolkit offers ready-to-use resources such as language portraits, posters, and forms to simplify interactions with families. Furthermore, it provides strategies on verbal, non-verbal, and written communication, including the use of plain language or diverse communication channels. The resources are divided into five categories, each designed to address various aspects of communication and integration in the school setting:
- General Part: This section focuses on overcoming language barriers and cultural differences, providing strategies for using multilingual communication channels and creating a more accessible school website. It shares ideas on how to help families better understand the school structure, the main rules, and frames within the school community, as well as how the education system in the particular country works.
- A second category emphasizes that All Languages Matter. This includes providing important school information, like health checks, invitations, and event details, in multiple languages via apps or templates. It also encourages the visibility of diversity through multilingual posters, events,

and libraries, helping to create a more inclusive school environment. In this regard, the project provides specific ideas for schools to expand on what is already in place and also offer further support in these efforts.
- Where parents can be involved is a third category, which focuses on involving parents more actively in school life. It explores reasons why some parents may hesitate to engage and suggests ways to use Parents' Association and Parents' Cafés to better integrate plurilingual and migrant families. It also includes resources to make these spaces more accessible and supportive to families who do not speak the school language or do not know exactly how to communicate and be part of the school community.
- The fourth category is dedicated to the topic of Parent-Teacher Communication: This area provides ideas and strategies to facilitate communication between teachers and parents, such as preparing for parent-teacher meetings, using simpler language, and creating more opportunities for questions. It also includes advice on how to build stronger partnerships by understanding each other's expectations and addressing cultural differences.
- The final category offers ideas that can be used by various school staff. It highlights the importance of understanding cultural differences, such as the unique eating habits of migrant families or challenges linked to specific religious traditions. It emphasizes the need for open communication with parents to show respect for their beliefs and traditions while also explaining the reasons behind certain school policies.

C. Chances and Challenges within the Frame of the Tonga Project

One of the significant challenges we faced in the Tonga Schools project was establishing solid partnerships with primary schools. On the one hand, while many schools express a strong interest in participating in the project and contributing to the development of strategies and resources for better communication with plurilingual families, their limited capacity poses a significant barrier. Building partnerships with schools under these conditions requires a flexible, supportive approach that acknowledges their limitations while fostering their involvement.

On the other hand, even when schools are interested and partnerships are established, their capacity to adopt and implement the new approaches developed by the project is another considerable challenge. While schools express a clear need for resources and methods to bridge communication gaps and integrate diverse linguistic and cultural practices, many lack the time, personnel, or infrastructure to take on additional responsibilities. Thus, building trust and encouraging schools to prioritize these strategies amidst competing demands is complex, particularly when school staff are already operating under tight constraints.

To address both challenges, the project proposes the creation of a Tonga Schools Network, offering a platform for collaboration and mutual support.

D. Looking at Real Life

During our interviews, we saw how much families are grateful when school stakeholders go to the trouble of communicating with them in a language they understand. They feel more welcome, and their language is respected. When families arrive in a new setting without knowing the school system and what the school would expect from them or even from their children, it is quite daunting. A mother from a Sri-Lankan background was telling us that it is like becoming a child again, and that everything has to be re-learnt. As a child, she had to translate for her parents, and it destroyed her childhood and teenage years. The tools created by the Tonga Schools Network have a powerful impact on the relationships and communication between the school and the family. They are helping to make the connections easier and improving relationships, creating the trust that is needed for the children to feel good at school. Other families are also seeing the positive effects of the advice given by the Tonga Schools Network. Parents are grateful that the principal took the time to explain the school system and the way the school operates. Parents' Cafés are also wonderful places where parents can meet other families and ask questions on how to navigate the school system and how they can best help their children in the new host country, while keeping their heritage language. Even if Parents' Cafés already exist in some schools, we have redefined the concept in order to meet the needs of the families and help them feel more involved in the school community. Families are thankful when schools show profound respect for their heritage languages. A family from Morocco was delighted that their children were allowed their home language within the school boundaries. A family from Angola arriving in Spain tells us that they were grateful that the school asked translators to help understand what was happening, as suggested in our Toolkit; however, even if their language ["Portuñol", a mix of Spanish and Portuguese] was not a problem, their skin color and culture were.

Inviting Schools to Become Members of the Tonga Network

We want to invite all the schools to become part of our Tonga Schools Network.

First of all, what is a Tonga School? It is important to recall here that the word "Tonga" means "welcome" in the language of Madagascar, and this is the reason we decided to call those schools "Tonga Schools." Those schools choosing to call themselves Tonga value all the languages of their students and welcome them. They accept the principles that we developed in our project. A Tonga school recognizes and embraces the plurilingualism of its students while fostering an environment where they can grow and study. Each Tonga School can decide to create its individual language roadmap in accordance with its own situation and in collaboration with us. This roadmap, which focuses on linguistic and cultural inclusivity, should involve all school stakeholders, whether they are teachers, staff, parents, or the students themselves. This roadmap will be created according to the specific needs of the school. The Tonga Schools have also adopted a good methodology to facilitate the relationships between the families and the school stakeholders. We are hoping to create a label.

Becoming a Tonga school has many benefits. It benefits the students as it is aimed at making them feel well at school and thus be able to learn in a linguistically and culturally inclusive environment, and be more successful. It also benefits the educators, the parents, and the whole school community.

Why would a school wish to become a member? There are several reasons for this. The first reason would be to acknowledge officially that your school is open to all languages and welcomes them. The second reason would be that you have adopted a good mechanism to communicate with the families. Another reason would be to become part of a Network of schools that are adhering to the same values, the values that we developed in our project. Language is a right, and it is used as a resource for teaching and communication with families. In entering the Tonga schools network, your staff will benefit from training online and regular meetings to help them develop the tools they need in their daily interaction with the students and the families, whether they are teachers or not.

One of the values is that the schools recognize and acknowledge the diversity of languages and cultures among the students that they have. Each language—and thus each child—is then valued for who and what they are. Tonga schools are making the languages visible and are celebrating them in many ways that we present in our project; this can go from posters presenting the languages, to multilingual events where the students can present their languages and where diversity is celebrated.

When getting the label of Tonga schools, the schools are getting more than being part of a Network. On our side, we will offer to support them in their daily work. We offer training on multilingual education as well as regular gatherings to support the schools. Tonga schools can help each other and share information and good practices.

In becoming a Tonga School, you will adhere to our manifesto, which presents the requirements to be a Tonga School, and agree with the following points:

- The school does not prohibit, discourage, or punish the use of other languages than the school language.
- The school uses appropriate tools to facilitate its communication with the parents.
- The school does not ask children to act as translators.
- The school has developed a roadmap with us to facilitate the languages in the school.
- The school has developed a Parents' Café with a coordinator in contact with us.
- The school has developed a multilingual library.
- The school's stakeholders are trained to value and encourage the use of any language.
- Positive collaboration and effective communication between parents and school staff are established to support the well-being of the children and their academic success.
- Teachers are celebrating the positive in their students.

We decided to create a Network

- To create synergies between the various schools.
- To support schools that value and bring to light the languages of their students.
- To shed light on the importance of fostering a linguistically and culturally inclusive environment for the students and the school community.

Communication between plurilingual families of migrant backgrounds can be improved with the right tools. It is time-demanding; however, our project provides you with ideas and tools that are aimed at facilitating the parents-schools relationships. Our Tonga Schools Project and Network seeks to encourage these relations for the well-being and academic success of the children.

Part II – Families, Identity, and Intergenerational Transmission

Chapter 6

Teachers of Portuguese as a Heritage Language: Their Profiles, Contexts, and Perspectives

Felicia Jennings-Winterle

As a complex and multifaceted process, immigration leaves individuals vulnerable in numerous ways. Yet, it may enhance intrinsic characteristics and even previous desires, while providing opportunities for new knowledge and experience. In one way or another, this process forces individuals to change. Migrant women go through such reinvention processes in many aspects of their lives; arguably, more than men. For instance, they tend to change professions and reposition their careers.

Taken abroad, for reasons that do not necessarily involve their previous occupation, women may reinvent themselves professionally and invest in alternative projects. Some start businesses that commercialize products and services that are characteristic of their countries of origin (involving food, arts, and crafts, among others). Others decide, often suddenly, to become teachers of their languages.

Specifically, it is noticeable among different groups that women predominantly develop various cultural and educational practices to subsidize the vitality of their languages, which, in the country of residence, becomes a heritage language. The need and the desire to develop an initiative that can materialize the continuity of their mother tongue, as well as the views and methods that sustain it, are tied to what those women judge important, considering the intrafamily communication – a way to maintain her original cultural identity – and future affordances that being a bi/plurilingual seems to guarantee – a way to invest in a new cultural identity, for their children.

The present contribution builds on this general trend and focuses on Brazilian teachers to discuss some of their social and professional characteristics. Drawing on studies about the profile of Portuguese Heritage Language (PHL) teachers and the discourses of Brazilian participants in a specific professional development program developed over 10 years, this discussion will highlight aspects of their profiles. These profiles will be described in terms of common social and cultural characteristics, contexts, and perspectives, and how they may contribute to their professional (re)invention. This reinvention often goes beyond their professional roles and involves changes in personal, intrinsic views and paradigms through discussions and formative experiences. Additionally, a few principles will be suggested to guide the development of educators with more diverse characteristics and perspectives.

What Does the Research Show?

Though scarce, there are a few studies done about those who develop the teaching, promotion, and maintenance of PHL. In general, women take the role of studying and promoting means for this goal. The higher numbers of women illustrate this fact present in conferences done by the *Heritage Language National Resource Center*,[263] which shows an overwhelmingly majority of women both as lecturers and as participants (Figure 1).

Within the milieu of PHL, only thirteen of the 98 initiatives mapped around the world have one man in their administrative body, which means that 86,74% of the initiatives are managed solely by women.[264] In addition, a study from 2023 shows that 90,09% of master's theses, doctoral dissertations, and articles published in specialized periodicals between 2010 and 2022, containing the concept "Portuguese as Heritage Language", or part of it in their titles, were written solely by women.[265] This phenomenon is

---

[263] Heritage Language National Resource Center, 2019
[264] Baldi, 2021
[265] Jennings-Winterle, 2023

instigating and alludes to multiple possibilities for cultural and feminine studies, as well as language education and sociolinguistics.

The Portuguese researcher Maria de Lourdes Gonçalves works in the *Ensino do Português no Estrangeiro* (EPE), the Portuguese-language teaching division of the prestigious Camões Institute, in Switzerland, and has published studies focused on teachers. As such, Gonçalves characterizes the teacher of PHL as someone who belongs to:

[...] a dispersed faculty body with diverse characteristics. They are unified by a passion for the Portuguese language and culture, and by an understanding of its importance to the identity formation of children and youth of Lusophone descent. (...) The way they see themselves as professionals does not seem to exist dissociated from their personal characteristics, practices, and interactions, since this representation is a mix of intrinsic traits of the individual and the concrete situations of their daily lives. They acquire the necessary knowledge about two contexts—the society of origin and that of residence—in order to respond to their students' characteristics. (...) In constructing their specific knowledge, different dimensions intertwine and interweave dynamically, articulating multiple perspectives from both local and global spheres and going beyond restricted views of the Portuguese language—a space in which a continuum encompasses the teaching of two extremes: Portuguese as a foreign language and Portuguese as a mother tongue. For this reason, their practice must be oriented toward the creation of a *third space*, common among professionals in transit, which is configured in creative, complex, and permeable ways, and is in constant construction.[266]

---

[266] Original in Portuguese, ... um corpo docente disperso e de características diversas. Une-os a paixão pela língua e cultura portuguesas e a consciência [de sua] importância para a construção identitária das crianças e jovens lusodescendentes ... O modo como se veem enquanto profissionais parece não existir dissociado das suas características pessoais, logo das suas práticas e interações, uma vez que essa representação é mesclada de características intrínsecas ao sujeito e às situações concretas do quotidiano.

Demographics of lectures		
	Women	Men
2010		
2014	5	2
2015	6	3
2016		
2017		
2018	3	2

Demographics of participants				
	Women	Men	Non specified	Total
2010	234	72	14	320
2014	232	78	4	314
2015	25	2	0	27
2016	53	14	3	70
2017	6	26	0	32
2018	235	64	2	301

Figure 1 – Data from the National Heritage Language Resource Center regarding demographics of their lectures and participants.

Gonçalves analyzed 50 questionnaires answered by the participants of a professional development event, done with 74% of the total of professionals involved in the EPE in Switzerland (a total of 71 participants).[267] The event had the active participation of half of the group — teachers who were invited to directly intervene in the

---

Assumem o necessário conhecimento de dois contextos – o da sociedade de origem e o da sociedade de acolhimento – para responderem às características dos seus alunos ... Na construção do seu conhecimento específico, entrecruzam-se e intervêm diferentes dimensões duma forma dinâmica, que articulam diferentes perspetivas do local com o global e ultrapassam uma visão restrita da língua portuguesa, espaço no qual se poderá melhor compreender o continuum no qual inscrevem o seu ensino, entre os extremos LE e LM. Por isso, a sua prática terá que se orientar para a criação de um 'third space' caraterístico de profissionais em trânsito, que se configura de forma criativa, complexa, permeável e que se entende em constante construção. Gonçalves, 2019, p. 51–52; italics in the original.
[267] Gonçalves, 2017

preparation and dynamization of the formative space by preparing the workshops, discussions, and posters of the program, and the other half of the group had a receptive participation.

The analysis of the questionnaires showed that teachers point out as positive aspects of the event the possibility of sharing practices while presenting activities, as well as exchanging experiences and ideas in peer discussion. Regarding the style of the formative sessions, teachers said they appreciate workshops, as opposed to the opening lecture, which had a more academic and theoretical essence. As the most valuable contributions for their individual professional development, participants pointed out the sharing of teaching experiences, strategies, and methodologies.

In another study, Gonçalves inquired about the profile of the PHL teacher working in the EPE in Switzerland based on their impressions.[268] Specifically, they were asked about their role as PHL teachers. Participants were first asked to complete the phrase "To me, EPE is ...". One year later, they were asked to present a metaphor that could illustrate the way they see themselves as teachers.

In the first part of the inquiry, twenty-two teachers participated, representing 27,5% of the total faculty body. In the second, there were sixty-eight participants, which represented 86% of the total faculty. The analysis of the data demonstrated three types of answers: the first showed how teachers perceived their role as teaching and celebrating the Portuguese language, while developing plurilingualism and sensibility to linguistic diversity; the second referred to identity as one of the main matters in the EPE, in which PHL teachers should support the development of a coherent identity, underlined by the different types of student involvement; finally, the third demonstrated teachers of PHL as the ones responsible for the transmission, maintenance and nurture of HL, while responsible for the construction of bridges and links within languages and cultures.

Another important contribution comes from the studies of Gláucia G. Silva and Everton Costa, who inquired into the

---

[268] Gonçalves, 2019

perceptions and beliefs of Brazilian PHL teachers and demonstrated that formative proposals are episodic and, therefore, their importance is seen by the participants as localized and with little relevance.[269] The study consisted of a questionnaire with four open-ended items to inquire about the perceptions and beliefs of teachers, using a metacognitive approach to analyze the results.[270] A total of 45 participants were involved, of whom sixteen answered online, and 29 answered on paper, at the end of a workshop.

The results demonstrated that 91% of the participants answered that they had previously been in professional development in various formats (they were, indeed, leaving one). Regarding content they deemed relevant, some participants highlighted the differences and specificities of teaching HLS; others mentioned curriculum, access to research, and practical training, but the majority did not specify, answering that the opportunity had been positive or relevant in one way or another. Regarding what they did not deem appropriate, participants pointed out the lack of connection between research and practice and, consequently, the lack of applicability in their classroom. In general, the results showed that participants valued the exchanges that were made possible in this kind of training.

A fourth study analyzed the discourses of 49 participants in the forum of a specific 12-week professional development program promoted to those who teach PHL.[271] The participants were asked about the importance of three chronological moments referent to the development of a HL, which had been previously discussed at length in the course: "beginning"[272] — which features the importance of the initial years of childhood, as well as actions and discussions about family language planning and primary experiences with the sounds of a language; "middle" — which refers to the years in which the

---

[269] Silva & Costa, 2020
[270] Barcelos, 2007; Pajares, 1996
[271] Jennings-Winterle, 2020
[272] These three "moments" refer to the philosophical proposal named The Philosophy of Beginning, Middle and End, created by Jennings-Winterle, 2015.

child starts going to school and negotiates her languages and cultures, amplifying, at the same time, their vocabulary and language skills; and "end" — referring to the final years of school, as well as the development of social and emotional autonomy of the now, teenager or young adult, highlighting the purpose and importance of the work of HL maintenance.

The discourse analysis of the pieces that participants wrote in the forum of the course showed that educators recognize the "beginning" as definitive to the development of the HL. While developing their answers, participants recalled experiences from the time they were pregnant and how those memories later formed the basis for a strong appreciation of the HL. This finding indicates a certain kind of intuition of the educator, represented in sentences like "I had no knowledge about which actions I would have to take," "my method was not conscious," "my intuition was the driving spring for my search on the internet for more competent guidance."

Participants also indicated reasons for their investment in the teaching, promotion, and maintenance of PHL. In order of prevalence, the reasons mentioned were 1. contact with family; 2. future advantages; 3. better cultural understanding. Moreover, participants highlighted the importance of the work of initiatives as a source of influence and renovation of the motivation of parents and HLS.

From this material, the author identified perspectives that participants have about bi/plurilingualism, cultural identity, and linguistic policies, as well as characteristics of their roles and specificities of their contexts. The data showed that 47,9% of the participants showed high proximity (i.e., appreciation) to topics about identity; 36,1% to topics about bi/plurilingualism; 10,6% to discussions regarding linguistic policy and planning; and 5,4% to other themes presented throughout their course.

The studies of Gonçalves, Silva, and Costa, and Jennings-Winterle clearly show the heterogeneity of those involved with teaching, promoting, and maintaining PHL, as well as their transversal positionings (whether between the place of training and the place of work, or within the fluency between the culture of origin and the host culture).[273] Furthermore, this brief literature review shows that generally, educators are more interested in formative sessions that focus on the practice itself. One could even say that there is a kind of resistance to more theoretical discussions. Accordingly, Costa identifies:

> A general eagerness to have access to a curriculum, activities, and lesson plans that can be used in their classrooms, somewhat akin to a recipe that can be followed and perhaps slightly tweaked according to the "ingredients" at hand. Instructors appear genuinely interested in teaching a good class, but without necessarily considering emerging issues in the field.[274]

This urgency arguably comes from the need teachers have to reinvent themselves, both personally and professionally, reaffirming social, cultural, and emotional positions. Let us not forget that in their professional identities, there is a mix of personal aspects — an immigrant subject, a woman who is also a mother. Even in the case of the Portuguese PHL teachers, generally more professionally capacitated, their urgency could be related to the need to guarantee that an important mission is accomplished: the transmission, maintenance, and celebration of a language that, to them, represents people, places, and events that anchor positive memories.

Profiles, Contexts, and Perspectives

It was a privilege to learn more about the characteristics, challenges, and needs of women who live among various languages and cultures and, consequently, reinvent their identities and socio-affective cultural values for fifteen years. Such an advantage called forth reflections about commonalities and specificities of the profiles, perspectives, and contexts of those involved in the teaching, maintaining, and nurturing PHL.

---

[273] Gonçalves, 2017; 2019; Silva & Costa, 2020; Jennings-Winterle, 2020
[274] Costa, 2013; Silva & Costa, 2020, p. 56

The concept *profile* was outlined as a description of common social and cultural characteristics. As previously mentioned, the vast majority of this group is women, a fact seen across various (if not all) HLs, which is why this gender is singled out.

Specifically, Brazilian PHL teachers are native speakers of Portuguese (rarely are they heritage speakers or additional language speakers) and immigrants. As such, they are subject to various challenges in the sociocultural and emotional spheres, inherent to their acculturation processes. Overall, they are subjects in transit, as Gonçalves describes, "between here and there, always articulating, mediating, transposing borders and building bridges."[275] There is a clear interplay between what is called cultural plasticity and cultural flaccidity, which can be seen amid processes of adaptation and socialization of these subjects.[276]

A previous study by Jennings-Winterle, da Costa de Sá and Nogueira showed, through a process of mapping Brazilian initiatives and teachers, as well as interviews and analysis of their discourses published on websites and social media, that the majority do not know about linguistic theories and practices with a more plural or critical essence, such as translanguaging, intercultural competence, integrative didactic approaches based on intercomprehension and interculturality, nor pluricentrism — an inherent characteristic of the Portuguese language.[277]

Moreover, it is possible to identify that most teachers did not go to university for a specialized academic development (i.e., in language education, for example), nor do they have access to training and discussions about general and essential knowledge of Linguistics

---

[275] Gonçalves, 2017, p 41. In the original, in Portuguese: "entre o cá e o lá, continuamente articulando, mediando, transpondo fronteiras e construindo pontes."
[276] Jennings-Winterle & Bittens, 2015
[277] Jennings-Winterle, da Costa de Sá, & Nogueira, 2018; Baldi, 2021; Jennings-Winterle, 2020; García, 2001; Yup & García, 2015; Bastos, 2014; Candelier et al., 2012; Ferreira & Melo-Pfeifer, 2015; Melo-Pfeifer, 2019; Pinheiro, 2020

and Pedagogy. They do not even have a background in education, something that is also seen across various HLs.[278, 279]

The concept *context* was outlined from the observation of intrinsic characteristics of the spaces in which there is a need and/or desire for the intergenerational transmission of an HL. As such, these are characteristics localized in a specific historical and sociocultural context. For example, the United States or, more exactly, the state of Massachusetts (where there is a large contingent of Portuguese speakers) will be significantly different than the state of Nebraska (where there is no large contingent of speakers nor initiatives).

These are spaces where immigrants and their children — either born in the host country or brought to it during school years — interact with others with the same ascendency and of different ascendancies, where various identities coexist. That means that they experience the similar and the distinct, daily. Cultures, languages, and identities collide in these contexts and, as a result, other, hybrid ones are formed as a consequence of the constant negotiations between what is worth keeping and what is worth acquiring.[280] The experiences with those with similar cultural and linguistic identities are also impactful and transformative.

Every context is inevitably reigned by linguistic ideologies proper to that region, conditioning, for example, how, when, and who can be (or could be) bi/plurilingual. That happens because ideologies determine policies, which, in turn, condition the availability of opportunities and various resources.[281] The sample of teachers'

---

[278] It is essential to emphasize, however, that this is not the case for a Portuguese educator: they are required to have an academic background in Literature and a B2 level of knowledge of the language of the host country, and these professionals are recruited in Portugal Gonçalves, 2019. Although they have to comply with this requirement, Gonçalves 2019 points out that the training of Portuguese teachers is not specific to teaching PLH. They adapt their pedagogical approaches to the contexts in which they work, but, above all, "the profile of the PLH educator is characterized by its dispersion and heterogeneity" p. 46. It is no different among Brazilian educators.
[279] Chik & Wright, 2017; Liu et al., 2011
[280] Berry, 1997; Berry, 2004
[281] Shohami, 2006

discourses analyzed highlights that, even when they plan or do not oppose the opportunity of offering a bi/plurilingual lifestyle, they face many challenges that are long ingrained in their contexts and in their minds (even the ones that might be perhaps better academically prepared).

Within the Brazilian context, the work of Instituto Guimarães Rosa (which has a similar proposal to that of Instituto Camões) is still very incipient regarding PHL. One could argue that there appears to be little, if any, interest in investing in the globalization of the Portuguese language, particularly through the linguistic and cultural development of heritage speakers.[282] From the teachers and cultural promoters' perspective, there are not enough financial resources, nor, many times, personal interest in financing their professional development. That is because the economic return from this kind of work is most definitely incompatible with the necessary investment and involvement. Not only do initiatives work once a week, often on weekends or once a month, but also most of them are free of charge or barely charge for their work, which does not cover costs related to their logistical functioning nor confer an expressive financial return to those involved.

It could be argued that while there is no direct or prescriptive involvement from government agencies or academic institutions in the context of PHL, there is no institutionalization of this field. As such, there seems to be more freedom to create and develop unique proposals. Of course, that also corroborates the dispersion and heterogeneity of the practice, as well as the perpetuation and

---

[282] It should be noted that the Ministry of Foreign Affairs MRE promoted, between 2011 and 2014, two-day workshops at the Brazilian consulates in Miami, San Francisco, Boston, Madrid, and Geneva Lico, 2012; Moroni, 2015. It is not within the scope of this contribution to analyze the programs mentioned, but it is clear that a two-day training is, at the very least, insufficient and, as Silva & Costa, 2020 were able to prove, "not very relevant", given the lack of initial training and, even more so, the specialization and dynamism that the field of PLH studies and practices requires. Once again, this scenario goes against the essential knowledge for teaching practice.

excessive repetition of projects and practices, including those that are not effective. Still, the context seems to be free from bureaucracy and hierarchization, as any institutionalization would impose.

Finally, the *perspectives* concept was outlined as the sum of personal evaluations, as well as values and views based on specific knowledge acquired in training, through experiences, or common sense. Silva & da Costa[283] further explain these values and opinions, characterizing them as

- *Rationale*: based on previous knowledge obtained in training and professional development, as well as through practice.
- *Affective:* built within families and communities through actions of observation and discernment, both as a subject in the situation or an observer.
- *Common sense:* constituted as the way through which one evaluates certain situations and is very much influenced by cultural views, by the capacity of encountering something without knowing it in full, and by associative thought.

The perspectives of PHL teachers are, mainly, driven by affective and sociocultural motivations to preserve (or create or develop) ties with the family members who stayed back, as well as guaranteeing that their own identities (as well as their children's) continue being nourished even during so many changes, assimilations, and adaptations. One can also observe the existence of adaptation and assimilation strategies that involve the host language and culture through the embodiment of manners and values of identity and cultural Brazilian aspects to the local ones.

Still, the practices and discourses that sustain teachers and their initiatives sponsor the perspective of separating languages and cultures in order to be more efficient. It seems that they intend to amplify the interaction with the HL, which has intrinsic time and space limitations. The teacher believes that she must preserve the

---

[283] Silva & da Costa, 2020

integrity—understood as a kind of purity—of the heritage culture, language, and identity in order to justify greater support for their learning and maintenance. This is a segregating strategy, based on colonial views,[284] contrary to heteroglossic views about bi/plurilingualism.[285]

Moreover, primarily, the teacher wishes to perpetuate the contact between their children (majority born in the host country) and the family members back in their birth country. There is a strong expectation among grandparents, uncles, and aunts to accompany their grandchildren or niblings as they grow up, alongside an often unconscious notion on the part of the teacher of how to be *mãe*—not *mother*, nor *Mutter*, nor *madre*. All that adds to the clear wish of developing their children's bilingualism, which can afford an advantageous future.

However, at the same time that the teacher stresses her primordial expectations, intrinsically emotional and affective, she undermines the whole extension of the concept of bilingualism or plurilingualism, and that PHL is part of the linguistic repertoire of their children;[286] much less that she is in front of individuals who are potential plurilingual. She also does not necessarily comprehend views that come from post-structuralist and decolonial schools of thought, not that she was allowed to discuss different opinions regarding the outdatedness of more traditional and structuralist concepts.

These teachers highlight the importance of the dialogue between their children and their spouse, as well as their children and their spouse's family. She is, however, painfully aware of the overwhelmingly more frequent offers for the nurture of local identities. Nevertheless, she is concerned and committed to the academic success of her children (irrefutably dependent on proficiency in the local language). That means that she is *mãe* and, at

---

[284] Cenoz & Garcia, 2017
[285] Garcia & Wei, 2018
[286] Megale, 2019

the same time, *mother/mutter/madre*.[287] As such, she deals with a variety of emotional, identity, marital, and familial matters. Indeed, she has (to have) answers ready to go to family and other society members regarding her children's linguistic and academic development.

Added to this already extraordinarily complex scenario, the fact that the teacher has what is called an emergent national identity,[288] in which an active and explicit desire to emphasize and celebrate the cultures of her birth country is evident. As such, she becomes a walking embassy, and that serves as the driving force behind her decision to create an initiative or to join one. That is, indeed, another acculturation strategy that becomes essential to some immigrants while dealing with the fact that they are no longer only Brazilian, and all the implications that this affirmation carries.

A Quest for New Profiles, Contexts, and Perspectives

Though created with teaching at the university in mind, a model proposed by Grillo & Gessinger[289] could be helpful to the quest of answering, *What does the teacher need to know to teach?* As such, the ideal teacher would be:

> Someone who (1) knows their teaching subject, seen as the area of knowledge in which they work, the discipline they teach, and the program as stated in the curriculum; (2) has knowledge related to Educational Sciences and Pedagogy, and (3) develops practical knowledge arising from their professional teaching experience itself (p. 36).[290]

---

[287] Of course, not all women involved in the field of PLH studies and practices are mothers, but, in one way or another, they are linked to mothers or perform functions associated with the role of mother, in a "false" and, definitely, complementary way.

[288] In the original in Portuguese, "identidade nacional aflorada." Jennings-Winterle, 2023

[289] Grillo & Gessinger, 2008

[290] In the original in Portuguese, alguém que 1 conhece sua matéria de ensino, entendida como a área do conhecimento em que atua, a disciplina que leciona e o programa conforme consta no currículo; 2 possui

That means that such plurality of knowledge that constitutes professional teaching makes her a professional in the area she teaches (ibid). Accordingly,

> The teacher is one whose teaching is built in a balanced way within the knowledge of specific knowledge, Pedagogy, and experience. It is plural knowledge, constituted by the amalgamation of a specific axis, a pedagogical axis, and an experiential axis. The greater emphasis on one of these axes will influence the practice developed in different ways.[291]

One can thus think of a professional identity that the teacher could (should) acquire once she receives appropriate professional training. It could be said that "the specific axis is responsible for mastering the knowledge of the professional specialty, from which the subject and curricular knowledge of the teacher's area of activity originates."[292]

In the case of PHL, the specific knowledge related to the Portuguese language itself (as well as, its grammar, history, and current positioning worldwide), as well as language teaching (concerning linguistic acquisition, development, and bi/plurilingualism) are, inevitably, themes explored by research — an activity that the teacher would also need to be able to understand and even produce.

---

conhecimentos relativos às Ciências da Educação e à Pedagogia e 3 desenvolve um saber prático oriundo de sua experiência profissional docente propriamente dita apud. Grillo & Gessinger, 2008, p. 36.

[291] In the original in Portuguese, o professor é aquele cuja docência se constrói equilibradamente sobre os saberes do conhecimento específico, da Pedagogia e da experiência. É um saber plural, constituído pelo amálgama de um eixo específico, um eixo pedagógico e um eixo experiencial. A ênfase maior a um desses eixos vai influenciar de forma diversa a prática desenvolvida. ibid.

[292] In the original, in Portuguese, "o eixo específico é responsável pelo domínio do conhecimento da especialidade profissional, de onde se originam os saberes disciplinar e curricular da área de atuação do profesor." Grillo & Gessinger, p. 36.

The pedagogical axis "is what characterizes the teaching profession because it deals with specific teaching content."[293] In the case of PHL, this is one of the least met axes, if we take into account the lack of training of most who are in charge of teaching programs. However, it is important to highlight the fact that most of them are mothers, which, even informally and subjectively, provides some experience about learning processes, childhood, and how struggling can be the growing-up process, being bi/plurilingual. This knowledge does not, however, provide sufficient support for understanding and applying theories and methodologies related to advances in research on cognition or language learning.

Finally, the experiential axis "refers to knowledge from teaching experience." From this perspective, experience is understood not as time of service, but in the sense proposed by Larrosa, as "that which 'passes' us, or touches us, or happens to us, and as it passes, forms and transforms us."[294] This perspective is in line with the observations that, even if there is experience in the area of education, or even in language education, such referentiality might not be sufficient for what makes up the multilingual context of reception, since it is exercised in a more homogeneous and monolingual context. Thus, thinking about experience reflectively and critically is fundamental, due to its capacity for formation and transformation.[295]

The field of studies and practices of PHL has been following a path of constant consolidation over the last fifteen years, at least. In this sense, it is necessary to focus on the training and improvement of the educators involved.

The following is a broad guideline created to improve and broaden PHL teachers' perspectives, implying the development of a set of

---

[293] In the original, in Portuguese, "é o que caracteriza a profissão de professor por tratar de conteúdos específicos da docencia." Grillo & Gessinger, p. 37.

[294] In the original, in Portuguese, the previous quote: "refere-se ao saber da experiência docente" Grillo & Gessinger, p. 37. The present, como "aquilo que nos 'passa', ou que nos toca, ou que nos acontece, e ao nos passar nos forma e nos transforma." Larrosa, 2004, p.163.

[295] Grillo & Gessinger, p. 39

skills that should make them even more capable of conducting their work more professionally. Some characteristics of this continuous training would be that the educator could:

- Be part of an immigration context, i.e., being an immigrant, and, thus, going through or having gone through the challenges of the acculturation process of experiencing languages in contact, valuing this multiple experience.
- Engaging in a network of HL teachers and continually participating in meetings for exchanges, training, and recycling.
- Seeking specific and updated training for teaching, promoting, and maintaining an HL.

Acquiring this training can be a process carried out in a guided or unguided manner, specifically because teaching an HL represents a non-institutionalized set of practices. In any case, the educator must be invested in this sense — considering Bonny Norton's concept[296]— to be able to:

- Create strategies and lessons that can contribute to the development of a plural identity, more than improving knowledge about the Portuguese language, and which include experiences and reflections on HL and the cultural practices and values related to it.
- Improve knowledge about HL, including grammatical and historical aspects, as well as its current positioning worldwide.
- Improve knowledge of the language of the country of residence, including grammatical and historical aspects, as well as its current positioning worldwide, in order to broaden their multilingual experience (and that of their students), by being able to point out transfers and interferences between languages.

---

[296] Norton, 2000; Norton, 2015; Norton, 2020

- Reflect on the understandings they have about the concepts of culture and identity, as well as with which cultural aspects and identity positions they identify, and finally,
- Familiarize themselves with research related to the field of HL, seeking to make connections between theory and practice, on their own and/or in a guided manner.

With these parameters, recommendations from other authors should also be considered. Among them, we highlight the fact that teacher education must mean multiple actions that foster professionalization, which means learning how to teach; developing skills and strategies to reflect on theory and practice; to narrate, explain, and justify choices in planning and decisions in the classroom; and, finally, to record and disseminate their experiences.[297] Therefore, it is essential to:

> (include) not only linguistic, cultural, and intercultural skills, but also digital skills, highlighting the flexible management skills of the teaching and learning process, which help teachers to operationalize more personalized and enriching approaches to the learners' linguistic-communicative repertoires, facilitating openness to others, in a process of construction and recreation of meaning about the world and oneself in the relationship with the Other.[298]

Furthermore, the aim is to make the teacher a teacher-researcher and a teacher-author, positions that will enable more effective exchanges

---

[297] Costa & Schlatter, 2017; Garcez & Schlatter, 2016; Perrenoud, 2002; Schön, 1983; Apud Silva & Costa, 2020

[298] In the original, in Portuguese: incluir as competências não só linguísticas, culturais e interculturais, mas também digitais, sublinhando as competências de gestão flexível do processo de ensino e aprendizagem, que ajudem os docentes a operacionalizar abordagens mais personalizadas e enriquecedoras dos repertórios linguístico-comunicativos dos aprendentes, facilitadoras da abertura ao outro, num processo de construção e recriação de significado sobre o mundo e sobre si na relação com esse outro. Pinho et. al, 2011.

between theory and research and practice and research, allowing the creation of culturally authentic and responsive materials and strategies (speaking of the culture of the language and its speaker). To this end, it will be necessary.

> To recognize the importance of the teacher's individuality in their development process, in addition to giving them a role as an active participant in the construction of their professional knowledge for understanding and consequent educational improvement [...] this action [...] is simultaneously individual and collective [...] in interaction with themselves, namely with their practices and representations, with peers, and with the context.[299]

We are witnessing a significant growth in the number of Portuguese language speakers around the world, who experience their variants and cultures through a specific bi/plurilingualism, involving PHL. The moment is critical — if, on one hand, it is notable that a greater and broader recognition of the concept has been achieved, with great success, thanks to numerous factors (especially the widespread use of social media); on the other hand, the need to train those who dedicate themselves to teaching, promoting and maintaining this culture-language-identity is becoming increasingly urgent.

It is necessary to empower them for the task that their work of convincing and enchanting entails, making this form of bilingual teaching a possibility for the development of a plural identity of competent bilingual individuals prepared for an increasingly

---

[299] In the original, in Portuguese: o reconhecimento da importância da individualidade do professor no seu processo de desenvolvimento, além de lhe conferir um papel de interveniente ativo na construção do seu conhecimento profissional para a compreensão e consequente melhoria educacional [...] essa ação [...] é simultaneamente individual e coletiva [...] em interação consigo próprio, nomeadamente com as suas práticas e representações, com os pares, e com o contexto. Gonçalves, 2017, p.1.

challenging future. In this sense, it is necessary to find ways for continuous training.

Furthermore, it is necessary to find viable and sustainable forms of training that are not only episodic but rather robust and complex, to meet the intrinsic needs of the profiles and specificities of PHL teachers, broadening their perspectives beyond a banking (Freire, 2016) or utilitarian form of teaching language, to provide truly plural experiences to their learners.

Nevertheless, it is necessary to develop questions for future studies, indicating the importance of research conducted by the teachers themselves on their practices, and emphasizing that PHL teaching is certainly a response to an intriguing phenomenon that alludes to multiple possibilities for investigation.

Finally, it is crucial to call on institutions (governmental or otherwise) and the community itself (family members and other speakers) to learn about the practices of teaching, promoting, and maintaining PHL, who carry them out, and how this complements formal and informal education offers, in the context of non-formal education. Preserving their non-schooled condition is important, but it is necessary to support them in many ways. This will only be possible and sustainable once the power of maintaining HLs and the importance they have, in a multiplicity of subjects, is considered. The search for a professional identity that fosters articulation between experience and practice, and that lends credibility to pedagogical work, is a central objective of the professionalization of teaching. In this context, the maintenance of heritage languages constitutes a fertile area for research and knowledge production in the field.

Chapter 7

Korean-American Parents' Efforts to Transmit the Korean Language to their Third-Generation Korean-American Children

Hanae Kim

The benefits of maintaining a heritage language extend beyond communication with family and community; it helps the learner to gain knowledge of their heritage culture, customs, and values; foster a sense of belonging and pride in their heritage; and expand job opportunities and social networks.[300] However, many immigrant families in the U.S. face significant challenges in transmitting their heritage languages to the next generation. These barriers include English-only policies in educational settings, societal pressures to assimilate, limited access to heritage language education resources, children's lack of motivation, and the dominant use of English in daily life.[301] Despite these obstacles, the effort to maintain a heritage language is deeply tied to developing a sense of belonging and pride in one's cultural heritage. Sociolinguistic theorist Fishman highlights the importance of heritage language maintenance as essential for preserving cultural identity and sustaining the cohesion of ethnic communities.[302]

Like many other immigrant communities, Korean-American families and the community have worked to transmit the Korean

---

[300] Bourdieu, 1986; Cummins, 1996; Fishman, 2001; Kim, 2017; Krashen, 2000
[301] Fillmore, 2000; Kondo-Brown, 2010; Liang, 2018; Shin, 2004
[302] Fishman, 1991

language to future generations. They have established community-based Korean weekend schools and cultural organizations to preserve their linguistic and cultural heritage.[303] Parents played a pivotal role in teaching the Korean language to their children by using diverse strategies such as enrolling their children in community-based, weekend schools and speaking Korean at home.[304] Many parents felt a strong sense of responsibility to pass on the Korean language to their children, and even some Korean heritage language learners also felt this responsibility for future generations.[305] These practices align with the theoretical framework of family language policy, which explores the relationship between parental beliefs, practices, and broader socio-cultural influence on heritage language transmission.[306]

However, as Fillmore notes, when children begin formal schooling in the U.S., English becomes their dominant language, leading to a decline in heritage language proficiency.[307] This language shift can limit children's ability to maintain and pass on their heritage language to future generations. Despite the growing number of third-generation Korean-American children in Korean language programs, there is a shortage of research on second-generation Korean-American parents, third-generation Korean heritage language learners, and multiracial and/or multilingual Korean heritage language learners.

This chapter examines how second-generation Korean-American parents in multiracial and/or multilingual families attempt to transmit the Korean language to their third-generation children. Specifically, this study seeks to answer the following questions:

---

[303] Cho, 2000; Lee & Shin, 2008; Shin, 2004
[304] Brown, 2011; Damron & Forsyth, 2010; Kang, 2015; Lee & Gupta, 2020
[305] Lee, 2002; Park & Sarkar, 2007; Song, 2016
[306] Curdt-Christiansen, 2013; King et al., 2008
[307] Fillmore, 2000

(1) What efforts do second-generation Korean-American parents undertake to teach the Korean language to their third-generation Korean-American children?

(2) What challenges do they encounter in this process?

By addressing these questions, this chapter aims to contribute to the broader discourse on heritage language transmission and intergenerational linguistic continuity, and the evolving needs of Korean heritage language education in increasingly diverse family contexts.

Literature Review

Korean-American Immigration History

Koreans represent one of the largest Asian ethnic groups in the U.S. Korean immigration to the U.S. began in the early 20th century, driven by social, political, and economic factors. The first wave of Korean immigrants was workers who came to Hawaii in 1903 to address a labor shortage in sugar plantations.[308] The second wave occurred after the Korean War (1950–1953), which included war brides and adoptees who came through the Refugee Relief Act and War Brides Act.[309]

Korean immigration shifted noticeably after the Immigration and Nationality Act of 1965, bringing a wave of predominantly educated professionals and middle-class families seeking better educational and economic opportunities.[310] This group contributed to the development of Korean-American communities in metropolitan areas such as Los Angeles, New York, and Chicago.[311]

The Korean-American population grew significantly during the 1970s and 1980s, driven by the family reunification provisions of the 1965 Immigration Act, South Korea's rapid economic development, and the pursuit of better educational and economic opportunities in

---

[308] Hong, 2018; Jo, 1999; Jung, 1991
[309] Jung, 1991
[310] Chang & Diaz-Veizades, 1999; Lee, 2018
[311] Fong & Shibuya, 2005; Shin, 2004

the U.S.[312] These immigrants established strong communities, including Korean-owned businesses, religious organizations, cultural centers, and community-based heritage language schools to support cultural preservation.[313]

Korean Heritage Language Maintenance

While community-based Korean language schools have made significant efforts to offer language education, these programs often face challenges that limit their effectiveness. These schools are typically small, offering limited classes and usually meet only once a week for a few hours. Such a schedule is generally insufficient for students to maintain proficiency, particularly in a language as complex as Korean.[314] Furthermore, these schools are not equally accessible to all learners; in areas with smaller Korean populations, limited resources and opportunities often make it difficult for students to find adequate support for their language development.[315]

Home environments also played a crucial role in Korean language retention, and studies show that parents' attitudes and family language policies greatly influence heritage language maintenance. For example, Shin and Lee, and Kang emphasize how parents' language ideologies shape family approaches to preserving the heritage language.[316] Families employ various strategies such as speaking Korean at home, engaging in home literacy practices, consuming Korean media, visiting Korea, and some even enrolling their children in dual-language immersion programs.[317] Despite these efforts, maintaining the heritage language remains a significant challenge.

---

[312] Hurh, 1998; Min, 2011
[313] Shin, 2004
[314] Byon, 2008; Shin, 2004
[315] Choi, 2016
[316] Shin and Lee, 2013; Kang, 2015
[317] Ee, 2016; Jeon, 2008; Kang, 2013; Kwon, 2017; Song, 2016

Heritage Language Learners

Heritage language learners (HLLs) are individuals raised in a home where a non-English language is spoken and/or those with a heritage motivation to reconnect with their family's heritage through language, even if they primarily speak English.[318] Unlike traditional foreign language learners, HLLs require tailored programs, materials, and pedagogical approaches that reflect their distinct linguistic backgrounds and cultural ties.[319]

Importantly, heritage language learners are not a homogeneous group; they bring diverse language proficiencies, language varieties, cultural backgrounds, motivations, and educational needs. This diversity complicates the planning and implementation of effective heritage language programs.[320] For example, learners may come from homes where the heritage language is actively spoken by both parents, spoken by only one parent, rarely spoken, or not spoken at all. These varying home language environments create various levels of linguistic resources and needs among learners, underscoring the importance of curricular materials and teacher training tailored specifically for heritage language education.[321]

Heritage Language Loss

Despite the efforts of families and communities, heritage language loss remains a significant challenge. Research shows that language loss occurs at both personal and familial levels, and intergenerational communication gaps arise between first-generation parents and their second-generation children.[322] For example, while first-generation immigrant parents may primarily speak Korean at home, their children often respond in English, gradually creating communication

---

[318] Fishman, 2001; Valdes, 2001; Van Deusen-Scholl, 2003
[319] Compton, 2001; Kondo-Brown, 2010; Valdes, 2001
[320] Wiley, 2001; Wiley & Valdés, 2000
[321] Compton, 2001; Kono & McGinnis, 2001; Schwartz, 2001
[322] Cho & Krashen, 1998; Haynes, 2010; Shin, 2004

barriers.[323] This shift accelerates by the third generation,[324] a pattern described by Fishman[325] as a three-generational language shift in the U.S. Language loss can lead to intergenerational communication barriers, cultural disconnection, and feelings of identity loss.[326]

Similarly, the Korean-American community also exhibits a similar pattern of heritage language loss like other immigrant groups. The social pressure to assimilate into an English-dominant society often prioritizes English for academic achievement and social integration.[327] Consequently, interest and participation in Korean heritage language schools frequently decline, especially as children grow older and face conflicting schedules between Korean schools and extracurricular activities.[328]

Research has documented that many Korean-American students value the importance of maintaining their heritage language, but feel that existing community-based Korean programs do not meet their needs.[329] Studies highlight students' dissatisfaction with outdated curricula, lack of engaging pedagogy, and inability to address the diverse needs of learners.[330] These programs often struggle to accommodate a wide range of students, including second-generation learners with English-speaking parents, Korean adoptees in non-Korean households, and children from multiracial families.[331]

Most research on Korean heritage language learning has focused primarily on first-generation parents and their second-generation learners. These studies often assume relatively homogeneous family dynamics, overlooking the unique challenges and motivations of third-generation learners, particularly those from multiracial and multilingual families. There is a need to better understand how

---

[323] Kang, 2015
[324] Fillmore, 2000
[325] Fishman, 1991
[326] Cho, 2000; Cho & Krashen, 1998; Shin, 2004
[327] Jeon, 2008; Kang, 2013a; Lee, 2002; Shin, 2004; Shin & Lee, 2013
[328] Damron & Forsyth, 2012; Jeon, 2008
[329] Lee, 2002; Shin, 2004
[330] Jeon, 2007; Lee & Bang, 2011
[331] Shin & Lee, 2013

heritage language transmission takes place within these more complex family structures, where parents vary in language proficiency, cultural affiliation, and access to heritage language resources.

To address this gap, this chapter investigates the strategies, motivations, and challenges faced by second-generation Korean-American parents as they transmit the Korean language to their third-generation children. By focusing on multiracial and multilingual families, this research aims to provide a deeper understanding of heritage language maintenance and intergenerational transmission within diverse family contexts.

Methodology

This qualitative case study examined three families living in a large city in the Midwest during 2020. Through prolonged direct observation and in-depth interviews, the study explored these families' efforts to transmit the Korean language to their children, who are third-generation Korean-Americans. Each family was treated as a distinct case due to their unique characteristics, such as ethnic diversity and the parents' varying levels of Korean language proficiency. A summary of the family structure and language proficiencies of the participants is shown in Table 1.

Table 1. Summary of Family Structure and Language Proficiency Levels

Interviewee's name	Role	Father's ethnicity	Father's Korean language proficiency	Mother's ethnicity	Mother's Korean language proficiency	Child(ren)	Age of the child(ren) at the study
Chris	Father	Korean	Conversational	Korean	Conversational	One daughter (Jenny)	10 years old
Olivia	Mother	Caucasian	None	Korean	Intermediate	One daughter (Melissa), one son (Paul)	Daughter – 16 years old Son – 13 years old
Michelle	Mother	African-American	None	Half Korean & African-American	Beginning	One daughter (Chloe)	16 years old

Participants

The data for this study came from a larger research project focusing on adult Korean language education, which aimed to study the motivations of adult Korean language learners. One parent in each family was actively studying the Korean language at the time of the study. During the interview, they shared their perceptions of the Korean language, its importance for their families, and the methods they used to teach Korean to their children. My role as a teacher at a community-based Korean weekend school and an instructor for adult Korean classes allowed me to interact with these families in various capacities, enriching the study's depth.

Chris's Family

Chris's family consisted of second-generation Korean-American parents born in the U.S. to Korean immigrant parents. Both sets of grandparents were deeply involved in the Korean community, fostering strong connections for the family. The grandparents frequently brought Korean books and resources for their granddaughter, Jenny, and invited her to Korean cultural events, exposing her to the language and traditions. Chris's family also arranged private lessons for Jenny over several years, and she also attended a Korean weekend school for one semester. Although both parents spoke conversational Korean, they primarily used English at home and with their own parents, who were also fluent in English.

Olivia's Family

Olivia's family consisted of a second-generation Korean-American mother and a Caucasian father. The mother, born and raised in the U.S., spoke some Korean at an intermediate level, while the father did not speak Korean. Their children, Melissa and Peter, initially attended a Korean weekend school at a local church for a few years but later transitioned to private lessons due to distinct reasons, including their children's progress in school and scheduling conflicts. Although Korean was not spoken at home, the children were motivated to learn the language to communicate with their maternal grandparents, who spoke limited English. Olivia's family frequently visited the maternal grandparents' home for Korean holiday celebrations, where they enjoyed Korean food prepared by the grandmother.

Michelle's Family

Michelle's family consisted of a half-Korean, second-generation Korean-American mother and an African-American father. Michelle was born and raised in the U.S., but during her early childhood, the family lived in Korea for a few years due to her father's military posting. This experience allowed her to speak fluent Korean as a child. However, after relocating to the U.S., her parents discouraged the use of Korean at home, encouraging her to learn English for school quickly. Michelle deeply regrets this loss of her heritage language and strongly believes in the importance of preserving cultural identity. As a result, she enrolled her daughter Chloe in a Korean weekend school. In this family, the maternal grandmother is the only fluent Korean speaker, though she rarely speaks Korean at home due to a lack of conversational partners.

Data Collection

Data were collected over one year, from January 2020 to November 2020, using online surveys, direct observation, and in-depth interviews. Direct observation took place in participants' homes and was documented through note-taking. In addition, my role as a Korean school teacher facilitated natural interactions with the families, who often sought advice on their children's language education.

Following the observations, semi-structured one-to-one interviews were conducted. The interview questions were based on the participants' responses to the online surveys as well as findings from the observations. These interviews explored the families' motivation for teaching Korean, their perceptions of the language, and the strategies they employed. The interview also provided an opportunity to address questions or explore topics that emerged during the observations. Each interview was conducted in English via Zoom, and it lasted between 60 and 90 minutes and was transcribed using pseudonyms to ensure confidentiality during data analysis.

Data Analysis

An iterative and inductive approach was used to analyze data from online surveys, direct observation notes, and interview transcripts. Patterns related to parents' efforts, motivations, perceptions, and self-assessed language proficiency were identified, providing a holistic understanding of each case and enabling meaningful cross-case comparisons.

The analysis began with a systematic review of each family's data to capture the context of their experiences. Observation notes and interview transcripts were coded to identify four primary themes: activities and efforts, motivations, experiences, and struggles. These themes provided insights into the families' language education experiences and practices.

To ensure the credibility of the findings, triangulation and member checking were conducted. Data from online surveys, observations, and interviews were cross-referenced for consistency, and participants reviewed preliminary findings to validate the interpretation of their experiences during the interview. These steps enhanced the reliability of the study, providing a nuanced understanding of the families' efforts, motivations, and perceptions regarding Korean language education.

Findings

Similar to previous research, the findings highlight a variety of efforts undertaken by these families to teach Korean to their children, including enrollment in Korean language schools, hiring private tutors, practicing the language at home, participating in local Korean cultural events, and visiting Korea. Regardless of their child's proficiency in Korean, parents expressed immense pride in their children's ability to read, write, or speak the language. The primary motivation behind these endeavors was the desire to foster a strong cultural identity in their children, along with a concern that the Korean language might be lost within their family. However, parents also reported significant challenges in teaching Korean, including their limited proficiency, as well as the infrequent use and accessibility of the language. These difficulties often left parents with a sense of regret and resentment about their inability to speak their heritage language fluently. All participants expressed an ardent desire to improve their own Korean proficiency.

Motivations: Heritage Identity Over Practical Language Needs

For third-generation Korean-Americans, the motivation to learn the Korean language was not rooted in a practical need to communicate with parents or grandparents, as even the grandparents often spoke some English. All families reported using English at home and rarely speaking Korean, even during family events. However, Olivia's family stood out, as they shared that their children were motivated to speak Korean to communicate with their maternal grandparents, who had limited English proficiency. Despite the lack of necessity for Korean as a communication tool within the family, parents unanimously expressed a desire for their children to speak Korean, understand Korean culture and history, and connect with their heritage. As Michelle shared:

> You know, Chloe looks like a little Black girl. And I don't want her to forget. She's not just Black. Well, Chloe's dad is Belizean from Belize, and she's Korean. So, I think it's important to know your heritage. Know where you come from. She's not around a lot of Korean people. So, I love that I found the Korean school for her to go to, encompassing all things Korean, you know. She's not just learning the language. She's learning how to play the Korean drum.[332]

Although Michelle is only half Korean and has limited proficiency in the language, she has a strong cultural identity as Korean. She and her sisters actively celebrate Korean holidays with her family and enjoy wearing Hanbok to special events, such as weddings. Michelle wants Chloe to maintain her Korean heritage through language and

---

[332] Michelle, personal communication, November 14, 2020

cultural education, which is why she drives 45 minutes each way to take Chloe to Korean school every Saturday.

Similarly, Chris's family began prioritizing Korean language education for their daughter, Jenny, when her school started teaching Spanish. Recognizing the importance of preserving their heritage and noticing Jenny's interest in Korean popular culture, the family decided to teach her Korean. They hired a tutor, enrolled her in a Korean school, and provided her with Korean books and resources to immerse her in the language and culture.

Regardless of the percentage of Korean ancestry in their family or the lack of Korean as a spoken language at home, all families shared a deep concern about the potential loss of the Korean language within their family. They viewed maintaining the language as an important part of their Korean identity. Olivia reflected on this with a mix of sadness and urgency:

> If I have enough capability to teach them, I would. But I don't. I need some kind of program. Because it's going to be lost. Like... It will be lost with my generation. It's so sad. But like me and my brother. If we don't pass anything on, it's gone.[333]

However, due to their limited ability to transmit the language themselves, all families sought external support, such as local Korean churches and private tutors, to help preserve their heritage language.

Challenges: Limited Linguistic Support in the Home Environment

Families faced significant challenges in supporting their children's Korean language learning due to limited linguistic support at home. Parents struggled to assist with Korean school homework, as their own proficiency was often insufficient. They acknowledged that their children's limited proficiency in Korean stemmed from a lack of consistent language exposure at home. Without regular use of Korean in the household, it was particularly difficult for third-generation Korean heritage learners to keep up with the materials

---

[333] Olivia, personal communication, April 15, 2020

taught at their community-based heritage language schools. These schools typically offered only a few hours of instruction per week, and many students came from homes with varying levels of Korean proficiency. This created substantial language gaps among students.

Parents expressed regret over their inability to help their children with Korean school homework because they never learned it, or they do not know enough Korean to help them. For example, Chris once asked me if I could assist Jenny with her Korean school homework, while Michelle shared feelings of helplessness when she was unable to help her daughter with learning. However, Michelle noted that this challenge also motivated her to study Korean and use the language more frequently at home.

Challenges: Struggles with Classroom Expectations and Language Proficiency

The linguistic challenges faced by the children also had a significant impact, with some losing interest and others experiencing embarrassment due to their language proficiency compared to their peers. For example, Chris shared that Jenny did not know any Korean until private tutoring, and after a few years of private tutoring, the family enrolled her in a Korean school to foster peer learning. However, Jenny lost interest in Korean school because her classmates, who were mostly second-generation Korean-Americans with parents speaking Korean at home, were far more advanced than she was. As a result, Jenny left the Korean school and continued with the private tutoring, which provided lessons tailored to her level.

Olivia explained that her son John experienced frustration and embarrassment when he failed to pass his class, and the school recommended that he repeat the year, despite spending considerable time on his homework/classwork. Although the teachers at his Korean school were understanding and supportive, they were limited in how much they could help given John's language proficiency compared to other students who spoke Korean at home. This led the family to withdraw both children from the school and switch to private tutoring.

In addition, Michelle shared that she had to switch Chloe's Korean school. At the age of 14, Chloe had no prior knowledge of Korean, so the school placed her in a class with first and second graders based on her proficiency level. This placement caused her to feel embarrassed being among much younger children. Additionally, Chloe was the only Black student at the school and felt isolated during lunch break because she did not have any friends. Despite these difficulties, Michelle strongly believed in the importance of Chloe learning Korean and ultimately found another school that had a more diverse student body, including biracial Korean students.

Although participants identified their children as Korean, they faced unique challenges in heritage language schools due to varying levels of their children's language proficiency. However, these challenges did not stop the families from pursuing Korean language education. They also expressed gratitude for having access to resources that allowed them to find programs better suited to their children's needs.

Parental Reflections: Regret and Lingering Resentment

During the interview, participants shared several reasons for their limited proficiency in Korean, such as prioritizing other activities during the school year or their parents' decision not to send them to Korean school when they were young. They expressed either regret for not studying harder or resentment towards their parents for not providing opportunities to learn the language. While a lack of Korean proficiency was not an issue for them earlier in life, participants now feel saddened by their inability to pass on this valuable aspect of their heritage to their children. All participants expressed a strong desire to improve their own Korean skills, both for personal reasons and as a way to support their children. While some participants were conversational in Korean, they hesitated to continue an entire conversation in Korean with me, while others only knew basic greetings. Also, at least one parent in each family was actively taking classes or receiving private tutoring to enhance their language skills.

Chris was the only participant who had the opportunity to learn Korean through his church when he was young, but he prioritized other commitments, such as academics and sports. Chris stated, "Either we didn't have time, or we were doing other things, like math or sports." As a result, learning the heritage language was often deprioritized. Chris shared that although his parents and his grandparents, who lived with them, spoke Korean at home and encouraged its use, they were not strict about him speaking Korean to them. Now, he regrets not being able to speak Korean fluently or professionally, nor being able to read and write in the language. To address this, Chris has taken private lessons and volunteered at a local Korean community center, creating opportunities to practice the language. He hopes to pass these learning opportunities on to his daughter and foster her connection to the Korean community.

Michelle and Olivia expressed resentment toward their parents for not teaching them Korean when they were young. Michelle, who was born in the U.S., lived in Korea for a year when she was four years old because her father was stationed in South Korea. At the time, Michelle spoke only Korean, so, upon returning to the U.S., her parents implemented an "English-only" policy at home to prepare her for school. Her mother stopped speaking Korean entirely, believing it would accelerate her English acquisition. Michelle now wishes her parents had maintained the use of Korean at home, allowing her to retain the language she had already learned. She acknowledges that bilingualism was not highly valued at the time, but feels sad about losing her Korean language skills. As an adult, Michelle is re-learning Korean through classes, private tutoring, and online resources. She not only aims to improve her skills but also hopes to set a positive example for her daughter by demonstrating her commitment to learning.

Olivia shared that she was never formally taught Korean, despite her parents frequently celebrating Korean culture, cooking Korean food, and speaking Korean at home; she responded to them in English. Olivia said that she was not sent to a Korean school, and her parents did not teach her formally. During the interview, she expressed regret and some resentment over her inability to speak Korean fluently. She reflected:

I think my whole life. It was a shame. Like, I know I was always ashamed that all my cousins, everyone, could speak Korean fluently, and my brother couldn't. And it's the last thing that I'm missing. I wish I had gone to Korean school and been forced to. Just because I think that would have helped so much. We did things that were Korean culture, but my parents never explained it. Like we just ate it. Yeah, we never knew why or what was the meaning like New Year's. My parents would make me put on the *Hanbok* (Korean traditional clothing) and bow down and all that. And I never knew why. I just knew that we had to do it.[334]

All three participants acknowledged that learning Korean was not a priority during their youth, either due to personal choices or parental decisions. However, they now deeply regret those choices and are making active efforts to improve their Korean language skills. They also expressed optimism about the growing acceptance and value of multilingual and multicultural diversity, particularly in light of the global popularity of Korean popular culture. Chris and Olivia shared that they could see that Korean culture has garnered significant international attention, inspiring them to improve their own language skills and feel pride in their heritage.

Conclusion and Implications

This study examined how three multiracial and/or multilingual families support their third-generation Korean-American children's heritage language learning as a means of fostering Korean identity and cultural connection. Unlike earlier generations who often learned Korean out of necessity to communicate with their immigrant parents,[335] these second-generation parents were primarily motivated by cultural identity, rather than by practical language needs. Regardless of the extent of Korean ancestry, all parents

---

[334] Olivia, personal communication, April 15, 2020
[335] Jeon, 2008; Kang, 2013

emphasized the importance of the Korean language as a vital link to their heritage and expressed pride in their children's progress.

Consistent with existing research on non-traditional Korean-American heritage language learners, such as biracial Korean-Americans and Korean adoptees,[336] participants noted that community-based language schools often do not meet the needs of children with limited exposure to Korean at home. Many children struggled to keep up due to low proficiency, leading to placement in lower-level classes with younger students, repeated coursework, or falling behind in class. These experiences frequently resulted in frustration, diminished interest, and, in some cases, withdrawal from the programs altogether.

This study highlights the need for Korean language educators in both community-based and higher education programs to better support the evolving needs of the next generation of Korean-American heritage language learners. Educators must be prepared to work with students from diverse linguistic and family backgrounds in a multicultural society, including those with minimal Korean language use at home. An inclusive and supportive learning environment and tailoring instructional approaches are critical to meet learners' unique needs.

At the same time, it is important to acknowledge the structural limitations of many Korean heritage schools. Prior research highlights challenges such as limited instructional materials, scarce professional development, and a shortage of trained language teachers.[337] Many of these schools are run by religious or community organizations, relying heavily on volunteers rather than professional educators. Therefore, broader community support is essential, such as involving Korean-speaking community members and creating additional language exposure opportunities beyond the classroom.

Shin emphasizes the value of home-based support and suggests leveraging popular culture like Korean music and television.[338] While

---

[336] Park, 2018; Shin, 2013, 2014
[337] Lee & Bang, 2011
[338] Shin, 2013

Chris and Olivia reported that their children enjoy Korean pop music, they felt it did little to support communicative competence. They also expressed difficulty in finding age-appropriate Korean-language TV shows for their children. However, they emphasized that increased exposure to the language and culture through media or educational mobile apps like Duolingo helped supplement their children's learning.

Although this study focuses on only three families and primarily on the perspective of parents, it offers valuable insights into the unique experiences of third-generation Korean-American heritage language learners. These cases illustrate the complex interplay of language, identity, and family dynamics across generations. As the number of third- and fourth-generation learners continues to grow, future research should expand to include larger, more diverse samples and incorporate learners' voices. This would help inform the development of effective programs, resources, and teacher training tailored to their needs.

Finally, ongoing investment in curriculum development, teacher training, and resource creation is essential to meet the evolving needs of heritage language learners in multiracial and multilingual contexts. As the Korean-American community becomes more diverse across generations, language programs must adapt to reflect this reality, ensuring that all learners, regardless of background or proficiency, can feel supported. By building on the commitment of earlier generations of educators, parents, and community leaders, this work can help sustain and enrich Korean heritage language education for future generations.

Chapter 8

Portuguese in the Heart: Identity, Belonging, and Heritage Language from Adolescents' Perspectives

Ana Lucia Lico

Adolescents and the Risk of Losing their Heritage Language and Culture

It is no news that the adolescent years are challenging. Regardless of families' and educators' cultural background or native country, most tend to agree that parenting and teaching adolescents can be quite hard. But that is not only for those around them. If we ask the teens, they would say that that period of life is tough for them too, even more so when they live in a different country than their parents' native one. Whether it is the host country's new set of cultural values and practices and linguistic systems or trying to keep up with the teaching and learning of the heritage language and culture (hereafter HLC), the entire process can be very demanding for everyone.

According to many authors in the field, families' efforts to ensure that children and adolescents maintain and develop their heritage language (as of now, HL) usually occur because this language represents an emotional and cultural connection expressed within the family and a small community that speaks the language. The role of the family is crucial in this process,[339] since it is grounded in the purpose of disseminating its linguistic and cultural roots. However, once children begin school immersion in the majority language, a tendency toward a decline in the use of the HL is observed, which may gradually intensify as they enter adolescence.

---

339 Lico, 2011; 2015; Lico; Pires, 2022

One of the typical issues of the teen years, identity affirmation, demonstrated by an increasing search for autonomy and a certain resistance to parental influence, takes on more complex contours in the lives of adolescents who live abroad.[340] As a result, these young individuals may drift away from their family's sociocultural roots. Furthermore, challenges related to age-specific issues—such as hormonal, physical, and psychosocial changes, and the limited number of suitable situations for adolescents to interact in their parents' language—can compromise their motivation to continue learning the HL.

I have worked with Brazilian Portuguese as a heritage language (hereafter, PHL) in the context of a community-based school since 2005, and given the risk of this gradual disconnection of the learners from their HLC, some questions intrigued me. I moved from Brazil to the U.S. to start a family with my American husband, and we were able to raise two multilingual sons, but that was not the case for many families. Over the years, these questions kept coming back. Is it possible to reverse that detachment or work to prevent it from occurring in the first place? Would it be reasonable to assume that if these young individuals continued learning PHL, for example, they could develop a sense of belonging or affinity with the Brazilian identity?

Although the teaching-learning of the language and culture of Brazil has been gaining increasing attention from native researchers of the country, there are still a small number of studies on PHL and even fewer that examine adolescent learners of PHL. Therefore, when the opportunity arose for an investigation project, part of a semester-long class I took in 2020, I chose to investigate what the adolescents do using PHL. That project, conducted in partnership with a colleague, revealed interesting data but also raised additional questions, one of which intrigued me deeply. What experiences had some of those young people gone through that led them to develop such a keen sense of connection with the Portuguese language and

---

[340] Wang, 2015

Brazilian culture, to the point of identifying (also) as Brazilians, even though they had never lived in Brazil?

This was the question that sparked my master's research. When I started my master's degree program in 2021, I knew I wanted to keep studying the connection Brazilian teenagers living abroad maintain – or not – with their HLC and how that would impact the way they see themselves close – or not – to the Brazilian identity. My research, using narrative methodology, focused on the perceptions of adolescents about their journeys as learners of PHL and their connection to Brazilian identity.

This study is rare in its depth of perspective from adolescent heritage language learners (HLL) – and even more so in its intimate exploration of acquisition within the family. Unlike much of the existing literature,[341] which often focuses on early childhood experiences or classroom settings, this chapter foregrounds the voices of adolescents as *active narrators of their own linguistic journeys*. It offers a unique lens into how HL learning is experienced, negotiated, and interpreted by those who navigate linguistic and cultural worlds during a formative life stage. Combining narrative inquiry with lived experience, the study explores how HL learning intersects with identity construction in adolescence.

Given the risk of a gradual disconnection of adolescents from their HLC, the topic of my research stemmed from the desire to understand the reasons why some of the children of Brazilian immigrant families have managed to maintain an increasing closeness to their HLC and to comprehend the choices made by their families that contributed to such a result. The main questions the research sought to answer were:

1. What are the perceptions of Portuguese heritage speakers regarding their language acquisition journey?

2. What relationship have they built with Brazilian identity through PHL?

---

[341] e.g., Duff 2008; Montrul 2016

The study aimed to elucidate relevant aspects of this trajectory, highlighting the role of the family and of the Brazilian community-based heritage language school. The participants demonstrated a strong sense of belonging to Brazilian identity and indicated that the factors that contributed the most to this are:

- The close contact with the language through interaction with their mother, in this case, this author.
- The meaningful social and emotional experiences lived in Portuguese from an early age, both in Brazil and in the U.S.
- The learning opportunities, social interactions, and friendships fostered by ABRACE, a community-based school that offers programs on PHL.
- The role of the non-Brazilian parent is of fundamental importance throughout the entire process.
- Portuguese is the language of the heart in the process of acquisition and use for young people, and in my journey of transmission and motherhood.
- Among the numerous factors influencing the construction of the learners' bond with the HL and their sense of belonging to their parents' country of origin, the mother's affection and the bonds she creates with the child in the HL are the base of this process.

In what follows, I outline the journey that led me to this research, describe the methodological approach of narrative inquiry, share the voices of the adolescent participants—my sons—and analyze how their emotional and linguistic experiences shaped their Brazilian identity. I hope these insights can be a source of inspiration for families and educators who work with heritage languages and cultures.

Heritage Language Acquisition: What are the Adolescents' Perceptions about Their Journey?

The transmission of the HLC to children is a process that starts within the family and depends on the family to advance. PHL is spoken by children of Brazilian parents[342] who grow up in countries where Portuguese is neither a majority nor an official language. Making it possible for children and adolescents to learn and develop PHL and establish a strong connection with their Brazilian identity requires significant effort. The role of the Brazilian parent in interactions with her children is crucial for them to develop emotional bonds with and through the PHL, and family involvement is essential in providing opportunities for language development and use.[343]

Many parents seek to create and/or find educational environments that enable their children to develop language beyond the household and to establish a strong emotional bond with their identity as Brazilian citizens. In many cases, the families find educational opportunities at community-based heritage language schools that offer programs to maintain and teach the language and culture of their parents' heritage. These programs also contribute to supporting the creation of affectionate ties between the HLLs and between them and a broader community, which, combined, foster the sense of belonging and identity development for the learners.

The primary objective of my research was to understand adolescents' perspectives on their PHL acquisition journey, particularly regarding their level of connection to Brazilian identity. Additionally, I aimed to investigate whether the process and the path of learning PHL influence the teenagers' understanding of Brazilian identity and to analyze their perceptions of the process of acquiring the language since childhood.

In order to capture rich, detailed accounts of firsthand experiences and to be able to have in-depth conversations, I invited my two sons to be the participants of my research. Initially, the intention was to invite multiple participants from Brazilian or mixed families.

---

[342] Brazil is one of nine countries where the official language is Portuguese, usually referred to as lusophone countries. Portuguese, as a pluricentric language, exhibits similarities and differences among the variants spoken in Brazil and other Portuguese-speaking countries. Despite all the differences, speakers of different lusophone countries are able to communicate, especially in a formal context.

[343] Lo Bianco & Peyton, 2013; Lico, 2015; Wang, 2015

However, through an intense reflection of the investigation's primary goal and my willingness to dig deeper, the idea of examining my own children emerged, and everything seemed to fall into place organically. I considered that the research findings could be enlightening for parents and teachers, as they could contribute to a better understanding of the adolescent profile in the transmission-acquisition of PHL.

I chose this context due to the desire to identify, analyze, and document the factors that influenced the relationship my children have with Brazilian identity, focusing mainly on the role of the Portuguese language acquisition journey within this relationship. On the one hand, having my own children as participants gave a special meaning to the research, as there was an opportunity for discoveries and new angles concerning their learning paths, as well as the chance to bring to light (about them and with them) striking and relevant aspects of their journeys as learners of HLC. However, on the other hand, researching people we are intimately related to and, in this case, having to consider the authority element in the mother-child relationship, was quite complex. In the next session, I will briefly present the theoretical framework and how I developed the investigation.

With Proper Input, Acquisition, and High-Level Proficiency, Adolescent HLL is Possible.

Given the risk of a gradual disconnection of adolescents from the language and culture of their parents, achieving success in the acquisition and maintenance of HLC takes a lot of work, dedication, and firm commitment from parents and their children.[344] Also, there must be consistency in the strategies adopted by the family and coherence in demonstrating the value of languages. Appreciation of the HLC is essential for the HLL to identify with the language and become fluent in it.[345]

---

[344] Wang, 2015
[345] Silva, 2016

One study, done in 2012,[346] presented that, for young children, although they learn the HL and the majority language simultaneously, in early childhood, he/she has greater competence in HL. However, as the child enters the school system, the skills in L2 (in this case, English) gradually increase, while the skills in HL (L1) decrease. According to this 2012 study, the absence of adequate academic support over the years impairs the development of HL and its use in adolescence and adulthood, as shown in Figure 1 below.

Figure 1: Typical development of an HL, without academic support, in a majority language context

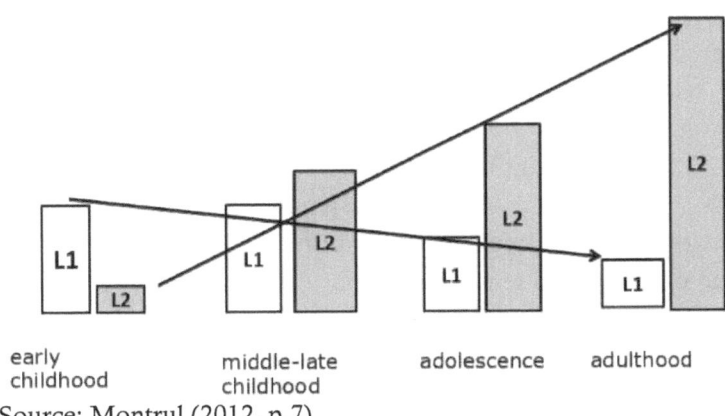

Source: Montrul (2012, p.7)

However, some authors oppose this notion of indiscriminate incomplete acquisition of HL, showing that the acquisition of HL may be delayed, compared to that of native speakers of the language. Nonetheless, with the proper input, the acquisition may not only occur, but their learners may reach a high level of proficiency. A study from 2015[347] found no evidence that HLLs would have

---

[346] Montrul, 2012
[347] Flores, 2015

deficient capacity or competence in HL; they only have a specific linguistic knowledge, resulting from the amount and type of input they received. If, over the years, HLLs remain exposed to the HL in situations that are relevant linguistic experiences, they will be able to consolidate and expand their repertoire continuously.

In addition to the language-rich environment at home, the programs offered by community-based HL schools usually present real-life opportunities for learning, interaction, and usage of the HL. These schools, which are typically non-profit organizations founded and operated by parents from the respective immigrant or HL community,[348] might offer programs for learners aged 2 to 17 years old, with classes that, in most cases, take place on weekends or after school. These schools or the events they organize are also fertile grounds for the formation of emotional bonds among the learners. Through these bonds, HLL develops a sense of belonging to this community, endorsing the dual function of these associations of being, simultaneously, a place of teaching-learning and bond-building.[349]

With regards to the Brazilian context, according to a survey done in 2021,[350] community-based schools that offer programs for teaching the language and culture of Brazil contribute to forging relationships among children and teens and foster a stronger connection with the Brazilian community and identity. These Brazilian schools offer a wide range of regular activities, as illustrated in Figure 2 below. The same association may provide more than one or all of these activities, to enable the development of different skills through varied resources. Still, they need parents' support for the programs in a variety of ways. The stronger the partnership between the parent, community, and school, the better the students' engagement and learning outcomes.

---

[348] heritagelanguageschools.org/coalition
[349] Aberdeen, 2016; Lico, 2015
[350] Lico & Silva, 2021

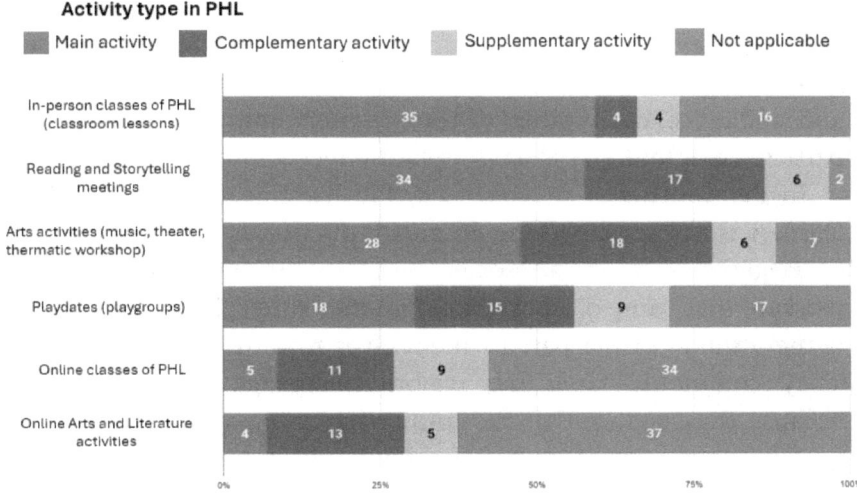

Source: translated from Lico & Silva (2021, p. 46)

The community-based HL schools' programs contribute to expanding and consolidating the linguistic and cultural repertoire of these students, but also to strengthening their process of identity development. There is a remarkably close relationship between language acquisition and the construction of identity. This connection can be further enhanced in group learning situations. Therefore, learning an HL at an HL school influences how young children perceive their own identity.[351]

The concept of identity is especially complex, since it is something continuously formed and reformed, characterizing a fluid and dynamic process.[352] As we think about these concepts in relation to the identity of an HLL, the notion that there are multiple identities, which are contextually negotiated, contested, shaped, and reshaped, becomes central in the learning of an HLL.[353] Identities are shaped by experiences of living in the host country and by narratives of belonging that young people construct about themselves in their

---

[351] Aberdeen, 2016; Seo, 2022
[352] Hall, 2006
[353] Seals, 2017

pursuit of acceptance or approval in certain social groups.[354] Considering the migratory circumstances, children and adolescents will develop multilingual skills in which identities and languages mix and influence each other. These learners must be prepared to participate in multiple social scripts and feel comfortable in them.[355]

In the context of my research, the learning of PHL for these learners is susceptible to the dominant discourses that favor the use of English in American society, and to the hegemonic internal pressure that some diasporic communities suffer. In addition, there is the attitude of the parents themselves towards such a situation. They commonly favor the majority language over Portuguese because they believe that the former has more value and is more useful than the latter, or that learning the latter would hinder the development of the former. According to Zhou and Liu:

> This pressure prevalent in immigrant minority groups is always reproduced within HL schools, internalised by children and their parents, and as a result, leads to forced positioning of HL learners as 'linguistically deficient and culturally inauthentic.' In a study of US-born Latinos, for example, Tseng shows how this imposed deficit positioning stigmatises HL learners, damages their identities and self-esteem, and contributes to HL insecurity and avoidance.[356]

Parents and educators should avoid adopting (or requiring) a model of speech and interaction based on an idealized native speaker, so as not to set unrealistic expectations for HLL in the context in which they live. Such situations can lead HLL to feel ashamed of their repertoire and afraid of not being considered legitimate members of that identity group. Therefore, these HLL may feel excluded from the group and, instead of looking for opportunities to improve their competence in HL, refuse to use the language.[357]

---

[354] Wang, 2015
[355] Boruchowski & Lico, 2015
[356] Zhou & Liu, 2022, p. 385
[357] Zhou & Liu, 2022

HL Learning: Cognitive and Emotional Dimensions

The parents' positive attitude towards their native language has a significant impact on the process of HL transmission and acquisition, as well as on the HLL's encouragement to continue learning the language.[358] This process is deeply influenced by affection (the mother's desires and motivations), just as the HLL choice to continue learning is shaped by emotions related to the language (connection with the mother, bonds with family members in the parents' country, among others).

In the context of emotional bonds, affection plays a crucial role in shaping connections between individuals, influencing how they interact, communicate, and develop a sense of belonging. The HL learning process may be guided by emotional investments in new identities and by language-related feelings,[359] which have a direct impact on their acquisition path, and can change it positively or negatively. It is necessary to observe the attitudes of the HLL towards their HL and towards other people, to identify if there are specific emotions connected to the language, and if they feel comfortable using it in this or that environment.[360] In HL acquisition, affectionate bonds can foster motivation, reinforce identity, and create meaningful connections between the learner and their linguistic and cultural heritage.

Narrative Methodology: Shared Stories that Bring Personal Histories to Life

Research that employs narratives as a means of data collection and/or analysis is a qualitative approach that is identified by narrative research or methodology.[361] This perspective of telling (with) stories to present or elucidate a phenomenon or situation offers numerous pathways that make it possible for one to understand, interpret, or explain a wide range of data and experiences.

---

[358] Ivanova, 2019
[359] Pavlenko, 2012
[360] Femia, 2021
[361] Barkhuizen, Benson & Chick, 2014

Narrative research enables a deeper understanding of the "inner worlds" of language learners and the nature of learning as a social and educational activity.[362] With this methodology, narrative research studies life moments as a story, as a way of reflecting on the experience, and the researcher's role is not merely that of an observer. At times, they act as researcher-observer; at others, as a researcher-participant, moving between levels of proximity with the research text.[363] This type of investigation *gives voice to the participant* and must be employed in a way that ensures the highest possible level of authenticity. When using this approach, the goal is not to expect a description of facts but rather to understand how the participants represent certain situations and interpret their experiences.

With this methodology, the research can be narrative or with narratives. When the study is narrative, storytelling is a way of analyzing data and presenting results, whereas in studies with narratives, the stories told by the participants are used as data. For my investigation, I employed both approaches: *narrative research* and *research with narratives*, which included my own autobiography and my children's language learning stories.

The use of narrative methodology is not merely a tool for data collection; it is deliberate to honor the complexity of lived experience, capturing the tensions, ambivalences, and moments of linguistic agency that more structured approaches might overlook. In this way, this chapter advocates an understanding of HL development as a deeply personal and relational process.

When working with this methodology, it is important to consider the risk that a narrative may present fabricated or projected content, depending on the context or conditions in which the research is conducted. This concern was highly relevant to my study, given the significant risk that participants might feel intimidated or inhibited by providing responses or accounts that could displease or disappoint their mother, the researcher. Considering the subtleties inherent in this situation, every possible precaution was taken to create a relaxed

---

[362] Barkhuizen, Benson & Chick, 2014
[363] Barcelos, 2020

atmosphere for interactions, allowing them to feel comfortable responding with spontaneity and sincerity.

Studying My Own Children: A Challenging and Rewarding Experience

For my master's degree, as I briefly mentioned, the research was narrative and based on narratives, and involved two young individuals, aged 19 and 16, born and residing in the U.S., who are my sons, Gabriel and Lucas. The data collection instruments included an individual narrative interview with the adolescents and a group conversation in which the three of us took part. I aimed to create a comfortable environment and allow them to feel at ease in choosing what and how to respond. The questions for the interviews and group conversation were open, making it possible for the participants to choose what to narrate, from their memories of experiences and situations lived throughout their journeys as Portuguese HLL.

The experience of researching my own children proved to be a lot more challenging than I had anticipated, not as much for the precautions or lengthy ethical procedures, but still, because of the profound emotional impact it had on me. The boys' narratives brought back many memories and emotions, and left me longing for moments of our lives that played like a movie in my mind.

According to the concept of relational ethics,[364] openness to discussing the investigation topics and emotional intimacy are essential elements for both the research and the family relationship. In terms of privacy, I took all the necessary measures related to consent, and even though I offered options to protect their identities, they chose to be identified by their names.

Given the risk that participants might feel intimidated or hesitant to provide answers or share experiences that could be displeasing to me (as their mother), I sought to present myself in the least hierarchical way possible, allowing them to feel comfortable responding (or not) with spontaneity. During the data analysis, I tried

---

[364] Ellis, 2007

The Construction of HLL's Identities: Meaningful Affective, Linguistic, and Cultural Experiences

My native language is the language of my heart. I only know how to be a mother in Portuguese.

Regarding the perceptions of the adolescents participating in this study, their responses in general showed a surprisingly deep self-analysis of their own beliefs and HLC learning paths. Gabriel, the oldest, is an extrovert and opted for a detailed narrative, full of memories and reflections. Lucas, more of an introvert, gave more succinct responses, which did not prevent him from sharing his perceptions – and perfectionism – with regard to his communicative performance in Portuguese.

Home Language Practices

They expressed a keen sense of *belonging to Brazilian identity*, attributing this primarily to their *close contact with the Portuguese language through interactions with me, their mother.* Gabriel and Lucas shared many recollections of exchanges in Portuguese since they were little and repeatedly stated that the communication in the language with me was seen as normal and comfortable. They described their journey of acquiring PHL as a natural process, as well as the use of Portuguese in the most diverse circumstances, whether in Brazil or the United States. For them, this sense of naturalness stemmed largely from the consistent use of Portuguese in our communication.

When asked about how he felt about the Portuguese language, Lucas responded, "I feel very connected to the language and culture of Brazil because of speaking with my mother every day in Portuguese, because of my background with ABRACE.[365] And I also have some friends who speak Portuguese as well. So, this

---

[365] A community-based PHL school in the Washington, DC area; find more at abracebrasil.org

Brazilian side of me has always been very important to me." Lucas indicates that the connection he feels with the Portuguese language and Brazilian culture is closely tied to the perception that Brazilian identity is part of him. Through language, an individual identifies as part of a society, and by engaging with their culture, they are in a constant process of identity construction.[366]

Whether at home, during routine activities such as family meals, giving instructions, or assisting with schoolwork, or outside the house, at American school events, medical appointments, or shopping at the supermarket, our interactions have always been conducted in Portuguese. Establishing and following this system was never difficult or a sacrifice for me; on the contrary, it would have required a significant effort or suffering to have communicated with them in a language other than my native language. In the same natural way, they have always communicated with me only in Portuguese, even if at times they asked me for help or sought words in their PHL repertoire to translate what they wanted to say. For HLL, the more natural and enjoyable they perceive the role of the family's language, the more natural and satisfying they can reproduce this use. When the family exposes the child from an early age to an environment rich in Brazilian cultural elements and to various situations in which the use of Portuguese is authentic, routine communication in the language is perceived as normal/natural by the child.

Travel to Brazil and Cultural Immersion

Another factor highlighted by the participants as having significantly impacted their improvement in PHL and their connection to Brazilian identity was the *meaningful social and affective experiences they had during vacations in Brazil*. Gabriel and Lucas' highlights of their memories of the periods in Brazil were the fun activities with children and teenagers of the same age, such as summer schools, soccer, or card games with friends or cousins, and biking in the park with the family. In one of Lucas' accounts, he said: "I have many memories from that time, and

---

[366] Hall, 2006

they are very important to me." This everyday exposure normalized Portuguese as a key part of Lucas's self-perception. Gabriel, at some point during the group conversation, referring to how he felt on the occasion when he could not go to Brazil with his family, said: "I always felt a deep longing because these things are also part of my childhood." This illustrates how physical absence can intensify emotional presence in identity formation.

These experiences demonstrate their *perception of having spent part of their childhood in Brazil*. Now that they are older, their leisure activities are no longer centered around children's games or playtime. While we keep some traditions, such as bike rides in the park and soccer games at the court of our apartment building in São Paulo, Gabriel and Lucas now prefer social and cultural programs, with music remaining a central element. Furthermore, their interactions with their uncles and grandmother in Brazil continue to be synonymous with affection and special treats.

Parental Roles and Mixed Families

Providing them with such a wealth of experience was only possible thanks to the unconditional support—both practical and emotional—of Tim, my husband, and their father. Despite being of American origin and not speaking or understanding Portuguese when we married, he fully supported the family language policy we established from the beginning. This policy ensured that each of us communicated with our children in our native language, regardless of the setting or the people present. This study also demonstrates that, in mixed families, the role of the *non-Brazilian parent is crucial* in helping children recognize the value of each language and culture, thereby fostering the development of multilingual and multicultural identities.[367]

In the process of HL transmission and acquisition, *family engagement* is essential. A HL is born at home, rooted in the desire of a father and/or mother to transmit their native language and culture to their children. It may start with conversations, storytelling,

---

[367] Moroni, 2017

cuddling time, and games when they are still babies. For the HL to continue developing, it is necessary to expose children and adolescents to *real opportunities* for contact, learning, and interaction in the language,[368] including in environments where it is a native language. I found that the *relevant experiences* that Gabriel and Lucas had when attending summer programs in schools or sports gyms in Brazil played a significant role in their bilingual development, expanding their PHL proficiency, fostering *affective bonds*, and creating *lasting memories* with people and places in Brazil.

Affection and Community

Gabriel and Lucas highlight another factor as highly relevant in their Portuguese acquisition journey: the *learning opportunities, social interactions, and friendships* fostered by ABRACE. In line with the perspectives of some authors,[369] community associations like ABRACE play a role that goes far beyond offering classes and organizing cultural events—they provide a sense of belonging and a welcoming space for both adults and children within the community. Both participants highlighted the experiences they had and the friendships they made at ABRACE as significant in their perception of connection to their Brazilian roots. When asked to reflect on his memories of attending ABRACE in his youth, Gabriel responded: "I always thought it was cool because it was a community outside of school. It was nice to have those friends and that identity, which was different from my everyday school identity."An excerpt from Lucas' response to that question: "I attended ABRACE every Saturday, and that helped me connect a lot with Brazilian culture. I made many friends who also spoke Portuguese." Many authors suggest that *friendships* play a key role in language acquisition and cultural connection processes. Combined with socialization opportunities, these bonds help children and teenagers develop pride in their roots.[370]

---

[368] Lo Bianco & Peyton, 2013; Wang, 2015
[369] Aberdeen, 2016; Lico, 2015; Lico & Silva, 2021
[370] Aberdeen, 2013; Moroni, 2017

As they both attended the Brazilian school since they were little and for many years, they met and hung out weekly with other children who, over time, became great friends with each of them. These *affectionate ties* built through PHL at ABRACE also contributed to maintaining their interest in continuing their PHL acquisition journey even when they reached adolescence. As they remained exposed to relevant linguistic experiences in PHL, they continued to develop the language.[371] In one of his accounts, Gabriel seems to make a direct association between socialization and proficiency in PHL, and self-perception of his identity/identities. In community associations that work with HL, students also learn sociocultural rules and values that help them develop a sense of belonging to their community and a connection with their identity—Brazilian identity, in this case.[372]

Connection and Communication in the HL

When asked what the key factor for him was to also identify as Brazilian, Lucas answered: "I think it's a *mix of many things*. Besides having more Brazilian *friends* now than ever before, with whom I speak Portuguese, I have Brazilian *music* that I listen to... I interact more and more with my *mom*... And I message my *cousins*, who are in Brazil. But it is a combination of all these things that have helped me identify as Brazilian more and more over the years." This suggests that Lucas's connection to Brazilian identity is rooted in his growing identification with his HLC, the proficiency he has developed in Portuguese, and the emotional bonds built through his experience with PHL.

The short study a colleague and I did in 2020 (published in 2022[373]), as I mentioned earlier in this chapter, had 21 speakers of PHL, ages 13 to 17, who first responded to a questionnaire. Then, among those who manifested interest, I selected five to be interviewed individually. Even though I will not discuss the data of

---

[371] Flores, 2015
[372] Lico, 2011; Aberdeen, 2013; Seo, 2022
[373] Lico & Pires, 2022

the 2020 study in this chapter, I would like to share a couple of insights on the adolescents' choices for communication in PHL. For instance, from the questionnaire, we obtained a few surprising answers, among them, the frequency with which they said they watch videos or write in Portuguese, as shown in Figure 3 below.

Figure 3: What/how much they do in the HL, per activity

Activity	Responses (always, almost always)	What
Speaking	62%	Mostly with family and relatives
Listening	38%	Music (both traditional and popular genres)
Watching	43%	YouTube, movies, news, comedies, series
Reading	24%	Genres (Fiction, comic books, social media) + Authors (established and new ones)
Writing	33%	Text msg, social media, email, notes

Source: compiled by the author for a presentation in 2020

The high percentages in Watching and Writing were quite surprising, but also demonstrated that there are great opportunities for parents and educators to dedicate more time to offering materials and possibilities for HLL to keep developing those skills. Given easier access to many technological resources these days, with some guidance, teenagers can improve their writing significantly with social media and texts. The more confident learners feel about their communicative abilities in the HL and the closer they are to the cultural elements of the speech community of that language, the greater the chances that they will *identify with and feel a sense of belonging* to that community.[374] According to their narratives, they identify with and as Brazilians and feel that Brazilian identity is part of who they are, as if affirming '*I am part of this identity, and this identity is part of me.*'

Even though many families cannot travel regularly to Brazil, as mine did, I argue that children can build a connection and a sense of belonging to their parents' linguistic and cultural roots. I advocate that factors such as the attitude of the Brazilian parent towards HL and the quality of their interaction with children in that language play a key role in fostering a strong connection to their cultural heritage.[375] When HL serves as the primary means of communication with children from an early age, it can become the foundation of the affectionate relationship between parents and children, establishing itself as the *language of the heart* and the family. Furthermore, as demonstrated by my study, it is crucial to provide opportunities for children to interact and build friendships with children of families who speak the same language, as well as structured pathways to learn their HLC.

Language and Sibling Connection

I want to highlight the strengthening of the bonds between Gabriel and Lucas with me, experienced through Portuguese as HL. This close bond through the HL also contributes to the HLL feeling encouraged to continue learning and connecting with their parents' cultural roots. The ability of adolescents from immigrant families to communicate in their HL may also have important consequences for their identification with their heritage cultures.[376]

I also observed that, over time, moments of *companionship between Gabriel and Lucas*, shared in PHL, became more frequent, and the

---

[374] Aberdeen, 2013; Zhou & Liu, 2022
[375] Lico, 2011; 2015; Ivanova, 2019
[376] Oh & Fuligni, 2010

types of interactions using the language gradually evolved. During the group conversation, when I asked about their frequent joking around and teasing each other in Portuguese, part of Gabriel's explanation was: "Our life now is basically what we are consuming (Brazilian pop culture), so that translates into how we interact with each other. So that is why almost all the jokes we make are in Portuguese with each other. We only do this in Portuguese, like, in English, we don't necessarily joke around in the same way." For teenage HLL, the ability to understand and make jokes in that language is a significant achievement in terms of vocabulary and communicative competence.[377] Gabriel's statement—"we only do this in Portuguese"—which stems from his close bond with his brother, is yet another example of the social-emotional value behind unique and meaningful experiences that HLL can only fully experience in their HL. I observed that this process of deepening their emotional bond through the HL contributed to them having - and continuing to have - certain experiences that are only possible in this language.[378]

Similarly, moments of closeness and affinity between them and me have been evolving; after all, I can no longer carry them in my arms or completely envelop them in my hugs. However, our relationship remains marked by deep affection and togetherness, which I can only genuinely express in Portuguese. Thus, I can say that, in the profound connection I have with my children, *my love is monolingual*. These moments of emotional nurturing through PHL were essential in fostering and maintaining the connection that Gabriel and Lucas have with each other and with their HLC.

Belonging and Identity

Before I conclude this section, I want to share one narrative of each participant that sheds light on relevant aspects of the HLC learning, which can serve as insights for observation and inspiration for parents and educators.

---

[377] Wang, 2015
[378] Pavlenko, 2012; Moroni, 2017

Lucas had a meaningful experience attending a seven-day summer camp in the countryside of São Paulo, Brazil, when he was 16 years old. Part of his account on this experience was: "It was a super, super good opportunity to, like, meet more people my age who live in Brazil, with, um, with real Brazilian Portuguese, like, from people who have only ever lived there. So, it was really great because I was able to practice my vocabulary, my speaking in general, and all that. Yeah, it was really great."

He makes an indirect comparison between his communication in Portuguese, as someone living abroad, and that of his peers, which he perceives as the "original" version. In more than one of his narratives, Lucas demonstrated a level of insecurity towards his performance in Portuguese, sharing that often he felt his proficiency (or lack of) was being analyzed and/or assessed. When asked what he thought was the reason for that, he answered: "Since my mom is Brazilian, people expected me to speak Portuguese well, right? So, I think that... I don't know if other people thought I felt this way, but I felt there was pressure not to make mistakes." To expect from HLL a spotless performance or compare it to the idealized native speaker from the parents' country of origin is unfair, can cause insecurity, and be demotivating for them to continue learning. The HL learning or acquisition process must create conditions that allow HLL to question labels or classifications so they can develop "linguistic confidence and claim their identities as legitimate speakers of the HL."[379]

Gabriel had the opportunity to work as a volunteer in the Brazilian presidential elections of 2022 held abroad. When asked to share his impressions about this experience, he described it as exciting, as it is evident in this excerpt: "When the opportunity came to be a poll worker, I thought it would be cool, so I went for it. And it was an amazing experience! It was truly unique. I didn't expect to like it so much. And it was also emotional to know that you are making a difference in your country. And as someone who was born and raised

---

[379] Zhou & Liu, 2022, p. 396

abroad, being able to do this helps me feel even more Brazilian." That election day was a Sunday, and the labor was very intense and exhausting, but Gabriel did not have a single word of complaint, during the day or after. He even wrote an almost poetic note about the experience that same evening. In the narrative above, he refers to Brazil more than once as "his country," indicating a sense of belonging to Brazilian identity and the active role it plays in his life.

Language use experiences that HLLs undergo in real and meaningful situations, like the one Gabriel had, can simultaneously be both a manifestation and a reinforcement of the bond with the HLC. A strong sense of belonging to one's family origins can result from a continuous and consistent process of experiences in HL. It can contribute to the heritage speaker establishing a *deep connection with the elements that shape their "inherited" identity.*[380]

Consistent with studies of the affective dimension of language learning,[381] when Gabriel and Lucas recalled memories related to language and friendships, many times affectionately sharing them, I was able to see how deeply emotional memory is involved in language learning. I identified that, in a reverse mechanism, I also experienced emotional memory during some of their narratives, when certain words brought back recollections and meanings linked to joy and affection. As I have already stated in this chapter, *I only know how to be a mother in Portuguese*, and experiencing motherhood, for both them and me, involves *both affective and cognitive dimensions*. Through my narrative and those of Gabriel and Lucas, it is evident how Portuguese is the *language of the heart* in their journey of acquisition and use, as well as in *my journey of teaching and being a mother*.

Upon concluding this research, I realized that I could not have chosen another methodology that would give voice to the three participants with such freedom and authenticity. Through my children's accounts, I was able to revisit (with them) their experiences and discover new lenses into the life stories of each of

---

[380] Zhou & Liu, 2022
[381] Pavlenko, 2012

us, as well as uncover untold narratives about myself. With this study, I managed to share, transparently and genuinely, elements of my personal experience and that of my family.

Summarizing...

The investigation for my master's degree has changed me as a researcher and as a mother, providing me with a journey with plenty of reflections, emotions, and learning. While listening to the stories my sons shared as remarkable memories since their childhood, I reviewed countless choices we made as a family, linguistic and logistic strategies we put into place to provide a multilingual environment at home – and wherever we were.

The research was developed from an innovative perspective, as, to my surprise, I did not find many studies that directly presented the learner's perspective on their HL acquisition journey. Among the numerous factors influencing the bonds learners form with their HL and their sense of belonging to their parents' country of origin, the mother's warm cuddle and the bond she creates with the child in the HL are the foundation of the process.

Studies of programs that teach HLs show that adolescents' connection with their parents' language and culture tends to weaken as they grow up. Thinking about ways to avoid or reverse that situation, my research aimed to understand the adolescents' perspective on their journey of learning the HL, specifically Portuguese, in relation to the level of connection they have with their inherited (Brazilian) identity. HLLs *build their identity* in a process full of complexities, deeply marked by social, cognitive, linguistic, and affective aspects. The concept of identity for these learners is fluid and dynamic, and results from the experiences they had in the host country and the country of their parents, long before they reach the age of adolescence.

The acquisition of HL by teenagers is influenced by affectivity and is intrinsically linked to the opportunities created by families for them to use the language. Although there is a high rate of adolescents who, over the years, move further away from their origins, others keep close ties to their HLC.

By positioning adolescent narratives at the heart of the study, this chapter contributes a vital and often-overlooked dimension to HL acquisition – one that insists on the value of emotional truth, relational dynamics, and the messiness (with its beauty) of language learning in real life.

I aspire for this chapter to contribute new insights to elucidate some critical issues related to the process of HL acquisition by adolescents and the connection they establish with their cultural roots. Hopefully, the findings from my research can inspire parents and educators to value their language and culture of origin as a precious linguistic-affective heritage and to encourage children and students to continue (or resume) their journey of HL acquisition. I also wish my study could shed light on the relevant role of community-based schools in the teaching-learning process of HLC, where the best outcomes are a result of a close partnership between parents, educators, and the community.

Chapter 9

"Harmonizing Hyphens": Navigating Multiracial Identities in Mandarin-English Bilingual Classrooms

Jasmine Pham

"I have this one core memory from when I was in grade two. I was at my Chinese dance dinner, where all the kids and teachers gathered after our performance. I remember we were eating at the round table, and we had our chopsticks, but I couldn't use them, so I had to ask someone to get me a fork. And then the next day at school, the kids were making fun of me like, 'You can't use chopsticks?' So, I remember grabbing two pencils and just practicing all day. I would use them to grab things over and over again. That was basically how I taught myself to use chopsticks." (Tien Minh, Interview)

Multiracial Students in Canada

As Canada becomes increasingly diverse, the number of students who identify as multiracial continues to grow.[382] Research indicates that multiracial students frequently encounter issues of belonging and identity, feeling like they must conform to multiple cultural expectations simultaneously.[383] Some students choose to present as white because of the privileges that being white-passing provides.[384] Meanwhile, others form stronger attachments to their minority heritage, with those able to speak their heritage language feeling the most connected to monoracial groups of their non-white identity.[385]

---

[382] Hou et al., 20203
[383] Chang, 2016; Harris, 2014
[384] Ginsberg, 2017; Hsu, 2019; Park & Chung, 2023
[385] Johnston-Guerrero & Pecero, 2016; Park & Choi, 2022

Many multiracial students also find themselves never belonging to either group, flipping between their racial identities depending on their surroundings.[386] While fluid, this duality can lead to isolation from their multiple racial identities,[387] particularly in school environments where racial diversity is not adequately acknowledged.[388] Additionally, multiracial students may face monoracism, where they face racism from both sides of their heritage identities.[389] This, in turn, exacerbates their sense of otherness and negatively impacts their mental health.[390]

In Canadian schools, the integration of multicultural education and anti-racist policies is crucial in addressing the needs of multiracial students.[391] Programs that promote cultural awareness and inclusivity can help these students feel more accepted.[392] For instance, the integration of heritage language programs, such as Mandarin bilingual classrooms, can significantly impact the identity development of multiracial students. Findings from numerous studies indicate that these programs help students navigate their mixed racial identities; engaging with their heritage language and culture can enhance their sense of belonging and identity.[393] Despite the benefits of heritage language programs, multiracial students still face challenges in both educational and social contexts. Multiracial students report experiencing racial microaggressions[394] and a lack of representation in their school curriculum, highlighting the need for ongoing advocacy and reform.[395]

---

[386] Lane, 2013; O'Brien, 2019; Wallace, 2004
[387] Patte et al., 2021
[388] Dutro et al., 2005; Museus et al., 2016
[389] Song et al., 2022; Song & Liebler, 2022
[390] Fisher et al., 2014; Harris, 2014
[391] Taylor, 2008
[392] Taylor, 2008
[393] Lane, 2013; Park & Choi, 2022
[394] Nadal et al., 2013
[395] Baxley, 2008; Boyle, 2022; King, 2008

Alberta's Mandarin Bilingual Program

Alberta's Mandarin bilingual programs were initiated in the 1970s to promote multiculturalism and multilingualism across Canada.[396] The program is currently offered in both Calgary and Edmonton and teaches students from kindergarten through grade 12 the Alberta curriculum in both Mandarin and English.[397] The program emphasizes balanced instruction, with a 50% split between Mandarin and English in elementary, 25% Mandarin instruction in junior high, and 20% in high school.[398] Chinese and Taiwanese teachers teach the Mandarin courses, while any Alberta-certified public-school teacher teaches the English courses. The program aims to enhance students' language skills, cultural understanding, and academic achievement, preparing them for a multilingual and multicultural world.[399]

While the program predominantly serves students of Han Chinese descent, there has been a growing number of multiracial students of various Southeast and East Asian backgrounds enrolled in the program as well.[400] While the program's initial aim was to foster bilingual proficiency and cultural understanding for Chinese Canadian students, the growth of their diverse student body means the program must also evolve to meet the needs of underrepresented students. This has created a unique social environment that influences multiracial student experiences and shapes their cultural identity.

Purpose and Research Questions

Part of a larger qualitative study which investigated how racial stereotypes and anti-Asian racism are mitigated in Alberta's Mandarin bilingual programs, the following chapter speaks to the experiences of the study's three half white and half Asian participants. This chapter explores the experiences of multiracial

---

[396] ECBEA, 2024
[397] ECBEA, 2024
[398] Alberta Education, 2009; ECBEA, 2024
[399] Alberta Education, 2009; ECBEA, 2024
[400] Confucius Institute in Edmonton, 2014

students in Alberta's Mandarin bilingual schools, focusing on how they navigate their racial identities and the impact of school culture on their sense of belonging. By examining these experiences, we can better understand the unique opportunities and challenges faced by multiracial students and identify strategies to support their well-being. My research questions were as follows:

1. What experiences do multiracial students have with their linguistic and cultural development within Mandarin-English bilingual programs?

2. How do multi-racial students perceive the program's impact on their identity and sense of belonging?

Methods

Researcher Positionality

As with all research, knowing my positionality as a researcher is essential, as my background and lived experiences will impact how I analyze the data. I am a Queer, Asian Canadian woman who was born and raised in Edmonton, Alberta. Due to my own experience as a graduate of Alberta's Mandarin bilingual programs, as well as my experiences as both a racial and sexual minority, I was able to develop a strong rapport with my participants. We often shared stories of how our experiences were similar or different. As such, I recognize my own background and lived experiences may influence my interpretation of the data. Thus, reflexivity and an awareness of my role in this study, both as a researcher and a former bilingual student, were addressed every step of the way.

Data Collection and Analysis

I conducted 17 one-on-one semi-structured interviews on Zoom with Asian Canadians who graduated from high school between 2020 and 2023. Participants completed at least three years of Alberta's Mandarin bilingual programs. Participants were recruited using the snowball sampling method[401] through individual emails and posters shared on Twitter, Instagram, and Facebook. These semi-structured interviews allowed the conversation to flow naturally and offered each participant the opportunity to share their experiences and stories without the rigidity of structured questions.[402] The interviews were then transcribed using Zoom and underwent two rounds of coding on NVivo. I then conducted a separate thematic analysis for the three multiracial students.[403] Below is their demographic information.

Table 1. Participant Demographics

Pseudonym	Age	Background	Languages Spoken at Home	Grades in Program
Tien Minh	20	Chinese, Vietnamese, White	English	K-12
Gary Nguyen	20	Ukrainian, Chinese, Vietnamese	English	K-12
Katherine Wu	19	Vietnamese, Chinese, Ukrainian, Irish	English	K-12

Participant Profiles

At the time of our interview, **Gary Nguyen** was a 20-year-old electrical engineering student. He considered himself a 2.5-generation Canadian with half Ukrainian and half Chinese Vietnamese heritage. Gary's father was born in Vietnam with Chinese ancestry from his paternal side, while Gary's mother was born in Canada. At home, Gary speaks English with his parents and often struggles with Mandarin. Yet, Gary was valedictorian of his

---

[401] Woodley & Lockard, 2016
[402] Marvasti & Tanner, 2020
[403] O'Reilly & Dogra, 2017

high school graduating class. To him, the bilingual program was a rewarding journey both socially and academically.

Katherine Wu was a 19-year-old biology student. She considered herself a 2.5-generation mixed-heritage Asian Canadian. Her father was born in Vietnam and of Chinese Vietnamese heritage, while her mother was Canadian-born and of Ukrainian and Irish descent. At home, Katherine primarily speaks English, which she considers her first language. Although Katherine has limited Mandarin-speaking abilities, she has been involved in Chinese dance since elementary school. Katherine often spoke of how she appreciates the unique perspective of being Wasian (white and Asian) in her cultural upbringing.

Tien Minh was a 20-year-old student who had moved to British Columbia to study Kinesiology at the time of our interview. Originally from Alberta, Tien considered herself a 2.5-generation mixed Asian Canadian. She was raised by her single mother, who encouraged Tien to enroll in the bilingual program. The bilingual program left a lasting impact on Tien. Although challenging, it provided Tien with a solid foundation in the Chinese language and culture. Despite struggling at times due to being half white, Tien appreciated the program's influence and now embraces her unique "Wasian" identity.

Findings

Findings associated with the students of mixed heritage suggest that the integration of Chinese language and culture in Mandarin bilingual classrooms can help students navigate their mixed racial identities and foster a deeper connection to their Asian roots. In fact, the ability to speak their heritage language has also helped multiracial students feel more confident in identifying with their "Asian side." While some participants expressed feeling like outsiders both in the Asian and Canadian communities during their teenage years, they have also developed a great pride in being both Asian and Canadian as young adults. Although their mixed ethnicity was a source of contention and struggle during their K-12 schooling days, these same students grew into adults who sought to reclaim and redefine their hyphenated identities; they developed a strong sense of self and created their own definitions of what it means to be Wasian Canadian.

Why the Bilingual Program?

To begin, I would like to share my participants' reasons for enrolling in the Mandarin bilingual program. Through their narratives, we explore the motivations behind their parents' decisions and the impact of these decisions on the participants' cultural and linguistic development.

When asked why she was enrolled in the Mandarin bilingual program, Katherine shared that her parents "thought it'd be a good idea to learn a second language" and because her dad "comes from the culture." Her parents hoped that by being a part of the program, Katherine "could learn something about the culture too." Katherine's narrative highlights the importance of cultural heritage in her parents' decision to enroll her in the bilingual program. She mentioned her father, who is Chinese Vietnamese, saw the program as an opportunity for her to learn about her cultural roots. Although her father never got to learn Vietnamese or Mandarin formally, he wanted Katherine to make use of this opportunity. Not only did Katherine pick up Mandarin, but she was also actively involved in various Chinese cultural clubs.

Likewise, Tien, who was raised by her white Canadian mother, shared that her mother put her in bilingual school so she could learn more about herself:

> It was my mom who put me in bilingual school. I didn't grow up with my dad at all. He was out of the picture. So, my mom, being white, she wanted her children to grow up in some Asian atmosphere. My mom also went to a Mandarin program in high school, and she did that for like 3 years, and she picked it up really well, which I think is why she also put me in the program. (Tien Minh, Interview)

Tien's reasons for enrolling in the bilingual program illustrate the significant influence of parental decisions on children's educational paths. Despite not growing up with her Asian father, her white mother prioritized an Asian cultural atmosphere for her children. Tien further clarified that her mother wanted to make sure Tien made Asian friends and could learn about various parts of Chinese culture that she herself could not teach her as a white Canadian woman. This decision was influenced by Tien's mother's own positive experience with a Mandarin program, demonstrating how parents' educational backgrounds and values shape their children's schooling.

Meanwhile, Gary's parents enrolled him in the bilingual program for practical reasons:

> So, of course, language and culture is important. But I think a big contributing factor in my case was that I live right beside [my elementary school]. So, it was really easy to get there. And you know, for my parents, with the school being so close, and if it was an option for me to learn Mandarin, they were thinking, "Well, why not?' (Gary Nguyen, Interview)

Gary's account emphasizes the practical considerations in choosing a bilingual program. Living close to the school made it a convenient option for his parents, reflecting how logistical factors can influence educational decisions. Although learning a second language and being immersed in Chinese culture were important factors, Gary felt like proximity was the primary reason he ended up enrolled in the program.

My participants' narratives reveal that the decision to enroll in a Mandarin bilingual program is multifaceted, involving cultural heritage, parental influence, and practical considerations. These findings suggest that the Mandarin bilingual programs serve not only as educational tools but also as bridges to cultural identity and heritage. Understanding these motivations can help educators and policymakers design programs that better support the diverse needs of multiracial and multicultural students.

Language Fluency and Cultural Identity

Language plays a crucial role in shaping and affirming the identities of Asian Canadians. It serves as a bridge to one's cultural heritage, a means of communication within families, and a marker of identity in broader social contexts. The following section explores how Gary, Tien, and Katherine navigated their relationship with their heritage language, highlighting themes of conversational proficiency, linguistic confidence, and the impact of fluency on one's identity.

First of all, both Tien and Gary struggled with their heritage language and often felt insecure or disconnected as a result. Their narratives delve deeply into the reasons behind their limited fluency and the emotional impact this has on their identities. For Tien, her low confidence in speaking Chinese was tied to being half white:

> I'm not very confident in my Mandarin. Yeah, actually very insecure. And I think it's mainly because I'm half white, and that's what started it. I think the biggest thing that prevented me from progressing my Chinese was honestly cause I'm white. And everyone is gonna judge me in some way. At first, I just thought, 'I'm not good at Chinese anyways so I'm not even gonna try,' and then I just never spoke it. (Tien Minh, Interview)

During her interview, Tien often reflected on the challenges of navigating her multiracial identity within the program. Unlike her fully Asian peers who spoke Mandarin or another Chinese dialect at home, Tien's Chinese Vietnamese father was absent from her life, and it was her white mother who enrolled her in the program to help her connect with her Asian heritage. Without opportunities to speak the language at home, Tien struggled to improve and felt judged for both her lower proficiency and her appearance, which she felt made her stand out. These experiences fueled her insecurities and hindered her progress. Although she now regrets not working harder as a child, Tien shared that moving to British Columbia for university gave her a new perspective. There, she realized her Mandarin skills surpassed many of her Asian peers who had never attended a bilingual program. Her story demonstrates how external perceptions and internalized insecurities can shape language learning, while also illustrating how the value of such programs may become clearer with time and distance.

Like Tien, Gary also did not speak Mandarin at home and, as a result, rated his fluency in Mandarin a "2 out of 10." Unlike Tien, Gary did not feel that being Wasian or looking "whiter" than his peers made learning Mandarin more difficult. For Gary, even though he did well in his classes and had a strong community and friends in the bilingual program, he felt that not having any help at home was a significant "part of the problem" for his lack of fluency. Gary had some high points and some low points while learning Mandarin; his fluency ebbed and flowed depending on his Chinese teacher and how much he was using the language in his classes, but no matter how hard he studied, he could not keep up with his peers who spoke Mandarin at home. Yet, Gary felt like it had less to do with being Wasian, as some of his fully Chinese classmates also struggled with Mandarin if their parents did not speak the language at home.

Despite his low fluency, Gary also reflected on how learning Mandarin was still a big part of his life growing up. Gary shared an experience where he was on a school trip to visit his junior high's sister school in China. He recalled:

> I mean, one thing that comes to mind is when we went on the China trip in Grade 8, I got to give a speech to our sister school when I was there. And it was, you know, probably the most complex speech I've ever said before, and I didn't do a horrible job of it. So that was definitely a highlight. It kind of proved that, you know, I did have the skills that I needed to use Chinese to the fullest extent that I could. It's like, wow I didn't even think about how great that was until you're an adult. And it's like, wait a second, most people don't get that. (Gary Nguyen, Interview)

On this trip, Gary's experience validated his language skills and helped him realize just how unique the opportunities provided by the program were. The complexity of the speech and the subsequent reflection on its significance also illustrated the depth of his learning experience. Although Gary has struggled to retain Mandarin due to the fact that his family only speaks English at home, the opportunities offered by the program still supported him in his cultural development. He also shared how, despite his current lack of fluency, "it was nice" that he was able to speak the language at least when he was "younger."

Meanwhile, Katherine shared that she had basic conversational fluency and thanked the bilingual program for her excellent pronunciation. Unfortunately, due to not speaking the language at home, Katherine struggled with her vocabulary:

> I can have basic conversations with people. That's not the issue. But I have to have really specific conversations with certain topics. It's kind of funny cause with some topics, if they taught you in the textbook then I would know how to have a conversation with that, because I've learned about that specific topic. But then there's some topics for even elementary-level conversations I couldn't have because I just didn't learn that specific topic while I was in school, so I wouldn't even know the vocabulary to have a conversation about that topic. (Katherine Wu, Interview)

Katherine's experience illustrates the specificity of language learning. She can engage in basic conversations but struggles with topics not covered in her education. This highlights the gap between textbook learning and real-world application, suggesting that a more comprehensive and practical approach to language education could better prepare individuals for diverse conversational contexts.

When asked to elaborate more about her fluency, Katherine said she did not speak the language at home, so it made it a bit harder to keep up compared to her friends, but it did not stop her from practicing. In fact, Katherine spoke of how tight-knit her friend group from the Mandarin bilingual program was and how she has a lot of fun memories from her Chinese classes. Although Katherine was slightly less fluent than some of her friends who spoke Mandarin at home, she believed her fluency was still "pretty good" because she had been in the program for 13 years.

The varying levels of fluency depending on the social context, as well as the different experiences that Gary, Tien, and Katherine had with their sense of self, demonstrate how language is more than a tool for communication; it is a vital component of cultural identity. Tien's insecurity about speaking Chinese due to her appearance and perceived judgment illustrates how language skills are intertwined with personal identity and confidence. On the other hand, positive reinforcement and supportive environments, as seen in Gary's experience with his Mandarin speech during his China trip, can alleviate these anxieties and promote a healthier relationship with the language. Likewise, Katherine's close friend group encouraged her to keep learning the language and building a connection to her heritage language. Proficiency in a heritage language enhances cultural engagement, strengthens social relationships, and fosters a sense of community and belonging. Thus, addressing the emotional aspects of language learning, along with providing supportive environments and practical opportunities for use, is essential for affirming and sustaining cultural identity among Wasian Canadians.

Cultural Connections

In addition to linguistic development, Alberta's Mandarin bilingual programs offered numerous extracurricular activities based on Chinese cultural traditions. From martial arts to lion dance, students enrolled in the bilingual program were often heavily engaged in cultural activities. In fact, Chinese dance is a well-known, significant part of the bilingual program. Students can join the Chinese dance team starting in kindergarten, with many continuing throughout their K-12 educational experience and beyond. For instance, Katherine saw Chinese dance as a large part of her bilingual experience, and participating in this activity helped keep her connected to the Asian side of her mixed heritage:

> I did a lot of cultural activities. I did dance, and I'm still doing that. So, I've been doing dance since grade one. That was

really a big part of my elementary school. I was in dance throughout the entire time in the program. I actually think that all the schools offered Chinese dance, and it was a big part of just being in the program. I think dance was, I mean cause, I'm still dancing, it's always been a really big part of participating in Chinese culture for me. (Katherine Wu, Interview)

Katherine's long-term involvement in Chinese dance reflects how dance has been a continuous and meaningful part of her life. Likewise, Tien spoke of how Chinese dance was also a big part of her life:

In elementary, I started Chinese dance. It was a pretty big part of the bilingual program, and everyone did it at least from elementary. Yeah, and actually I was in Chinese dance from kindergarten to grade 12. It was my way of being connected to Asian culture. (Tien Minh, Interview)

Tien's participation in Chinese dance from kindergarten through grade 12 highlights the program's ability to foster a deep and lasting connection to cultural practices, especially for students with multiracial backgrounds. Tien also shared how it was nice that Chinese dance was treated as a "normal" activity, the same way soccer and track are treated. This helped her stay engaged with Chinese dance and retain a deep connection to her "Asian roots."

Lion dance and dragon dance are also indispensable parts of the bilingual program, offering students a vibrant way to engage with their cultural heritage while having fun with their friends. When asked about his participation in extracurricular activities, Gary shared that lion dance and dragon dance were embedded within his elementary program due to the emphasis on the Lunar New Year:

So, our school placed a lot of emphasis on Chinese New Year. We did a lot of preparation for that. We did lots of art. We did and we also got engaged in, you know, certain dances in grade 2. Like, in grade 2, the whole class got to participate in lion dance and take turns being the tail or the head of the lion. Then in grade 6, all the grade 6 students go to do dragon dance. That was very fun. (Gary Nguyen, Interview)

During our interview, Gary recalled the emphasis his school placed on Lunar New Year, which involved extensive preparation and participation in cultural activities. When asked to elaborate, he shared that the school had a lion dance club, but they wanted everyone to get a chance to experience it. So, the second graders would get to practice and play with the smaller lions. Meanwhile, the dragon used for the dragon dance was quite heavy, so it was delegated to the sixth graders to ensure that everyone was strong enough to hold it up. When describing his experiences, Gary seemed to recognize that these opportunities offered to him were more than just "a fun time," but memories that many Asian Canadian students in other programs would not have experienced. From lion dance in grade 2 to dragon dance in grade 6, these experiences were fun memories for Gary, but just a dream for other students.

In summary, the extracurricular activities offered in the Mandarin bilingual program are essential for not only promoting cultural engagement but also normalizing the cultural traditions of Asian students. Other Asian Canadian students in non-bilingual programs likely do not have the opportunities to learn the various traditional Chinese dances that exist, nor do they have the equipment and tools necessary to learn lion or dragon dance. In offering these extracurricular activities and treating them the same as soccer or band, these activities enrich student educational experience while also helping them grow into well-rounded individuals who are proud of their cultural heritage. For Wasian Canadian students in particular, being able to participate in a variety of extracurricular activities affirms their dual identities.

Community Bonds

The Mandarin bilingual program provided participants with a rich cultural experience that extended beyond language learning. When asked about what their program experience was like, Gary talked about how their school was more than just a place for academic learning; it was also a "socially rewarding space" and a "community where we belonged." Along the same vein, Katherine described the program as a cohesive community where students from Asian backgrounds shared their educational journey from kindergarten onwards:

> Everybody in my classes, they all come from Asian backgrounds. So, I think it was kind of just like a big Asian community. And then, like from pretty much kindergarten, we'd all be in the same classes. (Katherine Wu, Interview)

For Katherine, this program allowed her to make friends with students who shared her cultural and linguistic background. She found that being in this program helped their bond as they would stay in the same class from kindergarten until the end of high school if they remained in the bilingual program. Katherine herself talked about how, even as an adult in university, she was still close friends with those she attended the bilingual program with.

Finally, Tien emphasized the strong sense of community and cultural ties she developed through the program. Despite not being fully Chinese, she was able to integrate aspects of Chinese culture into her identity:

> So, I have such a strong sense of community, and ties back home with my Asian friends, and like Chinese dance and everything. I was able to create that Asian community when I didn't have it growing up from my father's side in a way. And so, even though I'm not fully Chinese, I was able to adopt the culture into you know my white side. (Tien Minh, Interview)

Throughout our interview, Tien mentioned both her positive and negative experiences with the program. Tien struggled with trying to become "fully" Asian and often felt like she was not a "good Asian" because she did not do well in math. Yet, after moving to a different province, Tien recalled a lot of her memories fondly. Tien was happy she was able to be a part of such a close-knit Asian community in

Alberta and felt like the program helped her with "adopting" Chinese culture alongside her white identity.

The program's emphasis on community and cultural connection ensured that students did not just learn the language but also embraced the cultural context in which it is used. Gary, Katherine, and Tien felt like the Mandarin bilingual program fostered a strong sense of community and cultural connection, enriching their schooling experience and personal growth.

A Cultural Middle Ground

For many participants in my larger study, defining what it meant to be Asian Canadian came easily because the Mandarin bilingual program supported their sense of self and identity. They were able to embrace both their cultural heritage and Canadian culture in a way that many Asian Canadians struggle with.[404] For Katherine, Tien, and Gary, though, the question of what being Asian Canadian meant to them was a bit more challenging to define; they spoke of how they grew up in this cultural middle ground that differed from people who are fully Asian.

Katherine started answering the question from the perspective of what she looked like physically:

> I think physical appearance is definitely a part of it, like, I don't really look that Asian. So, then it's hard to claim that you're Asian when it's like, you don't even really look the part. The way I think about it is, I don't think I would ever like to introduce myself and just be like I'm Chinese. There's a lot of things that you don't experience as somebody who's half compared to somebody who is completely Chinese. They're completely just Asian in general. And it's just a different experience. And I think that lived experience is kind of what influences, kind of how you grow up and how you behave in certain situations. I think it's kind of hard to introduce myself as someone who's Chinese, just because I

---

[404] Cui, 2019b

haven't had that lived experience of growing up as somebody who both looks and has you know two Asian parents. (Katherine Wu, Interview)

Here, Katherine recognized that due to her appearance, she did not and will not experience life the same way that someone who is fully Asian might. Katherine shared how some people might get bullied for being Asian or experience racial stereotypes, but because she looks white, that is not an experience she has. And so, because these are not experiences that Katherine can claim, she does not feel like she could ever fully introduce herself as "just Chinese." However, Katherine also shared that she had "always been more culturally connected to that side" of her heritage. Katherine was a part of the bilingual program for thirteen years and continued to take Chinese dance classes in her university years.

Katherine then went on to reflect on the complexity of her mixed heritage, where cultural and linguistic connections play a crucial role in her sense of identity:

> I find it really complicated to answer that kind of question just because I'm only half so then it's like, I'm kind of Asian Canadian, but not really Asian Canadian. So, I think, like culturally and the language is a really big part of just being kind of connected to that culture in general. (Katherine Wu, Interview)

Although Katherine does not physically look the part of someone who is "just Chinese," she recognized the importance of cultural ties in defining what it means to be Asian Canadian. And for her, she tried her best to maintain cultural ties with her Asian roots and does see herself as Asian Canadian. Following this comment, I personally interjected and shared that I fully see Katherine as Asian Canadian. She had been taking Chinese dance for years and was fully engaged with the culture. She spoke Mandarin and listened to music in Cantonese. And while no one is required to do all of the above to be recognized as Asian Canadian, I wanted to offer Katherine a perspective from someone who looks fully Asian that her engagement with Chinese culture was even deeper than mine. My physical appearance does not make me any more Asian Canadian than her.

Katherine appeared to have been reassured by this response and went on to share that she did enjoy that she was able to experience being both Asian and Canadian. She shared:

> Thank you for that. And yeah, I mean, I talk to a lot of people who are half who just don't like being half cause they find it really confusing. And then they're just like, 'Well, I'm like, not Asian, but I am Asian.' I just think it's really cool to be honest, cause you get a bit of both. So that is kind of exciting. And it is kind of exciting to introduce a lot of my friends who aren't white to you know, activities, like I took some of my friends to try snowmobiling. Yeah, stuff like that, so it's kind of fun to introduce this to them. And then they always introduce me to different things like Asian culture. So that's kind of a nice exchange, almost. (Katherine Wu, Interview)

Katherine acknowledged the confusion that often accompanies a mixed heritage. While hers stemmed from her physical appearance, she was more confident in her cultural connections to being Asian. And, despite the challenges, she found excitement in having a bit of both cultures and enjoyed sharing and exchanging cultural experiences with friends.

Next, we have Tien, whose experience with the bilingual program was more challenging than Katherine's. Tien previously spoke of her experiences with racism from her teachers and classmates. When asked what it meant to be Asian Canadian, Tien shared:

> That's hard, I think. Yes, specifically for me, it just means not fitting in anywhere. Because again, you've probably heard this, but when you hang out with white people or anyone other than Asian, you're seen as full Asian, and when you hang out with Asian people, you're seen fully as white. So, to me, I actually really struggle hard with identity, and not really sure who I am or where I belong. (Tien Minh, Interview)

Tien also talked about the struggles that came with being raised by her white mom and going between her father's side of the family and then her mother's. Because her father is Chinese Vietnamese while her mother is white Canadian, they are culturally quite different. Add to the fact that they were separated since Tien was young, the lack of intermingling between both sides of the family made it even harder for Tien:

> And they don't mesh either! Like my mom. My white side has no idea what's going on with the Asian side, and the Asian side has no idea what's going on with the white side. So, it's like, I'm like two people, literally being two people. (Tien Minh, Interview)

Here, Tien highlighted the disconnect between her two cultural sides, with each side being unaware of the other's cultural nuances. This lack of integration contributed to her feeling of being "two people" and complicated her sense of identity growing up.

However, Tien noted a shift in her perception during university, where the growing acceptance and celebration of mixed-race identities have helped her embrace both sides of her heritage. This acceptance has led to a greater sense of pride and self-acceptance:

> Growing up. I really just wanted to be full Asian. And like my dream, I remember I was just like, 'Oh, I just wish I wasn't white at all.' And then come like, yeah, high school wasn't a big thing. I was in a school with people, the distinction between cultures kind of disappeared. In university, I feel like now I'm a little prouder of it because there is this hype of being Wasian. It's definitely giving me some of those advantages. So, I've come to love myself as cheesy as it is, you know, and accept both sides of everything. So. No, I'm proud. I love being both. And yeah, love both sides. (Tien Minh, Interview)

Contrary to the experiences of many multiracial students who try to "pass" as white, Tien, who is half white, half Vietnamese Chinese, felt like she had to relinquish her "white side" to fit in and not be excluded. For Tien, her multiracial identity made her a "minority" not only in Canadian society, but in the Mandarin bilingual program as well. Not only did Tien face bullying from her peers for not being a "smart Asian," but she also encountered discrimination from her Chinese teachers. And while she was still thankful for the experience and saw it as a crucial part of her upbringing, it does not negate the discrimination she experienced. As such, Tien's experience diverges from studies that assert how Asian students often "wish to be seen as Canadian as possible."[405] In Tien's case, the unique environment of Alberta's Mandarin bilingual programs, at least at the elementary level, is predominantly Asian. As a result, Tien wanted to be "fully Asian" instead of half white and half Asian.

While Tien struggled a lot with her identity growing up and had mixed feelings about parts of her experience with the bilingual program, ultimately, she has grown to love both sides of herself. She even used Mandarin "like a party trick." She would shock her university classmates with her Mandarin, and she would talk about her experience in the Mandarin bilingual program and how she was able to learn the language and celebrate Chinese holidays. As our interview came to a close, Tien shared she was happy she got to talk about what the program was like for her, both the good and the bad. She stated that the program was "super rare" and that it was hard to talk to other people about something so few people get to experience.

Meanwhile, Gary appeared to have struggled a little less than Katherine and Tien when it came to his identity. When asked how he felt about being Asian Canadian, Gary responded with "proud? Yeah, proud." Gary's succinct affirmation demonstrated a strong and straightforward sense of pride in his Asian Canadian identity. When asked to elaborate, Gary shared that he felt like the Mandarin program really helped him with developing a strong cultural understanding and connection with his Asian roots, which made being "mixed" easier. He believed it laid a foundation for his cultural identity that he continued to build upon:

---

[405] Bablak et al., 2016, p. 66

> I got to connect with people that kind of understand that half of me, because, you know, I'm mixed. So, it's not as clear cut. But yeah, if I could go back and choose whether I did it again, I would certainly choose to do it again. It was a good experience to connect with peers that I was, you know, culturally somewhat similar to, and I got to learn more about the culture and being an environment for my whole childhood, that at least lays some foundation for me to build on in my older years. (Gary Nguyen, Interview)

Although Gary is of mixed heritage and is only partially Chinese due to his Asian roots being a mix of Vietnamese and Chinese, he felt like he was at least able to connect with that half of himself while in the program. And as he said, it laid a "foundation" for him to build upon. Not only was Gary selected to present a speech during his China trip in junior high school, but he was also valedictorian for his high school graduating class and remained heavily involved in volunteer activities in the bilingual program. Gary saw an opportunity to connect with half of his cultural identity and went for it.

Katherine, Tien, and Gary's experiences reflect both the challenges and triumphs of having a mixed heritage. They highlight the influence of physical appearance, the struggle to fit in, and the journey towards embracing and celebrating a dual identity. While the three of their bilingual school experiences differed, they were all able to connect more deeply with their Asian roots because of the program. The increased visibility and acceptance of mixed-race identities in the university also contributed to Tien's pride and self-acceptance. Their journeys underscore the dynamic nature of cultural identity and the importance of societal context in shaping self-perception.

Conclusion

By focusing on multiracial students in Mandarin-English bilingual programs, this study highlights the unique challenges these students face, such as navigating multiple cultural identities and struggling with their sense of belonging. My findings suggest that Mandarin-

English bilingual programs help multiracial students harmonize their hyphenated identities by fostering a sense of belonging and cultural pride, enabling them to navigate and integrate their diverse cultural backgrounds more effectively. This supportive environment promotes inclusivity and reduces feelings of isolation. By exploring these experiences and identifying effective strategies for fostering belonging, this study empowers multiracial students to reclaim and redefine what it means to be Wasian Canadian.

Chapter 10

Between Two Worlds: The Arabic Language and Identity in Italy's Second Generation

Haifa Alsakkaf

When asking young people of non-Italian origin who were born and raised in Italy how they self-identify, the answer is usually that they feel — and in most cases are — Italian citizens who also carry an additional value: their cultural heritage. This aspect is not always easy to harmonize and can sometimes present a significant challenge. The fact is that these young people want to feel integrated with others of their generation in an Italian society that has been typically, till recent times, monolingual and monocultural. The presence of people from diverse cultural backgrounds has determined a change that the new generation has to face and live through. But how does Italian society deal with this new phenomenon?

The Issue of Identity in the Second Generation of Immigrants

In the past few decades, there has been debate about the issues related to young immigrants, not only regarding the topics of integration, assimilation, and reception policies, but also addressing the topic of cultural identity, which is a fundamental aspect of the human experience,[406] representing the sense of belonging to a group culture. The identity development of young immigrants is of significant importance and has become a central issue for Italian society. The identity of these young people is of crucial importance. This raises the question of how they navigate—and sometimes clash with—the reality in which they grew up while building their lives as citizens in a multicultural society. On the challenging path of self-identification,

---

[406] Khudayberdievich, 2024

there are many important encounters and many places where they feel at home, but just as many conflicts and hostile places. For young immigrants, as well as for the children of families of non-Italian origin, the construction of identity is extraordinarily complex. Striking a balance between seeking what is familiar and losing oneself within an undefined whole is not easy.

> I had doubts because I thought I had to choose, then I realised I didn't. I am Italian with an important added value given by my Arab origin, which is part of my identity, that I cannot remove. For me now, my culture of origin is a fundamental support to who I am, which influences my being and influences my identity. B.N.(age 20) [407]

The search for a psychological balance is particularly difficult for individuals with multiple cultural references, as they are presented with simultaneous developmental challenges that require different strategies to interpret the situations they face.[408] Young people belonging to second generations and ethnic minorities, who are aware that they live immersed in a context that offers them multiple stimuli and ways of living, understand that there is no single point of view or tradition. They do not want to be restricted to one category, and they know that they are carriers of multiple characteristics and qualities.[409]

---

[407] This and the following quotations are obtained from dissertation research conducted by Haifa Alsakkaf, 2021, in which 11 males and 14 females heritage learners were interviewed about their experience in learning the Arabic language as a heritage language. The respondents' backgrounds fairly reflect the migration situation with regard to countries of origin. The interviewees' countries of origin were Morocco 7, Egypt 5, Tunisia 3, Algeria 3, Syria 3, Jordan 2, Somalia 1 and Yemen 1. The age range was 18-24 and included children of mixed couples; 2 with an Italian mother and Arab father and 1 with an Italian father and Arab mother. They were asked about their experience in learning Arabic and the influence that it had on them on a social and personal level and on the formation of their identity.
[408] Nigris, 2015
[409] Ambrosini & Pozzi, 2018

> I think I am a mixture of the two cultures, Italian and Arab.
> I definitely have a different way of thinking and seeing things
> because of this. O.R. (age 21)

The way in which they position themselves in society determines whether they are able to define which side they are on or whether to move from one side to the other, shifting between their ethnic group and the mainstream. This oscillation is influenced by cultural, religious, linguistic, and socio-economic aspects that affect their social interactions.[410] Most importantly, these aspects are transmitted and inherited for the most part from previous generations, as well as from other societies.[411] In the identity construction of the second generation, both family dynamics and social capital play an important role. Family dynamics are crucial because they are determined as much by the migration history of the family unit and the redefinition of roles in the receiving country, as well as by the link to the traditions of the ethnic group of origin that individual members keep alive in the new context. Social capital arises from the networks of relationships formed at school, in the workplace, and in other social settings. These networks are crucial, as they provide opportunities for professional emancipation and personal growth. Within the various contexts of social life, young people express different facets of their identity. Language, deeply intertwined with identity, shapes values, worldviews, and the sense of belonging, with the mother tongue holding particular significance in this regard.

The Mother Tongue and the Other Languages

Language is one of the elements that shape identity. The language a person thinks in and the one he or she prefers to speak allows the construction of identity with a view to belonging to a certain culture. The language element thus enables the second generation to choose sides when they are in difficulty due to their moving between the culture of origin and that of the country in which they were born

---

[410] Lannutti, 2016
[411] Lannutti, 2014

and/or are growing up. The importance of learning the host country's language is well emphasized by various immigration regulations and policies as an indispensable tool for successful integration.[412] Nevertheless, it should not be forgotten that the language of origin, or heritage language, the mother tongue, is the language of affection, the language that underpins all learning, and the construction of one's own view of the world.[413] It is the vehicle for passing on norms, rules, values, and traditions from one generation to the next. It plays a fundamental role in the primary socialization process conducted by the family. Through this process, individuals acquire the skills that enable them to become fully integrated members of society. This aspect seems to influence not so much the manner of acquisition as the extent to which linguistic input is used to express openness toward the surrounding reality.[414]

Children and young people who navigate two or more languages on a daily basis develop sociocultural skills that enable them to empathize more readily with others. This ability comes from the fact that their language skills are different from those of monolingual people; they are aware of the existence of more than one way of seeing and thinking about things. In addition to the heritage language with which one communicates within the family, one learns other languages that are a way of thinking, recording memories, and imagining the world in a way that is personal and subjective to each person, but that contributes to shaping one's personality.[415]

> With my parents, we speak in Arabic, but with my brothers, I speak in Italian. I find it easier. A. K (age 18)

The advantages of multilingualism, although still a vast and open field, have been studied and demonstrated. From a psychological perspective, preserving one's heritage language is an essential component of individual identity. It also provides a fundamental

---

[412] Ciliberti, 2012
[413] Pozzi, 2014
[414] Di Lucca & Masiero, 2005
[415] Kara & Schmitt, 2020

contribution to his or her linguistic-cognitive development, which means the acquisition of skills that allow language development and the ability to communicate, understand speech, and express verbally. For this reason, it is desirable that schools, starting from kindergarten, promote the appreciation of all the languages present, with curiosity, intercultural projects, and bilingual materials.[416]

> My primary school experience went well; I had other classmates of non-Italian origin. There were times when the teacher would ask us to talk about our culture of origin and would ask us some questions. I was always very glad to talk about it, and I felt especially happy when I would notice the curiosity of my teachers and classmates. H.F. (age 19)

Maintaining one's language of origin, as well as other traditional features, does not imply a lack of integration. On the contrary, it can constitute a series of additional resources, because successful integration is not linked to the total renunciation of one's own values and traditions in favor of those of the host country.[417] The accomplishments of the new citizens of the second generation are strongly linked to the maintenance of their own cultural references, integrated with the satisfaction of the host society's demands for acceptance, in our case, the Italian society.

Compared to the past, the concept of multilingualism has taken on a more open character. Children of immigrants of Arab origin who use their heritage language at home—whether a dialect or a regional variety—and the national language of the host country at school are considered multilingual.

> With my parents, I only speak in Arabic; sometimes, if I don't remember a word, I would say it in Italian. I. A. (age 20)

---

[416] Lannutti, 2014
[417] Desinan, 1997

> I used to use only the Jordanian dialect, and I could not distinguish the dialect from the classical language, which I learned at the Arabic language school. S. O. (age 23)

Even though properly supporting the correct and constant use of these languages is not easy, research has shown that maintaining them strengthens self-esteem and makes the path to identity construction more conflict-free. There is a close relationship between language, culture, and identity; they form an inseparable whole and support personality and the implementation of cognitive skills. Successful integration, in which the school has a vital role, takes place when the individuals succeed in reconciling, integrating, and harmonizing their own culture/cultures, including the mother tongue, discovering that this does not penalize them, but rather enhances their success.[418] This is why it is important to learn and practice the heritage language, especially from an early age. This is not always easy, yet many initiatives have been taking place in the past few decades in Italy to teach the Arabic language as a heritage language. These initiatives are based on European and Italian indications that promote and encourage multilingualism.

Learning Arabic: How Does It Feel?

The Italian national regulations for education encourage an intercultural approach to teaching. The principles of intercultural pedagogy promote the understanding, acceptance of, and the importance of cultural diversity, fostering dialogue, cooperation, and exchange among learners from diverse backgrounds. Nonetheless, the Italian school curriculum does not offer sufficient intercultural teaching, nor courses on the culture and language of the students' countries of origin. Some immigrants from Arab origin are not very literate and, even if they speak Arabic with their children at home, they are unable to provide them with the tools to read and write it sufficiently. Because of these needs, the teaching of the Arabic language and culture in Italy is mainly conducted in cultural centers

---

[418] Demetrio & Favaro, 1999

of the various Arab and Islamic communities, in the form of courses held on weekends and in after-school hours. The schools for the Arabic language try to promote their activities through various channels, particularly through the various Arab communities in their area, but also in public schools and cultural associations. Although most of the students speak Arabic at home, albeit only in the dialect of their country of origin, most of them approach the teaching of the standard Arabic language through these schools, which they start attending at the same age they begin primary school.

A language is not an abstract tool, made up only of rules, morphology, and syntax, but it is also supported by a specific culture that manifests itself through it.[419] The teaching of the Arabic language, therefore, cannot be dissociated from the learning of the Arab culture and the references connected with it. Children and young people of non-Italian origin who attend schools for the teaching of the Arabic language move daily between two languages and develop socio-cultural skills that bring them closer to other cultures. They acquire a particular mindset through the different languages they learn. In addition to the language of origin with which they communicate within the family, they learn other languages as a way of thinking. People who move between cultures manifest different cognitive processes that are applied according to circumstances.[420]

> The social aspect was the most important one for me. Without the Arabic school, I would not have had friends and acquaintances from other cultures, and especially from the Arab culture with which I have a special bond. K. A. (age 22)

Till now, the experience of the Arabic schools in Italy has been continuous and positive. After a few decades of activity of these schools, the first students who attended are now young adults of a new generation who are no longer content just to be there, but who want to take an active part in the construction of meanings, and who

---

[419] Vygostskij, 1990
[420] Nigris, 2015

daily try to conquer their own spaces of action, both with regards to the first generations, as well as with regards to the Italian society which is becoming increasingly multicultural.[421] For these young adults, the acquisition of cultural identity has been a more emotionally intense journey than for adult immigrants. For them, the perception of self oscillates between the cultural system within their original nucleus and another system of meanings and symbols existing outside it, within Italian society. The ability to maintain a harmonious balance is an achievement that requires effort and various identity-processing strategies.

Finding the Balance

Through an investigation of some cases of Arabic language heritage learners, it appears that learning Arabic has been an overall positive experience. Of course, there have been difficulties and critical issues, but these were mostly related to organizational aspects and not to the concept of learning the language itself. Skills are put into practice through specific tasks such as the use and processing of texts and other sources of information. Cultural competencies of knowledge, attitude, and values are acquired through direct contact with other students of Arab origin and their families, as well as with the teachers. These competences manifest themselves in operational skills, problem-solving, and dealing with others.[422] Through the investigation of this experience, the most important aspect that emerges is the social and relational aspect and the construction of identity.

Language plays a central role in shaping a person's identity, as it embodies the values, beliefs, and experiences that define an individual or a group. In migratory contexts, families construct their identities in diverse ways—by choosing, accepting, transforming, and reinventing what is inalienable from their culture of origin and what can be adapted to facilitate integration into the new environment. All the foundational aspects of identity, such as the

---

[421] Portera, 2019
[422] Vollmer, 2010

sense of self and relationships within and beyond the family, are intricately linked to the language of origin. The feeling of belonging is tied to the stability of family bonds, from which relational elements are inherited.[423] Learning a language does not simply mean acquiring grammatical rules; it entails a long and demanding process of engaging with the world the language narrates, describes, and brings to life. Language is constructed through its relationship with the culture to which it belongs.[424] Thus, the Arabic language and culture carry with them a set of norms, rules, values, and traditions transmitted within the family, representing both a constitutive aspect of identity and a principle of social cohesion for children of Arab origin.

Identity formation is central for second-generation individuals in a context of pluralism and represents a fundamental need in the search for belonging and in overcoming a condition of uncertainty. Ethno-cultural identity[425] can be understood as the result of a process of negotiation with the different social groups a person comes into contact with, including that of the origin of their families and the one to which he or she belong.[426] For these young adults, the Arabic language represents the language of affection. It is the preferred means of maintaining emotional ties and communicating with their parents and relatives in the countries of origin. They need reassuring bonds and a sense of belonging that is reinforced at the family level through their heritage language.[427]

> At home, we have Arabic TV channels, my parents often watch Arabic news. I sometimes watch with them to know what is going on, and when I go to Egypt, I feel good because

---

[423] Cavaleri, 2007
[424] De Pascale & Filotico, 2018
[425] Ethno-cultural identity, from a sociological point of view, is a person's awareness of belonging to a certain ethnic culture or a cultural reference group, which allows him or her to determine their place in the cultural space. Smith, 2010
[426] De Vita, 2003
[427] Ferroni, 2010

> I can communicate well in Arabic. This makes me happy and surprises many of my relatives who know that I was born and live in Italy—N. M. (age 19).

Young adults who learn and speak Arabic as their heritage language are aware that they belong to several traditions that offer them multiple signals and ways of living. This is why they try both to maintain contact with their origins and to socialize in the contexts with which they come into contact. This allows them to choose sides when they are in difficulty due to the oscillation between the culture of origin and that of the country in which they were born and/or are growing up. For them, both identities are placed on an equal footing; they recognize the differences in values and behavior and adapt to concrete situations. Multiple identities for these young people can be an asset if they know how to make use of their different affiliations in the various environments in which they find themselves.

> I am Italian, but I am also Arab. I think both in Italian and Arabic, it depends on the context. This aspect is definitely part of and influences my life. M. S. (age 20)

These young people live and are molded in an international perspective and outlook; they acquire a sense of belonging that is no longer that of their parents, because their condition is pushing them to structure their identities in hybrid and multiple ways. They are young people who live in a globalized world. For them, the dual identity can be a resource but may also become a limitation depending on the context and how they manage to make use of this quality.[428] However, this may not always be the case, because an environment that is hostile to ethnic differences may provoke the reaction of an attachment to, and vindication of, one's ethnic traits and a closure towards society.

---

[428] Lannutti, 2014

Conclusion

The exploration of Arabic as a heritage language reveals that it plays a significant role in the integration and inclusion of children of Arab origin. Beyond issues of citizenship, many of them feel a genuine sense of belonging to Italy, the country where most of them were born. At the same time, their culture of origin remains deeply present in both their personal identity and family life. Through this experience, these young adults—situated within two dynamic, open, and plural cultures—manage to move beyond the notion of a single culture of belonging. The findings also show that they recognize and value various elements of their heritage language, seeking to adapt these elements so they can be meaningfully integrated into their own social and personal contexts. They assert their uniqueness and individuality, while rejecting both discrimination and assimilation, as well as the anonymity of indistinct equality.

This perspective highlights the importance of recognizing individuals and the specific groups to which they belong, affirming their right to develop their own lifestyles and cultural values. Such recognition strengthens the sense of identity and confirms the individual's acceptance within society, with all their particularities and specificities. The language of origin, as a heritage received from one's family, embodies a history that must be known and preserved. It serves as a vital means of transmitting the cultural traditions of the country of origin to the second generation, enabling them to achieve a deeper understanding of themselves and their identities.

Chapter 11

Bridging Worlds: Exploring the Dual Identities of Arabic Heritage Students

Issam Salameh Albdairat

This chapter examines the experiences of Arabic heritage students enrolled in Arabic language courses at Indiana University Bloomington, where Arabic is predominantly used as the medium of instruction in the classrooms. This case study investigates how these students, who come from Arabic-speaking backgrounds, navigate their linguistic and cultural identities in an academic setting that reinforces their heritage language. Focusing on classroom interactions, language use, and cultural engagement, the study explores the challenges these students encounter, such as balancing their proficiency in Arabic with the academic demands of formal language study and the broader linguistic influences they face outside the classroom. The study also highlights their achievements, demonstrating how immersion in their heritage language within the academic setting strengthens their cultural connections and enhances their educational experience. This case study identifies effective strategies for supporting Arabic heritage students in higher education, including culturally responsive teaching practices, integrating culturally relevant content, and developing a supportive learning community. By providing practical recommendations for educators and policymakers, this chapter contributes to a deeper understanding of the importance of heritage language education in preserving linguistic and cultural heritage while promoting social cohesion and integration within diverse academic environments.

Who Are Arabic Heritage Learners?

Heritage languages (HLs) are typically defined as languages other than the dominant language in a given social context.[429] Learners of Arabic as a foreign language can generally be divided into two categories. The first group consists of those who recognize the importance of Arabic for studying the Qur'an and understanding Islamic law. However, observations show that many of these learners study the Qur'an in isolation from the language itself. As a result, they may be able to recite or memorize the Qur'an but are often unable to write simple sentences or hold basic conversations with native speakers.

The second group comprises students who enroll in university programs that require the study of a second language. Some of these students choose Arabic out of curiosity or academic interest. Unlike the first group, they tend to focus on the language itself rather than on religious texts. This group requires comprehensive instruction in all four language skills—listening, speaking, reading, and writing.

Heritage language learners (HLLs) of Arabic can be divided into two broad categories: Geographical HLLs (G-HLLs) and Muslim HLLs (M-HLLs).[430] The geographical HLLs category includes students from Arabic-speaking families. The students in my classroom who fall into this category come from Jordanian, Iraqi, Moroccan, and Syrian families. In contrast, the Muslim HLLs (M-HLLs) category includes students from non-Arabic-speaking backgrounds who learn Arabic for religious purposes.

Inside the Arabic Classroom: Language in Action

The Arabic program at Indiana University Bloomington (IU) serves a diverse student population consisting of both heritage and non-heritage learners, reflecting the composition of Arabic language classrooms at the university level. To ensure appropriate placement, heritage learners must take a placement test before enrolling in the

---

[429] Kelleher, 2010
[430] ElHawari, 2021, p. 74

program. This process helps assess their proficiency and places them in the proper course level, ensuring an optimal learning experience.

The Arabic program at IU is structured into five levels, beginning with A100, which introduces students to the Arabic alphabet and foundational language skills. The curriculum emphasizes the development of four key language competencies: reading, writing, speaking, and listening. Instruction is primarily guided by a designated textbook, supplemented by external materials and worksheets provided by instructors to reinforce classroom instruction.

A distinguishing feature of the program is its immersive approach, as Arabic is the primary language of instruction in the classroom, even at the beginner level. This methodology accelerates language acquisition by encouraging students to engage with Arabic practically and meaningfully from the outset.

Connecting Culture and Learning

In the Arabic program, we acknowledge the differences between students who view Arabic as an integral part of their identity and those learning it for professional or academic purposes. Instructors also recognize the emotional and psychological impact of learning Arabic on heritage students' sense of identity.

For the above reasons, it is important to help heritage students connect their cultural background to their academic journey. To support them in our program, we incorporate various cultural activities into our curriculum that students must attend. These activities include Arabic Poetry Night, Arabic Dinner, and an Arabic Talent Show, where students sing, act in Arabic, and participate in a fashion show showcasing traditional clothing from different cultures, such as Moroccan dresses and Egyptian costumes.

For example, during the Arabic Dinner event, we bring food from restaurants specializing in cuisine from various Arab countries, allowing students to connect with their culture through food. At Arabic Poetry Night, students recite poems by famous poets from the Arab world, deepening their appreciation for Arabic literature.

Additionally, we invite several guest speakers to discuss various topics throughout the year, providing students with opportunities to engage with the Arabic language and culture beyond the classroom.

Navigating Different Paths to Arabic: Teaching Diverse Learners

Arabic language educators at the university level face a unique set of challenges due to the diverse linguistic backgrounds of their students. Heritage learners typically have a familial connection to Arabic and prior exposure to the language, yet many enroll in beginner courses. Despite their conversational proficiency, they often struggle with reading and writing, leading to an imbalance in skill levels among students.[431]

Additionally, the phenomenon of diglossia — a situation where two forms of the same language are used for different purposes[432] complicates the learning process. In Arabic, most people speak a local dialect at home but use *Modern Standard Arabic (MSA)* for reading, writing, and formal settings like school or news broadcasts. This means that heritage students often need to "relearn" Arabic in its formal version, which has a more complex grammar and vocabulary than what they are used to speaking with family.[433]

I once had two heritage students working on a speaking exercise in my classroom. One student, whose family was originally from Iraq, said أنا /احچي (*'anā aḥchī*), meaning "I am talking." In contrast, the other student, whose family was from Syria, said أنا بئول (*'anā b'ūl*), which also means "I am talking." While each used their respective dialect—Iraqi and Levantine—the Modern Standard Arabic (MSA) equivalent is أنا أتكلم (*'anā 'atakallam*). This example highlights how learning MSA requires heritage students to acquire vocabulary they may never have encountered before, despite their familiarity with Arabic in its spoken forms. Due to their informal exposure to the language, some heritage learners may develop complacent attitudes, believing they already possess sufficient

---

[431] ElHawari, 2021, p. 93
[432] Ferguson, 1959, p. 325
[433] ElHawari, 2021, p. 19

knowledge. Therefore, educators need to foster a supportive environment that validates their background while encouraging active engagement in classroom activities.

The primary motivation for heritage learners to study Arabic is often a desire to reconnect with their culture, frequently encouraged by family members who see language as a vital link to their heritage. However, in addition to cultural ties, heritage learners may share similar motivations with non-heritage students, such as academic or professional aspirations.

Conversely, non-heritage students typically enter Arabic courses with little to no prior exposure to the language. Their motivations often differ from those of heritage learners; some enroll to fulfill academic requirements, while others are drawn to Arabic for career opportunities in diplomacy, international relations, and political affairs involving the Middle East. Additionally, some non-heritage learners study Arabic to gain cultural insight or to enhance their ability to communicate effectively in a globalized world.

Educators must recognize these distinct linguistic backgrounds and learning motivations. One of the primary challenges in Arabic language instruction is designing curricula and classroom activities that address the needs of both groups simultaneously. Balancing the differing levels of linguistic proficiency and engagement requires pedagogical strategies that accommodate heritage learners' existing skills while ensuring that non-heritage learners receive the foundational instruction necessary for their progression in the language.

Balancing Language, Identity, and Expectations

Heritage language students often demonstrate strong oral proficiency in their home dialect but face challenges with Modern Standard Arabic (MSA), literacy, and formal academic writing.[434] Upon joining Arabic courses, one of the primary challenges they encounter is their expectation that instruction will focus exclusively on reading, writing, and grammar—areas where they lack proficiency. However,

---

[434] ElHawari, 2021, p. 80

our curriculum is based on the Communicative Language Teaching (CLT) approach, which emphasizes real-life communication, interaction, and fluency while integrating all four language skills. This methodology ensures that students develop not only their weaker skills but also enhance their conversational abilities.

Another challenge for heritage learners is their preference for studying only the dialect spoken by their family. For instance, a student of Egyptian heritage may resist learning about the Levantine dialect. However, university-level Arabic programs and standard textbooks incorporate MSA alongside major dialects such as Levantine and Egyptian. Textbook exercises often expose students to all three varieties, making it necessary for heritage learners to acquire new vocabulary in MSA and unfamiliar dialects.

Heritage learners' motivations for studying Arabic vary widely. Some are primarily interested in improving their ability to communicate with family members in their country of origin, making them less inclined to engage with other dialects. In contrast, learners who aim to work in diplomatic or international fields recognize the value of mastering multiple dialects in addition to MSA. These differing motivations influence students' engagement with various aspects of the Arabic language curriculum.

Heritage Arabic learners often face challenges in identity negotiation as they navigate their dual cultural and linguistic backgrounds. These learners frequently experience pressure to demonstrate fluency and cultural authenticity, which can impact their confidence and language use. Additionally, interactions with native speakers may reinforce or challenge their self-perception as Arabic speakers, influencing how they engage with the language and their heritage identity.[435]

Moments of Growth: Success Stories from the Classroom

Students in the Arabic program complete their studies and enhance their Arabic language proficiency by the end of their senior year at the university level. For many, this is not their first exposure to

---

[435] Trentman, 2015

learning Arabic. Throughout their elementary, middle, and high school years, they may have studied Arabic at home with family members or attended specialized Arabic instruction programs, such as Sunday Arabic schools. These programs, commonly found across the United States, are often held in mosques or Islamic schools where parents enroll their children to learn Arabic.

Following the COVID-19 pandemic and the widespread adoption of digital learning platforms, many parents began enrolling their children in online Arabic courses, where native Arabic speakers provide instruction remotely.

However, students entering the university's Arabic program often express concerns and doubts about their ability to succeed. Many have had prior experiences with Arabic learning programs taught by volunteers or individuals without professional teaching credentials. These experiences have sometimes led to a lack of confidence due to ineffective instruction. Additionally, resource limitations in these programs often result in mixed-level classrooms, where students with lower proficiency may feel hesitant to participate or speak.

At the university level, students benefit from a structured and professionally designed curriculum, guided by trained instructors who address their diverse learning needs. This approach significantly enhances their language proficiency and boosts their confidence in mastering Arabic. Many students report that they now feel equipped with the necessary skills to read and comprehend the Qur'an and other Arabic religious texts. Furthermore, they gain the confidence to pursue careers that require Arabic language proficiency, recognizing their ability to engage with the language at a professional level.

Beyond coursework, students have also excelled in Arabic language competitions. Notably, the IU Arabic Debate Team ranked first in the nation at the U.S. Universities Arabic Debating Championship.[436] This achievement highlights the program's success

---

[436] IU Newsroom, 2024

in fostering linguistic and critical thinking skills, preparing students for competitive and professional environments.

Another success story involves my students' participation in the Global Classroom experience, where I paired them with native Arabic speakers from Jordan to create meaningful international learning opportunities. The Global Classroom initiative enables instructors to integrate an international component into their courses through collaboration with partners abroad, allowing students to engage in cross-cultural academic experiences without leaving campus.[437]

In Spring 2024, students in Elementary Arabic II (A150) participated in this initiative. The course focused on developing foundational skills in reading, writing, listening, and speaking in Modern Standard Arabic (MSA) and one dialect (Egyptian or Levantine). Additionally, it provided insights into Arabic culture and customs to help students understand the language in its authentic context.

Through a partnership with Al-Balqa Applied University in Amman, Jordan, my students interacted with native Arabic speakers, enhancing their language proficiency and cultural understanding. This collaboration was facilitated by a faculty member in Applied Linguistics & Computational Linguistics at Al-Balqa's Language Center.

By engaging in this international experience, students not only improved their Arabic language skills but also gained a deeper appreciation for cultural exchange and global collaboration.

What Works: Strategies that Support Heritage Learners

In the Arabic program at Indiana University, we implement various strategies to support Arabic heritage students and enhance their learning experience.

One key strategy is Structured Placement Testing, which ensures that heritage students are placed at appropriate levels based on their

---

[437] Indiana University, n.d.

proficiency.[438] The placement test includes reading and writing components, as well as a section to assess their conversational skills, such as listening and speaking. This approach helps identify the most appropriate starting point for each student, enabling them to build effectively on their existing knowledge.

Another essential strategy is offering tutoring and conversation sessions in addition to regular Arabic courses. For example, we provide conversation sessions led by native Arabic speakers, where students engage in in-depth discussions about topics covered in class. These sessions are conducted entirely in Arabic and are limited to a maximum of four students, ensuring a more personalized and focused learning experience. In contrast, regular classroom settings may include up to 20 students, making it more challenging to give individualized attention. The smaller conversation groups allow instructors to understand each student's strengths and weaknesses better, helping them improve their speaking and listening skills more effectively.

Additionally, Indiana University hosts an Arabic Flagship Program, which provides even more comprehensive support for students aiming for higher proficiency in Arabic. Arabic Flagship Programs, supported by the National Security Education Program (NSEP), exist in select U.S. universities to help students achieve professional-level proficiency in Arabic. These programs offer intensive language courses, cultural immersion experiences, study abroad opportunities, and individualized support such as one-on-one tutoring sessions. Students in the Flagship program receive guidance from instructors on specific areas they need help with, further enhancing their fluency and overall language skills.

Another essential strategy is adopting innovative, student-centered pedagogical approaches, which can significantly enhance language engagement and proficiency. Instructors who implement this strategy take on the role of facilitators rather than traditional

---

[438] ElHawari, 2021, p. 64

lecturers, creating a more interactive and dynamic learning environment.

In my classroom, I apply this approach by providing students with handouts and assigning them to work collaboratively in small groups. This group-based learning encourages students to engage actively with the material and each other. After completing the activity, students present their findings and results to the entire class, fostering discussion and peer learning. These exercises are designed to integrate all four language skills—reading, writing, speaking, and listening—ensuring a well-rounded linguistic development.

By shifting the focus from passive reception to active participation, this method not only improves students' Arabic proficiency but also enhances their confidence and ability to communicate effectively in real-world contexts.

We also use an approach called *Interactive Peer Learning*, where heritage students are paired with non-heritage learners to work together and support each other's progress.[439] This encourages a practice known as *translanguaging*—when students switch between languages or dialects to help each other understand and communicate. For example, a student who is more fluent in Arabic might explain an unfamiliar word by relating it to an English phrase or by giving an example from their home dialect.[440] For instance, in this weekly exercise, I divide the students into groups to discuss the questions below. Each group is assigned to answer the questions from either Group ا (A) or Group ب (B).

Students first work together in small groups, asking and answering these questions in Arabic. Afterward, they write their responses and then switch to a new partner to ask and answer the questions again. These questions are designed to be personally relevant, allowing students to connect their responses to their own experiences.

This exercise is conducted weekly when I introduce new vocabulary. It is adapted from the Al-Kitaab textbook and fosters collaboration between heritage and non-heritage students, creating

---

[439] ElHawari, 2021, p. 93
[440] Abourehab, 2023, p. 418

an inclusive learning environment where students can share their unique perspectives and learn from one another.

اسألوا زملاءكم

Group ا (A)
1. What is your ethnic origin/descent? Do you know a lot about it? (عنه)
2. How many classes do you have this semester?
3. Which city in the United States is the best for living (للسكن) as far as you are concerned, and why? Give at least two reasons. Your partner should use the expression بالنِّسبة لي.
4. What do you do (تَفعَل\تَفعَلين) in the summer?
5. Do you like winter in Indiana? Why or why not? How do you feel in the winter?
6. What do you sometimes do on Saturdays?

اسألوا زملاءكم

Group ا (B)
1. What do you do (تَفعَل\تَفعَلين) when (عِندَما) you feel lonely?
2. What is the best season of the year, as far as you are concerned? Why? What kind of weather do you dislike?
3. What is the best restaurant in Bloomington, as far as you are concerned? What food (طعام) do you like?
4. Do you travel in the winter? If so, where?
5. Do you like crowds? Why or why not?
6. What do you do frequently?
7. What classes are offered in the fall/spring semester?

Another strategy we implement is integrating technology into our teaching. For example, I use YouTube to enhance students' understanding of various topics. Sometimes, I have them listen to Arabic music and songs, which not only helps them learn the language but also deepens their appreciation of Arabic culture. Similarly, I incorporate Kahoot, an interactive game-based learning tool, to engage students in a fun and competitive way. This tool can be particularly effective in language teaching by reinforcing vocabulary, grammar, and comprehension through quizzes and live interactive sessions.

Additionally, we use the companion websites for the textbooks "Alif Baa" and "Al-Kitaab", where students can complete listening exercises, quizzes, and other activities online to strengthen their skills.

I also use Quizlet to reinforce topics covered in class, particularly new vocabulary. For example, I design flashcards that display the Arabic word, its English meaning, and a corresponding image, making it easier for students to visualize and retain new words.

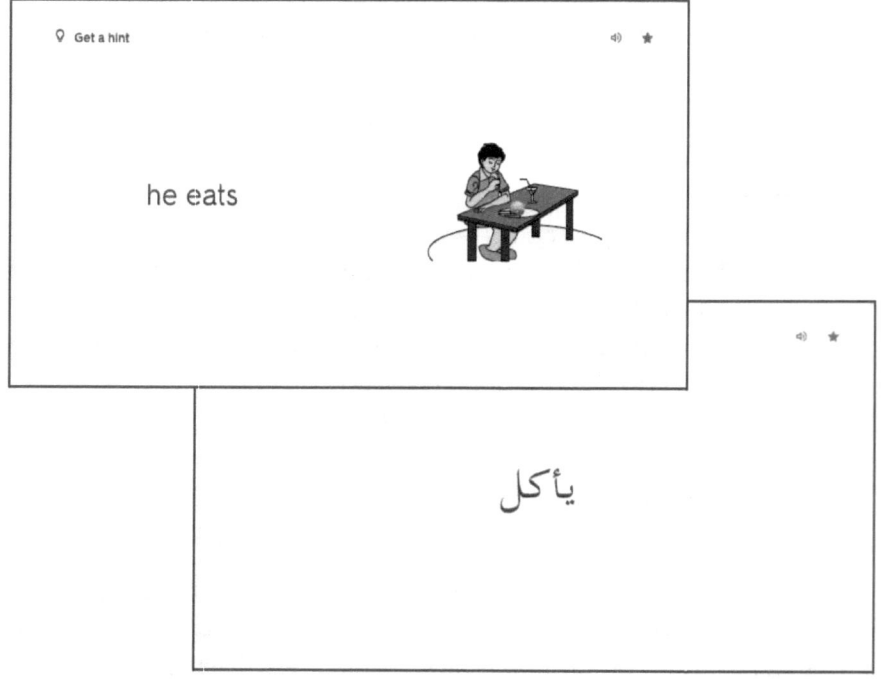

Additionally, this exercise allows students to click on the listening icon to hear the word pronounced correctly, reinforcing proper pronunciation. They can also view hints before revealing the answer, providing a gradual learning process that enhances retention. This interactive learning tool encourages students to engage in multiple senses. They see images, hear pronunciations, and interact with words, which strengthen their vocabulary acquisition beyond just reading and memorization. Incorporating multimodal resources and diverse instructional materials—such as music and digital media—provides heritage students with meaningful opportunities to engage with the language in ways that reflect their lived experiences.[441]

Another effective strategy to support both heritage and non-heritage Arabic learners is the integration of artistic and multimodal methods into language instruction. Incorporating artistic practices—such as text-based visual art, poetry, and digital storytelling—helps students bridge the gap between dialects and Modern Standard Arabic (MSA), while also affirming their linguistic and cultural identities.[442] These creative approaches make learning more engaging and relevant, especially for heritage learners who may be navigating complex relationships with their home dialects and formal Arabic.

In my classroom, I implement these strategies by embedding visual imagery into reading texts to aid comprehension and cultural association. Additionally, we host Arabic calligraphy workshops, where students learn about the aesthetic and historical significance of Arabic script. These activities not only enhance students' understanding of the language but also deepen their appreciation for Arabic art and identity. By engaging with Arabic through artistic expression, students connect emotionally and personally with the language, fostering a more inclusive and empowering learning environment. Below are photographs of students' calligraphy and visual projects, which showcase how these methods support student engagement and identity formation.

---

[441] Abourehab, 2023, p. 415
[442] Khaled & Anderson, 2024

This approach is supported by emerging scholarship emphasizing the role of creativity and multimodal expression in language learning. Artistic integration provides "alternative spaces of engagement," especially beneficial for heritage learners.[443] Multimodal learning environments enable learners to express themselves more authentically and interactively.[444] Incorporating students' cultural and linguistic resources through creative tasks can transform the classroom into a space of empowerment and linguistic ownership.[445]

Another effective teaching strategy is incorporating collaborative projects into the course. Throughout the semester, students engage in small-scale projects, fostering teamwork and language development. By the end of the semester, they collaborate on a larger-scale project,

---

[443] Khaled & Anderson, 2024
[444] Sierens & Van Avermaet, 2014
[445] Yazan & Ali, 2022

which includes preparing a PowerPoint presentation and creating a video where they interact in Arabic. These projects incorporate peer tutoring, allowing students to support each other in understanding and using the required vocabulary for successful completion.

Parental influence plays a crucial role in heritage language retention.[446] A study highlights that Saudi mothers actively invest in their children's Arabic proficiency by enrolling them in community language classes and reinforcing their learning at home.[447] Parents seek opportunities to maintain their children's Arabic skills through structured learning environments and cultural engagement.[448]

In our program, heritage students' parents play an active role in their children's Arabic education. For example, parents participate in our Arabic Dinner event, where we serve food from restaurants specializing in cuisine from various Arab countries, allowing students to experience their cultural heritage through food. Additionally, parents attend our Arabic Poetry Night, where instructors, students, and native Arabic speakers from the community recite works by renowned Arab poets. While these events are open to all parents, we have observed that heritage students' parents, particularly those who live locally, tend to be more actively engaged in these cultural gatherings.

Reflections and Future Directions

As an educator deeply involved in teaching Arabic at the university level, witnessing the linguistic and cultural growth of Arabic heritage learners has been both inspiring and humbling. This journey has reminded me of the power of language as a bridge, not only between words, but between generations, continents, and personal identities. I have seen students walk into the classroom uncertain about their place within the Arabic-speaking world, only to leave with a stronger sense of self, newfound confidence in their abilities, and a deeper appreciation for their cultural roots. Their stories, struggles, and

---

[446] Et-Bozkurt and Yağmur, 2022
[447] Al-Samiri, 2024
[448] Trentman, 2015

successes have not only shaped my teaching philosophy but have also reaffirmed my belief in the importance of creating inclusive, empathetic, and responsive learning environments that nurture both language skills and cultural pride.

This case study has shed light on the complex realities Arabic heritage students face as they navigate dual identities within the academic setting. By blending structured placement, student-centered pedagogy, creative methodologies, and culturally immersive experiences, we can more effectively support these learners in developing both linguistic proficiency and cultural competence. Programs must continue to evolve, recognizing the distinct needs of heritage learners alongside non-heritage peers. Future efforts should focus on expanding international collaborations, integrating community-based learning, and embracing technology to deepen engagement. Ultimately, investing in heritage language education is not just about language preservation—it is a commitment to diversity, inclusion, and the empowerment of students as global citizens.

Part III – Schools, Communities, and Innovation

Chapter 12

Transformation of Heritage Language Schools during the Pandemic: Connectivity, Community, and Identity

Nina Paulovicova, Renata Emilsson Peskova, and Marta McCabe

This chapter reports on research conducted during the COVID-19 pandemic in heritage language schools (HLS) in Alberta, Canada. Coping with the pressures of the pandemic without any governmental support, these schools provided grassroots assistance to their language communities. They even moved towards professionalization while facing multiple impacts of the pandemic, such as increased racism, cuts in funding, and denied access to their teaching spaces, including supplies, teaching materials, or school documents, with the onset of pandemic restrictions. HLS showed resilience by transitioning its teaching online, but more importantly, by connecting with other schools regionally, nationally, and transnationally. The increased virtual connectivity of the heritage language cyberspora[449] affirmed their respective heritage identities and empowered heritage language (HL) communities during the pandemic.

HLS are grassroots organizations that maintain the languages and cultures of immigrant communities and advocate for multilingualism and cross-cultural understanding. HLS play crucial roles in immigrant communities around the world, but their activities often go unnoticed, and little is also known about the challenges they face in their work. HLS are known by many names, such as community-

---

[449] Hatoss, 2013

based heritage language schools, ethnic schools, Saturday schools, supplementary schools, and community schools.[450] These schools' size and structure vary. Non-profit organizations and volunteers typically run smaller HLS, while the Alberta Ministry of Education accredits some larger HLS. They teach children and adults and usually meet on the weekends in libraries, community centers, or church basements.[451]

HLS provide their students with many benefits beyond simply delivering language lessons. By providing learning spaces in which children's linguistic and cultural heritage is activated and celebrated, HLS allow children to safely explore and develop their plurilingual identities[452] and learn literacy skills in their HL.[453] HLS thus complement the formal school system, which has traditionally failed to provide HL instruction and to value students' linguistic and cultural skills.[454] HLS also provide their community members with additional opportunities: by volunteering with HLS, teachers can develop a Canadian work history,[455] find meaningful work matching their professional skills outside of what might be available to them as new Canadians,[456] and remain connected to their HL communities.[457] Moreover, HLS offer leadership opportunities for their community members[458] and help new Canadians understand Canadian educational expectations and services.[459] As such, HLS serve as bottom-up integration channels for new immigrants, providing support to newcomers, refugees, migrant workers, and their families facing limited access to information and resources.[460] These services proved essential, especially during the pandemic, when HLS helped

---

[450] Chow, 2001; Lamb, 2020; Shibata, 2000
[451] Aberdeen, 2016
[452] Lamb, 2020
[453] Cui, 2011
[454] Emilsson Peskova & Ragnarsdóttir, 2016
[455] Aberdeen, 2016
[456] Bilash & Shi, 2011
[457] Aberdeen, 2016
[458] Hornberger & Swinehart, 2012
[459] Guo, 2013
[460] See, for example, Chi, 2020; OECD, 2020

compensate for the slow governmental response by facilitating communication, community engagement, and care.

With the social distancing measures of the COVID-19 pandemic, HL education moved online, transforming HL teaching and learning, but also shifting the relationships between connectivity, community, and identity. Some heritage classes were canceled; in other cases, they "virtualized with their 'old' structures"[461] or adjusted to the affordable technologies and available platforms that suited the goals of HL communities. This study focuses on what has changed, transformed, and been gained or lost during the transition to the online environment.[462] With the onset of the pandemic, new forms of transnational practices, spaces, networks, and strategies emerged.[463]

Considering the multiple roles that HLS play, and the unique model of integration and belonging, our study approaches HLS as a community of practice[464] where learners acquire their HL while engaged in socio-cultural communal practices. We use HL as an important analytical category to explore how the COVID-19 crisis affected ethnic communities, about which little is currently known. The following research questions shaped our inquiry:

1. Considering the inequitable governmental approach to HLS as opposed to public schools in Alberta, Canada, how have the unique immigrant integration channels of HLS been disrupted or altered as a result of the pandemic?

2. How have HLS transformed and adapted to the challenges of the pandemic in Alberta, Canada?

Theoretical and Conceptual Framework

To better understand the responses of HLS to the disruptions caused by the pandemic, we apply the theoretical concepts of the "community

---

[461] Svensson, 2004
[462] Cook, 2003
[463] Goldring & Krishnamurti, 2007; Levitt, 2010
[464] Lave & Wenger, 1991

of practice",⁴⁶⁵ "community of care",⁴⁶⁶ "spaces of immigrant integration through multilingualism,"⁴⁶⁷ and "fluid identities."⁴⁶⁸

We approach HL learning as a social process, where learners acquire heritage languages while engaged in socio-cultural communal practices, and apply the community of practice concept.⁴⁶⁹ Wenger, Dermott, and Snyder define communities of practice as "groups of people who share a concern, a set of problems, or a passion about a topic, and who deepen their knowledge and expertise in this area by interacting on an ongoing basis" and argue that "communities of practice are the ideal social structure for 'stewarding' knowledge."⁴⁷⁰ Communities of practice differ from traditional institutional structures in how they manage and develop knowledge and then reach out to the community. Communities of practice build their respective reservoir of knowledge via informal interactions, allowing for input from individuals who are directly acquainted with the challenges on the ground. Communities of practice typically display more spontaneity in knowledge building and project implementation compared to the centralized and bureaucratic processes of traditional educational institutions.⁴⁷¹ Employing this concept allows us to approach HLS as an analytical category and to examine the specific responses of HLS to the pandemic, including their short- and long-term impacts on a broader community.

This study further draws on Basu's conceptualization of three spaces of immigrant integration through multilingualism: a) unidirectional or traditional integration, b) reciprocal integration, and c) multifarious integration.⁴⁷² Whereas unidirectional integration is based on the dominance of one language (typically the official language), reciprocal integration also displays the dominance of one

---

⁴⁶⁵ Lave & Wenger, 1991
⁴⁶⁶ Tungohan, 2023
⁴⁶⁷ Basu, 2011,
⁴⁶⁸ Byram, 2003; Flores, 2013
⁴⁶⁹ Lave & Wenger, 1991
⁴⁷⁰ Wenger, Dermott, & Snyder 2002, p. 9
⁴⁷¹ Lave & Wenger, 1991
⁴⁷² Basu, 2011

language, which, however, accepts non-dominant languages, but "separates learning of a language by specific ethnocultural groups."[473] The multifarious model is the most democratic and rooted in solidarity, as none of the languages is dominant and their interaction is reciprocal.[474] Using this classification with respect to HL communities allows us to analyze which of these integration channels were disrupted by the COVID-19 pandemic—particularly, how the transition to online teaching altered the models of integration. While public schools represent a top-down approach to immigrant integration relying on the official language, HLS foster a vastly different model of integration and belonging.[475] HLS are operated by leaders and volunteers who respond directly to the community's use of the language and cultural norms of the community,[476] representing a bottom-up, grassroots approach to integrating immigrants into Canadian society.

In addition to HL teaching and supporting communities, HLS also promote the plurilingual identities of its members. We use the concept of plurilingualism to acknowledge that language learning and use impact individuals on personal as well as societal levels. HL speakers are not obliged to choose and prioritize one of their multiple identities. This knowledge soothes the inner tension and reconciles the various identities, cultures, and languages of an immigrant into one complex identity that is in flux. For instance, while the majority society often views mixing of languages as a weakness and a sign of the lack of English language proficiency, HLS acknowledge the competency in multiple languages and familiarity with different epistemologies as an asset. Such fluidity of identities[477] allows newcomers, refugees, and migrant workers to adjust to a variety of social, cultural, economic, and political environments. "Fluid

---

[473] Basu, 2011, p. 1313
[474] Ibid.
[475] Basu, 2011
[476] Paulovicova, McCabe, & Emilsson Peskova, 2021
[477] Byram, 2003, p. 8

identities" erode the "static language constructs"[478] and open space to "more fluid linguistic constructs," which are becoming more popular in identity and cultural politics and signal the increasing importance of plurilingualism.[479]

The concept of fluid identities nudges to question the "rigid, broad, ambivalent, and overused" analytical category of identity."[480] The shared interest of HLS and their connectivity proved to be more relevant than the concept of land-based identity. Shared interest and connectedness "disregard borders and other specific identity markers and fully embraces the relational aspect and mobilization around shared concerns."[481]

Politically speaking, plurilingualism aims to construct "a new citizenship" and aims to build "a new solidarity and a more democratic society."[482] At the same time, plurilingualism undermines monolingual (English) Western epistemologies and opens a new space for engaging with immigrant, migrant worker, and refugees' epistemologies, which in turn challenges the concept of "otherness" and humanizes HL speakers.[483]

Methodology

Overall, twenty-nine schools are affiliated with the International and Heritage Languages Association (IHLA), totaling over 150 teachers and over 2000 students. These community-based schools are similar in aim and hours of instruction; however, they range from small, tuition-funded schools of a dozen or so students to large schools with a student body of over 100 and an operating budget of over $100,000.[484] Some of Alberta's HLS offer a curriculum approved by the Ministry of Education, thus issuing high school credits for their students. The HLS in Alberta teach a variety of languages, including

---

[478] Flores, 2013, p. 509
[479] Piccardo, 2013
[480] Paulovicova, McCabe, & Emilsson Peskova, 2023
[481] Ibid.
[482] Flores, 2013, p. 512
[483] Vehabovic, 2020
[484] Aberdeen, 2016

Arabic, Armenian, Bangla, Czech, Farsi, Filipino, Greek, Gujarati, Hindi, Italian, Marathi, Nepali, Polish, Portuguese, Punjabi, Russian, Slovak, Somali, Spanish, Swahili, Telugu, Tigrinya, Turkish, and Ukrainian.

This 2020/2021 qualitative study is based on twenty-five interviews with HL school leaders and teachers at IHLA schools in Edmonton, Canada. Participants were interviewed online, and the interviews were transcribed, edited, and anonymized before being checked for accuracy by the participants.[485] Interviews were then coded for themes and analyzed in MAXQDA2020. The analysis focused on the HLS' transition to online teaching and learning. We specifically sought markers of three spaces of immigrant integration through multilingualism:

a) unidirectional or traditional integration,

b) reciprocal integration, and

c) multifarious integration.

As part of the analysis, we considered evidence of immigration integration channels pointing to resilience, transnational practices and connections, community support and volunteerism, identity negotiations, and the inclusion or exclusion of HL in society.

The study employed a participatory action research (PAR) lens, since "advocacy research provides a voice for... participants, raising their consciousness or advancing an agenda for change to improve their lives. It becomes a united voice for reform and change."[486] PAR builds a partnership between the researcher and the participant. Throughout this study, we invited participants to ask questions, check, and refine their answers, and even remove their data should they choose. Participant rights were outlined in an informed consent document.

To increase the credibility and validity of the findings, we used peer debriefing, member checks, accurate data recording, and thick

---

[485] This study has been reviewed by the Athabasca University Research Ethics Board. The participants were anonymized. No personal identifiers were used throughout the study.

[486] Creswell, 2009, p. 9

descriptions. We considered the identity biases of both the research assistant and the researchers.[487] To triangulate data, we conducted a document analysis of online and social media postings created by HLS in Canada. We maintained researcher field notes, in addition to 25 semi-structured interviews and a survey. An analysis of social media postings, such as Facebook or Twitter, as well as HLS announcements, informational emails sent to students and parents, and teaching materials provided more insight into attitudes, perceptions, responses, and challenges faced by HLS leaders, teachers, and families during the pandemic. Our purpose was to consider the relationship between governmental support – or the lack thereof – and the various aspects of HLS's transformation, adaptation, and resilience during the pandemic.

Findings: Transformation of Heritage Language Schools during the COVID-19 Pandemic

Two questions guided our research: *How have the unique immigrant integration channels of HLS been disrupted or altered during the pandemic in Alberta, Canada?* and *How have HLS transformed and adapted to the challenges of the pandemic in Alberta, Canada?* In the subsequent section, we discuss the three themes we identified as the major HLS's responses to the challenges and disruptions brought by the pandemic: connectivity, community, and identity.

Connectivity

In the early months of 2020, the COVID-19 outbreak forced many schools around the globe, from elementary to postsecondary institutions, into a partial or complete closure without any indication of when in-person classes might resume. Traditionally, HLS have always struggled with a lack of space. Classroom space became a critical determinant for the functioning or closure of HLS due to the possibility of distancing to prevent the spread of COVID-19. Many HL educators had to leave the security of their physical classrooms and provide virtual teaching, unprepared and without the

---

[487] Hendricks, 2017

support of technology advisors, curriculum planners, and grade-level teams. Without the availability of funding, HLS struggled initially with the transition.

Grassroots early online transition.

The Alberta government's late response to the pandemic forced HL communities to contact relatives in their respective countries of origin to receive updates on the spread of the pandemic and on the measures implemented in different countries. Such cross-border information exchange born out of the transnational diaspora-homeland community of practice inspired the early closure of two HLS in Edmonton *before* the official school closure in the province was implemented: "It was obvious to me that what was happening there [homeland] would come here, too," a principal said (HL15). Yet the news about the pandemic was received with fear about the future of HLS, as they had to suspend their in-person activities. At this time of uncertainty, interacting in online spaces was welcome as a solution and relief: "When those two or three weeks of anxiety were taking place at the end of March [2020], when nobody knew what was going to happen, I had a couple of phone calls saying, 'So, what's going to happen?', 'So, what's happening?' And when we started Zoom, everybody went 'Ahhh' (HL18). HL practitioners spontaneously shared their early experiences of trial and error while transitioning online and made decisions that were not subjected to the lengthy formal institutional approval processes. Sharing these earlier experiences and lessons learned among the community of HL practitioners, for example, condoned WhatsApp as a primary tool of HLS' communication with their larger membership.

Though improvised, these prompt responses of HL practitioners allowed for spontaneous knowledge building in crisis, which secured most (but not all) of these schools' survival. After the early phase of critical transition and finding ground during the crisis, some HLS reached out to the Alberta government not only for information and guidance but also to offer to translate vital information concerning the pandemic for HL speakers who were not proficient in English (HL17, HL13). Despite prompt stewarding of essential information among HL community practitioners, HLS faced financial insecurity and the absence of government assistance. Out of twenty-one schools, five HLS had to search for alternative means of funding, seven schools stated that their financial situation had slightly deteriorated, and eight schools stated that their financial situation had deteriorated significantly.

Transnational collaboration.

Similar to public schools, most HLS moved their instruction online with the start of the pandemic. However, HLS' move to online teaching allowed many more participants from different geographical locations – nationally as well as internationally – to participate. In one case, online HL classes were attended by students and teachers from four different time zones: Edmonton, Montreal, and Toronto in Canada, as well as towns in Slovakia, Germany, and Ireland. In another case, former community members who had moved out of Edmonton rejoined the school when it transitioned online. The possibility to retain students who were not physically located in the HLS vicinity provided an important motivation to implement a hybrid model of HL education even post-pandemic: "With this experience, one thing we learned is that probably running the online classes simultaneously might be a thing that we would consider ...we found that some of our students moved out of the city and ... wanted to join the online classes. So, people from other Canadian cities were actually joining the class and attending the class." (HL17). Needless to say, such grassroots transnational HL education bypassed the daunting bureaucratic hurdles and was affordable. HL practitioners were building their reservoir of online teaching knowledge via informal local, regional, and transnational interactions, benefiting from the input of HL practitioners acquainted with the challenges of online teaching and learning.

Grandparents as HL educators

A transnational community of practice that facilitated the survival of HL learning in Alberta during the pandemic also resonated through the increased engagement of grandparents who assisted in online HL teaching and cultural programming while living overseas. In addition, grandparents taught grandchildren school subjects in the HL. For example, a principal and teacher at one HLS shared: "I asked my mom, and she has no English... to explain it [math] in the heritage language, and I had to translate it because sometimes kids don't know all the details in the heritage language. But mainly the conversation is in the heritage language, and she's trying to explain all this math things in the heritage language." (HL1).

In some cases, other relatives overseas mitigated the pressures of the pandemic: "My other sister, she's a professor of art... teaching at university now. She had recorded videos about art, the philosophy of art, and my kids had to watch it ... and it's family time, I said, let's watch my sister... It was an amazing experience." (HL1). As grandparents were connecting with grandchildren in new ways, the pandemic provided an opportunity for children to use online platforms to expand learning beyond HL. Even in times of crisis, "you don't stop your learning" (HL1). Due to the grandparents' inability to speak English, the increased involvement of grandparents proved to be an excellent motivation for children to learn and use the HL.

Collaboration with homelands.

Some schools noted an increased interest of their respective homelands' governments in the challenges they faced. More importantly, some HLS leaders approvingly commented on the homeland's acknowledgment of the diaspora's sustenance of heritage language and culture. As HL15[488] noted in the interview:

> So, they [homelands] know about us here, and they really appreciate our work, what we do here in the heritage language community, because it pays back, honestly. It creates a good name for the homeland. They know that some families are coming back to the homeland and, you know,

---

[488] We anonymized the interviews with HLS principals and teachers as "HL" followed by a random number attached to the anonymized HLS.

their kids speak the language, you know. So, that was a good feeling to know that they know about us and they support us a lot. (HL15)

Some countries offered free access to libraries and teaching materials or free installation of HL teaching software. In one case, the ambassador and the Minister of Education of the country of origin arranged an online meeting with HL educators in the diaspora to discuss their needs and possible support that the homeland could provide. Additional transnational online events were organized, where HL learners in the diaspora and learners in the homeland participated together, such as 24 hours of reciting poems of a famous poet. In another case, the home country produced a series of interviews aired nationally on a weekly basis. HL diaspora thus provided the homeland with vital information on pandemic measures in school systems around the world. It allowed the homeland to compare possible approaches and measures to education during the pandemic. HL diaspora also provided information about problems as well as solutions to accessibility of educational materials, student motivation, and technology issues. They described instances of collaboration between the government and NGOs or businesses: In New York, students were asked to fill in a survey, and as a reward, they received iPads for free. In other instances, companies were installing the internet for free.

Increased engagement with non-Western epistemologies & multilocal fluctuating of identities

This increased online engagement between HL cyberspora and their homelands allowed for the engagement with epistemologies unrelated to the Western code of knowledge and culture, which boosted the usage of HL during the pandemic. The increased online cultural exchange between the HL diaspora and its homeland served not only as a means to overcome the harsh impacts of the pandemic; it opened vital spaces for identity negotiation and also involved a political dimension. Firstly, belongingness to a virtual HL community of practice is determined by "learning the ways of doing, ways of being, and ways of using language which fit with that of expert members of the community."[489] Virtual cyberspora of HL practitioners whose identity was negotiated through relationality to each other represented a site where "tensions between identity positions and choices and ideologies of language and culture are foregrounded particularly because issues of position, power, and control are less established and therefore more open for choice and negotiation."[490] In other words, in transnational virtual space HL practitioners' "senses of attachment are multilocal."[491] Hence, identity fluctuates between nodal points of HL practitioners' diasporic network and the homeland.[492] In this context, concrete political opportunities emerged. In one case, the HL diaspora was allowed to vote from abroad. In another case, the HL community pushed for the possibility to vote in their respective country of origin.

Increased global collaboration.

In the fall of 2020, Canada's federal government announced a new program to provide funding to the provinces and territories to support a safe return to the classrooms. Still, HLS were not considered for this funding even though they were struggling with the same crisis and operated on much lower budgets than public schools. The exclusion of HLS from financial assistance questioned the "reciprocal model" of HL societal integration, which is defined as inclusive yet "separate[ing] learning of a language by specific ethnocultural groups."[493] During the pandemic, the government assisted public schools. It acknowledged the presence of HLS as far as it benefited from HL practitioners' voluntary translation of vital COVID-19 official guidance to other languages. Still, it failed to reciprocate the relationship and help when HLS struggled

---

[489] Paltridge, 2015, p. 16
[490] Cruickshank, 2015, p. 84
[491] Cruickshank, 2015, p. 85
[492] Ibid.
[493] Basu, 2011, p. 1313

financially. Rather than being inclusive, such an approach was exclusionary and cemented the division between official and heritage languages.

The lack of governmental support and a deteriorating financial situation fueled the resilience of HLS as they sought support in HL cyberspora and its transnational resources and collaboration. When asked, "What kind of support could be offered to help your school right now?" HLS pointed to the need for support from both the country of residence and the country of origin:

> Right now, I have two kind of really dreams. The one is to have our own, as we talked about, our own space. The second thing would be if the homeland's government or some universities there could send to our school students from university, like the University of Education, and this person would help us with how to structure the class ... I know that a heritage language school in Calgary has one young lady there now who helped them with the teaching. I would love something like that. It would be really nice. So, the space, yeah, and a student from a university in the homeland to come here and help us teach the language. (HL15)

The global collaborations were not only embraced in the direction of the country of origin towards HLS in diaspora, but they were multidirectional in the sense that HLS principals and teachers participated in international online conferences, symposia, workshops, and professional development sessions where they shared experiences and solutions to the challenges presented by the pandemics to HL communities globally. HLS built resource banks of transnationally-shared teaching materials and other resources that substantially supported the overwhelmed HL teachers. As one of the principals noted,

> Even with the coordination of those in our community in Toronto, there was a lot of feedback about how the schools were dealing with things. We had schools in Montreal as well, so they were kind of ahead of us doing things and

dealing with things. So, we kind of learned from our school peers. And through IHLA, you know, sharing information... Like the mentorship program... We shared a lot as well, and it was needed. (HL12)

Transnational mobilization of HL organizations

Following this pattern, January 31, 2021, marked a milestone in the transnational mobilization of HL organizations prompted by the impacts of the pandemic on the HL communities and language learning. Leaders of five heritage language associations from the U.S., Canada, the Netherlands, Iceland, and Ireland launched a collaborative project to create universal international guidelines for professional practices for HLS.[494]

This transnational effort to define universal principles and best practices to guide heritage language schools (HLS) was only the tip of the iceberg in revealing the pandemic's far-reaching impact on heritage language learners. The main goal of this international community of HL practitioners was to establish HL as a recognized educational category and to design adaptable guidelines that could be implemented by diverse HL groups worldwide. These goals were particularly important given the uneven global recognition of HL as an educational category.

This collaboration also inspired the creation of the *Forum of Heritage Language Coalitions in Europe* (FOHLC Europe), modeled after the *Coalition of Community-Based Heritage Language Schools* in the United States.[495] Overall, the pandemic significantly increased the connectivity of HLS at the family, community, national, and transnational levels. These new connections enabled HLS to take important steps toward the professionalization of its work, rather than becoming further marginalized.

---

[494] Aberdeen et al., 2021
[495] FOHLC Europe, 2022

Community

HLS communities ability to maintain their HL through communal, national and transnational networking, support and mobilizing while still providing vital care for precarious migrant workers, marginalized and elderly underscores HL communities' importance in building "communities of care" and "caring citizenship", which as Tungohan persuasively argued "widens the ambit of democratic participation to encourage human beings to be more collectively engaged with civic life, encouraging a more active form of democracy."[496] HLS responded to the pandemic and adapted their program to provide support to the immediate community in a variety of ways: They assisted frontline workers and community members in general by providing language support, and protected community members from increased racism, xenophobia, and inequities.

Sixteen HLS that participated in our research reported that their community members served as frontline workers. Six HLS started sewing cloth masks for the homeless, the elderly, and the hospitals, and three schools cooked or distributed food via local churches and organizations. Seven schools provided mental health support, two schools took part in blood donation, and two schools helped migrant workers. Nine schools offered free services to seniors, including grocery shopping and hospital runs. One HLS donated money to mitigate the impact of the pandemic in their homeland and sent masks and hand sanitizers to another local community in Alberta in the early stages of the pandemic.

The community continuously checked on the well-being of temporary foreign workers. The support network of heritage language schools was important when racialized temporary foreign workers were blamed for the spread of the pandemic. One HLS helped temporary foreign worker families find a place to live where they could no longer rent apartments, provided financial support, and delivered food from a communal bakery to feed them:

---

[496] Tungohan refers to Tronto, 2013; Mingol, 2013

> We, with all of our families, we always wrote emails just asking how everyone was doing, how extended members of their families were doing ... most of our students were either dropped off or picked up by an extended family member, be it an aunt or a grandparent, as well as the parents. ...we chose and wanted to make sure that our extended community was doing okay. (HL6)

HLS as first responders

During the pandemic, HLS continued to be the first responders to the needs of marginalized community members. For example, almost half of HLS communities were heavily involved in translating and sharing critical information about COVID-19 with the communities that relied on them. As one principal noted, "I consider that it's very important to send bilingual emails. Because we have several that don't understand the heritage language, the second generation. We do have a second generation of people that don't know the heritage language." (HL12)

While assisting those in need, the volunteers' identity awareness, i.e., the importance of the role of their respective HLS in grassroots communal assistance and maintaining the appearance of normalcy despite the ongoing crisis, was critical:

> We also wanted to make sure that they knew [community members in need of assistance] that we are the heritage language school, and we are important as well. Like, it is important for the community to make sure that we find solutions in difficult times as well. And that was the main thing. We are visible, we are working, we are finding solutions for our kids, we are maintaining a certain normality. Like, you know, we used to have heritage language school on Saturdays, and you will keep having school on Saturdays, but in a different way. (HL12)

Similarly, positive messages to the community and assurance about the ability to resolve any situation further enhanced the sense of community:

> It was a stressful time; everyone was anxious, everything was up in the air, and we didn't know how it would go. I wanted to also have them understand that we are always there, and we will find solutions together. We are there to help and we wanted that continuity, and I wanted that continuity for teachers as well. And it was a matter of seeing what kind of solutions can be found from the get-go. (HL12)

Confronting racism and systemic inequalities

In addition, the pandemic clearly uncovered systemic inequalities affecting the diverse groups of immigrants and migrant workers. According to Project 1907, in September 2021, "Canada continues to report a higher number of anti-Asian racism incidents per capita than the United States by over 100%."[497] The pandemic spiraled anti-Asian, anti-Black, and anti-Indigenous racism and exacerbated systemic inequalities. HLS coped with manifestations of racism to support their members. One school made this public statement:

> It has been deeply bothering to read, hear and see the recent rise in attacks on the Asian community. We are personally affected by these incidents, which have shaken up deep-rooted issues of racism felt in our society and have provided an opportunity to reflect on our personal experiences ... We are here to listen and check in with our community to ensure everyone feels safe, heard, and protected.[498]

In another case, when a student in an online adult HL class shared the experience of being subjected to an anti-Asian racial slur, the teacher opened the space for students to discuss racism openly. The collegiality of cyberspora played a critical role in sustaining HL education during times of crisis. As one of the principals noted:

> I think the important thing is showing everyone that we are resilient as communities, right? We find solutions, and if we

---

[497] Project 1907, 2022
[498] Paulovicova, McCabe, Emilsson Peskova, 2022

work together, we find solutions, and, you know, we are in this together. It's really the resilience... And knowing our worth as well... (HL12)

In this time of crisis, the sense of relationality and community belonging increased. At the same time, identity among the HL groups was negotiated through multiple nodal points of diaspora locally, regionally, and transnationally as they worked together for a common purpose: to find solutions to the challenges presented by the pandemic.[499]

Identity & Plurilingualism

The pandemic offered HL communities an opportunity to temporarily withdraw from the public education system into the privacy of individual homes, safe cultural spaces where HL and identities could thrive. Families watched movies, sang songs, prayed, read books, or wrote letters to relatives in HL, cooked traditional heritage meals, or learned traditional dancing. These activities not only allowed for increased usage of heritage languages in families during the pandemic, but they also helped children more fully embrace the heritage culture and identity. An HL principal highlighted the importance of family time that the pandemic crisis offered: "Here were benefits for lockdown because families meet, parents are at home, all together they start watching heritage language movies that they never did; living in Canada they had no time because everybody was working..." (HL1).

In another case, a mother-daughter cooking time provided a treasured opportunity to embrace HL culture: "I started cooking heritage language country cookies, and my daughter, she was helping me. We're trying to learn recipes in the heritage language, and now she knows lots of things about homeland recipes." (HL1). Overall, mothers often played a significant role in facilitating HL education at home and in HL *cyberspora*. As one HL educator noted:

---

[499] Cruickshank, 2015, p. 85

> Moms were very happy because kids did very well. Some of them are very happy just being at home spending time on writing like you said, but there are lots of negative moments, actually, but there are some benefits as well. (HL1)

In addition to increased family time, the pandemic provided children with more time to participate in HLS programming, which was offered virtually at that time. The HL classes and programs further shaped identity and belonging for the children and families. As one HL educator noted:

> The heritage language school, in our case, like it's community, right? It's the culture, it's the identity that is there. It's another place where you can find information you can rely on. You can trust that the information is trustworthy... Okay, you have the schedule for your homework. Like the work that you do at the Canadian school, and at what time are you going to listen, to speak, to play, to read, to write in the heritage language? What's their commitment? You know, where will they find space for the heritage language in the week? We really wanted them to think about ... where are you fitting in the heritage language, right? Like it is important. (HL12)

The pandemic crisis confined many to their homes for a prolonged time, but this very outcome also inspired powerful transgenerational identity affirmations. Many third- and fourth-generation Canadians became motivated to learn more about their roots and utilized online space to reach out to their ancestors' countries of origin. According to one HL principal, the schools served adult students who "want to visit their home, their ancestral homeland. That's one of the major reasons. Or, to communicate with their relatives in their ancestral homeland, as well as communicating with some of their older relatives in Canada." (HL11).

The COVID-19 pandemic school closures physically removed HL speakers from the public education system, which marginalized HL and cultures and often dehumanized HL speakers. As a result, HL were confined to culturally familiar spaces of homes and the virtual space of HL cyberspora.

Discussion and conclusions

The following objectives shaped our inquiry:

1. To explore how the unique immigrant integration channels of HLS have been disrupted or altered during the pandemic in Alberta, Canada

2. To understand how HLS have transformed and adapted to the challenges of the pandemic in Alberta, Canada.

In this section, we summarize and discuss our findings about HLS's reactions to challenges caused by the pandemic. HLS schools as communities of practice employed spontaneous, bottom-up approaches. We further discuss the transformations that the HLS underwent as a response to the challenges.

Our research points towards an exclusionary approach of provincial government towards HLS, which abundantly showed the divide between the official languages and HL. Reciprocal relations between official languages and HL, as outlined in Basu's inclusive reciprocal integration channel,[500] were not maintained during times of crisis. In particular, HLS were accepted when the provincial government needed help with translating critical information to HL communities. Still, their marginal status was confirmed when they were left to their own fates without much-needed provincial support during times of crisis. Yet, despite financial challenges, HLS continued to respond directly to the needs of its communities, representing a bottom-up, grassroots approach to integrating immigrants into society. These findings confirmed that through their strong community involvement, HLS foster different models of integration and belonging than public schools. HLS represent a community of practice whose informal interactions and input from individuals directly acquainted with the challenges on the ground

---

[500] Basu, 2011

demonstrated spontaneity in knowledge building, prompt response, and implementation of the solution in crisis. Despite the existential threat during the COVID-19 pandemic, HLS reached out to the vulnerable in the earliest stages of the pandemic and provided community care spontaneously, as opposed to the centralized and bureaucratic official top-down processes.[501]

The support network of HLS became important when racialized minorities were blamed for the spread of the pandemic. This confirms Lave and Wenger's claims about the vital importance of the community of practice.[502] Canadian media covered the conditions of marginalized communities, but the systemic inequalities received less scrutiny. The disproportionate impact of COVID-19 on racialized communities, immigrants, and migrant workers has been well documented.[503] Fears of hate-motivated crimes represented a grave concern among Edmonton's Asian community, as visible minorities in Edmonton were exposed to verbal harassment, aggression, unwanted physical contact, and cyber-racism.[504] The pandemic "exposed the front-line nature of much of the work carried out by migrant workers."[505]

HL communities faced many challenges in the transition to the online environment as a result of the pandemic. The shift to the online environment yielded new forms of transnational practices, spaces, networks, and strategies that helped to mitigate the pressures caused by the pandemic.[506] In fact, our findings document strengthening of connectivity within a "grassroots 'cyberspora'"[507] and display the "cyber geography of languages"[508] that helped to mend the disruptive impact of the pandemic on HL education. HL cyberspora allowed for the engagement with epistemic communities

---

[501] Lave & Wenger, 1991
[502] Lave and Wenger, 1991
[503] Cross & Gonzalez Benson, 2021; Helps, Silvius & Gibson, 2021
[504] CTV News Edmonton, 2021; Dubey, 2020
[505] Foley & Piper, 2020
[506] Goldring & Krishnamurti, 2007; Levitt, 2010
[507] Hatoss, 2013
[508] Pimienta, 2021, p. 9

outside of the Western code of knowledge, which empowered HL learners.[509]

The lack of support from the Canadian federal and provincial governments contributed to the resilience and transformation of HLS. During the pandemic, the financial situation of most HLS significantly worsened. The lack of governmental support pushed HLS leaders to gain new skills and to seek help in transnational resources and collaboration. One of the critical outcomes of transnational collaboration was the creation of International Guidelines for Professional Practices in Community-Based Heritage Language Schools. The guidelines aspire to "preserve heritage languages as a way of nurturing diversity, mutual respect, and inclusion."[510] With these guidelines, HLS hopes to "send the message to the global community that community-based HLS provide a crucial service to plurilingual children, their families, language communities, and society as a whole."[511] This collaboration also motivated the establishment of the Forum of Heritage Language Coalitions in Europe (FOHLC Europe), which adopted the model of the Coalition of Community-Based Heritage Language Schools in the US. Additionally, some homelands showed increased interest in their diasporas and how they were coping with the pandemic.

HLS's move online erased borders and boundaries and provided equitable access to HL education[512] to students in all geographic locations.[513] Some schools reached out to sister HLS across Canada and coordinated online teaching synchronously across several provinces. Some HLS noted increased engagement of grandparents in homelands. Grandparents in homelands assisted in online HL teaching and culture display in the form of singing, storytelling, or even cooking traditional meals, and mitigated the pressures caused by the pandemic. Many HLS in Alberta benefited from the higher

---

[509] Mignolo, 2011
[510] Aberdeen et al., 2021, p. 3
[511] Ibid., p. 4
[512] Alban Conto et al., 2020
[513] Pimienta, 2021

engagement of grandparents or relatives overseas, who alleviated the pressures faced by immigrant families with several children. HLS's move online thus expanded nodal points of diasporic network[514] and opened space for negotiation of the fluctuating identities, and articulation and affirmation of relationalities.

In our research, we advanced HL as an analytical category. We intended to elevate studies of an individual's mother language within scholarly inquiries that scrutinize structural inequalities and injustices in society. Historically, race, ethnicity, gender, class, ableism, and age are more often the focus of study in these domains. Our findings deepen our understanding of the intersecting themes of multiculturalism, plurilingualism, identity, online education and pedagogies, equity, diversity, inclusion, community, immigration, and politics, ultimately advancing heritage language studies as a critical field of inquiry. This analysis of HLS' challenges, adaptations, and transformation during the COVID-19 pandemic can inform public debate on the place of immigrants, refugees, migrant workers, and HLS in society.

In addition, this study offers a foundation for better advocacy of HLS leaders among policymakers, which is crucial for the sustainability of HLS more generally. Grassroots nature of HLS, as opposed to meso- and macro-institutional governance, allowed these small community-based schools to display promptness and flexibility in their response to the pandemic, which, as some cases indicated, helped curb the spread of the pandemic at its initial stages. HLS became the first responders reaching those in need, as opposed to a late and sluggish response trickling through centralized decision-making channels, slowed by administrative hurdles. For future policymaking, it is essential to preserve the grassroots nature of HLS with its ability to maintain the momentum of prompt decision-making and action to assist the marginalized who need urgent and immediate help at times of crisis. Providing governmental (municipal, provincial, or federal) support that does not compromise

---

[514] Cruickshank, 2015, p. 85

HLS's grassroots decision-making would allow HLS to enhance the outreach of their first response at times of crisis in familiar communal environment that, as this chapter demonstrated, often transcends borders and builds HL communities of care.

Acknowledgments

This research was funded by Athabasca University's COVID-19 Research Study Grant in 2020. We want to express our gratitude to Graduate Research Assistant Evan Supple, who transcribed and coded the interviews, and to the former coordinator of IHLA, Dr. Gertrude C. Aberdeen, for interviewing half of the research participants. Finally, we would like to express our deepest gratitude to the IHLA heritage schools' principals and teachers for participating in this research project despite the challenges they faced during the pandemic.

Chapter 13

The Challenges of Albanian Heritage Language Schools in Canada

Marigona Morina

Heritage languages are a lifeline for preserving immigrant students' linguistic and cultural identities. However, the trend of second-generation immigrants shifting away from their parents' native languages, often towards English, is a cause for concern. This chapter is a wake-up call, aiming to understand and address the challenges and obstacles faced by community-based programs in preserving heritage languages in Canada. With little documentation available on the functioning of heritage language schools in smaller communities, this research focused on Albanian, a minority language not included in official school curricula. Interviews were conducted with six teachers from Albanian Heritage Language Schools across various regions. The study identified significant challenges these schools face through thematic analysis, including public support and funding, student recruitment and motivation, curriculum and teaching materials, and teacher recruitment and training. Although the research centered on Albanian as a heritage language, the findings highlight broader issues affecting underrepresented heritage language schools. These challenges pose serious risks to the sustainability of heritage language programs. Therefore, the chapter emphasizes the need for increased attention and support for these programs to maintain immigrant communities' linguistic and cultural identities and foster a multilingual society.

Heritage Languages and Community-Based Programs

The term *heritage languages* refers to the languages spoken at home that do not dominate the broader national society.[515] Contrary to the traditional belief that parents can maintain and pass on these languages solely by speaking to their children in the heritage language, research suggests that some form of formal instruction is necessary to achieve high proficiency.[516] Thus, while heritage language education typically begins at home, it often takes on a more structured format in community schools, which strive to transmit language and culture across generations and preserve familial and ethnic community connections through cultural values and practices.[517] Unfortunately, due to the unofficial nature of these programs, they lack legitimacy for academic credit, meaning students usually do not receive formal acknowledgment of their language proficiency.[518] Although there is increasing awareness of heritage language education, there is limited research on the functioning of these programs, especially in smaller communities.[519] This lack of research is particularly problematic for minority languages, which encounter heightened difficulties due to limited institutional support, reduced teaching resources, and smaller speaker populations. Therefore, there is an urgent need for institutional recognition and sustained support for heritage language programs to foster equitable access to multilingual education.

Lee and Wright provide a comparison of Korean and Khmer community-based service-learning programs in the United States.[520] While both the Korean and Khmer communities offer HL education programs, the resources available to them differ significantly. The Korean-American community, one of the largest Asian communities in the U.S., benefits from national-level support for language

---

[515] Rothman, 2009
[516] Lao & Lee, 2009; Lee, 2002
[517] Fishman, 2001
[518] Lee & Wright, 2014
[519] Aberdeen, 2016
[520] Lee & Wright, 2014

programs, financial backing from the Korean government, and well-established networks for language teachers, along with diverse instructional materials and standardized exams. In contrast, the Khmer-American community has considerably fewer economic and human resources, lacking governmental support, widely available teaching materials, or formalized language assessment systems comparable to those for Korean.

Given the challenges faced by minority, community-based language schools, this chapter explores the case of Albanian as a Heritage Language in Canada, highlighting its unique context. The 2016 census in Canada revealed that there are more than 140 immigrant languages spoken at home by more than 7 million residents.[521] Within this multilingual landscape, Albanian remains a minority language. Thus, this chapter examines how the status of Albanian as a minority language in Canada shapes the experiences of heritage language learning and teaching.

By investigating the challenges of Albanian community-based language programs, this study sheds light on the broader struggles faced by (minority) heritage language initiatives. The chapter underscores the urgent need for greater recognition and institutional support to ensure that heritage languages remain a vibrant part of Canada's multicultural identity. In the following section, I aim to provide a contextual background on the Albanian language, as well as explore the scholarship on Albanian as a heritage language.

Albanian as a Heritage Language

Albanian (endonym: Shqip) is one of the oldest languages in Europe, spoken by approximately 7.5 million people worldwide. It is the official and primary language of Albania and holds principal and co-official status in Kosovo. Albanian is also spoken across the Balkan Peninsula, especially in Northern Macedonia, Southern Serbia, Southern Montenegro, and Northern Greece, with some dialects present in Southern Italy and Türkiye. Thus, the Albanian language serves as a unifying force for ethnic Albanians, bridging various

---

[521] Statistics Canada, 2017

geographical and political gaps. While mainly spoken in the Balkans, though, Albanian is unique as the only non-Slavic language in the region, part of the Indo-European family but forming its own distinct branch. Despite this linguistic individuality, Albanian is not singular;[522] it consists of two primary dialects, Geg and Tosk, each containing further subdivisions. Figure 1 shows a map of Albanian dialects and their subdivisions,[523] color-coded and shaded.[524]

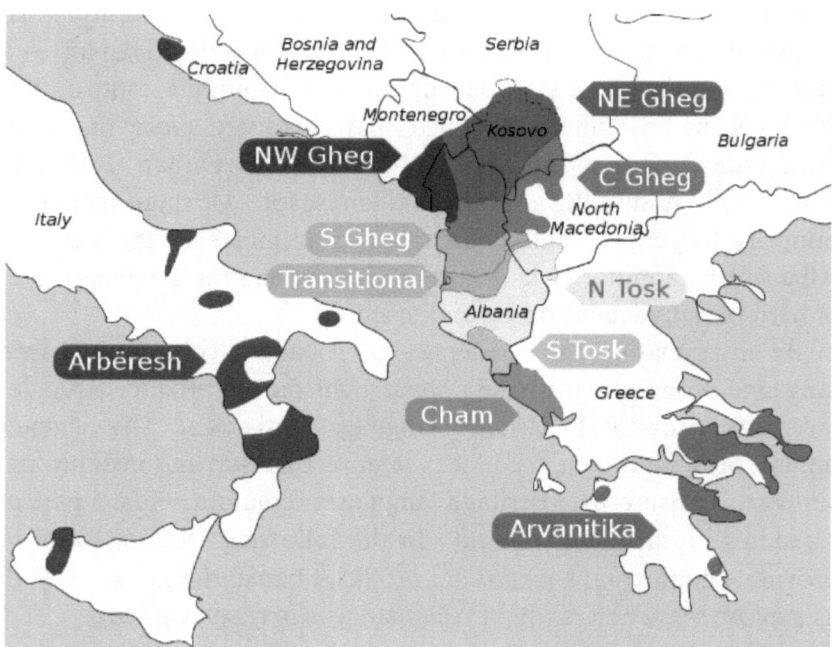

Figure 1. Map of Albanian-speaking areas with major subdivisions[522]

Despite the countries shown on the map above, the Albanian language has spread to Europe and beyond through the Albanian diaspora, which, according to the United Nations, is one of the largest diasporas, with 30.7% of the native-born population living abroad.[525] However, despite the overall size of the Albanian diaspora,

---

[522] Hyllested & Joseph, 2022
[523] as displayed by Coretta et al. 2022
[524] according to Gjinari 1988 and Elsie and Gross 2009
[525] United Nations, 2020

research on Albanian as a heritage language remains limited. The existing literature on Albanian as a heritage language is mainly in the context of Greece, where the Albanian community represents almost half of the registered immigrant population,[526] constituting the largest immigrant community.[527] While Greek studies provide insights into Albanian heritage language, it is crucial to recognize that the experiences of Albanian heritage language speakers can differ significantly across various countries due to differing social, political, and geographical contexts.

Therefore, this chapter focuses on the context of Canada, where over 7 million residents speak an immigrant language at home, excluding Indigenous languages.[528] This represents more than 20% of Canada's population and marks a nearly 15% increase since the 2011 census, reflecting the country's growing linguistic diversity. In this pool of languages spoken in Canada, Albanian holds a minority status as the mother tongue of 29,265 people and the most spoken language at home for 14,110 people.[529] Therefore, the chapter seeks to explore how the status of 'minority language' shapes the experiences of Albanian heritage language learning and teaching in this particular setting.

Gathering Teacher Stories and Perspectives of Albanian Heritage Language Learning and Teaching in Canada

This chapter draws from a subset of previously unpublished data generated as part of my doctoral dissertation,[530] which examined heritage language learner identities in Albanian Heritage Language Schools in Canada. The broader study adopts a qualitative research approach, using interviews to explore the perspectives of teachers, parents, and students. Within this larger study, this chapter specifically examines the challenges of sustaining and operating

---

[526] OECD, 2024
[527] Labrianidis & Hatziprokopiou, 2005
[528] Statistics Canada, 2016
[529] Statistics Canada, 2021
[530] Morina, 2025

Albanian Heritage Language Schools across Canada, as expressed by teachers. Participating teachers were recruited through Albanian associations and heritage language schools across Canada, which, upon being contacted by the researcher, informed teachers about the study, allowing those interested to volunteer for participation. A total of eight participants (seven language teachers and one traditional dancing instructor) from three provinces participated in one-hour-long, semi-structured interviews.

The interviews followed a structured yet flexible format, allowing teachers to share their experiences and perspectives in depth. The process began with participants introducing themselves, discussing their qualifications, and describing their experiences in teaching Albanian as a heritage language. This initial phase provided context for understanding their professional backgrounds and personal connections to heritage language education. Following this, teachers were asked about their perceptions of the importance of heritage language maintenance. They reflected on the role of the Albanian language in students' identities, academic development, and connections to their cultural heritage. Next, the discussion shifted to teachers' perspectives on how students and parents perceive the significance of heritage language maintenance. Participants shared their observations on students' attitudes toward learning Albanian and the level of parental involvement and support in the process. Finally, teachers were asked about the challenges they face in teaching Albanian as a heritage language. This included discussions on curriculum limitations, resource availability, student engagement, and broader systemic barriers that impact heritage language education. The structured flow of the interview allowed for a comprehensive exploration of teachers' insights while ensuring that key aspects of heritage language teaching were addressed.

The interviews were conducted online via Zoom, audio-recorded with participants' consent, and transcribed for analysis. The participants had the option to choose their preferred language to articulate their experiences and concerns. The audio-recordings were transcribed using the transcription software *Shqip.ai*, which transcribes audio to text in the Albanian language. The researcher then double-checked the transcription for accuracy. The transcripts were color-coded to identify the challenges as faced by Albanian Heritage Language Schools across Canada, and further discussed through a micro-, meso-, and macro- framework.

For this study, ethics approval was obtained from the Institutional Review Board of the University of Calgary. Participating teachers provided informed consent and were made aware that, due to the limited number of Albanian heritage language teachers in their area, their identities might be recognizable. However, all participants willingly chose to participate without anonymity.

Albanian Heritage Language Teacher Voices and Perspectives

The thematic analysis of individual interviews with Albanian Heritage Language Teachers in Canada revealed significant challenges the schools face, such as public support and funding, student recruitment and motivation, curriculum and teaching materials, and teacher recruitment and training.

Public Support and Funding

The study revealed that historically, finances have been one of the biggest challenges confronting Albanian Heritage Language Schools, as they do not receive any public support or funding. In provinces where Albanian is recognized as a heritage language, the government provides access to facilities, pays the teachers, and supplies some teaching materials. This is the case in Ontario, the province with the highest concentration of the Albanian population in Canada. However, participating teachers from Ontario explain that for their classes to be funded, they need a certain number of students to remain enrolled throughout the year, or otherwise they lose funding.

This also explains how the same level of support is unavailable in most other provinces, where Albanian is categorized as a minority language. Consequently, these schools do not receive any public funding from either the host country or the country of origin. To operate, Albanian Heritage Language Schools must rely on community fundraising and charge tuition to students who wish to enroll. Unfortunately, the small number of students means that tuition fees alone are insufficient to cover the school's operating costs. Furthermore, tuition cannot be set too high, as this would deter potential students from enrolling. For example, as Ms. Marsela Kola explained, the Albanian Heritage Language School in Calgary, which enrolls around 20 heritage language learners, estimates that the Albanian Canadian Association in Calgary contributes 10,000 CAD per year to help cover the school's operating expenses, as the school itself cannot meet all its financial needs. The school board, however, acknowledges that it receives some financial support from non-profit organizations to help cover the costs.

Diversity of Students' Age and Language Skills

Due to the small number of enrolled students, most of the Albanian Heritage Language Schools in Canada operate with only two class groups, encompassing a broad age range from 4 to 11 years old. In addition to age diversity, students vary significantly in their language proficiency, ranging from those with a strong command of the language to those with little prior exposure. This combination of differing ages and language abilities within the same classroom presents a considerable challenge for teachers, who must adapt their instruction to meet the diverse learning needs of all students. For instance, a current teacher in Calgary, Ms. Bedrana Berberi, explains how having students with various language skills is particularly challenging. In particular, she mentioned a recent case where one student in the class with older peers chose to leave the school because he felt embarrassed for being the only one who did not know any Albanian.

However, the experience of one of the former teachers in Ontario shows how even when children have similar proficiency in the heritage language, the varying ages across them create a layer of challenge for teachers. Specifically, Ms. Liri Leka explained how "the students' range when we first started with classes was from 4-15 years old who had zero or minimal [heritage] language skills, so we had to think how to make learning fun for all of them, and the challenge was that what was fun for the younger students definitely wasn't for the older ones.... like learning the alphabet... You couldn't just teach the 15-year-olds the basic ABCs the way you teach it to young students... You had to make it fun for them as well, otherwise they would not come."

As participating teachers explained, the diversity in students' age and language skills is problematic not only for teachers but for students as well, as sometimes it negatively affects their desire to attend the school. The topic of student recruitment and motivation is further elaborated in the following section.

Student Recruitment and Motivation

Many Albanian Heritage Language Schools across Canada are experiencing a decline in student enrollment, despite the fact that the Albanian community has grown over the years. For instance, Ms. Liri Leka, a former Albanian Heritage Language Teacher in the province of Ontario, explained how, "at the time, we were a small community with around 3000 people, whereas now we are over 40,000. But the interest was continuously growing, as from a group of 20 students we doubled, and then the venue could not host us anymore, so we started looking for alternatives." Whereas Ms. Mirka, a current Albanian Heritage Language Teacher in the same province, talks about how the class risks closure due to the small number of enrolled students. Furthermore, Ms. Mirka expressed how when teachers advocate for the significance of heritage language maintenance, they are often subject to community prejudice, as if their primary concern is self-interest.

Teachers attribute the lack of students' participation in heritage classes to several factors, including underestimating the importance of maintaining the heritage language. They also note that adolescent students are particularly reluctant to attend, leaving schools with mostly younger children. Specifically, participating schools claimed that they have students up to twelve years old, after which age the school claims that recruitment is almost impossible. Additionally, motivation among families has generally decreased over time, with many teachers recalling a period when these schools had significantly more students than they do today, although the community is growing. The decline in students' registration in heritage language schools raises concerns about the long-term sustainability of heritage language education and the ability of these schools to foster linguistic and cultural connections among younger generations.

Curriculum and Teaching Materials

The Albanian Heritage Language Schools across Canada typically use the formal textbooks that are utilized in Albania and Kosovo. Previously, this presented a challenge since Albanian-speaking countries, like Albania and Kosovo, had different textbooks. This was particularly problematic because the schools enrolled students originating from both countries, and there was a concern that students from one group might feel excluded if a different book was chosen over the other. Therefore, participating teachers explained that they often tried to utilize both books, which was overwhelming not only for them but also for the students. To date, however, progress has been made toward a unified textbook, and now only one version is in use.

Despite this step forward, teachers at Albanian Heritage Language Schools in Canada feel that the unified book still does not adequately meet the needs of children in the diaspora. For example, lessons in the textbooks assume that students have daily exposure to Albanian, using more complex vocabulary, grammar structures, and even cultural references unfamiliar to those growing up in an English-dominant environment. This disconnect often creates a need for teachers to modify content on the spot by simplifying language or creating additional materials that are more relatable to students' lived experiences in Canada.

Some argue that even a book specifically designed for all diaspora students would fall short, as it must also reflect the culture of the host country. For instance, one of the teachers said, "The Albanian Heritage Language School is more than just a language school. It's a place where children learn about history and culture, not only language. So, when teaching the language, we aim to incorporate many cultural elements. However, since most of these children were born here, we want to ensure they feel included and that we also integrate aspects of the local society." Similarly, another teacher mentioned how, especially during holidays, she prepares activities that incorporate both Albanian and Canadian traditions. This approach allows students to see their heritage as something that coexists with their Canadian identity, rather than as separate or conflicting.

As tailored materials and activities are essential in making heritage language learning meaningful and culturally responsive, teachers at Albanian Heritage Language Schools in Canada often need to create their own materials, such as posters and handouts. Since many teachers work on a volunteer basis or have other full-time jobs, creating customized materials outside of teaching hours adds considerable pressure and requires a significant personal commitment to sustain culturally relevant and engaging instruction.

Teacher Prep Time

Heritage language (HL) teachers often face a significant challenge in terms of the amount of preparation required for their classes, largely due to the lack of suitable teaching materials. Participating teachers shared that heritage language classes in their provinces are typically held on Saturdays. Since heritage language schools generally are held during the weekends, teachers, many of whom already have full-time jobs, often in teaching, find themselves having to balance the demands of their primary employment with the added responsibility of preparing and teaching HL classes. Specifically, five out of eight participating teachers indicated that while teaching at heritage language schools, they also worked at other schools. This workload effectively results in the loss of one of their weekend days, creating an additional burden on teachers who are already stretched thin.

The absence of appropriate resources further exacerbates this situation, as teachers are compelled to spend considerable time developing or adapting materials that can effectively meet the diverse needs of their student populations. For instance, during the interviews, Ms. Mirka Hallidri and Ms. Valbona Ahmeti shared copies of the handouts that they had created for students; handouts that reflect students' language needs as well as their hybrid identities.

However, participating teachers also expressed that creating such materials takes time and commitment. While this situation is deeply rooted in their passion for language and community, it can contribute to teachers' burnout, especially in the absence of broader institutional support.

Teacher Recruitment and Training

Teachers working in Albanian Heritage Language Schools throughout Canada exhibit a profound commitment to fostering community engagement and cultural preservation. Many of these educators are driven by a passion for teaching and promoting the Albanian language and heritage among younger generations. However, a notable challenge arises as some teachers may not possess formal education credentials or specialized training in language instruction, particularly in the context of Albanian Heritage Language education. For example, one of the eight participating teachers lacked an academic background in education, four teachers had a background in education but not specifically in Albanian, and three held degrees in Albanian language teaching. However, even among those who held degrees in Albanian language teaching, their qualifications were not specifically tailored for teaching the diaspora. This suggests that their training might have focused on general Albanian language instruction, rather than the unique cultural and linguistic needs of the diaspora communities. For instance, one of the teachers said, "Besides having taught for nearly twenty years in Albania, teaching the language in a different context presented unique differences that I had to adapt to to ensure effective learning." This reflection also reveals another layer of the challenges with teacher recruitment and training, as a lot of Albanian heritage language teachers begin teaching heritage languages as newcomers, often possessing little to no experience within the Canadian school context. They may also be unfamiliar with the specific pedagogical approaches and cultural nuances necessary for effectively engaging students in the classroom. This lack of structured training can impact their effectiveness in delivering a comprehensive and culturally rich curriculum, highlighting the need for further professional development and support in the field.

A Multilevel Analysis of the Identified Challenges

The findings of this study underscore the challenges and opportunities in Albanian Heritage Language (HL) education in Canada, which can be understood through the Micro, Meso, and Macro frameworks. This framework allows for a comprehensive analysis of the interconnected factors affecting heritage language schools, from individual teacher experiences to broader institutional and societal structures. Connecting this with the research from Lee and Wright,[531] it becomes clear that many of the issues faced by Albanian HL education in Canada mirror the challenges identified in community-based HL programs globally.

Micro-Level: Teachers and Students in the Classroom

At the micro level, the study highlights the significant role that individual teachers and students play in shaping the outcomes of Albanian HL education. The teachers interviewed in this study generally have formal education training, though not necessarily in Albanian language instruction. This contrasts with Lee and Wright's findings, where many HL teachers lack formal educational training. The Albanian teachers in this study, while proficient in pedagogy, still face challenges related to the specific needs of HL learners, such as the lack of formal heritage language teaching resources and strategies. However, as Lee and Wright suggest, the gap between teachers' general educational training and the specialized demands of HL education can hinder teaching effectiveness. Therefore, professional development focused on heritage language pedagogy could help teachers address these challenges and better support students at different proficiency levels.

Furthermore, the study mirrors Lee and Wright's findings regarding student perceptions of HL education. In Albanian HL schools, students' motivation and confidence are key factors

---

[531] Lee & Wright, 2014

influencing enrollment and retention. As Lee and Wright note, many students do not perceive HL education as valuable, especially when it conflicts with other extracurricular activities that hold greater societal prestige. However, it is important to note that in the current study, most ideas about students' motivation for HL are derived from teachers' perceptions rather than firsthand accounts from the students themselves, which may influence the findings and interpretations. The issue of a student dropping out due to embarrassment about their lack of proficiency underscores the need for more inclusive and supportive teaching strategies that foster a sense of belonging. Similar to the suggestions made by Lee and Wright, incorporating peer support and differentiated instruction would help address issues of isolation and encourage greater engagement.

Meso-Level: Community, Schools, and Institutional Support

At the meso level, the study reveals how community engagement, school administration, and institutional support play a significant role in shaping the sustainability of Albanian HL education. The reliance on community funding and volunteer work, as well as the lack of formal institutional support, mirrors the challenges described by Lee and Wright in community-based HL programs. Lee and Wright's research highlights the difficulty of sustaining HL programs without adequate financial resources, infrastructure, and organizational support. In this study, the dependence on textbooks from Albania and Kosovo presents both opportunities and challenges. While these resources offer a foundation for instruction, they often do not reflect the linguistic realities and cultural contexts of Albanian students in Canada, as Lee and Wright similarly find with textbooks used in community-based HL programs. The creation of locally relevant, culturally specific teaching materials could alleviate some of these challenges and improve student engagement and learning outcomes.

Moreover, the study indicates that the Albanian HL schools often struggle with logistical challenges, such as limited classroom space and resources. Lee and Wright similarly note that many HL programs face space constraints, which limit the ability to offer classes tailored to different age groups and proficiency levels. This often leads to older students being placed in classrooms with younger ones, creating mismatches that can hinder learning. The development of more flexible, resource-rich environments for HL education, supported by both community organizations and educational institutions, would help resolve these issues and improve the quality of education.

Macro-Level: Policy, Public Support, and Societal Attitudes

At the macro level, the study underscores the absence of public funding and institutional support for Albanian HL education in many provinces, reflecting broader issues of linguistic inclusivity in Canadian educational policy. In Ontario, where Albanian is officially recognized as a heritage language, schools benefit from government support in terms of facilities, teacher salaries, and teaching materials. However, in provinces where Albanian is not recognized as a heritage language, schools must rely on tuition fees and community fundraising, making them less accessible and more vulnerable to closure. Lee and Wright highlight how the lack of institutional recognition for HL programs is a major obstacle to their sustainability.

Furthermore, the broader societal perception of heritage languages as non-essential for economic or social mobility, as discussed in the study, reflects Lee and Wright's findings about the devaluation of HL education in many communities. The study suggests that advocacy efforts and awareness campaigns are needed to emphasize the cognitive, cultural, and social benefits of bilingualism. By promoting the value of heritage language education, these initiatives could shift public perceptions and increase enrollment and retention rates.

Implications and Call for Action

The challenges faced by Albanian HL schools in Canada necessitate immediate and targeted support from multiple stakeholders, including policymakers, educational institutions, and the Albanian-Canadian community. These schools play a critical role in preserving linguistic and cultural heritage, fostering bilingual competencies, and strengthening community identity. Without adequate support, their sustainability is at risk, which could lead to a gradual erosion of the Albanian language among younger generations. This reality is underscored by the fact that the challenges faced by Albanian heritage language schools remain strikingly similar to those identified in studies conducted a decade ago. This persistence suggests that little has changed in terms of policy support, institutional recognition, or community-driven interventions. While previous studies have identified these issues, the ongoing struggles of Albanian HL schools highlight an urgent need for targeted interventions, greater institutional support, and policy reforms.

Policymakers should consider integrating HL programs into broader educational initiatives by providing financial assistance, teacher training opportunities, and curriculum development support. Institutions of higher education and linguistic organizations can also contribute by offering research-based recommendations, professional development workshops, and resource-sharing platforms tailored to the needs of HL educators. Community engagement remains paramount in ensuring the longevity of these schools. Increased awareness campaigns highlighting the benefits of bilingualism, along with strategic partnerships with local businesses and cultural organizations, can facilitate fundraising efforts and advocacy work. Additionally, heritage language schools can explore innovative models, such as hybrid or online instruction, to reach a broader student base and accommodate the busy schedules of immigrant families. This chapter, therefore, calls for renewed attention to these challenges, advocating for meaningful action to support Albanian heritage language learning and maintenance.

Conclusion

This chapter demonstrates how challenges faced by Albanian HL schools in Canada are deeply interconnected across micro, meso, and macro levels. While teachers demonstrate remarkable dedication, their efforts are constrained by a lack of training, resources, and institutional support. Community-driven initiatives sustain these schools, but declining student enrollment and insufficient funding threaten their long-term viability. Addressing these challenges requires a multi-level approach, including improved pedagogical training, the development of diaspora-specific materials, enhanced community engagement, and policy advocacy for greater public support. By recognizing the importance of heritage language education and implementing targeted interventions at all levels, stakeholders can work toward a more sustainable and effective model for preserving Albanian linguistic and cultural heritage in Canada.

Although this research centers on Albanian as a heritage language, the findings reflect broader issues affecting underrepresented heritage language schools across Canada. The challenges of teacher training, resource scarcity, and limited institutional recognition are not unique to the Albanian community but are shared by many heritage language programs. Moreover, these challenges have been persistent through decades, posing serious risks to the sustainability of such programs, potentially accelerating language loss and weakening cultural ties within immigrant communities. Therefore, this chapter emphasizes the urgent need for increased attention and support for heritage language programs, not only to preserve individual linguistic traditions but also to foster a more inclusive and multilingual Canadian society.

Acknowledgement

I want to thank the Albanian Heritage Language Teachers in Canada, especially the participants of this study, Liri Leka, Adriana Fishta Bejko, Danjela Lumani, Zoica Dhamo, Ina Kocaqi Xoxa, Marsela Kola, Bedrana Berberi, Mirka Hallidri, and Valbona Ahmeti, for their enormous contribution to the community through Albanian Heritage Language Schools.

Chapter 14

Home is a Language: Building Diaspora Belonging Through Heritage Tongues.

Djeneba Deby Bagayoko

Human beings have moved across the globe since the dawn of time. Wherever they went, whether temporarily or definitively, of their own will or because of forces outside of their control, for trade, politics, religion, or in quest of more knowledge, humans have left their footprints on the earth and their linguistic mark on the societies they encountered. Moving is like breathing for the human race, for, as the Burkinabe scholar, writer, and activist Joseph Ki-Zerbo said, « N'an laara, an saara ». If we lie down (or sleep), we die. Staying still in one place, like when we sleep, is synonymous with death. Being awake and movement are, on the other hand, life. With movement, we have shifted and influenced cultures inside and outside our own from time immemorial.

Of those adventurers who travelled the world and settled elsewhere, we can say that they brought into being and birthed the concept of heritage language. Heritage in general discourse is what is passed down from one generation to the next. It is legacy, memory of the recent and not so recent past, material as well as immaterial treasures, things, and ideas that ground us and connect us with our ancestors. Language is what we use to communicate, to exchange ideas, and to know about one another. Whether it be speech, sign language, body language, or facial expressions, language is the key to interaction, knowledge, and community. But what happens when two people meet, and they do not share the same key to unlocking the door of comprehension? The very thing that builds communities that share the same idiom could cause isolation when tongues are unintelligible. This is what most people leaving home are faced with.

Heritage languages are the tongues that migrants pack with them, together with hopes and dreams of a better future for themselves and their families. It is the language that they will mostly maintain in the house in the new country and hopefully pass on to their children, whether born in their parents' country or in the new one. As a consequence, this means that most, if not all, children of immigrant parents are welcomed into the world by their parents' tongue, regardless of location, and the foreign country's national language. In the first 3 to 6 years, depending on whether or not the child is enrolled to attend kindergarten, they will almost exclusively be surrounded by the sounds of their family's tongue, which will be their first and mother tongue. As they age and are obligated to enter institutions like the school, thus exiting their bubble and entering the dominant culture, the first tongue could more or less speedily be downgraded. I emphasize the verb could because some families continue to use their language among themselves and in the house, while reserving the language of the dominant culture for the public sphere. Therefore, a child could become anywhere from a fluent speaker to a receptive bilingual. The latter is quite common, and I am one of the many children of immigrants who, although I can perfectly understand Bamanankan, as soon as I try to utter a complex phrase, the vocabulary I believed was anchored in my brain washes away. But even when we feel limited in our ability to communicate in our heritage language, our bi- and multilingual parents can engineer and build bridges across majority and minority cultures.

The vector and vessel by which heritage languages become such, through which they travel, and are contained, are immigrants and people with an immigration background. We can divide immigrants from the global South and hitherto colonized regions into two groups:

1. Those who migrate to the former colonizer.
2. Those who, out of spite or because of better opportunities in other countries, move to regions that do not share a colonial past with their homeland.

The advantage that the first group has over the second is represented by language. Although there are many exceptions, mainly due to education level, social and economic class, gender expectations when it comes to schooling, there is a non-negligible likelihood that any given person who decides to leave their country to travel to the former colonial power has a basic understanding and basic mastery of the latter's tongue. It is not by simple coincidence that citizens from Mali, Côte d'Ivoire, or Guinea Conakry migrate to France or Canada. At the same time, people from Kenya, Zimbabwe, and Nigeria pick the U.K. or the U.S. as their destination. They have already been acculturated and accustomed to those Western countries via media, education, and language. Although being the first wave or generation of the era to migrate is never easy, knowing the language is one less barrier to settlement.

The second group is made up of people who, like my family, decided to move to a country—Italy—that was not involved in any direct colonial effort toward our country of origin. Unbeknownst to many people in Mali even today, French is not the national language of *Lo Stivale* ("the Boot"). Those who lived through colonialism and still deal with its consequences equate their (ex) colonial master to the entirety of Europe or the West. France, thus, represents the whole continent of Europe. Linguistically unprepared, the first migrants either drew on their education to learn the new Romance language or relied on benevolent hosts—namely, the Church. The Church, improvised or well-established schools, and workplaces were the first nuclei where linguistic social networks began to form. These were the places and institutions where migrants could meet people of the same or similar cultural, ethnic, religious, and linguistic backgrounds and, in turn, create their own web of social connections. The main factors that determine which country to select as a destination are far from random. One does not simply spin the globe, close their eyes, and point their index finger anywhere like Prince Akeem did in *Coming to America*. Multiple elements are considered, and different influences play their part. First of all, the host country's reputation and renown. Depending on one's exposure, the home country's history, the host nation's world positionality, and prestige, the choice may differ. Until recent times, central and northern European countries, Canada, and the United States dominated aspiring immigrants' dreams; we now see a shift towards Asian countries when it comes to leaving Africa altogether. The second point that is considered is who has already migrated there. Word of mouth, hearsay, and visits back home can reassure aspiring migrants of the possibility of having an anchor in the new country. Knowing someone who knows someone abroad is as valid and important as securing paperwork.

Work and job opportunities are generally concentrated in big cities. Consequently, migrant communities often live in metropoles or their surrounding areas, which become focal points of attraction. The migrant communities that have already established themselves encourage, influence, and support newer flows. In *Heritage languages and socialization: an introduction,* Francisco Moreno-Fernández and Óscar Loureda Lamas state that these networks:

> Form a social capital that acts as a support system in the various phases of migration: in the selection of a destination as a knock-on effect created by channels of information about the opportunities in a given region; in the arrival phase, by providing information about the necessary procedures (e.g. bureaucracy, housing, work); and in the settlement phase, as agents for social integration (e.g. associationism, the maintenance of traditions).[532]

Most social networking is done informally. Institutions may facilitate purposeful encounters with events and initiatives created ad hoc for migrants, but it is often the individual who will search, establish connections, or further institutional work. A couple of examples include the following: a new kid who enrolls in school may

---

[532] Moreno-Fernández & Lamas, 2023

be classmates with someone with the same or a similar origin. The child or their parents may approach the newcomer and their family, offer a welcoming hand, and support with school bureaucracy and language acquisition, creating a new bond. If the school as an institution decides to interfere, it may be done through socially conscious teachers who see the benefit in bringing the newcomer together with more seasoned minorities.

When ethnic belonging is non-existent or a non-factor, religion can be the unifier. In the West, where the majority population is Christian, the adherents of other beliefs like Buddhism, Hinduism, or Islam may get together, especially when inquiring about places of worship where they can maintain their faith and practice it in community.

In religious communities, new migrant populations will find veterans as well as their offspring. It is safe to assume that because of age and place of birth, both sets of migrants will form relationships more quickly and more easily than a new migrant would with a second generation or child of an immigrant. Conversely, children of immigrants might find support with their agemates, especially if they are in school. The reason for choosing the word might lie here: connection and language proficiency are intertwined. The more in tune one is with their heritage language, the more comfortable they will be when interacting with people of the same background, fostering solidarity, support, and bonds that will strengthen integration efforts. According to Chen, Zhou, and Uchikoshi, the more a child is exposed to and uses their heritage language, the more positive opinions they will have in regard to their ethnicity.[533]

On the other hand, if the heritage language is neglected, a child might develop an adverse relationship towards all those associated with it, from the parents themselves to other migrants.[534] This holds particularly in contexts where non-Western cultures are dismissed, devalued, and are at the receiving end of stereotypes, xenophobia, and/or racism. Being a child of immigrants often means being

---

[533] Chen, Zhou, & Uchikoshi, 2020
[534] Chen et al., 2018

ashamed of one's culture and trying to assimilate into the dominant one by shunning any association with one's parents' ethnicity and origin. Internalized racism creates an obstacle that can take years to face and dismantle. When language is valued, however, children develop better attitudes towards their native culture and the ability to empathize with newer generations of migrants.

Families grounded in their mother cultures and idioms can create a site of resilience. On the one hand, parents hold on and pass down cultural norms, ethics, and values. On the other hand, children are taught pride and hold their heads up high despite individual, societal, or institutional attacks on their status as « perpetual foreigners ». Donald Lowe praised the sense of hearing and sound[535] and emphasized how speech is what really brings people closer to one another. Communication creates a site of comfort, reliability, and even resistance because, in spite of the external worlds and struggles, it connects people who are part of a minority. Language becomes the glue that holds together families and communities and offers a safety net to newcomers.

Empathizing and sympathizing with migrants, old and new, is one of the implicit teachings imparted to me, along with aiding them whenever possible.

The police are known for racial profiling, and anyone who « fits the description » or is already on file can expect constant surveillance and harassment. Having legitimate papers or being naturalized does not shield racialized people from scrutiny.

One sunny afternoon after work, as I walked towards my bus stop, I witnessed a scene that made my heart sink. On the other side of the road, a man I recognized was surrounded by around four police officers. At the green light, I walked right up to him and asked what was going on. I sensed the surprise of the officer to my left at my intervention, so I said that I was his interpreter. He was one of the many Malian asylum seekers I accompanied in their paper quest. My action gave courage to other bystanders, namely two men of

---

[535] Oyěwùmí, 1997

Senegalese origin and a woman of Moroccan descent. Had it not been for my exposure to my heritage language and my role as interpreter, I might not have intervened, as I would not have seen myself as a native and would not have identified as an immigrant.

The advantage I personally had was the ability to navigate two worlds and two languages as a child of immigrants and, in my professional capacity, as an interpreter. The relative power that comes with the job is the chance to provide assistance to asylum seekers, facilitate network building, and institutional processes. One Italian-speaking member of the commission that has to collect the story and reason of a person leaving their country, and one who speaks Bamanankan, Wolof, or even French, would never meet halfway. Interpreters make the encounter possible. The main limit to the role is the time constraints, which do not fully allow interpreters to transpose cultural and other norms from one idiom to another. For instance, life without Internet or Wi-Fi is now unfathomable to Westerners. For many Africans, however, the dependence on it is not as central to life as it is in Europe. Its prohibitive prices and, at times, unreliability make it an unjust struggle for Africans to be connected, whereas in the West, we can barely function without it. When an asylum seeker I worked for mentioned how the center he was hosted in offered him Wi-Fi « only », he meant that the Internet was not a priority. I could read those unspoken lines and simultaneously hear the irritation in the commissioner's voice. Thankfully, before I could bridge the cultural gap, he showed his cellular phone to demonstrate that it would not have connected to the World Wide Web anyway, since it was not a smartphone. Although interpreters are tasked with translating verbal words, in our translation, we have to include all the non-verbal cues to make sure the translation is accurate, and nothing gets lost, especially when the asylum seeker is not as proactive and cannot themselves see and decipher the commissioner's body language.

Conversely, a young Malian refugee could not really grasp the importance attributed to ID cards to prove his nationality. He kept reiterating that he was a real Malian. If that could have worked in his homeland as a native and indigenous inhabitant, in the West, that verbal statement as a foreigner was not sufficient to prove his national belonging. Two meetings were needed to try to make him understand the type of formality that Italian institutions required.

The above-mentioned are examples of higher social competence.[536] Being soaked in heritage languages means acquiring social and cultural sensitivities, knowledge of cultural values, ethics, and manners, age- and/or gender-related social protocols, which allow heritage language speakers to understand a range of cultural and linguistic cues.

Oral or written translation is not merely about transposing one word or sentence from language A into language B. There are nuances, double entendre, cultural and social references, registers, and the whole plethora of communication we perform through our bodies. And how does one get all of that onto cold paper? Italian, being my first language, and Bamanankan, my heritage language, put me in a perfect position where I knew how to give justice to asylum seekers' accounts and reasons for leaving. There is a certain poetry and drama that I could understand and capture while ensuring it transpired in Italian too. Weeks or months after the interview, refugees would see me on the street, recognize me, and thank me for helping them get their papers. But it was not my doing. The only thing I did was to guarantee an accurate and culturally adequate translation.

Completely disconnected and separate from my work, my parents were on their mission to create a network for newcomers to give them communal support. For about 7 years, my parents have welcomed a group of people into their household.

In more recent years, my mother, as well as my Nigerian neighbor, has been approached at bus stops or train stations by other African people trying to strike up a conversation or asking for help. At times, they attempt to speak Italian, but at times, just by looking at my mother's face, they guess or know the region she is from, so they start

---

[536] Chen et al., 2018

talking in Bamanankan, Jula, or Wolof. There is power in familiarity, or better yet, familiar faces. People who look and sound like us inspire trust. Three ladies came by the house to meet the rest of the family, talk more with my parents, and get some insight and advice as senior members. From family issues to adjusting to a new life, new language, and institutional barriers, my parents provide priceless guidelines on how to navigate the system and the dominant society.

Connections and community network building are crucial to the insertion of any person in a new context. Even enslavers knew this and, while relatively rare, some of them used common linguistic backgrounds as an asset. Idioms like Mandinka have left their mark in the world through one of the most brutal institutions in human history: the human trafficking enterprise known as the Trans-Atlantic slave trade. Enslavers generally forbade the use of African languages on the plantation to prevent enslaved Africans from communicating among themselves. At the same time, masters would have been left clueless about the nature of their speech. There were, however, two places that went against this trend.

In *Bound to Africa: The Mandinka Legacy in the New World*, Schaffer noted that slavers in Charleston and Georgia preferred to enslave Africans belonging to the Mande nation. The rationale behind this choice was an amazingly simple and practical one. Slave masters created a homogenous linguistic network so that the more seasoned enslaved Africans could bridge the linguistic gap between new enslaved people and enslavers.[537] They needed people already familiar with the system, the plantation, the big house life, as well as colonial languages, to quickly insert the newly enslaved Africans into the slavery production chain and institution.

Aside from the crude and cruel reality of chattel slavery, displacement in the form of immigration creates similar conditions where home travels with the people and in the language. Without a community, however, the home pillars would crumble. So how does the network build and sustain itself? There are many examples, such

---

[537] Schaffer, 2005

as cultural and religious celebrations, weddings, independence days, new births, funerals, and what we call pare in Bamanankan. Known as tontine on this side of the Mediterranean, it is a system that, although monetary and economic in nature, actually centers trust and solidarity. Pare is a great tool to mobilize and pool resources, which can be used to help people save money, buy a ticket to travel back home, or put a down payment on a mortgage. In some instances, religious communities come together to help transport a defunct person's body to their place of origin. This is how a community solidifies itself.

Through informal channels, new migrants get priceless advice and support from filling out papers to finding jobs and a place to rent. Older generations can provide job recommendations and can go as far as offering training or keeping an open line for bosses and managers when there is a linguistic chasm. If they are in touch with their former landlord and have maintained cordial relationships, they can aid in securing accommodation. Although the fear from the majority culture that a minority will form a community within a community is ever-present and weaponized, the fear is unjustified. The examples provided above show that minorities work and provide support to actually become part of the wider society. Schooling and jobs are the two main avenues to achieve this, and migrants with prior experience and know-how make the insertion less clumsy. Insularity appears to exist when visible (and hearable) cultural aspects are displayed: celebrations, festivities, outfits, music, food, and language. One is quick to see, hear, and smell what is different from their own perspective and point to those as a sign of stubborn unwillingness to integrate. Accompanying a fellow immigrant to an office to sort their paperwork, helping them buy the correct schoolbooks, talking in the majority language to help secure a job, and suggesting that their children join a gym or learn to swim go unnoticed. Immigrants will always face the dominant culture: from the media, to having to go to school, work, the doctor's, grocery shopping, or the post office. Insularity is virtually impossible and thus a non-issue.

Heritage languages allow migrants to see themselves in the new host country. The reference point provided by the shared way in which people of a minority group communicate ensures the creation and sustenance of social networks, which facilitate and lead the way to wider social insertion.

Maintaining heritage languages in families and communities makes it exponentially easier for communities to build themselves and include newer generations of migrants. Generational differences, such as age, year of migration, and cultural shifts, can limit first-generation migrants. Their children, being even more soaked in the majority culture due to birth or being in the host countries since childhood, push the envelope in how they are able to navigate two or more worlds. Many receptive bilinguals like me are passive speakers because of the shame attached to being the Other and the ridicule we may face from our own families when we try to speak. We have, however, been sufficiently exposed to the language to have a full understanding of it, and although becoming an active speaker may look like an insurmountable task, practicing it in an environment void of embarrassment and judgment, coupled with consistent immersion, can flip the switch rather quickly. My work as an interpreter is a testament to this. While there was initial doubt, fear, and unease, I promptly managed to turn Bamanankan into an active tongue as I was more and more called to translate for people hailing from Mali, the Gambia, and Côte d'Ivoire.

As stated above, the more proficient a person is in their heritage language, the more culturally confident they are. Parents must carry that pride too in order to instill it in their children through their idiom. By establishing a family language policy that promotes the use of heritage languages,[538] children will become active participants in the creation of multicultural societies.

The linguistic rope of pride and confidence that veteran migrants and people with a migration background weave is what newer waves can hold onto to rebuild their lives elsewhere.

---

[538] Bose et al., 2024

Chapter 15

The Arabic Speaking Competition: A Tool for Heritage Language Motivation and Identity Affirmation

Tony Calderbank, Janine Elya, and Chase Smithburg

Qatar Foundation International (QFI)'s Arabic Speaking Competition (ASC) in the United Kingdom was established in 2021 to promote Arabic language proficiency by encouraging students across all U.K. schools to improve their proficiency in Modern Standard Arabic (MSA), otherwise known as fuSHa or فصحى. At the same time, the ASC provides an opportunity for classroom Arabic teachers to encourage students to practice and demonstrate growth in their speaking ability. The ASC was set up for all learners of Arabic, with no specific focus on a student's previous exposure to Arabic. However, the ASC has become particularly popular with heritage learners of Arabic over the last four years, supporting student motivation, providing positive reinforcement of heritage language identities, and celebrating students' multilingual skills as an asset. Rather than heritage learners shying away from using their Arabic, the ASC has given them a platform to proudly display their linguistic profile and showcase and celebrate their cultures on a stage that is not necessarily specific to heritage communities.

As such, the ASC has the potential to make a significant difference to people's lives. The parent of one participant, whose family had moved from an Arabic-speaking country to the UK, reported: "We have been going through a lot of challenges, including cultural differences, language, and even the weather was different. It was important for my daughter to stay connected to her roots and to maintain her connection to the Arabic language. Participating in the competition allowed her to show her language skills in an unfamiliar environment. It was also a way for her to build confidence in her identity while adapting to life in a different country." After taking part in the ASC, the student summed up the experience: "After the competition, my self-confidence increased, which helped me interact better at school and with friends. Overall, it was an inspiring experience that led to considerable personal growth."

In this chapter, we will first discuss the various terminologies being used to describe students who are learning Arabic in U.K. schools. We will also give an overview of how and where Arabic is being taught. Next, a conceptual model for language revitalization that examines the importance of opportunity creation and desire is presented, followed by a brief literature review on the use of competitions for motivation in language learning. The ASC and its history will be detailed before we dive into analyzing surveys conducted with student participants, teachers, and parents. We will conclude by demonstrating how the ASC acts as an additional motivational tool for heritage learners to develop their speaking skills alongside their previous exposure to the language through their respective communities, which likewise motivates them to take part in the competition in the first place.

Terminologies

Ramezanzadeh raises the question of what is meant by "heritage learner" in the context of Arabic education in the UK.[539] Terms such as "heritage speaker," "mother-tongue speaker," "heritage learner," and "native speaker" are all used. Furthermore, different terminologies are employed to describe the Arabic language itself—"community language," "home language," "heritage language," "mother tongue," and even "native language." While each term has its own definition, some of these are used interchangeably in different contexts. To make the best curricular decisions, teachers need to understand a student's linguistic profile fully, and these labels are one way they do that. However, the labels are used differently by different

---

[539] Ramezanzadeh, 2016

teachers, which could take away from the nuanced understanding of a student's linguistic abilities that comes with assigning them a certain label. Heritage learner, for example, can mean so many different things.

Referencing Valdés' commonly used description, a heritage language learner (HLL)[540] is someone who: is raised in a home where Arabic is spoken but lives in a country where Arabic is not a majority language; may speak or merely understand Arabic; and is to some degree bilingual in the language of their country of residence and Arabic. Building on this, we also looked at Ibrahim & Allam's definition, which broke this down further into four types of HLL:[541]

a) Students whose parents are both of Arab origin and who hear or speak one of the Arabic dialects at home.
b) Students who have only one parent of Arab origin and do not speak Arabic at home.
c) Muslims who came from non-Arab countries and are exposed to only one variety of Arabic through their learning of the Qur'an or aspects of religion.
d) An Arab who lived in Arab countries, attended international schools, and has never had any formal education in Modern Standard Arabic.

It is important to be aware of the complex and nuanced language profiles that heritage students bring to the classroom in U.K. schools. Not only are children growing up in homes where both or one parent speaks Arabic, but also where parents/caregivers speak other languages alongside Arabic. Some students are managing a linguistic repertoire that contains two or three languages alongside English, only one of which is Arabic, and are mixing with peer and friendship groups where an even wider range of languages are used. These students are truly plurilingual individuals in a multilingual environment.

---

[540] Valdés, 2000
[541] Ibrahim & Allam, 2006; this definition was also used by Allaf et al., 2026

Sometimes it appears that the term "mother tongue" is being used interchangeably with "heritage" because both terms refer to the language one is exposed to from their family from when they were a baby. "Mother tongue," some argue, is the language that remains with a child despite where they live, but heritage language can be crowded out by the dominant (or host) language. Some are keen to distinguish between "mother tongue" and "heritage learners" because they believe that students in these categories have different educational needs. To further complicate terminology usage, "native speaker" is also used and generally refers to a person who speaks and writes using a native language or mother tongue.

It is also important to note that certain negative connotations are often associated with "heritage language." Kircher states that, "heritage languages, whether indigenous or from immigration, often face negative stereotypes and are undervalued, particularly within the educational system."[542] This discrimination originates from linguistic attitudes, which are the beliefs people develop about languages and their speakers. These attitudes are acquired early in life and associate certain languages with socially low-status groups. This leads to the stigmatization and marginalization of children using these heritage languages." Heritage language speakers themselves may perceive that their heritage language links them to being an immigrant or minority, which can lead to feelings of marginalization, discrimination, and pressure to assimilate.

While we can operationalize the phrase "heritage language learner" using any one of the various definitions that exist, it is vital to recognize that heritage language learners, as we define them, may reject being categorized as such when

1) It does not align with their own definition,
2) They do not want to be assigned a unidimensional identity (just "Arab"), or

---

[542] Kircher, 2024

3) The stigmatization of their heritage language makes them feel powerless.[543]

Criteria that these learners may use to exclude themselves as heritage learners can include affiliation, cultural artifacts (e.g., stereotypes), self-positioning, and positioning by others.[544]

One common criterion that students use to reject their assigned heritage learner label is the level of language expertise, which can affect students at both ends of the proficiency spectrum.[545] A study by Hillman found that students of MSA who were fluent in their regional dialect rejected the "heritage learner" label.[546] Instead, they identified with "native speaker," but only of their specific dialect (e.g., Syrian). In the same study, Hillman also observed two heritage language learners who minimized their in-class participation and experienced low self-esteem because they were labelled as "heritage learners." Of these two students, one was the only non-Arab Muslim in the class, and being classified as a heritage learner led to her feeling "like an artificial Arab." She received the same expectations for oral proficiency as the other heritage learners, even though most of her exposure to Arabic had occurred via perceptive skills (reading and listening). Both students felt afraid of making mistakes in front of their peers and embarrassed for not having a native-like level of proficiency. This fear of embarrassment actively prohibited the development of these students' language skills and, in turn, led to their proficiency levels being lower than those of the two absolute beginner, non-heritage learners at the end of the class. These observations by Hillman underscore a powerful assertion by linguists Nancy Hornberger and Suhan Wang that "without the recognition that HLL identity is as much chosen as assigned, the efforts of language educators to instruct these learners may not be maximally effective."[547]

---

[543] Hornberger & Wang, 2008
[544] Dressler, 2010
[545] Dressler, 2010
[546] Hillman, 2019
[547] Hornberger & Wang, 2008, p. 14

This plays out with Arabic in the UK. Students tend to downplay their proficiency in their own heritage language, Arabic, and only focus on that of the dominant language, English. Teachers we have spoken to describe how their heritage students of Arabic feel awkward or uncomfortable speaking Arabic outside the home, and do not use it in the classroom or the playground with other Arabic-speaking students for fear of seeming "different." Sometimes, Arabic-speaking parents may downgrade the use of the language at home as well, to encourage the use of English, in the belief that this will help children assimilate into the mainstream language and culture. Even mainstream schools can give heritage language speaking students the impression that English is more important than the language they speak at home. Alongside these factors are the feelings of shame or guilt that young speakers of the heritage language may experience if they are not fluent in their heritage language.

The 2021 England and Wales census reports that 204,000 people in those countries consider Arabic to be their "main language," up from 159,000 in 2011.[548] The UK's Arabic-speaking communities include those who have lived in the U.K. for many generations, such as the Yemeni communities of Liverpool and Newcastle. Some have arrived more recently and continue to come, often as refugees or asylum seekers, fleeing conflict in their home countries. The designation of "main language," however, further highlights the difficulty with all these labels, as the term can easily be interpreted as referring to a heritage speaker, a mother tongue speaker, or a native speaker. If a child from one of these families enters an Arabic classroom, their linguistic profile is still quite nuanced, and a teacher must fully understand what they know to be able to teach them. This difficulty in labelling students who come from homes where Arabic is the main language has been strongly highlighted in the ASC. Additionally, there are many Muslim families in the UK. According to the 2021 U.K. Census, 6% of the population identified as Muslim, and most of those Muslims have a South Asian background, where

---

[548] Office for National Statistics, 2022

Arabic is not used as a daily communicative language but rather is encountered and experienced as the language of the Qur'an.

Ramezanzadeh reviews various definitions of heritage learners.[549] These include a proficiency-based definition, which refers to those who have learned the language in childhood but not necessarily attained native speaker ability, and an ancestral-based definition, which "centers around a personal, historical, ethno-linguistic connection to the language in learners who may have had no previous exposure to the language putting them, in terms of competence, on a par with L2 learners."[550]

It is clear from the way in which teachers submit their student registration information for the ASC that there are vastly different ideas of what constitutes a heritage and native speaker, despite the efforts of the competition guidelines to define them. Additionally, the categorization of a particular individual can vary significantly depending on who is distinguishing between categories. There have been many cases where ASC judges have felt the need to recategorize a particular participant because they are clearly a native speaker, even though the teacher has entered them as an intermediate heritage speaker or vice versa.

Another crucial factor to bear in mind is that since Arabic is a diglossic language, with a standardized variety (MSA, used for specific formal spoken contexts but the most common medium of written communication) existing alongside the spoken colloquial forms used by native speakers in their daily lives, it is common that many of the heritage learners have minimal to no literacy skills. It is not uncommon to see learners who have grown up speaking their heritage language fluently but struggle to read or write in that same language. Indeed, as far as Arabic is concerned, one of the main motivations for families to enroll their children in Arabic supplementary schools is to enhance and develop their knowledge of MSA to access literature and religious texts.

---

[549] Ramezanzadeh, 2016
[550] Ramezanzadeh, 2016, p. 6

Despite using their heritage language regularly, the ability of many young Arab heritage learners in the U.K. to communicate fluently and fully comprehend may not be as natural as that of a native speaker. They may have a more limited vocabulary, make grammatical errors, or struggle with certain pronunciation. Despite these limitations, they may still identify strongly with their heritage language and culture. For this chapter, we use the term "heritage learner" as an umbrella term that includes native speakers and the full spectrum of students with a connection to Arabic living in the UK. These include heritage learners of the language, both with familial or ancestral connections to the Arab world or of Muslim background with religious attachments to the language.

Arabic in U.K. Schools

The teaching and learning of Arabic in the U.K. has witnessed significant growth in recent years, as can be seen through national examination numbers. GCSE entries for Arabic rose from 2,707 in 2011 to 5,171 in 2023.[551] By comparison, in 1995, there were just 1,000 entries.

Recent research conducted by Shift Insight in 2022 sheds light on where students are learning Arabic in the UK. This research identifies 232 schools known to be teaching Arabic, of which 170 (75%) were Islamic faith schools and supplementary Arabic schools.[552] 106 (almost half) were independent schools. Of the 61 non-Islamic faith schools offering Arabic, there were 23 academies, 12 independent schools, and 12 community schools. Looking at the geographical distribution of schools teaching Arabic, most (94) were within London, followed by the Northwest (41) and the West Midlands (24).

The Arabic provision in these schools follows a variety of models. Some have Arabic in the curriculum as a time-tabled subject, and all pupils take the language. In contrast, others provide Arabic as an enrichment subject or extra-curricular club, which students elect to take. In some cases, schools offer Arabic support to those pupils

---

[551] Alcantara Communications, 2016
[552] Wild & Graham, 2022

taking the GCSE, often pupils of Arab heritage, although other pupils in the school do not learn the language. Ramezanzadeh examined the demographics of learners of Arabic in 2015.[553] She interviewed 102 pupils learning Arabic at Muslim faith schools, of whom 77% were of Asian origin (Indian, Pakistani, or Bangladeshi), while 20% were of Arab heritage. Describing the diversity of learners that can be found in an Arabic language classroom, she says:

> Not only do some classes contain students of Arab heritage, but also those of different ethnicities who have lived in an Arab country during childhood. These students are being taught alongside those who, whilst not exposed to Arabic for communicative purposes in their homes, may be familiar with the language through religious observance.[554]

It is important to include the role of supplementary schools (sometimes also called complementary or weekend schools) when it comes to the teaching of Arabic to school-aged children in the UK. Much has been written about the history and role of supplementary schools in the UK. Lamb describes them as spaces of hope and resistance, a way that language communities ensure that their languages are maintained and learned, "semi-formal communities that choose to meet in the evenings and at weekends to ensure autonomously and collectively that their languages and cultures are passed on to the younger generation ... creating spaces in which their linguistic and cultural identities can be safely nurtured and maintained."[555] Soliman and Khalil state that "It is well known that in almost every major city in the UK, there is a supplementary school for each Arab community such as an Iraqi, Libyan, Saudi, etc., with each following the curriculum of its respective country, albeit with some local variation in the curriculum and teaching approach to suit

---

[553] Ramezanzadeh, 2015
[554] Ramezanzadeh, 2015, p. 46
[555] Lamb, 2020, p. 102

children growing up in the U.K. attending English schools during the week."[556]

While the methodology and approaches to teaching vary enormously from one supplementary school to another, these institutions are often well attended and seen by students as spaces where they can be themselves. Teachers who were interviewed for a research project on the teaching of Arabic as a mother tongue/heritage language in 2023 pointed to the social aspect of the mother tongue classes as a crucial factor in enhancing learning.[557] They said their learners enjoyed the opportunity to get together and improve their Arabic. They reported that their students feel safe with each other and that they appreciate the opportunity to express themselves by socializing with peers in an environment where they can easily show their identity: "They feel very happy to be gathered as Arabic speakers, and they can express their social identity more freely when all the students in the class are Arabic speakers and have common points in their heritage and language."

Our research and observation indicate that educators in the supplementary sector are evolving innovative teaching approaches that reflect and address the unique identities of their plurilingual learners. Some employ project-based learning and community action projects that allow their learners to develop their language skills in a way that is stimulating, exciting, and relevant to their lives. One teacher we spoke to, who works in a supplementary school in London, told us how her school has adapted its teaching approach to focus on more creative ways of teaching Arabic, an approach she calls اللغة العربية والابداع (The Arabic Language and Creativity). The school's understanding of heritage learners has changed as they have done more work on the creative side, and lessons are much more connected to learners' needs, interests, and lived experiences. As a result, interest levels have improved as students have become more involved in choosing the themes and stories that are taught.

---

[556] Soliman & Khalil, 2022, p. 3
[557] Allaf et al., 2026

A Model for Language Revitalization

To prevent host languages from completely dominating heritage languages, a strategic approach to language maintenance and revitalization of these heritage languages that can be applied at multiple levels of the social ecosystem is vital. One framework discussed by Bianco and Peyton specifies that capacity development, opportunity creation, and desire are three conditions that must be met to revitalize a minority language successfully. The authors discuss how, in practice, policy solutions that support heritage language maintenance overwhelmingly prioritize capacity development, or the teaching and learning of the heritage language.[558] They also emphasize that in English-dominant countries in particular, opportunity creation is especially important, as opportunities to authentically use heritage languages in third places (other than in school or at home) are limited. In the United States, it was discovered that the creation of additional academic and professional opportunities for heritage learners of Hindi, another less commonly taught language, fostered a sense of pride in Hindi-speaking communities.[559] Seals and Peyton similarly found that creating opportunities for heritage learners to share their language and culture with their peers helped foster self-confidence and build leadership skills.[560] As discussed later in this chapter, the Arabic Speaking Competition provides more opportunities for Arabic heritage learners to authentically engage with the language and culture in a way that affirms their identities.

The third condition in the framework, desire, is immeasurable yet perhaps the most crucial: learners must *choose* to study and use the language they are learning, which involves both sustained motivation and behavior change.[561] The authors suggest that this condition of desire requires the presence of an internalized motivational system, in which a learner incorporates images of their future self as a

---

[558] Lo Bianco & Peyton, 2013
[559] Gambhir & Gambhir, 2014
[560] Seals & Peyton, 2016
[561] Lo Bianco & Peyton, 2013

proficient speaker of the target language into their present sense of self. In other words, the desire to identify as proficient in the target language is essential to increasing a learner's actual proficiency and usage. A common source of intrinsic motivation for Arabic heritage language learners is the desire to strengthen relationships with their family members overseas and to connect with Arabic speakers from other backgrounds (locations, religions, etc.).[562] Additionally, results from a study by Wang suggest that heritage learners who maintain or improve their proficiency can significantly benefit the well-being of their family, promote deeper connections with their parents, and evoke positive parental emotions like pride, fulfilment, and accomplishment.[563] Thus, even without the provision of material prizes, in theory, the Arabic-Speaking Competition has the potential to provide both intrinsic and extrinsic motivation for heritage learners.

Language Competitions and Motivation

Student competitions can serve as powerful motivators for learning a new language in school settings. Research suggests that engaging students in competitive activities, such as language contests, speech competitions, or debate tournaments, can enhance their intrinsic and extrinsic motivation to learn a language. These events encourage students to set clear goals, practice regularly, and apply their linguistic knowledge in authentic, high-stakes scenarios, fostering deeper engagement with the language material.[564] One study by Marashi and Dibah even found that the use of a competitive learning approach generally led to better oral proficiency outcomes for second language learners, as compared to a cooperative learning approach.[565] Competitions can be part of a useful teaching strategy to inspire children and young people, and they can be a fun way to bring

---

[562] Cruickshank, 2019
[563] Wang, 2022
[564] Usher & Kober, 2012; Fowler, 2022
[565] Marashi & Dibah, 2013

excitement to the language curriculum, sparking conversations about the importance of language learning.

Collaborative contests, like team-based quizzes or role-playing activities, can also build confidence and promote peer learning.[566] For instance, students who see their peers excel in language competitions are often inspired to improve their own skills, leveraging the social aspect of competition to create a positive learning environment.[567] Research has also shown that such activities support the development of a healthy self-concept, coping with subjectivity, dealing with competition, and interacting with role models.[568]

Additionally, the recognition and rewards associated with competitions, such as ceremonies, certificates, medals, or scholarships, can reinforce the value of language learning. These tangible outcomes not only boost students' self-esteem but also highlight the importance of bilingualism or multilingualism in globalized education and careers. By integrating well-designed language competitions into school curricula, educators can nurture long-term motivation and interest in language acquisition.[569]

There is limited research specifically examining the impact of student competitions on the motivation of heritage learners in school settings. While competitions have been shown to enhance motivation among language learners generally, further studies are needed to understand their effects on heritage learners specifically, who may be affected by different motivational factors compared to non-heritage learners. Understanding these dynamics is crucial for developing effective educational strategies that support heritage language maintenance and development.

The Arabic Speaking Competition (ASC)

---

[566] Madrid et al., 2007
[567] Deci & Ryan, 2000
[568] Ozturk & Debelak, 2008
[569] Dörnyei, 2001; Papi & Hiver, 2020

The ASC, supported by QFI since 2021, was initially modelled after the Mandarin Speaking Competition in the U.K. and was developed in partnership with the British Council. From its initiation, the goal of the ASC has been to nurture the learning of the Arabic language among primary and secondary school students while also celebrating their linguistic achievements and creativity. Open to all students in U.K. schools learning the Arabic language, the competition has been extremely popular, with the number of competitors rising from 50 in 2021 to 463 in 2023. The competition involves a short (no more than two minutes) presentation on a topic previously selected by the student from a list of issues, including home, family, local area, interests, travel, celebrations, and festivities, followed by a live (not pre-prepared) question-and-answer session with a panel of two or three judges. This two-part format allows students to prepare in advance some of their contributions, to check the vocabulary and structures they need, and to practice before the event. It also provides for spontaneous interaction with the judges and a chance for the participant to display their extemporization skills. The participant's performance is judged using a rubric against a series of criteria that include communication, language use, fluency, and pronunciation. Both parts are considered together with a mark out of five for each of the four criteria, equaling a total of 20 points.

While the overall goal of the competition has remained the same over several years, the competition has evolved into an inspiring and inclusive event that encourages young learners, particularly from heritage learner communities, to become confident speakers and advocates for the Arabic language.

In the first iteration of the ASC in 2021, the goals of the event were to:

- Raise the profile of Arabic as a language.
- Increase students' motivation for learning Arabic.
- Develop students' vocabulary and improve pronunciation and speaking skills.
- Raise confidence for oral examinations.

- Inspire students to discover more about Arabic cultures.
- Celebrate the skills of those who have Arabic as a home or heritage language.

Quickly, QFI saw that many students taking part in the ASC had some identity link to the Arabic language. While students learning Arabic as a world language also took part in the competition, the ASC has proven to resonate especially with students from a heritage background, whether through exposure to Arabic as a home language or connection to it via religion. Still, for both, the ASC provides an avenue for expressing pride in aspects of their identity in a UK-specific context. For those who use Arabic at home, it allows students to present their home language as an asset and a strength on a stage that is not necessarily specific to those heritage communities.

There are several areas where the ASC appears to prove meaningful and important to the Arabic-learning community. The ASC provides motivation and a platform for students to practice speaking in preparation for the compulsory speaking component of the GCSE. Teachers have responded positively to the need for more enhancement opportunities to encourage students to practice their speaking skills for these assessment purposes. Moreover, another advantage of the ASC is that it capitalizes on the strength of heritage learners' speaking skills, when assessments in the field of pre-college language learning typically tend to privilege non-heritage learners and focus on reading and writing, which are usually heritage learners' areas of weakness.[570] Indeed, both teachers and parents have actively supported the participation of their children and students in the competition. The ASC also appears to contribute to the creation of a sense of community among Arabic learners and educators in the UK, fostering collaboration and shared enthusiasm for the language.

The ASC also raises the profile of the Arabic language itself. It acts to showcase Arabic as a versatile and adaptable world language that can be used creatively for various forms of expression, including

---

[570] Malone, Peyton, and Kim, 2014

poetry, storytelling, and music. It also aims to highlight its importance as a global language in areas of diplomacy, trade, media, and international relations. The competition reinforces the idea that Arabic is an important and useful language for a young person to learn.

From a more specific language learning perspective, the ASC seeks to develop vocabulary and improve pronunciation and speaking skills. By providing new avenues for speaking Arabic, it contributes to building confidence for language learners in demonstrating their speaking skills. The ASC requires that participants use MSA, or fuSHa (فصحى). There are several reasons for this: MSA is the language that students of Arabic learn at school in the UK; it is the language of the GCSE examination and the variety of Arabic that is expected to be used in the speaking component of that examination. It is also the language that heritage learners, who may well speak a colloquial variety of Arabic at home and with their peers, most commonly learn in their supplementary schools. Furthermore, MSA is the language of public speaking used by many speakers in the Arab world in formal and professional situations such as presentations, speeches, and interviews. We believe that the fact that the ASC is conducted in MSA has been one of the reasons heritage communities have so positively received it, as we will discuss in more detail below.

Contestants in the ASC have hailed from a wide range of backgrounds and have learned Arabic in a variety of ways, very much reflective of the varieties in labels and the nuances that they bring. Some are native speakers of Arabic who have learned MSA in schools in their home countries, others are born and raised in the U.K. and use Arabic at home, often speaking a colloquial dialect of the language fluently but with limited formal learning of MSA. Some have learned Arabic (MSA) from an early age for religious reasons, although they do not speak it as a home language. Yet, others have come to the language with no prior knowledge or connection to the Arab world and are at the very beginning of their Arabic journey (those who are studying Arabic as a world language in school). The

ASC reflects this variety with categories for heritage and non-heritage as well as beginner, intermediate, and advanced learners.

As seen in Figures 1 and 2, nearly all ASC participants in both 2023 (97%) and 2024 (97%) were heritage learners, and participation at the secondary level was greater than participation at the primary level for both years. Between 2023 and 2024, only one non-heritage student participated at the primary level.

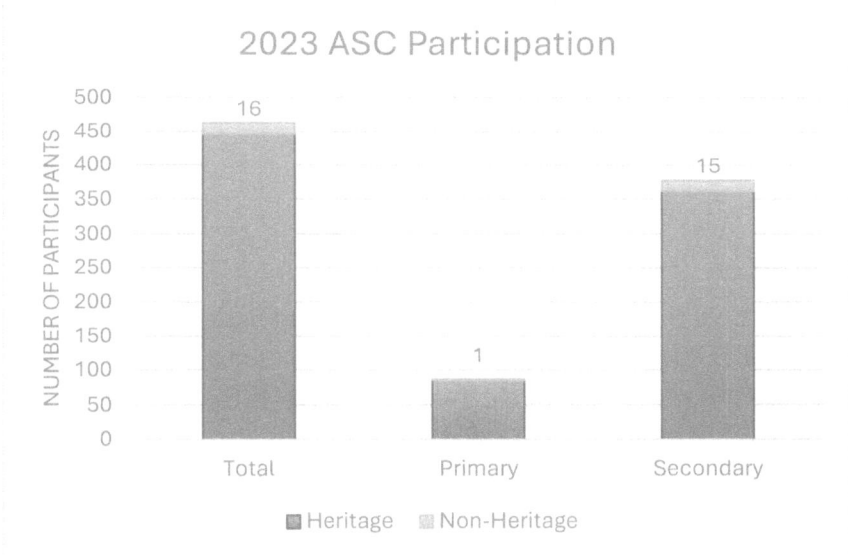

Figure 1. Of the 463 students who participated in the 2023 ASC, 447 (97%) were heritage learners. Heritage learners accounted for nearly all participants at both the primary (99%) and secondary (96%) levels.

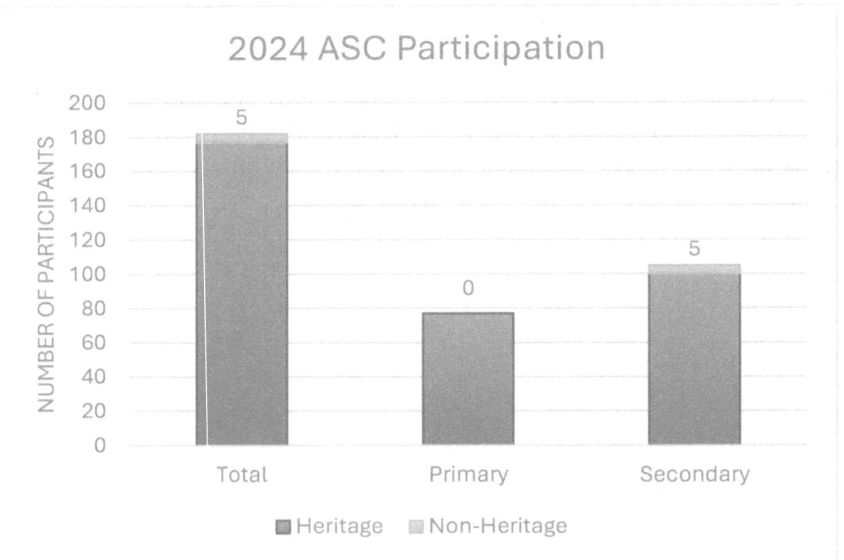

Figure 2. Of the 182 students who participated in the 2024 ASC, 177 students (97%) were heritage learners. There were no non-heritage learners at the primary level, and most participants at the secondary level were heritage learners (95%).

Figures 3 and 4 display the representation of three types of schools in the U.K. – state-funded, independent, and supplementary – in the 2023 and 2024 ASCs. In 2023, most participants (70%) were students enrolled in state-funded schools, and supplementary schools accounted for 28% of all participants. This changed significantly in 2024, when state-funded schools and supplementary schools each accounted for nearly 50% of participants. In both years, independent schools accounted for less than 10% of all participants. Figure 5 displays the representation of the three school types specifically for heritage learners' participation, which is virtually the same as the representation when including all participants.

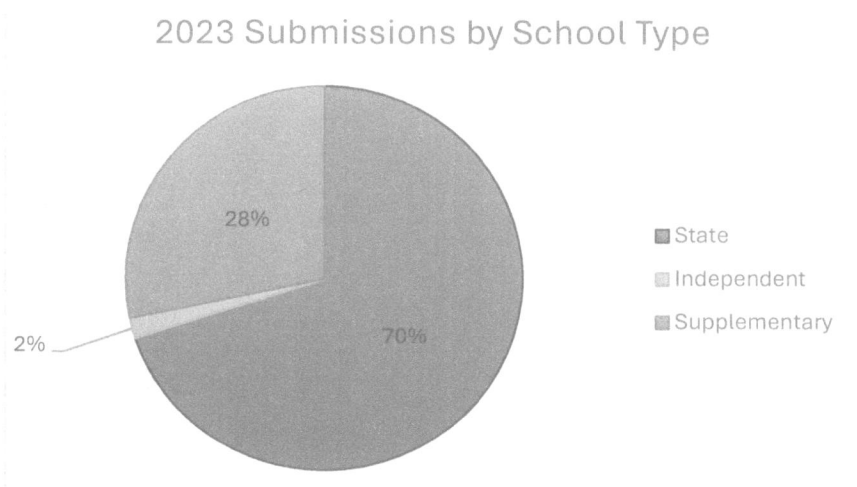

Figure 3. In 2023, most participants in the ASC were students at state-funded schools (70%), while nearly all other participants were students at supplementary schools (28%). Students at independent schools accounted for only 2% of all ASC participants.

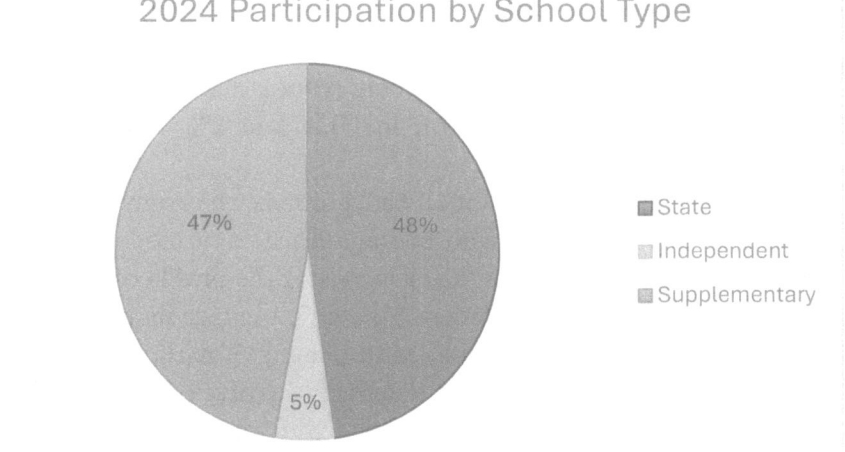

Figure 4. In 2024, nearly all ASC participants were students at state-funded schools (48%) or supplementary schools (47%). Students at independent schools accounted for only 5% of all ASC participants.

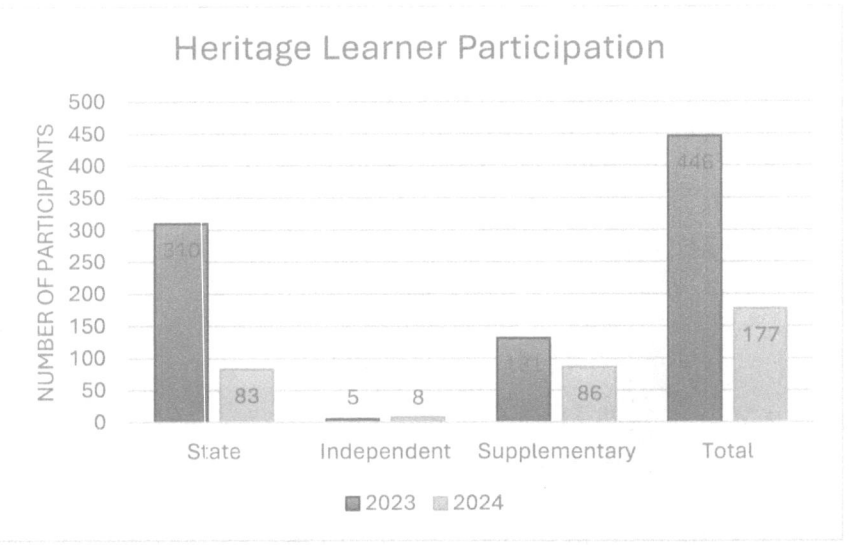

Figure 5. Nearly all ASC participants in 2023 (97%) and 2024 (97%) were heritage learners. State-funded schools accounted for the majority of heritage learner participation in 2023 (70%), in contrast to 2024, when supplementary schools accounted for most heritage learner participation (49%). In both years, students enrolled in independent schools accounted for less than 10% of all heritage learner participation, with independent schools accounting for 5% of all heritage learner participation in 2024 and 2% of all heritage learner participation in 2023.

While targeting students of all backgrounds, the competition has proven especially popular with heritage learners of the language. It has emerged as a significant factor in raising the profile of Arabic as a heritage language and a Modern Foreign Language in the UK. The ASC has also resonated strongly with parents of participants in the competition, many of whom are actively involved in their child's preparation for the event and who attend with immense pride and joy the award ceremony if their child is one of the winners. In the 2024 ASC, 19 of the 20 winners were of Muslim or Arab background, who we are referring to in this chapter as heritage learners.

That a considerable proportion of the entrants for the ASC are heritage learners of Arabic is no surprise and may be seen to reflect the interest of those learners and their families in strengthening their knowledge of MSA. If the heritage language is not supported either at home or at school, it will soon weaken as the dominant language, in this case English, takes over with the child's journey through formal education. As language is affected, so too is the sense of identity associated with that language. As we shall see below, maintaining identity is one of the main factors that lead parents to enroll their children in mother tongue language classes.

Feedback from Participants, Parents, and Teachers

As part of the preparation for this chapter, QFI included the results of surveys of three teachers whose students had participated in the Arabic Speaking Competition (12 entrants to the 2024 competition and 12 entrants to the 2023 competition). The teachers surveyed by QFI then interviewed those students and their parents. Ten parents and 16 students responded.

Survey questions asked about why the teachers signed up their students to participate, the backgrounds of their students who participated, how their students felt about participating, and the impact of the competition on students' language abilities, heritage learners' attitudes towards their mother tongue, and the cultural identity of the greater Arabic-speaking community. Parents were asked related questions, including whether the ASC was viewed positively by the Arabic-speaking community and whether the ASC improved students' self-confidence. Students were asked about why they participated, what participating was like, and whether they would participate again.

Teachers

All three teachers saw the ASC as an opportunity for their students to develop their language skills, and in particular speaking and presenting, as well as building confidence and improving fluency. "I think the ASC is a powerful tool for enhancing students' language skills and related abilities," said Teacher AB. Teachers also reported that their students felt a deep sense of pride in participating and found it a meaningful opportunity to connect with their mother tongue and heritage language: "It was a chance for them to celebrate their roots, express themselves confidently, and feel empowered by representing their language and heritage on a broader stage," said Teacher NS. At the same time, Teacher OM noted: "A number of them joined to celebrate their language, others aimed to strengthen their academic pursuits, and others felt an increase in confidence by speaking Arabic in front of unfamiliar audiences."

The teachers acknowledged the motivational aspect of the ASC: "It gives participants a clear purpose and an exciting challenge," commented NS, while AB observed: "Even if they don't win, the act of participating can foster a sense of achievement, enhance their confidence, and encourage continued learning. Teachers agreed that preparing for the competition encourages students to focus on their speaking and listening skills, which helps them engage more deeply with the language.

The teachers also reported how the ASC impacts students' attitudes towards their heritage language. NS observed how Arabic heritage speakers often have "complex feelings about their mother tongue, which are shaped by community attitudes, educational experiences, and social interactions." She pointed out how positive reinforcement from families and communities that value the Arabic language can instill pride and a keen sense of identity in heritage learners. All three teachers agreed that creating a positive atmosphere is essential for encouraging young heritage speakers to embrace and maintain their Arabic heritage, and that the ASC contributes to this.

Parents

When asked why they wanted their children to participate in the ASC, parents' responses focused almost exclusively on identity and linguistic ability. "As a proud Arab parent, I wanted my child to participate in the Arabic Speaking Competition because I wanted them to feel proud of their heritage and connect with their roots," explained Parent One. Parents clearly recognize the importance of Arabic in maintaining a sense of identity: "I believe that speaking

Arabic can enhance his culture and identity," said Parent Two, while Parent Nine told of her child: "I wanted her to express herself in her native language, especially after facing difficult challenges when moving to the UK."

Other parents said that the ASC was an opportunity to enhance their children's Arabic skills and express themselves in their mother tongue, to express themselves clearly and eloquently, and to have a chance to explore the cultural and historical connections that Arabic, as their mother tongue, offers. Parent Two also commented on the social aspect of the ASC, "I wanted him to enjoy sharing and learn something new, connecting with other children, and sharing their experiences to help him build new friendships and increase his self-confidence."

When asked if the Arabic-speaking community views the ASC positively, all parents we surveyed agreed that it was. "It fosters a sense of pride in our language and culture, bringing people together and encouraging young generations to embrace their heritage. This support helps strengthen our identity and inspires a love for Arabic among children," said Parent One. "This competition is a positive and very important event for the Arab community in the diaspora," said Parent Three, "because it creates the spirit of competition between the children of the Arab community."

Parents recognize that the ASC provides positive reinforcement of heritage language identity. "It really helps kids feel proud of their Arabic language and culture," said Parent One. Parent Two remarked that the ASC "greatly enhances the heritage identity of the language. When they learn and compete in the use of language, they understand the stories of their heritage, their songs, and proverbs. This helps them better connect with their family and grandparents and increases their connection to their history." The parents were also in general agreement that the ASC promotes student well-being and is an opportunity to develop character and build self-confidence, and had encouraged their children to continue their Arabic studies and to read Arabic.

Students

Sixteen students who participated in the ASC gave feedback for this chapter. When asked why they had taken part, participants reported several reasons. "I wanted to challenge myself and connect more with my language and culture," said Student One. Student Nine had similar motives: "I wanted to test my limits and expose myself to a challenge." Student Five shared, "I participated because I wanted to test my Arabic skills." Student Two agreed: "Participating in the Arabic speaking competition was a great opportunity to express oneself and improve language skills."

In responding to how the ASC had impacted them, a considerable number of respondents mentioned increased confidence. "Winning the competition made me believe in myself more," said Student One, "I started to feel proud of my language and who I am. It helped me open up, and now I'm more confident when I speak, not just in competitions but in everyday life, too." Student Two said: "The experience was positively impactful, as I felt proud when speaking in front of the audience and realized the importance of my voice and my ability to influence. Overall, it was an inspiring experience that led to considerable personal growth." Student Ten echoed these sentiments, sharing, "It built my ability to convey and articulate myself in Arabic, which has built my confidence and belief that I can network using the Arabic language."

Respondents also commented on more personal aspects of their relationship with Arabic: "The Arabic language is a significant part of my identity," said Student 14, "This Arabic speaking competition was an exceptional opportunity for me to demonstrate my skills and get to know other young people who are passionate about the Arabic language." Student Seven commented on the sense of pride they felt when participating. "I felt proud when speaking about myself and my personality."

Respondents were generally positive about the experience of participating in the ASC. "Participating in the Arabic speaking competition was a positive and beneficial experience," said Student Two, "despite the stress at first, self-confidence increased over time," while Student One exclaimed: "Overall, being part of something like this made me feel really proud. It made me realize I can accomplish things I never thought I could."

All the students surveyed said that they would participate in the ASC again. They gave many reasons: wanting to win, improving their Arabic, increasing academic opportunities, and because it was "fun," "enriching," "beneficial," and "motivating." And of course, there is the sense of achievement, as Student One confirms, "Yes, I would totally participate again! Winning the competition was such an awesome feeling."

Future Directions

Building on the success of the last few years and considering the lessons learned from the different iterations of the competition, QFI plans to make the ASC an opportunity in other geographies. In the 2025/2026 academic year, QFI will hold the competition in the different geographies where we work (the US, Canada, Ireland, Italy, Germany, Spain, and Sweden) as well as continuing it in the UK. Heritage learners of Arabic make up a large part of the student population of Arabic classrooms all over the world. And while the contexts of Arabic learning may be different, the lessons learned from the ASC in the UK, and the nuances of the profile of a heritage language learner, indicate that ASCs would be welcomed and impactful in other contexts. The unique aspect of the ASC is that it is a motivational tool of learning not just for heritage language learners – as demonstrated in this chapter – but also for students learning Arabic as a second or foreign language. Holding ASCs in other geographies will provide an opportunity to build connections between learners of the language in different countries and contribute to raising awareness of Arabic as a major world language worthy of study and deserving of celebration.

Additionally, the profile of a heritage language learner deserves even more research and attention. Heritage Language Learners is an umbrella term that does not fully convey the nuance of what a learner with that label can do with the language in their everyday lives and across the four modalities of speaking, reading, writing, and listening.

Teachers need to understand a student's full linguistic profile – no matter what they are labelled as – to be able to teach them so that they reach their full Arabic language potential. Specific teacher training for Arabic teachers on this is necessary, and is currently not widely available or offered. While there is professional development on differentiation, or perhaps how to accommodate having heritage language learners in class with other types of language learners, a full understanding of heritage language learners and the possibilities for advancing their Arabic language skills is not widely known by Arabic teachers.

Conclusion

The ASC has achieved a particular resonance with heritage learners, and those that we surveyed shared how the ASC is now perceived. Both parents and student participants spoke about how the competition engenders confidence and pride in their identity. One parent commented how they see it as "a valuable initiative that unites us and keeps our traditions alive" (Parent One). At the same time, another believes that such competitions "promote belonging and help prevent our culture from becoming extinct" (Parent Two). The ASC is seen as something that motivates the younger generation to preserve and master the Arabic language and enhances their ability to speak it. One parent even commented on how the ASC has impacted family ties, sharing, "the bonds between students and their families have become stronger because students rely on their parents as a reference for the Arabic language and culture. Families themselves have also become proud of their children" (Parent Three). Overall, we can see positive impacts of the ASC for teachers, parents, and students in confronting the marginalization of Arabic; challenging the negative connotations of the term "Home, Heritage, and Community Language;" reinforcing heritage language identity; and celebrating the benefits of multilingualism.

While targeting students of all backgrounds, the ASC has proven especially popular with heritage learners of Arabic, which was not necessarily the original intention of the ASC. Without explicitly setting out to do so, the ASC has helped heritage learners be proud of having prior exposure to Arabic or having heritage linked to an Arabic-speaking country. Rather than shying away from the spotlight, the ASC has motivated students with Arabic as a heritage language to want to showcase their linguistic profile to a wider audience. The ASC has shown that despite Arabic not being readily offered as a language in mainstream schools, families and students still value their heritage language and are ready to invest critical time and effort in preparation to allow them to use it with sophistication and proficiency to win.

Lastly, this chapter has also shown the challenges with using terminologies and how they do not support teachers in their planning because they could mean so many different things. Rather, teachers should think of all learners as individuals, coming to the classroom with their own linguistic profiles and varied purposes for taking Arabic in school. While heritage learners – those with some background linked to Arabic, the Arab world, and/or Islam – have an additional asset when they come to the Arabic language classroom, it does not set them up immediately for success. Because students come with various feelings associated with their heritage language, in addition to students who come to Arabic as a brand-new language, differentiation is essential to meet all their needs as learners. Competitions like the ASC with varied categories allow students to partake in a way that makes sense for their own learning.

Chapter 16

English as a Heritage Language: A Case Study in Calabria, Southern Italy

Elizabeth Wardy, Jessica Salerno, and Steven J. Sacco

When one thinks of "building worlds" and "the power of heritage languages in social cohesion," one seldom points to Southern Italians, possessing intimate ties to egalitarian havens such as Argentina, Australia, Canada, or the United States of America. Many of these Southern Italians, known as the "birds of passage," were usually young men who came to America (or, in the case of our two senior authors, to Australia) with the goal of earning enough money to support their families back home in the *Mezzogiorno*.[571] Generally, Italian immigrants remained permanently in their adopted country to start a new life. Still, Simkin reports that between 30 and 50 percent would return to their homes in Southern Italy, in our case, Calabria.[572] Most "birds of passage" immigrated to their temporary countries during the late 19th or early 20th centuries.[573] Many saw the era of American industrialization and the power of the American dollar, backed at that time by the gold standard, while the pubescent Kingdom of Italy was undergoing volcanic social and political change. An egalitarian America or Australia liberated peasants from medieval feudalism that still existed in the late 19th and early 20th centuries.[574]

---

[571] Rohlf, 2023
[572] Simkin, 2020
[573] "The Italian-Americans," 2020
[574] Many of the students in the third author's Italian-America Studies class Cultura et letteratura italoamericana at the University of Calabria were descendants of "birds of passage" who left Calabria in the mid-20th century. Their stories can be found in Calabrian Voices: Diaspora Stories from the

According to Anne Kelleher,[575] a "heritage language" is any language used in a social setting that represents the culture of immigrants or the children of immigrants. In the United States, English is the dominant language, whereas Spanish, Italian, Polish, Greek, and others are heritage languages. In the United States, even though there is no official language, English is the *de facto* dominant language used in all formal settings, such as government, education, and public communication.[576] Some Italian residents chose to immerse themselves linguistically and culturally in American life, while others decided to preserve their "heritage language," creating a bilingual home. Joshua Fishman viewed the preservation of immigrant heritage languages as an attempt to maintain traditional cultures. He asks minority-language activists to "view local cultures (all local cultures, not only their own) as things of beauty, as encapsulations of human values which deserve to be fostered and assisted (not merely 'preserved' in a mummified sense)."[577]

In this essay, we will discuss three case studies of immigrant heritage languages. The first refers to an Australian woman's case of Italian as a heritage language: Elizabeth Wardy is primarily an English speaker because she was born and raised in Australia, but she is also the daughter of an Italian migrant woman who decided to start a new life overseas and who spoke to her daughters in Italian, mostly as a secret code never to be understood by non-Italians. When Elizabeth got married and moved to Calabria (a region in the South of Italy), she became an "outsider" despite her native-like proficiency in Italian. *L'Australiana* is what Calabrian townspeople called her. The second case is a unique one in which English, the dominant language of America and Australia, became the heritage language for Jessica Salerno, Elizabeth's daughter. She is a native Italian speaker, but as the story repeats itself, she was raised in a bilingual context

---

Younger Generations Rubbettino. Giordano, 2015; "The Italian-Americans," 2020
[575] Kelleher, 2010
[576] Kelleher, 2010
[577] Fishman, 1991, p. 33

because her mother never ceased to speak English to her since she was a child. Juxtaposed with the first two case studies, the third case involves the language history of the third author, whose father, uncles, aunts, and grandparents refused to teach him Italian or the local dialect *miglierinese*. All wanted him to be fully immersed in America's melting pot. He later became an Italian professor, although he learned Italian in language schools in Florence at age 51.

Testimonials

Elizabeth Wardy

My story begins on the 23rd of July 1963, on a cold, wet winter morning in Sydney, Australia, where I was born. Surprisingly, there is no official recording, not even on my birth certificate. It was after midnight when my mother, Maria, a young Italian woman of 32 who had been married for one year, was rushed to the delivery room to give birth to her first child, me, Elizabeth. It was a very difficult birth because I came into the world two months before the expected delivery date, and shortly after I was born, I was rushed to the emergency room because something had gone wrong. I required two life-saving blood transfusions. I have a rare blood type, AB negative, which can receive only Rh-negative blood. I was suspended between life and death.

"It's a girl!" said the nurse, but my parents' reactions were completely different: my mother forgot all the pain and thanked heaven, while my father, Joseph, a self-made Lebanese businessman, was disappointed and said, "What? A girl?" "Girls are trouble. Where is the boy, my heir?" By the time my two other sisters, Yvonne and Laura, were born, the mistake was already a forgone conclusion.

"A name for the baby?" asked the nurse, and this is when the war was declared. Joseph wanted to call me Armini after his mother, and today it is my middle name, while Maria wanted Melanie, from *Gone with the Wind*. In this classic film, Melanie was a kind, beautiful, graceful, quiet, grounded young woman with a pure heart who always did the right thing. Funny enough, that is exactly how I would describe my mother. There were many arguments between the two, but thank goodness Aunty Winnie, an authentic English woman who had arrived in Australia as a two-year-old orphan in the early 1900s, stepped in and saved the day, choosing Elizabeth as my name. Her choice was an appropriate tribute to Queen Elizabeth II, who reigned at the time of immigration to Commonwealth countries such as Australia and Canada.

Elizabeth was the perfect name, a timeless name used by saints, royalty, and VIPs, and I was lucky because it never gave me any trouble: it was easy for me at school because everyone could say my name, unlike many of my friends who were saddled with strange names. I remember children being ridiculed for names like Pasquale, Rosina, and Maria, which became "Lino," "Rose," or "Mary," and so on. I hated it when Australians shortened my name to "Betty," "Lizzy," or "Ely."

In Italy, it is even worse because people cannot read my name and cannot write it properly, which is why the easiest way to identify me became *Elisa Australia*—my newly acquired surname—because "Wardy," at best, becomes "Wendy." In addition, even today, many people do not know what my name is, as in town I am known as *A mugliera i Giovanni* or *A mamma i Jessica,* meaning "Giovanni's wife and Jessica's mother." No one ever knows me as Elizabeth, except for close friends.

My parents' marriage was not the climax of a wonderful love story. It was clear to everyone who knew them that it was a disaster from the start. How could two people who did not know each other and did not speak the same language even think of getting married? But they did. They had their own reasons. Maria had come to Australia on a large ship, *The Conte Grande*, on the 30th of January 1961, with Melbourne as the port of disembarkation. She was heartbroken because the love of her life had not found the courage to marry her. Nicola, a handsome young man in medical school, had decided to follow the strong advice of his parents and marry someone from their circle, not the butcher's daughter. Maria spent 31 days sailing toward new horizons, distancing herself from her homeland and trying to forget Nicola and her past. During this never-ending journey across the seas, she decided that she would marry the first man she met in Australia and offer this marriage to God as a sacrifice, because no one could ever replace Nicola.

Joseph was the owner of a café and was looking to get married. He wanted an Italian wife because he had heard that Italian women made good wives and mothers and ran impeccable households. Australian women in 1960 were considered too independent and emancipated. Most men wanted the comfort of good old-fashioned, accommodating, and obedient brides. This way of thinking reminds me of the Italian comedy *Bello, onesto emigrato Australia sposerebbe compaesana illibata,* directed by Luigi Zampa, literally meaning "Handsome, honest migrant in Australia looking for a single woman from his own country to marry," which was translated in English as *A girl in Australia.*

It was filmed entirely in Australia with real-life immigrants, telling both the story of post-war migration to Australia and of men with moral values typical of the 1930s and 1940s who were looking for women to share their lives with. The introductions took place at the port on the day Maria arrived, thanks to Tony, my father's best friend, who was also the matchmaker and the chaperone on the ship Maria had sailed on; his role was to introduce lonely men to single young women.

This was not just a film; it was real life and reflected how things were done at that time. The meeting between Maria and Joseph consisted mostly of smiles, glances, and nods, and they both found what they were looking for: they were two lost souls trying to move on with their lives, seeking nothing more than companionship. They got married on the 3rd of March 1962, without any romantic courtship.

They did not speak the same language, and English became their common ground. Joseph had been in Australia much longer and could speak good English, albeit with a Lebanese accent. On the other hand, Maria spoke only Italian and attended a crash course on the ship: migrants learned basic greetings and a few odd English words. They were also instructed in the British/Australian customs they would encounter. Survival skills included drinking tea, a beverage seldom consumed in Italy: "Never refuse a good Cuppa!"

"Cuppa" in Australian slang means "a cup of tea," and of course, it was the first step toward resolving any problem. The same applied for the advice "Eat your scones with whipped cream and handmade strawberry jam," an art which Maria had mastered over the years while welcoming guests into her home. Basically, Maria had to learn everything from scratch: the English language, Australian culture, how to become a good wife and mother, how to run a bar, and how to manage daily tasks.

For as long as I can remember, the first and only rule in our house was that we were to speak only English, both at home and in public; no other languages were allowed in my father's presence. Nevertheless, my father spoke to me in Lebanese and my mother in Italian when he was not around. Unfortunately, I have lost all my Lebanese language skills because Joseph worked all day, spent little time with his daughter, and later abandoned us.

We also rarely had anything to do with his side of the family. I do not recall family gatherings, and today I am only able to count from one to ten, although I have a strong liking for Arabic fragrances. Growing up, my father did not want secret conversations between his wife and children that he could not understand. Before this rule was imposed, "communication" had already been a matter of smiles, frowns, glances, stares, and nods; very few words were uttered. There was constant screaming between my parents in three languages, and we quickly learned to disappear during these heated moments.

I learned the rule that "silence is golden," and as an adult, I still resort to it, preferring it to arguments. As a child at home with my parents, I spoke very little, but in public, I would never stop. The best conversations I had were with "Tinkerbell," the next-door neighbor's dog, through a hole in the back fence. My conversations with my parents were always private affairs: I whispered so that the other parent would not hear and would not know what was being said. It was like being in a spy story, like James Bond "007"; the second language became a code so that the other parent would not understand.

Obviously, because I spent more time with my mother, I was more advanced in Italian, but this was a secret to be kept from my father. As the first child, my mother had more time to devote to me—time to pass on the language, its customs, its cuisine, the family tree, and family stories. I had fallen in love with Italy and Italian culture, and I already knew that I would make my way to Italy to stay. Strangely enough, my sisters, Yvonne and Laura, were not as interested as I was; they used to call me *la fanatica*.

Then one day, when I was six, my father went out to buy some cigarettes and returned only months later. He had gone to Lebanon to take a break and to see his family—maybe even to find another wife. This was when my mother made her move and filed for divorce. We moved back to Melbourne, where social services found us a home and a different life, one in which our voices could finally be heard. Within the walls of our new home, everything became Italian; English was used only for visitors and guests, and outside the house.

I was able to live my Italianness openly: I could speak Italian, eat Italian food, read Italian newspapers, listen to Italian music, watch Italian movies, meet Italian *paesani* at home for birthdays and special occasions, together with *la commara,* my godmother. She was my mother's best friend, and they worked together. To be raised by an Italian mother is to be showered with unconditional love, but there is a fine line between love and discipline, and all children knew this. My mother's disciplinary tools were *la pantofola* (her slipper for small problems) and *la cucchiaia* (her wooden spoon for big issues), as in many Italian households. One's life depended on *la bella figura* (a set of unspoken guidelines for life, which were passed down from generation to generation). The goal of every good Italian mother was to pass them on; it was all about how to behave. *Comportati bene*—behave properly—echoed wherever you went.

I remember that in primary school, at lunchtime, my teacher and classmates eagerly awaited the knock on the door from my Italian mother, who would always bring me my hot lunch, mainly *lasagne* and *cotolette*—nothing like the cheese-and-Vegemite cold sandwiches that my Aussie friends ate. "Vegemite" is a salty vitamin paste made of yeast, vegetables, and spices, a typical Australian food spread given to children as part of their diet. It has the same status in Australia as Nutella does in Italy. Desserts included sweets like *bignè* and *tiramisù*. "Wogs"—the Australian derogatory term for migrants—were famous for food that Australians, deep down, envied. Her kitchen was *la migliore del mondo*, the best in the world, and her recipes were top secret, never to be revealed to anyone outside the family. Dishes such as *pastina in brodo*, small pasta in broth, were a remedy to fix everything from a cold to a broken heart.

Finally, I could do everything and anything I wanted to do in Italian and no longer hide. When I was a teenager, I painted my room the colors of the Italian flag, and I would always watch *Sanremo* on TV. I also went to Italian school every Saturday morning, where mothers and daughters alike admired the Italian professor because he embodied Italian style and fashion with his clothes, leather shoes, and accessories coming straight from Italy: *tutto firmato*, with visible brand names like Gucci and Valentino. I studied Italian up to university.

There was a special Sunday church service for the large Italian community, so we always went to Italian mass. Every Sunday afternoon, my best friend Collette and I went to Lygon Street to "Little Italy," a main street full of Italian restaurants with authentic food, shops with the latest Italian items, music, and cultural attractions, libraries, and museums where the only language spoken was Italian—music to my ears. *Gelatissimo* was our first stop.

Lygon Street still exists today, but with very few Italians, as new migrants—mostly Greeks, Asians, Indians, Lebanese people, and those from the Middle East—have settled there. The turnover of migrants is so sad for us, second-generation Italians, that with our university degrees, we have gone on to bigger and better things, leaving behind the traditional family businesses. During my last trip to Australia in November 2023, all that was left of "Little Italy" was its name. There were very few businesses run by Italians, such as the

Italian restaurant "Piccolo Mondo," a three-generation family business where we spent Christmas Day celebrating with family and friends in an Italian atmosphere.

When I was 25, during my first trip to Italy, I met what was to become my future husband, Giovanni (Gianni). At 26, I moved to Italy, to Paola, and a whole new chapter began: even though I had studied Italian all my life, Calabrese was a completely different story because people mostly speak in dialect. It felt like an entirely new language to me. Everybody called each other *Cumpà,* the dialect version of the Italian *Compare,* as an affectionate greeting to a friend or acquaintance. In addition, the ways of greeting someone for the first time were somewhat overwhelming because, in Calabria, kissing, hugging, and touching were inevitable, along with the hundreds of personal questions people asked to learn all about you and your life.

Many of these topics are strictly avoided in English, such as *Chi fa?* meaning "what do you do," *Quantu guadagni?* meaning "how much do you earn," or *Chin a votato?* meaning "who did you vote for?" There were also many cultural differences: as a small child, I remember hearing the word *malocchio,* literally meaning "evil eye," so I dismissed it, thinking it was a medical condition, an eye infection. At school, I discovered it was a Calabrian superstition meaning "the evil eye"—a jinx, a curse bringing misfortune and negative energy, and sometimes illness.

Once in Calabria, I discovered, thanks to my mother-in-law Aquilina, that it was believed to be caused by a powerful stare, an intense look of admiration, or a bad intention from an envious person. I was introduced to the ideas of *sfiga* or *jella,* words used to refer to bad luck, which could be warded off by using the famous Italian bull horns or red hot chili pepper charms made of red coral. I saw them hanging everywhere: in cars, in homes, as jewelry or keepsakes, generally carried in pockets or handbags, and designed to protect against the *malocchio.* The same applies to the hand gesture of raising the pinky and index finger while the others are folded; people usually say: *fa i corna!*

Purpett'i mulingiane—*polpette di melanzane* in Italian, or eggplant meatballs—accompanied every meal. Almost everything could be turned into a *purpetta*: rice, tuna, potatoes, and, obviously, everything was fried. *Pi Samprancisc*—in Italian, *Per San Francesco*—was a common expression of wonder or disapproval in which the patron saint of the town was invoked. Almost everything in the city revolved around him: religious tourism, the wind, his blessing on any new venture, and weddings—like mine—celebrated in the main church of San Francesco di Paola.

At 28, I had my one and only daughter, Jessica. This is when history repeats itself: I found myself reliving many of the experiences my mother had gone through in Australia, here in Calabria—probably all of them and more. If I had a penny for all the times I was called *L'Australiana*, the foreigner who sees, thinks, and acts differently from everyone else, I would be rich—even now, after 36 years of living in Calabria. Interestingly enough, they call my daughter and me "the Italians" when we go back to Australia to visit.

From day one, I spoke English to my daughter and made sure she studied English at school. I remember when she was in primary school, her pronunciation was better than the teacher's, and this created problems for Jessica, who banned me from going to school and talking with the teachers. Today, we still usually insert English words into our conversations, like "wash basket," "vegemite," and "stingy." Still, I only speak English on two occasions: when I teach English lessons and when I am on the phone with my sisters.

I have also told my daughter everything I could about Australia, and we still talk about something Australian every day for one reason or another. I helped her forge ties with the Australian side of the family, and we recently went to Australia for a three-month study program at the University of Melbourne. How proud I was of her. Like it or not, she is an *Australiana* too. What will she do with her future—stay here in Calabria or go there? Who knows? She has the same opportunity I had, a choice not everyone has. We are the sum of all the experiences we go through: our past is never truly past; it lives on in our present and our future.

Jessica Salerno

Looking back at my childhood, I might say that it was hard to be raised in a bilingual context and to be caught between two distinct cultures: the English one within the family and the Italian one outside of it, in my social life in Calabria. I remember the feeling of being both surprised and confused when I started to realize that it was as if my brain were set to think in English while I was acting and living according to a purely Italian lifestyle. It is well known that each culture carries with it its customs and manners, its way of thinking, ideals, and beliefs, and, as you all can imagine, English culture and Italian culture are quite different in many aspects. For this reason, I found myself in tricky situations when I was younger, and that is also why I started to consider bilingualism a burden too heavy for a child to carry: although it may seem a harsh judgment, it comes from experiencing bilingualism in an inappropriate environment.

Here is the thing: I was born to an Australian mother and a Calabrian father who ended up living in Paola, a small town in Calabria, a region located in southern Italy. Historically, it has been an underdeveloped area that has also experienced a high rate of migration toward the United States and other destinations, mostly for economic reasons. Unfortunately, this has affected—and continues to influence—the lives of its inhabitants and its numerous dialects. Italian is obviously the native language; there are also many local dialects, but there were few traces of English use, which was mostly linked to the phenomenon of return migration. This means that people who had once migrated and later returned to their country of origin brought with them some linguistic expressions learned in the host country, which was most often an English-speaking country.

Those relatives returning from America had adopted an American accent—one that was incomprehensible to the locals. They had no chance to speak English as freely as in the host country because no member of the community was able to hold a conversation in English; it was mostly unknown to the vast majority. At this point, you may wonder how an Australian woman and a Calabrian man managed to meet. My family history starts in Carpinone, a small town in Molise, the smallest Italian region, where my great-grandparents, Rosina and Costantino Iamurri, owned a butcher shop and gave birth to my maternal grandmother Maria and her four siblings, Pasquale, Nicola, Rita, and Emilia. *Zio Pasquale* (as we usually call him) refused to join the army and escaped to Australia, sponsored by a family friend from Carpinone who was already living there.

Once there, he sponsored his brother Nicola, who also wanted to start a new life overseas. After a few years, my grandmother Maria (whom I will refer to as *Nonna Maria* from now on), heartbroken by a not-meant-to-be love story due to social class differences, also joined them overseas. Motivated by an impossible future with the man she loved and by Australia's job opportunities as a seamstress, she decided to live on the other side of the world, where she eventually created a family with my grandfather Joseph Wardy, a Lebanese man and owner of a café in Sydney.

Two faraway cultures and languages, the Italian and the Arabic, found a meeting point through a third culture, English, which was the culture in which my mother, Elizabeth, and her two sisters, Yvonne and Laura, were raised in Australia. My mother has already provided an in-depth analysis of her personal experience in her testimony. As she explained, she was aware of her Italian heritage, developed a great interest in Italian culture, and decided to return to her Italian roots in Carpinone. During one of her trips, a case of overbooking brought her to my father's workplace in Rome, at the Hotel *Portamaggiore*. They fell in love and got married in Italy; their plan to live in Australia was never realized because of my father's *caffè* opening in Paola, my birthplace, in December 1991.

I grew up as an English-speaking child. My mother never completely gave up her English side; that is why she has taught me English since I was little and applied for Australian citizenship by descent for me. When I was a child, I hardly remember there being English-speaking people around me apart from my mother, her relatives calling from Australia, and my primary school teacher, who, in the end, was able to say only a few basic English words. In addition, none of my classmates could understand English because they had only just begun learning the language.

Nothing changed in secondary school: even though I was attending a linguistic high school in which English, French, and German were taught, it was almost impossible to speak any language outside the classroom. None of my classmates were really interested in learning English, and most of the time, they were nearly ashamed of reading it aloud. Can you imagine speaking a different language freely? This made it really hard for me to develop my linguistic skills outside my family circle.

I can provide many examples of different customs between my Italian friends during our childhood. Let us consider film. In the 1990s, movies were recorded on videotapes. Still, today I keep them in a drawer, both as memories and as part of my English heritage: exactly like a perfect English child, I grew up only with the English versions of movies; that is why they all have English titles. I still remember that I was obsessed with both *The Lion King* and *The 101 Dalmatians,* and I used to watch them more than once a day.

As most children probably do, I learned all the names of the characters and the songs. Linguistically, of course, the names were the same in both languages—they only seemed a little strange to me when pronounced with an Italian accent—while it was a completely different story for the songs. Even if the rhythm and sounds were more or less the same, the lyrics were different because they were created according to the needs of each language to preserve the same meaning. I was accustomed to associating songs with specific movie scenes, which usually brought out strong emotional feelings in me. Still, when I discovered the Italian versions of the movies, I could not feel the same things; I was not experiencing the same emotions without the English version.

I was almost shocked and disappointed because it all felt so weird and strange in another language. As we all know, the film's iconic opening song, "The Circle of Life," was sung by the American singer Carmen Twillie and was performed by the well-known Italian singer

Ivana Spagna in the Italian version. The Italian song, also known as *Il Cerchio della Vita,* contains more or less the same meaning as the original. There is nothing to complain about in Spagna's voice and skills, for which Italians are obviously proud, but I soon realized that, in my mind, the delicacy and sensibility of Twillie were replaced in Italian with a less emotional spirit. The same applies to the well-known songs "Hakuna Matata" and "Can You Feel the Love Tonight." The worst thing was that my friends could not really understand what I was trying to say, because I was accustomed to the English version, while they were accustomed to the Italian version, which, for them, was equally emotional.

Therefore, what was normal to me was strange to them. Another example, which also demonstrates a completely different setting for my growth—and which was clearly oriented toward English culture—was cartoons. I remember that I found it hard to talk about cartoons with my friends because they did not know anything about *Bananas in Pyjamas* or *The Muppets,* which became popular in Italy only later on, more or less in my twenties. At the same time, T*he Wiggles* or the *Hi-5* series never appeared in the Italian preschool entertainment collection, so they remain equally unknown to them. I always had to explain to my friends that *Bananas in Pyjamas* were two funny bananas called B1 and B2, that the Muppets were strange and absurd puppets, that the Wiggles were a children's musical group also made up of costumed characters such as Dorothy the Dinosaur or Henry the Octopus, while the *Hi-5* were people performing educational songs and dances for children.

I like all of them very much, but they were considered "so Australian," and this made me feel different. At the same time, it was also strange to try to teach my friends the correct pronunciation of their names in English because "banana" (/bəˈnɑːnə/—or, in American English, /bəˈnænə/) is pronounced so that the "a" sound of the first syllable is almost silent. In contrast, in Italian /baˈnana/, it is clearly pronounced, because Italians are used to reading each letter of the alphabet as it is, except for the "h." This brings us to the pronunciation of *Hi-5* as if the "h" were not there: they lost the aspiration of the "h" which, in English, makes a difference. The same difficulty occurred with the pronunciation of *Wiggles*, in which they usually emphasize each letter.

In contrast, in English, the final part of the word is almost unified into a single closing sound. Finally, the term "Muppets" (/ˈmʌpɪts/) was also pronounced differently, as Italian speakers tend to stress double consonants. Of course, young children do not really expect much understanding of language rules while playing, but this clearly affected me emotionally and culturally.

I also had similar problems at school: I was always happy to receive presents from my Australian aunties, such as pens, pencils, books, personalized stickers with my name on them, and all this cute school stuff. Unfortunately, most of the time this puzzled my friends because it was decorated with "the same strange characters from Australian cartoons"— I had *Bananas in Pyjamas* all over, starting with my backpack and ending with my rubber. By contrast, all my friends had Spiderman and Barbie school supplies. My things also featured prints of Australian animals, such as kangaroos and koalas, which became known from that moment on. As children, they were all interested in kangaroos and koalas because one was funny, jumping around and carrying its baby in its pouch, while the other was more like a cute, soft puppet to squeeze. Yet again, I could really feel the difference.

The same was true of my typical English habits, such as "biscuits and tea at 5 o'clock" or "fruit as a snack." I still remember the shame I felt at school when I took out an apple from my Tupperware container. I cannot tell whether my classmates were more surprised by the apple or by the plastic container itself. The lunch box was one of the strangest things I took out of my school bag every day because it looked so odd to my classmates' eyes. Food habits were also a big issue: at school, they were used to eating panini with ham or salami or packaged snacks, and no one needed a container for them. In the 1990s, Tupperware was not as common in Italy as it is today. I remember some ladies organizing meetings at their homes to sell them among friends as the newest thing ever, which really surprised my mother. I was also the only one to eat "cereal" for breakfast and the only one to drink green hot tea in the afternoon instead of Fanta and Coke. I also did not like to eat many of the most common and traditional Calabrian dishes: *rape e salsiccia* (broccoli and sausages) *polpette di melanzane* (eggplant balls), *parmigiana* (a dish made up of layers of eggplants mixed up with tomato sauce and Parmesan cheese), *verdure sott'olio* (vegetables in oil, usually olives, eggplants, zucchini) as well as *insaccati* cured meats. I was probably the only *Calabrese* who hated them. On the contrary, I was addicted to English breakfast dishes such as pancakes or toast with butter and jam.

For snacks, I always preferred an apple pie or "cornflakes biscuits with raisins" that my mother used to cook for me instead of buying packaged biscuits. Mangoes are one of my favorite fruits, and I always struggled to eat them in Italy because I compared their taste to Australian ones. I can tell you they are completely different: the mangoes you find in Italian supermarkets are clearly imported, usually not ripe, and most of the time they taste like soap. In Australia, I have always been lucky to eat mangoes directly from the tree because Nonna Maria had a big mango tree in the backyard, and the taste was delicious. I remember Nonna Maria climbing up the tree to grab a mango for me for breakfast; she was used to cutting two big slices on both sides of the pit and then cutting them into little squares so they were much easier to eat.

One of my favorite photographs portrays Nonna Maria in the tree with a mango in her hands. Dealing with the English language in the family also meant that it was hard for us to render some words in Italian, such as "the wash basket" (*cestino dei panni sporchi*), which is one of the luckiest words that survived in our everyday speech. The same applies to "fluff" (*polvere*) or "cereal and milk" (*latte e cereali*); "tea" and "coffee" are always stressed with an English accent.

In addition to some lucky words that survived in our everyday speech, there are also idiomatic expressions, such as "to put lipstick on a pig," that my mother likes to use when someone wants to make us think that things are better than they really are. Fortunately, we never completely gave up speaking English as we frequently talked on the phone with my aunties and had long conversations. I also kept using English as much as I could in the university context and, possibly, at work.

Of course, things have changed, and today I am a 33-year-old woman completely conscious of the gift of being bilingual and belonging to two cultures—or maybe even three. I have re-evaluated Arabic culture because I feel connected to it, apart from the clearly visible Arabic traits on my face, such as my kittenish eyes. I feel more attracted to the Arabic style, especially when it comes to clothing patterns, home design, and perfumes, but, as I said before, I am also aware of my "Aussie" habits and way of thinking. I have been to Australia several times in my life. I have a few memories of my early trips as a child, mainly flashbacks triggered by specific smells and tastes. It may seem a bit strange, but sometimes, while walking along the Italian seaside, the smell of the water suddenly reminds me of the scent of Australian beaches and the sea.

During my last trip to Australia, I was able to visit Kurrawa Beach in Broadbeach, a suburb in the City of the Gold Coast, as well as Brighton Beach and St Kilda Beach, two beachside suburbs of Melbourne. I can say that the smell of these places was the same one I had magically remembered from my youth. Even stranger is the scent of Australian water from the tub; it is hard for me to explain the difference between types of waters, because it is a very personal perception, but it is a distinctive trait that takes me back to the long baths I used to take in my grandmother Maria's bathroom. It feels like an emotional bond that I have experienced throughout my whole life—magical moments that make me move from one place to another. I have also been to Australia to complete my master's research at the University of Melbourne. Studying in Australia has always been my dream, also because I wanted to experience the difference between the educational systems.

While living in Italy, it was hard for me to properly understand the Australian educational system, with grades from 1 to 13. Of course, I only experienced university life and, probably in this case, felt more Italian than Australian. When I was younger, I strongly defined myself as *Italiana*, reinforcing my Italian identity and appealing to my birthplace: *Sono nata a Paola, Città di San Francesco, in provincia di Cosenza, Calabria,* meaning "I was born in Paola, Saint Francis' town, close to Cosenza, Calabria." In primary school, all my classmates and teachers identified me as *l'Australiana*—the Australian—exactly as my mother was called when she first arrived in Paola. This still happens even today.

In the beginning, I felt uncomfortable with this nickname; I nearly hated it, just as I hated the Australian customs my mother raised me with, but today it is a completely different story because I am so proud of my Australian heritage. I understand how important it is and how lucky I am to have dual citizenship, which also means being able to move freely around the world. Many people would like to be in my shoes, because it is not easy to obtain Australian citizenship, or to speak and understand English fluently in a globalized world that increasingly requires it.

Steven J. Sacco

While Elizabeth and Jessica were each known as *l'Australiana*, I possessed two identities. I was *the Italian* on the West Side of Chicago and *l'Americano* in my grandparents' village in Calabria. No one in my neighborhood identified as American, except for those who were unsure of their immigrant identity. In Chicago, a common question between two people when meeting for the first time was "What are you?" I discovered later that outside of Chicago, no one understood that question. In response, a Chicagoan would say "Polish," "Lithuanian," or whatever immigrant group they came from. No one ever said, "I'm American" or "I'm Italian American."

I am a 73-year-old Italian-American born in Chicago in 1952. My story is different from Jessica's and Elizabeth's, but my linguistic history mirrors that of many Americans whose families wished their children to be linguistically submersed in America's melting pot. I had no heritage language—until I was asked to learn Italian by my academic department at San Diego State University when I was 51 years old. I learned Italian at an immersion program in Florence because my academic department needed me to teach elementary Italian. At that moment, Italian suddenly became my heritage language.

As a child, I participated in three-generational family gatherings, which took place every Sunday and on holidays. The three generations included my grandfather, who immigrated to the U.S. in 1914, my uncles and aunts, my father, and finally my cousins. My grandmother had died in 1952, three months after my birth. I mention her because he was the heart of the family, which I documented in my article for the book *Italian Women in Chicago*. My grandfather remarried, and Grandma Lucy became the only grandmother I would know in person.

When they were not speaking English, my grandfather, father, uncles, and aunts communicated in *miglierinese*, the dialect of Miglierina, especially when they wanted to exclude us from "adult" conversations, they never taught us Italian or *miglierinese,* even though my cousins and I, talented language learners, acquired Calabrese words, mostly insults, in our conversations. "Look at that guy! He's a *giucci*." *Ciuccio* is the Italian word for a donkey, an ass.

We acquired a dozen or more Calabrese words or phrases, interspersed in our English, which we still use today. Though my cousins and I were excluded from becoming bilingual, we were bicultural. We all suffered through dual-identity issues, which I describe in my memoir *Growing Up Calabrese*. We identified ourselves as Italian or Calabrian, never as Americans. Our Polish-American, Lithuanian-American, or Greek-American friends and classmates also used this identifying marker. Being Italian enabled us to join the in-group among other Italian-Americans in Chicago.

Unfortunately, like Jessica, I was excluded from the in-group of my grandparents' village, Miglierina, which was hidden deep in the mountains in the Calabrian province of Catanzaro. First, I spoke to my distant cousins in Italian, the language of the outsider, instead of in *miglierinese*, a dialect I still cannot speak. I am known as *l'Americano*, which I probably will not ever shed that label, even if I live there for the rest of my life.

My wife, Sandra Luz, is bilingual in Spanish and English, and it is her bilingualism that I envy every time she speaks Spanish *senza* accent and *senza* anglicisms. Instead, I speak Italian with a pronounced accent, and my anglicisms will never totally disappear, even though I work daily to improve it. My Italian will never approach my French, my first foreign language, which I was forced to learn in high school and college because Italian was not offered. Ironically, my high school now gives Italian, which could have become my heritage language had it been provided a half-century earlier.

Conclusion

In this chapter, we have identified and described a unique "heritage language" experience in which English has become a heritage language in Calabria, a region of Southern Italy. In a rare linguistic phenomenon, English has attained the status of "heritage language" for University of Calabria students whose grandparents had once emigrated to the U.S., Canada, and Australia. Their grandparents became affluent in these countries, attained professional proficiency in English, but then decided to return to Calabria.

Many "birds of passage" returned home to Calabria heroes and role models. Their affluence enabled them to purchase beachfront property, affluent homes, college education for their children, and even, in one case, a 1955 Cadillac Seville.[578] Lo Bianco describes the case of her great-grandfather, who shipped home to Calabria in a Cadillac only to discover that the streets of Briatico were too narrow for it to cruise around town in triumph.[579] As a result, the Cadillac remained in the town square, where it served for decades as a

---

[578] When I, Steve Sacco, met my first class at the University of Calabria in 2020, I expected them to all be first generation college students as Calabria is the poorest region of Italy and the European Union. To my surprise, all were second or even third generation college students—unlike me. That was the power of the affluence acquired by the "birds of passage" in America, Argentina, Australia, and Canada. All have professional careers, in large part, as a result of their grandparents and great grandparents.
[579] Lo Bianco, 2022

monument of affluence. Lo Bianco's grandfather returned as an outsider, even by his best friend, even though he was born and raised in Briatico.

Today, at the University of Calabria, a university that did not exist during the time of most "birds of passage," there are students representing new heritage languages such as Russian, German, or Albanian. All have either a Calabrian father or mother. They left Calabria to find employment and then returned as a new generation of "birds of passage." Today, they are *la Russa*, *la Tedesca*, or *l'Albanese*, new "outsiders" trying to fit in.

Chapter 17

Translanguaging in a Third Space: Enhancing Multilingualism and Literacy Through a Bilingual Buddy Reading Program in South Africa.

Sibhekinkosi Anna Nkomo

Learners in many African countries have limited access to culturally and linguistically relevant reading resources in their homes and learning environments. Additionally, in the case of South Africa, the mismatch in the learners' home languages and the language of teaching and learning hinders their academic success. This disconnect can impede learning outcomes as learners may struggle to relate to and engage with the content. South African learners have consistently performed poorly in international assessments such as the Progress in International Reading Literacy Study (PIRLS), revealing the country's low literacy levels. According to the PIRLS 2021 report, 81% of Grade 4 learners cannot read for meaning in any language.[580]

According to Mkhize & Balfour, multilingual education in South Africa remains controversial despite legislative policies implemented to support multilingual education.[581] Linguistic diversity is still a problem as African languages are far more dominant in the education system, thus not visible in the curriculum in many primary schools. This shows that language inequality and monoglossic ideologies are still prevalent in South Africa despite Constitutional and legislative policies being in place to support multilingual education. This limits

---
[580] Mullis et al., 2023
[581] Mkhize & Balfour, 2017

students' linguistic development and affects their overall academic performance. This chapter seeks to show how translanguaging as a pedagogy was used to promote inclusive, quality education and heritage languages and nurture reading in emerging bilinguals. Heritage languages are integral to cultural identity and heritage, with significant implications for social cohesion. The chapter also highlights the importance of community-based language schools, bilingual education programs, and cultural activities in preserving heritage languages.

Multilingual Education and Literacy Challenges in South Africa

South Africa is a multilingual country with 12 official languages, including sign language. Despite this linguistic diversity, English remains the dominant language of instruction in many educational contexts. This dominance of English affects many African language-speaking learners' access to quality education and hinders their academic success. While the Language in Education Policy advocates for multilingualism, the implementation of such practices has largely been unsuccessful, especially within formal educational settings. In the Foundation Phase (Grade R-3), many learners are being taught in their home language, transitioning to English as the language of instruction in Grade 4. In addition, in the Foundation Phase, learners are still learning to read, and they begin reading to learn in Grade 4. This important transition occurs between the foundation and intermediate phases. Before learners "read with meaning," they need to be able to decode and read fluently. Once their reading accuracy and automaticity develop, their fluency develops. Their cognitive resources will be free, and they can now focus on comprehension. However, this switch has been criticized as abrupt, with insufficient support provided to learners, leading to considerable challenges for learners, yet the ability to read forms the foundation of all future learning.

The issue of language learning and teaching offered in many teacher training programs does not align with the South African realities of indigenous languages. Teacher training programs are offered in English, yet the African indigenous language is used as the language of learning and teaching (LoLT) in the Foundation Phase in more than 80% of the schools in Quintile 1- 3 (These are no fee-paying schools). Thereafter, from Grade 4, indigenous languages are relegated to be learned as a subject, at either a home language (HL) or a First Additional Language (FAL). The LoLT becomes English for many schools from Grade 4 onwards. Given the South African population demographics, more than 80% of teachers and learners do not use English as their home or native language.[582] Due to insufficient teacher training, research shows that South African teachers do not know how to teach reading. In addition, there are limited teaching and supplementary reading resources. Of relevance to this study is the absence of multilingual literacy-rich environments, linguistically and culturally relevant reading resources, and libraries to support reading practices. These are some of the contributing factors to the poor reading culture and performance of South African learners in reading and comprehension. However, it is important to highlight that there has been emerging and notable support from stakeholders, including the education department and communities, in promoting native-language instruction through the provision of linguistically and culturally relevant reading resources and other literacy development initiatives, such as in and out-of-school reading clubs being established.

Buddy Reading Programs

This chapter reports on a multilingual Buddy Reading Program that was implemented for primary school learners in South Africa as a strategy for enhancing multilingualism and literacy. Buddy reading involves pairing children of similar or varying reading abilities to engage in shared reading activities. Children take turns reading aloud to one another, providing feedback, discussing comprehension, and sharing their interpretations of the text.[583] Studies on the buddy reading strategy are scarce in South Africa, and this reveals a gap in national research. Learners must be provided with varied reading

---

[582] Mkhize & Balfour, 2017
[583] Topping, Duran, & Keer, 2015

opportunities to nurture reading. Reading resources should be culturally relevant materials to support language development and identity. In this study, it was observed that outside of the reading program, the participants had limited exposure to and use of culturally relevant texts reflecting South African Xhosa traditions. Thus, in the established reading program, the participants had an opportunity to engage with isiXhosa (and English) language resources, and this contributed to their self-esteem and motivation to read as they were familiar with the texts. They could see themselves and their lives depicted in the texts. In addition, adopting a buddy reading strategy presented reading as a social activity rather than a chore. The benefits of adopting reading as a social activity have been reported to be positive in nurturing reading and creating a reading culture.

Considering a Translanguaging Pedagogy

Classrooms around the world are becoming more diverse with an increase in multilingual learners in the classroom. This has necessitated the need to recognize multilingual pedagogies and practices to promote multilingual teaching and learning.[584] Translanguaging is one pedagogy that has gained popularity with teachers and researchers around the globe to encourage multilingual teaching and learning in diverse contexts. There are two frequently cited definitions of translanguaging, which are 'the act performed by bilinguals of accessing different linguistic features or various modes of what are described as autonomous languages'[585] and the 'deployment of a speaker's full linguistic repertoire without regard for watchful adherence to the socially and politically defined boundaries of named ... languages'.[586] Simply put, McKinney & Tyler state that translanguaging describes language practices where bilingual and multilingual speakers draw on their full linguistic repertoires without concern for the boundaries of named languages to co-construct

---

[584] Krulatz, Christison, Lorenz & Seviç, 2021
[585] García, 2009, p. 141
[586] Otheguy, García & Reid, 2015

meaning.[587] This happens spontaneously as a naturally occurring phenomenon in a range of domains (in linguistic terms, the use is unmarked), as well as deliberately, as in the case of pedagogical translanguaging in classrooms.[588] Thus, translanguaging can be described as a purposeful pedagogical approach using language interchangeably, whether it be spoken or written.[589]

Within the context of this study, translanguaging is defined as a pedagogical approach used by researchers or teachers that allows learners to switch between different languages in the reading program (classroom) to create an understanding of the content being read and taught. The main aim of translanguaging is to use multiple languages to progress a person's competence in the target language.[590] This pedagogical approach allows teachers and learners to use their linguistic collection flexibly within the classroom. Teachers can build on the learners' bilingual language practices strategically and with ease to ensure that they access the content knowledge and develop their language skills.[591] In the context of South Africa, translanguaging is, therefore, central to enabling epistemic access as well as challenging and changing the marginalization and exclusion of African languages from education.[592]

Researchers of multilingual language practices and interventions in different South African education contexts have adopted the concept of translanguaging. For example, at the university level (higher education), several studies have been conducted on translanguaging, while in the primary school context, other researchers have also explored this concept in depth. In addition, studies have investigated translanguaging in science teaching and learning in high schools.[593] The overall research findings show that

---

[587] McKinney & Tyler, 2024
[588] Probyn, 2015, 2019
[589] Makalela, 2015
[590] Heugh, Prinsloo, Makgamatha, Diedericks & Winnaar, 2017
[591] Menken & Sánchez, 2019
[592] McKinney & Tyler, 2024
[593] Mbirimi-Hungwe, 2016; Motlhaka and Makalela, 2016; Krause & Prinsloo, 2016; Makoe, 2018; Kerfoot & Bello-Nonjengele, 2014;

applying the translanguaging approach in multilingual classrooms can support learners' literacy, language acquisition, and epistemic access.[594]

Besides the translanguaging pedagogy being taken up by researchers in different learning contexts in South Africa, there is a dearth of research that examines the application of translanguaging in the Primary years.[595] In many primary schools, learners often have a different Home Language from that of the teacher, and this requires the teacher to create an environment that helps build the learners' confidence, provides support, and enhances the learners' emotional well-being. However, not all Foundation Phase teachers are creating these environments to support learners whose Home Language is not English to thrive in the classrooms. Hence, this study sought to bridge this gap by adopting the translanguaging pedagogy where translanguaging activities were implemented within a third space (reading program), which included a group of 10 Foundation Phase and 10 Intermediate Phase learners. This was to demonstrate how the linguistic and the whole linguistic repertoires of emergent bilingual learners can be drawn into the classrooms to open dialogue and transform learning spaces.

Theoretical Framework- Social Constructivism Theory and the Third Space Theory

- The theoretical framework guiding this study was a combination of the social constructivism theory[596] and the Third Space theory.[597]

The Social Constructivism Theory

Social constructivism suggests that individuals interact with one another, their culture, and society for enhanced meaning-making.

Schoeman, Geertsema, le Roux, & Pottas, 2023; Probyn, 2015, 2019; Tyler, 2023
[594] Carrim & Nkomo, 2023
[595] Carrim & Nkomo, 2023; Schoeman et al., 2023
[596] Vygotsky, 1978
[597] Pahl & Rowsell, 2005

The key concepts of this theory that were applied in this study are mediation and scaffolding. Vygotsky defines mediation as the use of tools that are adapted to resolve an issue or accomplish a task. In this study, language and reading resources were considered important mediating tools. Scaffolding refers to the support that is provided to a learner throughout the learning process, whether it be by an individual or by textbooks.[598] Teachers must be taught how to implement different strategies to scaffold teaching.

The Third Space Theory

The reading program was conceptualized and set up as a translingual third space. According to Gutiérrez, a third space "is a transformative space where the potential for an expanded form of learning and the development of new knowledge is heightened."[599] A third space is considered a hybrid space or an in-between space, between home and school, or between different practices of literacy that blend elements of home and school cultures and literacies.[600] In addition, Scheckle states that the third space theories offer alternative spaces of possibility for the co-construction of knowledge and the negotiation of meaning.[601] They are essential sites for drawing on the different repertoires of learning or literacy, which eschew any dominant practice as they involve learning through vernacular practices in informal, networked spaces outside strict school environments.[602]

Third spaces allow inclusion and bridging between different knowledge domains and rejection of binaries between categories like public and private, physical, and virtual.[603] While schools control formal learning spaces, third-space learning involves more tactical appropriation of space by learners and everyday resistance to imposed structures. The concept of third spaces was adopted in this study, where learners were encouraged to use their linguistic and

---

[598] Vygotsky, 1978
[599] Gutiérrez, 2008, p. 152
[600] Pahl & Rowsell, 2005
[601] Scheckle, 2022
[602] As evidenced in Guzula, McKinney & Tyler, 2016; Scheckle, 2022
[603] Guzula, McKinney & Tyler, 2016

cultural resources flexibly, fostering both academic and personal growth. Thus, the bilingual buddy reading program is considered a third space. Figure 1 neatly summarizes the third space theory.

In this study, an after-school buddy reading program (Grade 7 learners reading with Grade 3 learners) was established in a social learning environment. Reading was presented as a social activity rather than a chore for the participants. In contrast to formal language and literacy classrooms, where teachers often frame hybridity as a problem,[604] the researcher created a linguistic third space, where bi/multilingualism was promoted, and translanguaging was encouraged in both spoken and written words. The researcher modelled dynamic bilingualism,[605] and the participants were positioned as competent multilinguals. By allowing them to translanguage, both in spoken and written language, the researcher repositioned the learners as linguistically resourceful.[606] Li supports the notion of establishing the translanguaging space.[607]

---

[604] Palmer, Mateus, Martinez, & Henderson, 2014
[605] García & Wei, 2014
[606] Palmer et al. 2014
[607] Li, 2011

Figure 1: Application of Third Space Theory[608]

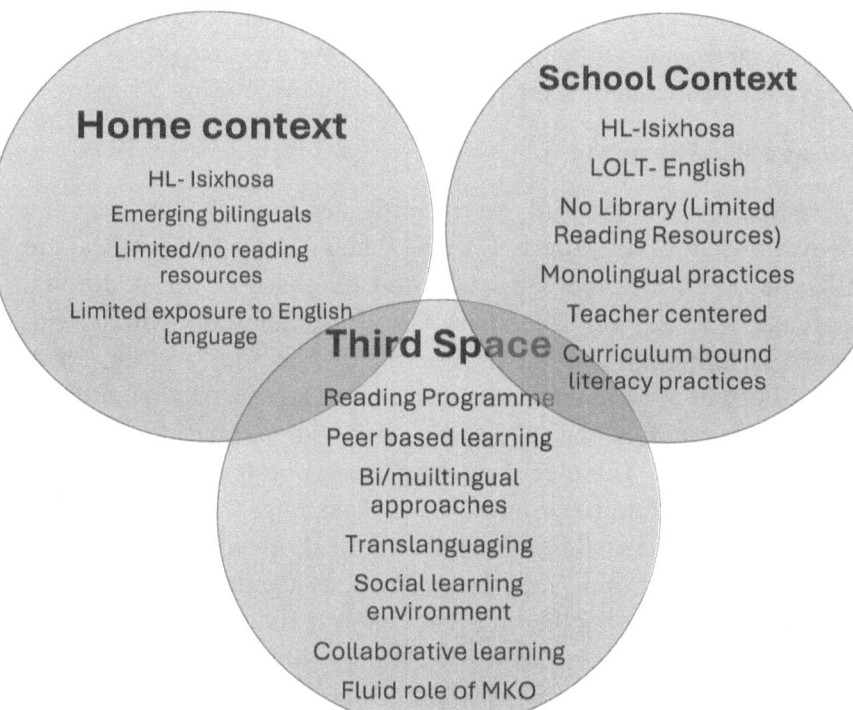

Translanguaging creates: [S]social space for the multilingual language user by bringing together different dimensions of their personal history, experience, and environment, their attitude, belief, and ideology, and their cognitive and physical capacity into one coordinated and meaningful performance and making it into a lived experience.

---

[608] Theory Adapted from Pahl & Kelly, 2005, p. 1223

Methodology

This was a mainly qualitative study, which enabled the researcher to observe and engage with the participants to understand their experiences and outcomes of the bilingual buddy reading program.[609]

Site and Participants

The participants of the study were Grade 3 and Grade 7 learners in a township school in South Africa. Their linguistic profiles are isiXhosa as the home language and English as an additional language. The Grade 7 learners (12-year-olds) were paired with Grade 3 learners (8-year-olds) to read together once a week, for at least 1 hour in a social learning environment for 7 weeks. The role of the older learners is that of a tutor, while the younger learners are considered tutees. The older learners model good reading habits, and support and scaffold the young learners' reading, assuming the role of the More Knowledgeable Other (MKO). It was important to include both age groups, mainly because they would be transitioning to a new Phase in the following year (Intermediate Phase and Senior Phase), so this shift must be scaffolded and supported. In these new phases, teaching and learning mainly happen in English, which is their first additional language.

The structure of the Reading Program

The bilingual buddy reading program was designed in such a manner that Grade 7 learners were paired with Grade 3 learners to read together for fun as a way of nurturing reading and inculcating a culture of reading. Taking into cognizance that the young learners were still learning to read, and using their mother tongue, isiXhosa, as a language of learning and teaching, while the older learners were at a stage where they were reading to learn, and using English as the language of instruction, a multilingual program informed by a translanguaging pedagogy seemed viable for this project. The older learners were first trained on how to assume the 'Tutor' role. Each

---

[609] Barrett & Twycross, 2018

week, 1-2 hours were set aside for reading together. This was an after-school program to not interfere with the already overloaded school curriculum. All sessions were facilitated and monitored by the researcher to ensure that learners were on task during the weekly reading sessions.

The overall reading program was led by the researcher, who implemented translanguaging pedagogy within the program. Applying the translanguaging stance, during the initial training and at the beginning of each reading session, the researcher told the participants that they did not have to speak English or worry about speaking 'proper English'; instead, the researcher reminded the learners that they could communicate in whatever style of language they were comfortable with. In addition, the researcher included a variety of reading resources, which included bilingual books, storybooks in English, isiXhosa, and picture books. Learners were shown how authors of bilingual books used language to convey meaning, and they were encouraged to do so, which resulted in them producing/reproducing translingual texts.[610] Different pre-, while, and post-reading activities were included, where learners were allowed to switch between isiXhosa and English to support self-esteem, confidence, reading, and comprehension. Finally, the researcher and the learners made use of strategies such as code-switching, translation, and code-mixing, known as translanguaging shifts.[611]

Data Collection and Analysis

Observations and video recordings were mainly used as methods of data collection to note the participants' changes in literacy, self-esteem, and confidence. Data was collected throughout the seven reading sessions that were conducted. Each reading session was observed. The researcher focused on the interaction between the participants, literacy events such as book swaps, reading, talking, and writing about their reading, and the way learners used language in

---

[610] Seltzer & García, 2020
[611] Seltzer & García, 2020, p. 36

their engagements. All the reading sessions were video recorded for later analysis.

Data were analyzed from the reading program session observations and video recordings. A thematic analysis was done both deductively and inductively.[612] The researcher read through each reading session observation transcript in comparison with the researcher's journal notes many times. Thereafter, these data sets were transcribed and coded using the NVivo transcription to provide an accurate verbatim transcription. During coding, excerpts that contained changes in literacy, self-esteem, and confidence were identified, coded, and sorted into themes that accurately represented the data. Recurring themes were selected for analysis, and verbatim codes were analyzed and interpreted in line with the objectives of the study.

Research Findings

Due to the established learning environment regarded as a third space, the following measurable changes were observed in the participants:

Impact on Literacy Development: Measured by observations, study participants showed improvement in reading fluency, comprehension, vocabulary in both English and isiXhosa, and writing. The following samples of their writing show evidence of improved vocabulary and writing skills:

---

[612] Thornberg & Charmaz, 2014

Figure 2: Example of a dual language storybook written by learners.

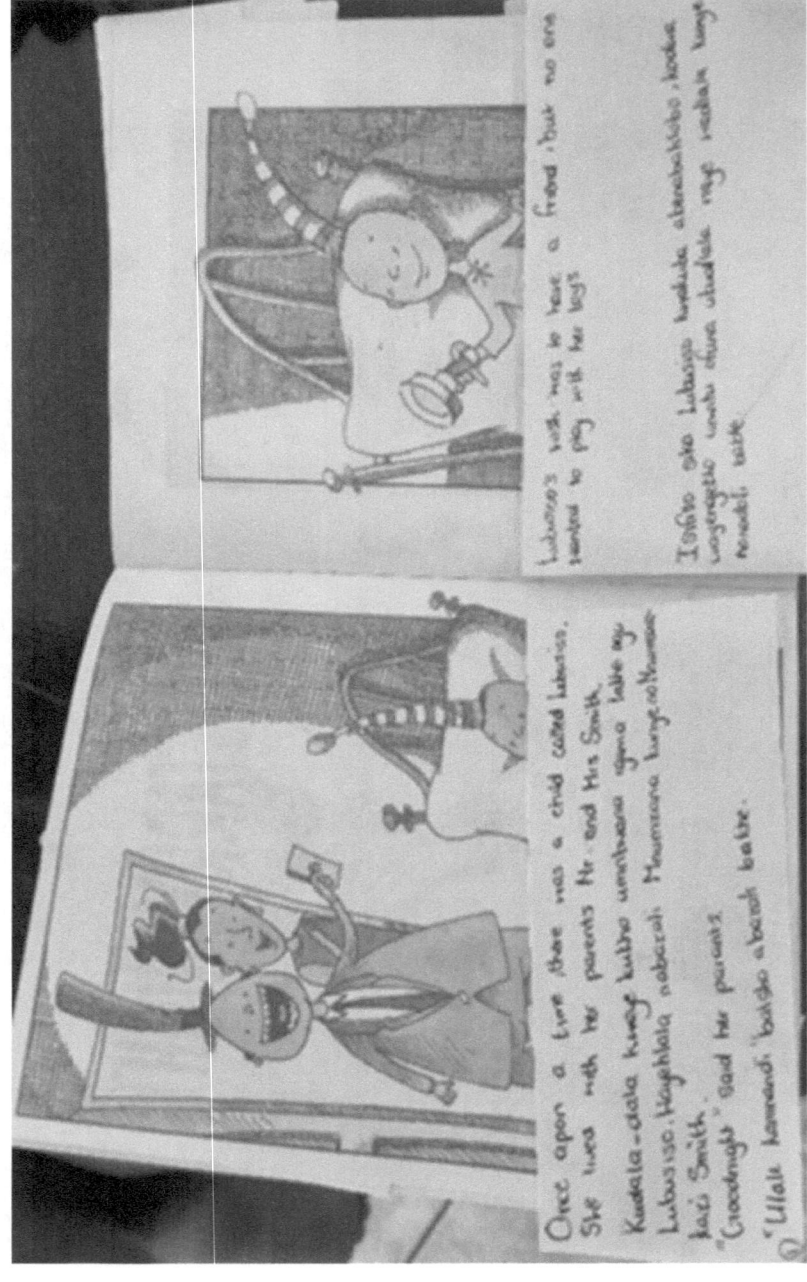

Figure 2 illustrates learners' ability to produce written content in both English and isiXhosa, showcasing improvements in vocabulary, sentence structure, and narrative coherence. It supports the argument that dual-language/bilingual instruction contributed to enhanced literacy and vocabulary development across both languages.

The researchers instructed the learners to use any language resources they liked and to write their own story. In this way, she constructed and established a translanguaging space. The example in Figure 2 shows a (Trans)languaging-for-learning activity using fluid languaging. The above samples of learners' written work in isiXhosa and English show that during the reading sessions, learners and researchers alternated between isiXhosa and English, enhancing vocabulary and comprehension through flexible language use. Learners were given opportunities to work on their understanding through either exploratory talk or writing using their full linguistic repertoire.

Boost in Self-Esteem and Confidence: Participation in the bilingual buddy reading program affected learners' self-esteem and confidence, both as individuals and as bilingual speakers. Concerning their self-esteem, the researcher noticed an increase in participants' willingness to participate in activities like book talks and reading aloud. During book talks, learners who were initially shy to stand in front of everyone improved their body language and verbal expressions of self-worth.

Similarly, their confidence was evident in increased risk-taking behavior, such as confidence to read, speak, and write in English. In addition, I observed a greater willingness to speak in front of the group and try new tasks such as free writing and storytelling, where they could shift between languages. They also volunteered to read and talk about their reading.

Role of Translanguaging: The use of both isiXhosa and English supported learners' understanding of the reading materials and allowed them to express themselves more freely, ultimately aiding in literacy development. During book talks, learners could flexibly switch between languages as they were aware that all languages were recognized. Example 1 shows how what is considered separate named languages (such as IsiXhosa and English) were meshed in the researchers' talk without diglossic separation (languages were integrated spontaneously and not used for different domains or distinct functions). As alluded to by Creese & Blackledge (2010), 'it is the combination of both languages that keeps the task moving forward' (p.110). In example 1, the researcher is translanguaging using the resources of isiXhosa and English, making use of familiar language to explain the new English vocabulary found in the story. Initially, the learner's talk was limited to short one- or two-word responses, mostly in monolingual English or isiXhosa.

Example 1: Translanguaging in researcher talk in one reading session:

> Researcher: The Fox and the Crow. Liyayazi iFox ngesiXhosa? What about i-Crow? Kukho i-Crow, ihleli on a branch...umthi. Lentaka, the Crow, was sitting on a tree branch with a i-piece of delicious cheese. U-delicious uthetha into enjani? If mhlawumbe ubona ichomie yakho iphethe something delicious, what would you do?
> Learners: Ask
> Researcher: Yes, uyayihalela, you can ask, or just like the fox, uyacinga, about how to get the cheese.

The above example of the reading program talk illustrates that TL 'is the combination of both languages that keeps the task moving forward' (Creese & Blackledge 2010:110). The naming of separate languages as well as meshed languaging is used. They were also exposed to bilingual and dual books, which they could read for pleasure. The following figure shows some of the bilingual resources that were used in the reading program.

Figure 3: Example of Bilingual Resources used in the reading program.

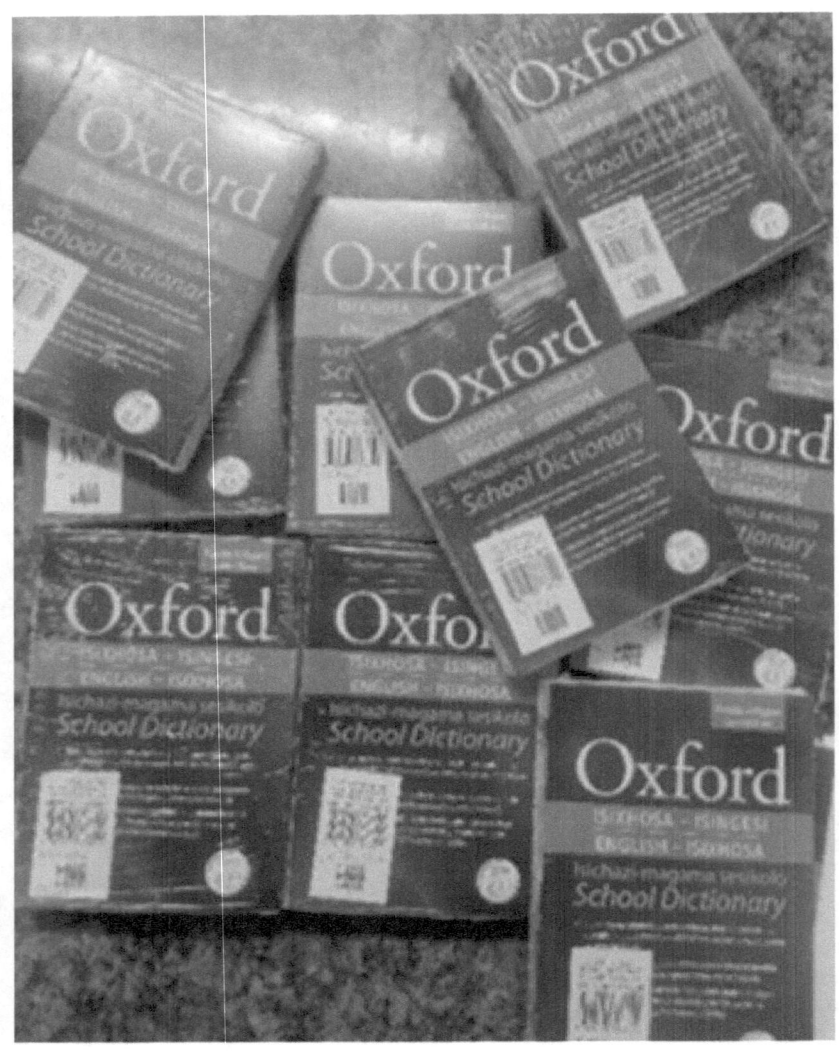

Figure 3 highlights the culturally and linguistically relevant materials employed during the reading program. These bilingual resources supported learners' translanguaging practices, fostered engagement, and encouraged reading for pleasure by reflecting the learners' lived experiences and home languages. It is important to note that not only were the resources linguistically relevant, but they were also culturally relevant. Learners could see themselves and their communities depicted in the stories, which resulted in more dialogical engagements.

The Third Space Effect: The reading program created a third space in which learners could move beyond traditional language boundaries. Firstly, A social learning environment was established, which entailed that learners had a choice to read what they wanted to read, and they had an option to choose whom they wanted to read with. They also had a choice to sit where they wanted to sit or where they felt comfortable sitting and reading, rather than being bound to a desk and table (see Figure 4).

Secondly, within the reading program, reading was viewed as a social practice rather than an isolated activity. Learners had opportunities to read in pairs and groups. Thus, the reading program was more peer-based learning, rather than the researcher always taking the lead in all the activities. This set-up led to a space where the role of the More Knowledgeable Other (MKO) was fluid. Everyone was regarded as a knower, and their knowledge, values, voices, and skills were all valued.

Finally, the 'third space' that was established allowed for bi/multilingual approaches such as translanguaging, code-switching, and translation so that all the learners had equal access to learning. Initially, learners did not understand what was meant by that they could use any language with which they were comfortable. They also found it difficult to flexibly switch between languages, as in the normal classroom context, languages are treated as separate entities. Through the researcher's modelling of language use, learners enjoyed the incorporation of both English and isiXhosa in the reading program. In addition, the use of wordless picture books, which offered them an opportunity to interpret signs, symbols, and images freely, was another unique activity that learners enjoyed.

All these mentioned design characteristics of the reading program are rare in many normal classroom environments, and they facilitated both academic and cultural engagement.

Figure 4A: social learning environment.

Figure 4 above illustrates the flexible, learner-centered setup of the reading program, where learners were empowered to choose their reading materials, peers, and seating arrangements. It visually represents the creation of a 'third space' that disrupted conventional classroom hierarchies, promoted social learning, and supported bi/multilingual engagement.

Discussion

The findings of this study suggest a notable impact on literacy development, self-esteem, and the overall educational experience of learners participating in the bilingual buddy reading program. These results highlight the importance of an integrated, flexible, and culturally sensitive approach to literacy in multilingual settings, especially in South Africa, where linguistic diversity plays a key role in social and academic life. To further contextualize the findings, the following discussion examines these findings, drawing on the literature and theoretical frameworks, including social constructivism, bilingual education, and translanguaging.

Impact on Literacy Development

The study participants' improved reading fluency, comprehension, and vocabulary in both English and isiXhosa. According to Garcia and Wei, bilingual learners can develop stronger cognitive skills, such as enhanced executive function and metalinguistic awareness, through regular engagement with multiple languages.[613] By alternating between English and isiXhosa, improvements in the learners' vocabulary development and comprehension were observed. Moreover, the bi-language approach adopted in the study is supported by Cummins, who states that bilingual learners benefit when both languages are used to scaffold learning, particularly in literacy practices.[614] By promoting the flexible alternation between languages, the study concurs with the findings of Creese and Blackledge that translanguaging fosters an environment where learners are empowered to make meaning in ways that extend beyond rigid language boundaries.[615]

---

[613] Garcia & Wei, 2014
[614] Cummins, 2001
[615] Creese & Blackledge, 2010

The improved writing samples of the learners further support the hypothesis that bilingualism can contribute to better literacy outcomes. Research by Bialystok has consistently shown that bilingual children exhibit better writing skills due to their ability to navigate different linguistic systems.[616] In this study, learners demonstrated improvement and creativity in their written work, suggesting that translanguaging facilitated both lexical and syntactic development. In particular, the flexibility to move between languages enhanced their vocabulary and grammatical structures in both English and isiXhosa.

Boost in Self-Esteem and Confidence

The findings of the study show improvements in learners' self-esteem and confidence, particularly their willingness to participate in book talks and express themselves orally and in writing. These findings resonate with social constructivist theories, such as those proposed by Vygotsky, which emphasize the role of social interaction in cognitive and emotional development.[617] By participating in a peer-supported environment where learners were encouraged to take risks, learners gained confidence not only in their academic abilities but also in their social identities as bilingual speakers. This aligns with the work of Norton, who argued that learners' sense of identity and self-worth is intricately connected to their language learning experiences.[618] Through the safe, supportive environment of the reading program, learners were empowered to take risks in their language use, thereby boosting their self-confidence.

The improved self-esteem was evident in the learners' increased willingness to participate in collaborative activities, such as book talks, where they could express themselves in both English and isiXhosa. Similarly, findings of the study by Molefe indicate that learners who felt their linguistic and cultural identities were acknowledged and celebrated showed greater engagement and motivation in learning

---

[616] Bialystok, 2001
[617] Vygotsky, 1978
[618] Norton, 2000

activities.[619] Moreover, the practice of engaging with bilingual resources, which depicted learners' communities and experiences, reinforced positive self-identity and social belonging.

Role of Translanguaging

Translanguaging emphasizes the fluidity of bilingual and multilingual language use and the process of communicating.[620] The flexibility of alternating between isiXhosa and English during the reading sessions supported the participants' literacy development. As observed in this study, translanguaging allows learners to access their full linguistic repertoires, thus facilitating deeper comprehension and richer expressions of meaning.[621] By engaging with bilingual and dual-language books, learners were able to draw upon their knowledge of both languages to enhance their understanding of the text. Canagarajah argued that translanguaging provides a means for learners to use their multilingual skills to negotiate meaning and foster more interactive, participatory learning environments.[622]

Furthermore, availing culturally relevant resources such as bilingual texts, reflecting learners' communities, increased engagement, and created a space where learners' diverse cultural backgrounds were acknowledged.[623] This is particularly significant in the South African context, where language plays a pivotal role in identity and community dynamics. The use of resources that are both linguistically and culturally relevant ensured that the reading program was a pedagogical success and a culturally affirming experience for the learners.[624]

The Third Space Effect

The concept of a third space, developed by Gutiérrez et al., guided the design of the reading program.[625] The reading program presented

---

[619] Molefe, 2022
[620] McKinney & Tyler, 2024
[621] García & Wei, 2014
[622] Canagarajah, 2011
[623] Hornberger, 2008
[624] Vasquez, 2020
[625] Gutiérrez et al. 1999

a unique space for learning that was fluid, collaborative, and social by allowing learners to fully utilize their linguistic repertoires and engage in more flexible forms of communication. This aligns with the theoretical framework of the More Knowledgeable Other (MKO),[626] where the teacher and the students co-construct knowledge. The findings of the study suggest that the role of the MKO was fluid, with learners taking on the role of both teacher and student, depending on the demands of each activity. This approach to learning helped create an inclusive environment where every learner was encouraged to contribute their knowledge and insights.[627] The flexibility of the third space was further enhanced by giving learners access to resources, such as wordless picture books. The resources allowed learners to engage with content through visual and symbolic interpretation. Skerrett argued that multimodal resources, such as pictures and symbols, support learners in expressing themselves creatively and in a way that goes beyond linguistic limitations.[628]

Finally, the learners' ability to translanguage, code-switch, and translate within this third space ensured equitable access to learning. While learners initially struggled with the idea of using both languages interchangeably, the study demonstrates that with adequate support and modelling, learners were able to develop the skills necessary to navigate these flexible language practices successfully. This result highlights the importance of teacher scaffolding in the development of bilingual literacy.[629] Creating a third space provided a legitimate after-school time and space for learners to talk about their reading. Through book talks in the reading program, learners had an opportunity to think about the books and provide evidence from the texts to support their interpretations; thus, discussion is a key tool for learning both language and content.

---

[626] Vygotskian, 1978
[627] Pahl & Rowsell, 2012
[628] Skerrett, 2013
[629] García & Wei, 2014

Conclusion and Recommendations

The findings of this study indicate that the bilingual buddy reading program, implemented within a socially supportive learning environment, positively influenced learners' literacy development, self-esteem, confidence, and appreciation for multilingualism. By creating a 'third space' that encouraged fluid language use and peer collaboration, the program highlighted the transformative potential of learner-centered, multilingual pedagogies in diverse classrooms. Translanguaging, as the central pedagogical approach, resulted in an inclusive and culturally affirming educational space where learners were not only allowed, but encouraged to draw on all their linguistic resources. This approach helped to dismantle rigid language boundaries, giving rise to more equitable learning experiences and improved literacy outcomes.

While the study is grounded in the South African context, its implications extend well beyond. In multilingual societies globally, especially those where linguistic hierarchies marginalize indigenous or home languages, this model offers a low-cost, scalable intervention that promotes both academic success and linguistic equity. Educators and policymakers in such contexts should consider the integration of bilingual buddy reading programs and reading clubs, both in and out of school, as accessible ways to support multilingual learners. The study strongly advocates translanguaging as a tool to enhance literacy development and learner engagement. Coupled with culturally relevant resources, this pedagogy cultivates interactive, inclusive classrooms that validate learners' identities while building crucial academic and social skills. It also contributes to broader national goals, such as South Africa's aim for all children to read for meaning by age 10 by 2030. Ultimately, this research adds to a growing body of evidence supporting the role of bilingual and multilingual education in nurturing not only linguistic proficiency but also socio-emotional development and equitable participation. It calls on educators, curriculum developers, and policymakers, locally and globally, to reimagine literacy instruction in ways that reflect and respect the linguistic realities of learners.

AI For Heritage Language Learning: Insights from Mind Genomics

Angela Popovic

Language is more than a system of words and rules-it is a living symbol of cultural identity, belonging, and continuity. Heritage languages, defined as those spoken within families or minority communities, serve as bridges between generations, connecting speakers to shared histories and emotional traditions.[630] Yet in a rapidly globalizing world, these languages are vanishing. UNESCO estimates that more than half of the world's 7,000 languages could disappear by the end of this century, an erosion that represents not just linguistic loss, but also the disappearance of entire worldviews and ways of remembering.[631]

Within diasporic populations, language attrition typically occurs within one or two generations. Younger speakers often adopt the dominant language of their host country for education, work, and social mobility, while their ancestral tongue becomes confined to ritual or nostalgic use.[632] Heritage language programs, such as weekend schools and community classes, frequently struggle to maintain relevance. Many rely on rigid textbooks and grammar-heavy instruction that feel outdated and disconnected from learners' real lives. Learners may enter these programs with strong emotional motivation, desiring to connect with family, heritage, and identity, but disengage when content fails to reflect their modern experience or cultural realities.

Artificial intelligence offers new ways to bridge this gap. AI-driven systems have the capacity to personalize instruction, adjusting in real time to learner needs, interests, and emotional cues.[633] When applied

---

[630] Fishman, 1991
[631] UNESCO, 2021
[632] Baker, 2018
[633] Woolf, 2010

thoughtfully, these systems can provide learning that is culturally relevant, interactive, and deeply human. However, despite widespread enthusiasm about AI in education, empirical research on how it can best serve heritage language learners remains limited.

This study seeks to fill that gap by exploring how AI tools can be designed to balance personalization, culture, and motivation. Using Mind Genomics, a behavioral and preference-mapping methodology, this pilot study investigates which AI-powered features resonate most with heritage language learners. The study addresses two primary research questions:

1. Which AI features most effectively enhance motivation and cultural connection for heritage language learners?
2. How can AI tools be designed to support diverse learner mindsets and sociocultural contexts?

Heritage Language and Social Cohesion

Heritage languages are central to cultural identity and intergenerational continuity. They transmit values, traditions, and emotional connections that sustain community cohesion.[634] As Baker notes, language functions not only as a communication system but also as a repository of shared meaning, enabling individuals to participate fully in their cultural heritage.[635] When these languages decline, the result is more than linguistic loss-it represents a fracture in community identity and a weakening of familial bonds.

In multilingual societies, especially those shaped by migration, younger generations often prioritize the dominant societal language, perceiving it as the key to success and social integration.[636] As a result, heritage languages can quickly become relegated to ceremonial use or private memory. Reversing this trend requires teaching approaches that engage both intellect and emotion, methods

---

[634] Portes & Rumbaut, 2001
[635] Baker, 2018
[636] Edwards, 1994

that reinforce the learner's sense of belonging and pride while fostering communication across generations.

Artificial Intelligence and Adaptive Learning

Artificial intelligence allows for individualized learning experiences that respond dynamically to user behavior. Algorithms can analyze a learner's progress, identify patterns, and modify instruction accordingly.[637] In language learning, this means that the same system can deliver extra support to a struggling learner while challenging another with more advanced tasks, creating a balance between engagement and difficulty.

For heritage learners, adaptive systems can also incorporate cultural relevance. For example, if a learner frequently interacts with vocabulary related to cooking or family gatherings, the AI can automatically generate lessons around recipes or holiday traditions. Similarly, if a learner prefers conversation to grammar drills, the system can emphasize speaking practice, providing just-in-time feedback that mirrors real communication. This type of learning not only builds skill but also affirms identity, turning language practice into a personal, meaningful act.[638]

Mind Genomics as a Behavioral Lens

Mind Genomics, developed by Dr. Howard Moskowitz, is a behavioral science method that identifies the factors influencing human preference and decision-making.[639] It operates through combinatorial design, testing multiple feature combinations (called vignettes) to uncover which elements have the greatest emotional and cognitive impact. Unlike traditional surveys, which isolate single variables, Mind Genomics captures how people respond to ideas in realistic combinations, similar to how they make decisions in daily life.

---

[637] Shute & Zapata-Rivera, 2012
[638] Woolf, 2010
[639] Katz, 2020

The method has been widely applied across consumer research, healthcare, and education.[640] By combining statistical modeling with behavioral data, it uncovers "mindsets"-patterns of preferences that reflect how different individuals engage with a concept. In this study, Mind Genomics offers a way to understand not just what heritage learners like, but why they like it. It bridges the emotional and functional aspects of learning, showing which AI features best resonate with heritage learners' goals, motivations, and cultural values.

Methodology

Participants

This pilot study included eight adult participants, all heritage language learners or educators residing in the United States. Their linguistic backgrounds included Serbian, Vietnamese, Korean, and Spanish. Participants ranged in age from 20 to 40 and demonstrated varying degrees of proficiency in their heritage languages.

While the sample size was small, it was suitable for exploratory Mind Genomics research, which seeks depth of insight rather than broad generalization. Participants were recruited through university-affiliated networks and cultural community groups. Several participants reported acting as informal language mentors to family members or younger peers, offering dual perspectives as learners and facilitators. This added qualitative richness to the study, as participants could reflect both on personal experience and on how learning tools might benefit others.

Data Collection

This study used the Mind Genomics method, implemented through the BiMiLeap online survey platform, to investigate which AI-driven features appeal most to heritage language learners. The approach, pioneered by Dr. Howard Moskowitz, is well known for its application in identifying consumer preferences, such as which

---

[640] Moskowitz, 2022

combinations of flavors make a soup or beverage more appealing. The same principle applies here, only the "ingredients" were AI features instead of food components.

The Analogy: Testing Recipes Instead of Ingredients

Imagine developing a new soup recipe. Rather than asking whether someone likes carrots or noodles separately, you give them spoonfuls that mix several ingredients and ask whether they want that combination. After many trials, you learn which blends work best. Mind Genomics functions the same way: instead of testing one feature at a time, it evaluates combinations of ideas, revealing how elements interact in real-world decision-making.

In this study, each "recipe" consisted of three or four short descriptions of AI features, combined into a vignette designed to feel realistic. Participants rated whether they found each vignette appealing or not appealing. Examples included:

- "The app highlights words you haven't mastered yet and gives you quick refreshers."
- "If you're progressing quickly, it adds harder exercises to challenge you."
- "You get reminders to record a short voice message to share with family."
- "Short folktales help you experience the language the way your grandparents did."

Each vignette represented a small simulation of what an AI learning experience might look like. Reaction times were also recorded in seconds to measure intuitive (fast) versus reflective (slow) responses, providing insight into both cognitive and emotional appeal.

Survey Design and Procedure

Each participant completed a sequence of 24 randomized vignettes generated by BiMiLeap. Before beginning, participants responded to background questions capturing their linguistic and motivational profiles. These included:

- Which heritage language did they speak, and how often do they use it?
- Their primary motivation for learning (e.g., family connection, identity, education, or career),
- Their preferred learning modality (speaking, reading, writing, or group activities), and
- Whether they preferred learning alone or collaboratively.
- Collecting this data provided context for interpreting preferences and identifying subgroups based on motivation or learning style.

Feature Categories

The study draws from six primary categories of AI-driven features, developed through a review of existing adaptive learning literature and pilot interviews:

1. Personalization – Adaptive pacing and content based on learner progress.
2. Cultural Narratives – Folktales, family stories, or diaspora experiences embedded in lessons.
3. Reminders – Automated prompts that encourage consistency and re-engagement after breaks.
4. Progress Tracking – Visual indicators such as badges, milestones, or skill trees.
5. Social Learning – Peer challenges, group goals, and family-centered activities.
6. Multimedia Integration – Audio, video, and interactive storytelling features connecting learners to community experiences.
7. Each vignette blended elements from these categories, enabling researchers to analyze how feature combinations influenced user appeal and engagement.

Why This Method Works

The strength of Mind Genomics lies in its realism. People do not evaluate technologies one feature at a time-they experience them as integrated systems. This approach allows for a more natural, behaviorally valid understanding of user engagement. By identifying which "recipes" of AI features generate the most positive responses, developers and educators can design heritage language tools that align with real user motivations rather than assumptions about what learners should want.

Analysis

Data were analyzed using regression-based modeling to determine which individual features most strongly influenced appeal within each vignette. Positive coefficients indicated higher appeal, while negative coefficients represented disinterest or aversion. Reaction times were coded as either fast (intuitive) or slow (deliberative), offering insight into the depth of user preference.

Through this process, patterns of response were clustered into distinct learner mindsets, groups of participants who shared similar motivational and behavioral tendencies. These mindsets reflected not only surface-level preferences but also deeper psychological orientations toward learning. By identifying these patterns, the study laid the groundwork for a more nuanced understanding of how AI tools can be designed to meet diverse learner needs, balancing personalization, cultural connection, and social engagement.

Results

Adaptive Personalization

One of the most compelling findings of this study is the significant role of adaptive personalization in AI heritage language tools. Participants consistently rated features that adjusted lesson content and pacing according to individual performance as highly appealing. For example, when an AI feature offered more challenging tasks after a learner demonstrated mastery, or slowed down when the learner struggled with it, it helped sustain confidence and reduce frustration.

Similar adaptive designs in educational systems have been shown to increase persistence and self-efficacy.[641] Participants described these tools as making them feel "seen" by the technology, a quality associated with higher learner agency and ownership of the process.[642]

Another frequently praised feature involved the AI's ability to recognize a learner's personal interests-such as favorite travel destinations, traditional recipes, or family memories-and generate mini-lessons around those topics. This approach positioned language learning as something alive and personally meaningful rather than abstract or purely academic. Participants reported that such adaptive lessons reduced anxiety, enhanced enjoyment, and helped them emotionally connect with their heritage. Prior research likewise links personalized, interest-driven learning with deeper engagement and long-term retention.[643]

Cultural Connection Through Storytelling

Cultural narratives were not merely appreciated-they were perceived as essential. Features that incorporated folktales, legends, family stories, or diaspora experiences received the highest average appeal ratings. Heritage learners emphasized that these stories transformed language practice into identity exploration. Comparable results have been documented in studies of narrative-based instruction, which improves vocabulary acquisition while reinforcing cultural awareness.[644]

Participants explained that storytelling made them feel "closer to their grandparents" or "finally able to understand the meaning behind family traditions." Whether they were learning through the vocabulary of a holiday recipe or hearing migration stories, these experiences cultivated empathy and belonging. This aligns with heritage language research showing that emotionally resonant

---

[641] Shute & Zapata-Rivera, 2012; Woolf, 2010
[642] Means et al., 2014
[643] Fryer & Bovee, 2016; Park & Yun, 2017
[644] Kramsch, 2013; Kim & Lee, 2018

content increases both motivation and community attachment.[645] Therefore, AI designers should embed storytelling features that honor heritage rather than treating language as decontextualized words and grammar.

Motivational Features

Gamification elements-such as visual progress trackers, timelines, and digital badges-were widely endorsed by participants. These mechanisms were valued not as decoration but as concrete signs of achievement. Prior work in language-learning apps supports this finding: goal visualization enhances motivation by making incremental progress visible.[646]

Another strongly rated feature was the inclusion of supportive reminders or "nudges." When framed in culturally relevant language (e.g., "Your grandfather would be proud of you today"), reminders felt like gentle encouragement rather than external pressure. This resonates with behavioral design studies demonstrating that positive, personalized prompts significantly improve persistence in self-paced learning.[647]

Finally, social interaction features-group challenges, family learning circles, and shared milestones-elicited enthusiasm, especially among participants aligned with the "Collaborative Goal-Oriented" mindset. Prior research also finds that social accountability enhances language retention and emotional engagement.[648] Together, these results affirm that motivation in heritage language learning arises from a mix of personal meaning, visible growth, and community connection.

Learner Mindsets

A major outcome of this study was the identification of three distinct learner mindsets, derived from statistical clustering of participant

---

[645] He, 2010; Fishman, 1991
[646] Deterding et al., 2011; Looyestyn et al., 2017
[647] Fogg, 2009; Hattie & Timperley, 2007
[648] Vygotsky, 1978; Gee, 2017

responses and reaction times. Each mindset represents a unique orientation toward learning, culture, and motivation. Recognizing these profiles helps designers and educators avoid "one-size-fits-all" solutions and instead build flexible systems that meet learners where they are.

Mindset 1: Adaptive Individualists

These learners prefer autonomy and control. They seek tools that adjust to their personal pace, offering immediate support when they struggle and greater challenge when they excel. They value efficiency and visible results. Research on self-regulated learning echoes this pattern, showing that independent learners thrive in systems providing real-time feedback and adjustable complexity.[649]

Cultural content matters to Adaptive Individualists only when it directly supports linguistic progress. For them, stories or traditions are valuable as long as they teach functional language. They are pragmatic and goal-oriented, often motivated by personal growth or professional utility rather than nostalgia. For instance, a cooking video would be engaging only if it advanced vocabulary mastery.

Mindset 2: Cultural Connectors

Cultural Connectors emphasize emotion, heritage, and continuity. They view language learning as a way to honor family and preserve traditions. Their engagement stems from meaning rather than metrics. They prefer lessons infused with storytelling, family interviews, or diaspora narratives. This echoes findings that identity affirmation drives persistence among heritage learners more than academic incentives.[650]

They are less impressed by gamification and more drawn to authenticity. A simple voice-recording task, inviting them to interview a grandparent, may carry more emotional weight than earning badges. For them, technology succeeds when it feels like a cultural bridge rather than a digital challenge.

---

[649] Zimmerman & Schunk, 2011
[650] He, 2010; Montrul, 2016

Mindset 3: Collaborative Goal-Oriented Learners

These learners thrive on interaction. They enjoy sharing progress, competing in friendly challenges, and celebrating group success. Their engagement increases when they feel accountable to others, mirroring research on cooperative learning and peer scaffolding.[651]

They respond strongly to communal experiences-family leaderboards, joint storytelling, or "Family Word Challenges." Conversely, isolated or self-paced formats may reduce their motivation. This group benefits from gamified social structures that balance fun with meaningful connection.

Why These Mindsets Matter

These three orientations highlight the diversity of heritage learners. A badge system may motivate a Collaborative Learner but leave a Cultural Connector unmoved; a reflective storytelling task may resonate with a Connector but feel slow to an Individualist. Therefore, effective AI design must blend personalization, emotional relevance, and social flexibility. Mind Genomics excels precisely at uncovering such segmentation, revealing how distinct user groups interpret the same experience differently.[652]

Personalization as a Core Strategy

Findings reinforce a broader pedagogical shift from standardized curricula toward learner-driven experiences. Adaptive personalization enables learners to progress at their own pace while maintaining motivation, an outcome long supported by research on differentiated instruction.[653] For heritage learners, who span wide proficiency ranges and emotional attachments, this flexibility is essential.

By dynamically adjusting lessons, AI tools can make language learning less mechanical and more responsive. This mirrors human tutoring in which guidance scales with learner needs.[654] The result is

---

[651] Johnson & Johnson, 2009; Warschauer, 2000
[652] As Katz, 2020 and Moskowitz, 2022 argue.
[653] Tomlinson, 2017
[654] VanLehn, 2011

improved confidence, sustained effort, and stronger linguistic retention.

Culture as Curriculum

The study also underscores that culture is not an accessory to language-it is the curriculum itself. Cultural storytelling, imagery, and traditions transform abstract grammar into lived experience. Learners were more engaged by lessons featuring family recipes or folktales than by repetitive drills, echoing Kramsch's argument that language learning should foreground symbolic and emotional meaning.[655]

When designed intentionally, AI systems can host community-generated content, creating authentic intercultural literacy opportunities. Integrating cultural modules reinforces identity affirmation and encourages intergenerational dialogue.[656]

Motivation Through Gamification and Social Learning

In digital environments saturated with distractions, sustained engagement requires intrinsic motivation supported by visible progress. Studies on gamified education confirm that micro-goals and feedback loops maintain user persistence.[657] However, surface-level entertainment is insufficient for heritage learners, who seek emotional connection in addition to enjoyment.

Social learning further deepens engagement by positioning language practice as a shared endeavor. As Vygotsky noted, knowledge develops through social interaction, and AI platforms that facilitate family or peer collaboration align with this sociocultural principle.[658] Features like family challenges or joint voice recordings blend emotional bonding with communicative practice, making learning both meaningful and sustainable.

---

[655] Kramsch, 2013
[656] Fishman, 1991; Portes & Rumbaut, 2001
[657] Deterding et al., 2011; Su & Cheng, 2015
[658] Vygotsky, 1978

Ethical, Equity, and Access Considerations

Participants raised valid concerns about ethics and accessibility. Chief among them was the need for cultural respect in AI content generation. Including community elders or cultural experts in design stages can mitigate risks of misrepresentation or stereotyping, aligning with participatory design principles.[659]

Data privacy emerged as another priority. Since heritage learners often share personal stories and voice data, transparency regarding storage, consent, and deletion is essential.[660]

Finally, equitable access must remain central. Many heritage speakers live in contexts with limited digital infrastructure. Offline functionality, multilingual interfaces, and partnerships with local institutions can help bridge the digital divide.[661]

Practical Recommendations for AI-Powered Heritage Language Tools

Drawing on participant insights and Mind Genomics analysis, seven key recommendations guide future tool development:

1. Design for Learner Diversity.

Create flexible pathways addressing each mindset—customizable modules for Individualists, cultural storytelling for Connectors, and group challenges for Collaborators.[662]

2. Embed Cultural Storytelling.

Partner with community storytellers and elders to build multimedia lessons that humanize heritage.[663]

3. Use Adaptive Feedback Loops.

---

[659] D'Ignazio & Klein, 2020
[660] Floridi & Cowls, 2019
[661] UNESCO, 2021
[662] Tomlinson, 2017
[663] Kramsch, 2013

Employ AI analytics to deliver just-in-time feedback, maintaining optimal challenge and motivation.[664]

4. Gamify Progress Meaningfully.

Reward culturally significant milestones rather than arbitrary points.[665]

5. Enable Community and Family Integration.

Facilitate shared projects that strengthen intergenerational ties.[666]

6. Ensure Cultural Respect and Data Privacy.

Implement transparent policies and community review processes.[667]

7. Expand Access and Inclusion.

Design low-bandwidth, intuitive interfaces accessible to all learners.[668]

Final Thought

These recommendations provide a framework for designing AI systems that do more than teach language-they sustain identity, family connection, and cultural continuity. When paired with ethical design and inclusive infrastructure, AI can help ensure that heritage languages continue to thrive as living expressions of community life.

Conclusion

Preserving a heritage language is ultimately an act of maintaining identity. As this study demonstrates, AI tools guided by human-centered design can make learning more adaptive, culturally resonant, and socially connected. The Mind Genomics method revealed that learners value three intertwined dimensions-

---

[664] Shute & Zapata-Rivera, 2012
[665] Deterding et al., 2011
[666] Warschauer, 2000
[667] Floridi & Cowls, 2019
[668] UNESCO, 2021

personalization, cultural storytelling, and social engagement-that together create meaning and motivation.

By uniting technology with cultural empathy, educators and developers can transform AI from a neutral platform into a cultural lifeline. Such tools can empower individuals to reclaim, sustain, and celebrate their linguistic heritage, ensuring that heritage languages live not only in memory but in daily, joyful use across generations. Ultimately, the survival of heritage languages may depend not just on remembering the past, but on designing technologies that carry it forward.

Future research directions

- How do we make AI-powered speech recognition adaptable for regional dialects and minority languages?
- How do we ensure adaptive storytelling preserves cultural authenticity?
- Compared to conventional methods, how do AI-driven heritage language courses affect long-term retention?

Addressing these questions will allow future research to hone AI-powered language preservation, helping communities, rather than having an adverse effect on their linguistic identity.

Conclusion
Toward a Transformative Multilingual Future

Fabrice Jaumont and Jane F. Ross

The chapters in this volume collectively show that heritage languages are not merely preserved—they are constantly reshaped in response to social, political, and technological change. Their maintenance is not a nostalgic act confined to diasporic enclaves; it is a dynamic process that reflects how individuals, families, and institutions negotiate belonging and cohesion in an era of global interdependence. Together, these studies demonstrate that heritage languages are as much about creating futures as they are about sustaining cultural memories.

Across contributions focusing on family and identity, a consistent theme emerges: emotional connection drives intergenerational transmission more powerfully than formal instruction alone. Research on adolescents and families (Lico, Pham, Kim) underscores that the strongest motivation to maintain a heritage language stems from its role as an emotional anchor and a marker of belonging, even when proficiency is uneven. Educators working in community contexts (Jennings-Winterle) add another layer, revealing how teachers act as cultural brokers, bridging private family efforts and public community life. These findings collectively suggest that any attempt to sustain heritage languages must address not only pedagogical methods but also the affective bonds that keep these languages alive.

In chapters examining policy and institutional frameworks, a clear tension appears between symbolic recognition and structural support. Initiatives like the Seal of Biliteracy (Rivière Copa) and the

French for All program (Gaboriau) illustrate the potential of formal recognition to reframe multilingualism as a civic asset. Yet comparative studies (Emilsson Peskova, and colleagues) remind us that policies often fail to translate ideals into equitable access, leaving grassroots communities to fill the gaps. Brecht and Peyton, as well as Barth, Hristozova, and Kanikli, show that collaboration between community schools and mainstream institutions can foster social cohesion, but only when institutional support is meaningful and sustained. The implication is clear: heritage languages thrive when policy and community action reinforce rather than replace one another.

At the level of community innovation, the chapters highlight resilience and creativity in the face of systemic challenges. Studies of pandemic-era adaptations (Paulovicova, Emilsson Peskova, McCabe) and underfunded programs (Morina) show that community mobilization can sustain language maintenance even with limited resources. Grassroots initiatives such as diaspora networks (Bagayoko) and youth competitions (Calderbank, Elya, Smithburg) illustrate how heritage languages can move from private family use to public affirmation, fostering pride and countering negative stereotypes. Meanwhile, Nkomo's translanguaging initiatives demonstrate that inclusive pedagogy not only improves literacy but also empowers learners culturally and socially. Together, these studies suggest that heritage languages are most vibrant when learning spaces—whether physical or virtual—become sites of community-building and identity affirmation.

The chapters also push us to rethink what counts as "heritage." Sacco, Salerno, and Wardy's analysis of English in Calabria, shaped by reverse migration, challenges linear narratives of language loss, showing that languages can gain heritage status in new and unexpected contexts. Popovic's exploration of AI-driven learning tools points to an emerging frontier, where digital technologies—if guided by ethical and culturally responsive design—may become catalysts for intergenerational transmission. This combination of reversed migration, transnational communities, and technological innovation highlights the fluidity of heritage itself in a globalized world.

Taken together, the volume points to five interrelated imperatives for research, policy, and practice. First, heritage language scholarship must adopt intersectional approaches, linking language maintenance to broader social determinants such as economic resources, migration patterns, and racial and gender equity. Second, collaborative policymaking is essential, aligning federal, local, and community efforts to extend the reach of programs like the Seal of Biliteracy. Third, technological innovation holds promise, but it must be developed with a human-centered ethos that respects cultural specificity and empowers users. Fourth, transnational dialogue is increasingly necessary, as reverse migration and digital diasporas reveal how linguistic borders are shifting. Finally, educational transformation must integrate heritage languages into mainstream schooling through teacher training, inclusive assessment practices, and an institutional belief that linguistic diversity is a civic and academic strength.

This book ultimately argues that heritage languages are blueprints for more inclusive futures. They mediate between generations, connect communities across continents, and provide the tools for intercultural understanding. If supported through thoughtful policy, innovative pedagogy, and community engagement, heritage languages can move from being seen as private family matters to being valued as public goods that enrich education, civic life, and cultural diversity. The challenge now is to act: every policy choice, classroom decision, and family conversation shapes whether these languages will continue to thrive. Heritage languages are, in the end, not only markers of identity but also instruments for building trust, empathy, and social cohesion that diverse societies urgently need.

Closing Reflection and Call to Action

Heritage languages are more than words carried across generations; they are living acts of connection, resilience, and hope. Every choice to speak an ancestral language at home, to create inclusive curricula, to fund a community program, or to design culturally responsive digital tools shapes whether these languages will continue to thrive. The stakes could not be higher: heritage languages are not only threads of cultural memory but also instruments of empathy, civic trust, and shared belonging. The chapters in this volume have shown that when families, educators, policymakers, and innovators work together, diversity need not divide; it can instead be the foundation of stronger, more inclusive societies. The challenge now is to act—to recognize heritage languages as collective resources and to nurture them as vital public goods. In doing so, we choose a future in which linguistic diversity is not feared but celebrated, and where heritage languages continue to build the bridges—between generations, cultures, and nations—that our interconnected world so urgently needs.

About the Authors

Issam Salameh Albdairat is a linguist whose work explores Arabic dialectology, sociolinguistic variation, and heritage language use in diaspora communities. He authored A Sociolinguistic Study of Phonological Variation in Jordanian Arabic in Al-Karak (Indiana University, 2021). His research examines the intersection of language, identity, and bilingualism among Arabic heritage speakers.

Haifa Alsakkaf is an intercultural education researcher and practitioner focusing on migration, multilingualism, and second-generation immigrant identity in Italy. Founder of Good World Citizen, she promotes multilingual education and inclusion. Her research investigates how Arabic heritage language learning shapes identity and belonging in migrant youth.

Djeneba Deby Bagayoko is an Italian-born Maninka and Bamana linguist of Malian and Senegalese heritage. Her research bridges African and diasporic linguistic traditions, showing how features of Bamanankan, Wolof, and Esan are retained in Ebonics. She advocates for linguistic recognition of African diasporic languages and comparative African linguistics.

Isabelle Barth holds a Ph.D. in Communication, Arts & Spectacles from the University of Bordeaux Michel de Montaigne. She founded the Association pour la Promotion et l'Avancement du Multilinguisme (APAM) and co-founded FLAM Monde. Her work promotes multilingualism and heritage language learning through European Erasmus projects and global networks.

Marie Boccou Kestřánková teaches at the Institute of Czech and Deaf Studies, Charles University. An expert in linguodidactics, language testing, and Czech as a heritage language, she authored the Czech for Foreigners textbook series. She has led several international projects supporting Czech language education for diaspora communities worldwide.

Richard D. Brecht is a linguist and policy expert recognized for shaping U.S. federal language education policy. Co-founder of the National Heritage Language Resource Center, his scholarship has advanced understanding of bilingualism, national language needs, and heritage language instruction in the United States.

Tony Calderbank is a British scholar of Arabic and Persian, currently a Consultant for Qatar Foundation International. He studied at the University of Manchester and holds an M.A. in Applied Linguistics from Salford. A former British Council director, he has translated major Arabic literary works and supports Arabic heritage education initiatives worldwide.

Michaela Chlostová Muñoz is a lecturer at the Faculty of Psychology and Sciences of Education, University of Geneva. Her research focuses on student engagement and perseverance in special education, with an emphasis on mathematics and language learning. She explores how teachers can support students with diverse linguistic and learning needs.

Fabien Rivière Copa is a multilingual educator and researcher whose work centers on U.S. heritage language policies and their impact on national cohesion and cultural diversity. Originally from France, he has taught French, German, and Spanish in American schools and contributed to policy studies promoting equity and multilingual education.

Janine Elya works on Arabic language education and heritage learner development at Qatar Foundation International. She holds degrees from Tufts University and Johns Hopkins University. She has led initiatives expanding access to Arabic instruction in the U.S. Her research interests include multilingual education and educational equity.

Renata Emilsson Peskova is an Associate Professor at the School of Education, University of Iceland. Her project Plurilingual Pedagogies for Diverse Classrooms explores how teachers and students use linguistic repertoires to enhance learning. Her expertise includes plurilingualism, heritage language education, and language policy in diverse contexts.

Yann Gaboriau directs the French Heritage Language Program in the United States, promoting bilingualism and cultural integration for Francophone students. His work fosters linguistic and cultural identity among French-speaking immigrant communities and strengthens connections between home languages and formal education.

Miglena Hristozova holds a Ph.D. in Slavic and Cultural Studies from the University of Freiburg. She has experience in diversity and multilingual education, serving as a researcher, consultant, and education manager at IMIB e.V. Her work focuses on multilingual identity, integration, and innovative education models across Europe.

Fabrice Jaumont is a French-born scholar-practitioner, author, and non-profit leader based in New York. He holds a PhD in Comparative & International Education from New York University and serves as Education Attaché for the Embassy of France in the United States. He is President of the Center for the Advancement of Languages, Education, and Communities, and the author of multiple books on bilingualism and heritage language education, including The Bilingual Revolution.

Felicia Jennings-Winterle is a language educator, author, and independent researcher specializing in language pedagogy. Founder of Brasil em Mente, she pioneered initiatives in Portuguese as a Heritage Language (PHL), including the annual Day of PHL. She holds a master's from NYU and is completing a degree in Applied Linguistics at UMass Boston.

Antri Kanikli holds a PhD in Linguistics (University of York, UK) and specializes in generative grammar, language disorders, and multilingual acquisition. She leads the Erasmus+ "Planting

Languages" project and has published widely in international linguistics journals. Her research bridges multilingualism, heritage language education, and the intersection of grammar and language policy.

Hanae Kim coordinates Korean Studies in the Department of Linguistics at the University of Illinois Chicago. Her research explores Korean heritage language education, teacher preparation, and community-school partnerships. She investigates how peer, family, and school networks shape the transmission of Korean across generations.

Ana Lucia Lico has worked in heritage language education since 2005 and holds a Master's in Linguistics. Her research explores the role of families and community schools in heritage language transmission, focusing on belonging and identity among adolescents. She co-founded ABRACE in the Washington, D.C. area and the Coalition of Community-Based Heritage Language Schools.

Marigona Morina holds a PhD in Educational Research with a focus on Language and Literacy from the University of Calgary. She has experience in language education and research in sociolinguistics, focusing on the intersection of culture, heritage languages, and English language learning among immigrant students. Her work promotes inclusion and multilingual identity in education.

Marta McCabe is an educator and researcher specializing in heritage language schooling and multilingual education. Her research addresses the transformation of community-based schools, particularly during the pandemic, and the role of language education in preserving cultural identity and fostering community resilience.

Sibhekinkosi Anna Nkomo is an educator and researcher whose work centers on translanguaging, multilingual literacy, and heritage language instruction in South African schools. She investigates how bilingual peer-reading programs enhance literacy and identity formation, fostering inclusive and culturally sustaining pedagogy.

Nina Paulovičová is Associate Professor of History at Athabasca University and founder of the Slovak Heritage School in Canada. Her work examines the history and memory of genocide and identity politics. She has served as president of the International and Heritage Languages Association (IHLA) in 2020-2021.

Joy Kreeft Peyton has over 30 years of experience in heritage language education and multilingualism. She served as Vice President at CAL for 16 years and was a founding member of the Alliance for the Advancement of Heritage Languages. She co-edited *Heritage Languages in America: Preserving a National Resource* and *Handbook of Heritage, Community, and Native American Languages in the U.S.* Her work spans teacher development, curriculum design, and policy for heritage and home language programs across the U.S., Africa, and Asia.

Jasmine Pham, Ph.D., is a course instructor in the Master of Teaching program at the Ontario Institute for Studies in Education (OISE), University of Toronto. Her research focuses on Mandarin–English bilingual programs, the Model Minority Myth, and Sinophobia. She employs Critical Race Theory, AsianCrit, and Culturally Responsive Pedagogy in her work.

Angela Popovic is a linguist and educator specializing in heritage language acquisition, computational linguistics, and AI-enhanced learning. She holds a B.A. in English Language and Literature and an M.A. in TESOL. At San Diego State University, she integrates technology into language instruction and supports Serbian heritage language programs.

Jane F. Ross has decades of experience in international education and philanthropy. As co-founder of the Alfred & Jane Ross Foundation and a leader in the French Heritage Language Program, she has supported multilingual and heritage language initiatives in the United States and globally, advancing intercultural understanding through language education.

Steven J. Sacco is Professor Emeritus at San Diego State University, where he specialized in linguistics, intercultural communication, and foreign language pedagogy. His research explores bilingual identity and English as a heritage language in Italian contexts, with a focus on Calabria and transnational cultural exchange.

Jessica Salerno is a researcher and educator whose work examines heritage English education and bilingual identity in Italian communities. She co-authored English as a Heritage Language: A Case Study in Calabria, Southern Italy, highlighting the intersections of diaspora, language preservation, and cultural belonging.

Chase Smithburg joined QFI in 2024 and brings over six years of experience leading Arabic language programs for U.S. students overseas, including Morocco and Egypt. He holds an MA in Arab Studies from the School of Foreign Service at Georgetown University and a BA in Arabic & Political Science from the University of Oklahoma. His work supports Arabic heritage learners and speaks to identity, motivation, and multilingual education.

Lenka Vaněčková teaches Czech at the Department of Slavic Studies, Sorbonne University. With experience in heritage language instruction, she coordinates Czech language education through the Association pour l'Enseignement Franco-Tchèque de Saint-Germain-en-Laye. Her research focuses on heritage language transmission and intercultural communication.

Elizabeth Wardy is an educator and researcher focused on English as a heritage language and bilingualism in Southern Italy. Her work explores the social and linguistic dynamics of English maintenance among Calabrian diaspora communities and the role of heritage language programs in identity development.

References

Aberdeen, C. G. (2016). *Understanding heritage language schools in Alberta* [Doctoral dissertation, University of Alberta]. Education and Research Archive. doi.org/10.7939/R39K45Z33

Aberdeen, T. (2016). Six things you might not know about heritage language schools. *Language Issues: The ESOL Journal, 27*(1), 13–20. academia.edu/28266619/Six_things_you_might_not_know_about_Heritage_Language_Schools

Aberdeen, T., Cannizzaro, G., Douglas, M., Emilsson Peskova, R., Lu, T., Ludanyi, R., McCabe, M., Paulovicova, N., Peyton, J. K., & Sobrevía, S. (2021). *International guidelines for professional practices in community-based heritage language schools.* heritagelanguageschools.org/coalition/article/249073

Abourehab, Y. (2023). Pedagogical translanguaging in community/heritage Arabic language learning. *Journal of Multilingual and Multicultural Development, 44*(5), 398–414.

Alban Conto, M. C., Akseer, S., Dreesen, T., Kamei, A., Mizunoya, S., & Rigole, A. (2020). *COVID-19: Effects of school closures on foundational skills and promising practices for monitoring and mitigating learning loss* (Innocenti Working Paper No. 2020-13). UNICEF Office of Research – Innocenti.

Alcantara Communications. (2016). *The teaching of Arabic language and cultures in U.K. schools.*

Alcimed. (2023). *AI for language preservation: How it can help.* Alcimed Publishing.

Allaf, C., Calderbank, T., & Tarabishi, O. (2026). Heritage language learners' identity and educator teaching decisions: Gothenburg, London, Detroit Metropolitan Area (DMA), and Drogheda. In A. Elgibali (Ed.), *Arabic as a heritage language: Issues and approaches.* Routledge.

Al-Samiri, R. A. (2024). "It's difficult, but it's worth it": Saudi mothers' investment in their children's Arabic heritage learning in the U.S. *International Multilingual Research Journal, 18*(4), 395–410.

Alvear, S. A. (2019). The additive advantage and bilingual programs in a large urban school district. *American Educational Research Journal, 56*(2), 477–513.

Ambrosini, M., & Pozzi, S. (2018). *Italiani ma non troppo? Lo stato dell'arte della ricerca sui figli degli immigrati in Italia*. Centro studi MED – Migrazioni nel Mediterraneo.

American Academy of Arts and Sciences. (2017). *America's languages: Investing in language education for the 21st century*. Commission on Language Learning.

American Community Survey. (2019). *American Community Survey (ACS)*. United States Census Bureau.

American Community Survey. (2022). *American Community Survey (ACS)*. United States Census Bureau.

American Councils for International Education. (2017). *The State of Language in the U.S.*

American Councils for International Education. (2021). *Canvas of dual language and immersion (DLI) programs in U.S. public schools*.

Aravossitas, T., Volonakis, S., & Sugiman, M. (2021). Perspectives on heritage language programs in early childhood education in Canada. In X. Sun, A. García, & P. Guo (Eds.), *Handbook of early language education* (pp. 1–37). Springer.

Arvanitis, E. (2016). Culturally responsive pedagogy: Modeling teachers' professional learning to advance plurilingualism. In P. P. Trifonas & T. Aravossitas (Eds.), *International handbook of heritage language education research and pedagogy* (pp. 245–262). Springer International Publishing. doi.org/10.1007/978-3-319-38893-9_29-1

Baker, C. (2018). *Foundations of bilingual education and bilingualism* (6th ed.). Multilingual Matters.

Baldi, A. (2021). O português desenvolvido pelas iniciativas de PLH: Língua minoritária ou pluricêntrica? *Lincool, 5*, 87–116.

Barcelos, A. M. F. (2020). Compreendendo a pesquisa (de) narrativa. In R. C. Gomes Junior (Org.), *Pesquisa narrativa: Histórias sobre ensinar e aprender* (pp. 17–37). Pimenta Cultural.

Barcelos, A. M. F. (2007). Reflexões acerca da mudança de crenças sobre ensino e aprendizagem de línguas. *Revista Brasileira de Linguística Aplicada, 7*(2), 109–138.

Barkhuizen, G., Benson, P., & Chick, A. (2014). *Narrative inquiry in language teaching and learning research*. Routledge.

Barrett, D., & Twycross, A. (2018). Data collection in qualitative research. *Evidence-Based Nursing, 21*(3), 63–64. doi.org/10.1136/eb-2018-102939

Bastos, M. (2014). A competência de comunicação intercultural: Olhares sobre a natureza do conceito e suas dinâmicas de desenvolvimento. *Cadernos LALE*. UA Editora.

Basu, R. (2011). Multiculturalism through multilingualism in schools: Emerging places of "integration" in Toronto. *Annals of the Association of American Geographers, 101*(6), 1307–1330.

Baxley, T. P. (2008). "What are you?" Biracial children in the classroom. *Childhood Education, 84*(4), 230–234.

Berry, J. W. (1997). Immigration, acculturation, and adaptation. *Applied Psychology: An International Review, 46*(1), 5–68.

Berry, J. W. (2004). Fundamental psychological processes in intercultural relations. In D. Landis, J. Bennett, & M. Bennett (Eds.), *Handbook of intercultural training* (3rd ed., pp. 166–184). SAGE.

Bialystok, E. (2001). *Bilingualism in development: Language, literacy, and cognition*. Cambridge University Press.

Bialystok, E. (2022). *Bilingual children: Families, education, and development*. CALEC / TBR Books.

Bilash, O., & Shi, W. (2011). Immigrant graduate students, employability, and citizenship: Transformation through experience and reflection. In C. Rolheiser (Ed.), *Citizenship Education Research Network (CERN) collection* (pp. 57–78).

Boccou Kestřánková, M., & Hrdlička, M. (2024). Czech as a heritage language and the need for its systematic state support. *Journal of Slavic Linguistics, 29*(2), 183–197.

Boccou Kestřánková, M., & Hubáčková, I. (2023). Podcasty týkající se české diaspory, vzdělávání žáků s češtinou jako jazykem zděděným a českých škol v zahraničí [Podcasts about the Czech diaspora, educating pupils with Czech as a heritage language, and Czech schools abroad]. msmt.cz/vzdelavani/zakladni-vzdelavani/podcasty-tykajici-se-ceske-diaspory-vzdelavani-zaku-s

Boruchowski, I. D., & Lico, A. L. (2015). Como manter e desenvolver o português como língua de herança: Sugestões para quem mora fora do Brasil. Consulado Geral do Brasil em Miami; MUST University. gov.br/mre/pt-br/consulado_toquio/toquio-arquivos/como_manter_e_desenvolver_o_portugues.pdf

Bose, P., Gao, X., Starfield, S., & Perera, N. (2024). Understanding networked family language policy: A study among Bengali immigrants in Australia. *Current Issues in Language Planning, 25*(4), 416–443. doi.org/10.1080/14664208.2024.2349405

Bouffard, S. (2008). *Tapping into technology: The role of the Internet in family-school communication*. Harvard Family Research Project.
Bourdieu, P. (1986). The forms of capital. In J. G. Richardson (Ed.), *Handbook of theory and research for the sociology of education* (pp. 241–258). Greenwood Press.
Bowen, G. (2009). Document analysis as a qualitative research method. *Qualitative Research Journal, 9*(2), 27–40. doi.org/10.3316/QRJ0902027
Boyle, R. C. (2022). We are not "mixed," we are "all": Understanding the educational experiences of mixed ethnicity children to enhance learner agency. *Education 3–13, 50*(4), 471–482. doi.org/10.1080/03004279.2022.2052237
Brecht, R. D. (2016). *America's languages: Opportunities and challenges*. Commission on Language Learning, American Academy of Arts & Sciences. amacad.org/multimedia/pdfs/AmericasLanguagesChallengesandPromise.pdf
Brinton, D., Kagan, O., & Bauckus, S. (Eds.). (2008). *Heritage language education: A new field emerging*. Routledge.
Brown, A. B. (2017). *Emergent strategy: Shaping change, changing worlds*. AK Press.
Brown, C. L. (2009). Heritage language and ethnic identity: A case study of Korean-American college students. *International Journal of Multicultural Education, 11*(1), 1–17.
Brown, C. L. (2011). Maintaining heritage language: Perspectives of Korean parents. *Multicultural Education, 19*(1), 31–37.
Byon, A. S. (2008). Korean as a foreign language in the USA: The instructional settings. *Language, Culture and Curriculum, 21*(3), 244–255.
Byram, M. (2003). *Intercultural competence*. Council of Europe Publishing. coe.int/t/dg4/autobiography/source/aie_en/aie_context_concepts_and_theories_en.pdf
Canagarajah, S. (2011). Translanguaging in the classroom: Emerging issues for research and pedagogy. *Research on Language and Social Interaction, 44*(3), 269–283.
Candelier, M., Camilleri-Grima, A., Castellotti, V., De Pietro, J., Lőrincz, I., Meißner, F., Schröder-Sura, A., Noguerol, A., & Molinié, M. (2012). *Le CARAP: Un Cadre de Référence pour les Approches plurielles*

des langues et des cultures – Compétences et ressources. Strasbourg, France: Conseil de l'Europe.

Carreira, M., & Chik, C. (2014, April 10). Identity: The driving force behind heritage language learning. *National Heritage Language Resource Center.* nhlrc.ucla.edu/nhlrc/article/205553

Carreira, M., & Kagan, O. (2018). Heritage language education: A proposal for the next 50 years. *Foreign Language Annals, 51*(1), 1–11.

Carrim, A., & Nkomo, S. A. (2023). A systematic literature review of the feasibility of a translanguaging pedagogy in the Foundation Phase. *Journal of Language and Language Teaching, 11*(2), 195–210.

Cavaleri, P. A. (2007). *Vivere con l'altro: Per una cultura della relazione.* Rome: Città Nova Editrice.

Cenoz, J., & García, O. (Eds.). (2017). Breaking away from the multilingual solitudes in language education: International perspectives. *International Journal of Language, Identity and Education, 16*(4).

Center for Applied Linguistics. (2023). Heritage Language Education in the U.S.: Research, Policies and Practice. March 31, 2023.

Český statistický úřad. (2023). czso.cz/csu/czso/obyvatelstvo_lide

Chang, A. (2016). Multiracial matters: Disrupting and reinforcing the racial rubric in educational discourse. *Race, Ethnicity and Education, 19*(4), 706–730. doi.org/10.1080/13613324.2014.885427

Chang, A. (2022). *The meaning of multiraciality: A racially queer exploration of multiracial college students' identity production.* Lexington Books/Fortress Academic.

Chang, E. T., & Diaz-Veizades, J. (1999). *Ethnic peace in the American city: Building community in Los Angeles and beyond.* New York University Press.

Chang, W.-C., & Viesca, K. M. (2022). Preparing teachers for culturally responsive/relevant pedagogy (CRP): A critical review of research. *Review of Educational Research, 124*(2), 197–224.

Charles University. (2018). *Code of Ethics.* cuni.cz/UKEN-731.html

Chen, J., & Patel, R. (2024). Learning an Indigenous language with the aid of AI. *Journal of Computational Linguistics, 45*(2), 112–130.

Chen, L., & Patel, R. (2024). Conversational agents and engagement in AI-supported language learning. *Journal of Applied Linguistics and Technology, 15*(1), 45–63.

Chen, M. J. (2020). Language education policy research in the United States: Review and inspiration. *Canadian Social Science, 16*(9), 36–41.

Chen, S. H., Zhou, Q., & Uchikoshi, Y. (2018). Heritage language socialization in Chinese American immigrant families: Prospective links to children's heritage language proficiency. *International Journal of Bilingual Education and Bilingualism, 24*(8), 1193–1209. doi.org/10.1080/13670050.2018.1547680

Chi, X. (2020). *Cross-cultural experiences of Chinese immigrant mothers in Canada: Challenges and opportunities for schooling.* Palgrave Macmillan.

Chik, C. H., & Wright, W. E. (2017). Overcoming the obstacles: Vietnamese and Khmer heritage language programs in California. In O. Kagan, M. Carreira, & C. H. Chik (Eds.), *The Routledge handbook of heritage language education: From innovation to program building* (pp. 222–236). Routledge.

Cho, G. (2000). The role of heritage language in social interactions and relationships: Reflections from a language minority group. *Bilingual Research Journal, 24*(4), 369–384. doi.org/10.1080/15235882.2000.10162773

Cho, G., & Krashen, S. (1998). The negative consequences of heritage language loss and why we should care. In S. D. Krashen, L. Tse, & J. McQuillan (Eds.), *Heritage language development* (pp. 31–40). Language Education Associates.

Choi, E. (2016). The current status of Korean language education in the United States: Class offerings in K–16 schools and Korean community schools. *The Korean Language in America, 20*(1), 29–52.

Chow, H. P. (2001). Learning the Chinese language in a multicultural milieu: Factors affecting Chinese-Canadian adolescents' ethnic language school experience. *The Alberta Journal of Educational Research, 47,* 369–374.

Christenson, S., & Sheridan, S. M. (2001). *Schools and families: Creating essential connections for learning.* Guilford Press.

Churkina, O., et al. (2023). The labor market outcomes of bilinguals in the United States: Accumulation and returns effects. *PLOS ONE, 18*(6), e0287711.

Ciliberti, A. (2012). La nozione di competenza nella pedagogia linguistica: Dalla competenza linguistica alla competenza comunicativa interculturale. *Italiano LinguaDue, 2.*

Coady, M. R. (2019). *Connecting school and the multilingual home: Theory and practice for rural educators.* Multilingual Matters.

COERLL. (2025). *America's Languages: Model Programs & Practices.* University of Texas at Austin & American Councils for International Education.

Compton, C. J. (2001). Heritage language communities and schools: Challenges and recommendations. In J. K. Peyton, D. A. Ranard, & S. McGinnis (Eds.), *Heritage languages in America: Preserving a national resource*. Delta Systems.

Conus, X., & Fahrni, L. (2019). Routine communication between teachers and parents from minority groups: An endless misunderstanding? *Educational Review, 71*(2), 234–256.

Cook, G. (2003). Various shades of grey: The losses and gains of contemporary multimodality. Paper presented at the BAAL/CUP Seminar on Multimodality and Applied Linguistics, University of Reading, 18–19 July.

Coretta, S., Riverin-Coutlée, J., Kapia, E., & Nichols, S. (2023). Northern Tosk Albanian. *Journal of the International Phonetic Association, 53*(3), 1122–1144. doi.org/10.1017/S0025100322000044

Costa, E. V. (2013). *Práticas de formação de professores de português língua adicional em um instituto cultural brasileiro no exterior* (Unpublished MA thesis). UFRGS, Porto Alegre, Brazil.

Costa, E. V., & Schlatter, M. (2017). Eventos de formação de professores: Uma perspectiva etnográfica sobre aprender a ensinar. *Trabalhos em Linguística Aplicada, 56*(1), 37–63.

Council of Europe. (1992). *European Charter for Regional or Minority Languages* search.coe.int/cm/Pages/result_details.aspx?ObjectID=09000016808f2232

Council of Europe. (2007). *From linguistic diversity to plurilingual education: Guide for the development of language education policies in Europe.*

Cour des Comptes. (2016). ccomptes.fr/sites/default/files/EzPublish/20161020-enseignement-fran--ais-etranger.pdf

Crawford, J. (2004). *Educating English learners: Language diversity in the classroom*. Bilingual Education Services.

Creese, A., & Blackledge, A. (2010). Translanguaging in the bilingual classroom: A pedagogy for learning and teaching? *The Modern Language Journal, 94*(1), 103–115.

Creswell, J. W. (2009). *Research design: Qualitative, quantitative, and mixed methods approaches*. Sage Publications.

Cruickshank, K. (2015). Community language schools: The importance of context in understanding hybrid identities. In D. N. Djenar et al.

(Eds.), *Language and identity across modes of communication* (pp. 83–106). De Gruyter. doi.org/10.1515/9781614513599.83

Cruickshank, K., Lo Bianco, J., & Wahlin, M. (Eds.). (2024). *Community and heritage language schools transforming education: Research, challenges, and teaching practices.* Routledge. doi.org/10.4324/9781003302704

Cruickshank, K., & Tsung, L. (2026). *Languages, cultures and schools: Community and heritage languages in a changing world.* Multilingual Matters.

Cruz, R. A., Manchanda, S., Firestone, A. R., & Rodl, J. E. (2020). An examination of teachers' culturally responsive teaching self-efficacy. *Journal of Education, 43*(3), 197–214.

CTV News Edmonton. (2021, March 18). Fear of hate-motivated attacks a concern for Edmonton's Asian community. edmonton.ctvnews.ca/fear-of-hate-motivated-attacks-a-concern-for-edmonton-s-asian-community-1.5352409

Cui, D. (2011/2012). Two multicultural debates in the lived experiences of Chinese-Canadian youth. *Canadian Ethnic Studies, 43–44*(3.1), 123–143.

Cummins, J. (1981). *Bilingualism and minority-language children.* Ontario Institute for Studies in Education.

Cummins, J. (1992). Heritage language teaching in Canadian schools. *Journal of Curriculum Studies, 24*(3), 281–286.

Cummins, J. (1996). *Negotiating identities: Education for empowerment in a diverse society.* California Association for Bilingual Education.

Cummins, J. (2000). *Language, power and pedagogy: Bilingual children in the crossfire.* Multilingual Matters.

Cummins, J. (2001). Bilingual children's mother tongue: Why is it important for education? *Sprogforum, 7*, 15–20.

Cummins, J. (2021). *Rethinking the education of multilingual learners: A critical analysis of theoretical concepts.* Multilingual Matters.

Cummins, J. (2024). Multilingualism in English language education. In *The Routledge companion to English studies* (p. 13). Routledge.

CUNY–NYSIEB (City University of New York–New York State Initiative on Emergent Bilinguals) (Eds.). (2021). *Translanguaging and transformative teaching for emergent bilingual students: Lessons from the CUNY–NYSIEB Project.* Routledge.

Curdt-Christiansen, X. L. (2013). Implicit learning and imperceptible influence: Syncretic literacy of multilingual Chinese children. *Journal of Early Childhood Literacy, 13*(3), 348–370. doi.org/10.1177/1468798412455819

D'Ignazio, C., & Klein, L. F. (2020). *Data feminism*. MIT Press.
Damanakis, M. (2017). Identity, language, and language policies in the diaspora: Historical-comparative approach. In P. P. Trifonas & T. Aravossitas (Eds.), *International handbook of heritage language education research and pedagogy* (pp. 671–690). Springer International Publishing. doi.org/10.1007/978-3-319-38893-9_29-1
Damron, J., & Forsyth, J. (2010). Korean heritage students and language literacy: A qualitative approach. *Cross-Cultural Studies, 20*, 29–66.
Damron, J., & Forsyth, J. (2012). Korean language studies: Motivation and attrition. *Journal of the National Council of Less Commonly Taught Languages, 12*, 161–188.
Davin, K., & Heineke, A. (2024). *The Seal of Biliteracy in higher education: Harnessing students' cultural and linguistic strengths at colleges and universities*. Routledge.
Davin, K. J., & Heineke, A. J. (2018). The Seal of Biliteracy: Adding students' voices to the conversation. *Bilingual Research Journal, 41*(3), 312–328. doi.org/10.1080/15235882.2018.1481896
Deci, E. L., & Ryan, R. M. (2000). The "what" and "why" of goal pursuits: Human needs and the self-determination of behavior. *Psychological Inquiry, 11*(4), 227–268. doi.org/10.1207/S15327965PLI1104_01
Demetrio, D., & Favaro, G. (1999). *Immigrazione e pedagogia interculturale: Bambini, adulti, comunità nel percorso di integrazione*. Edizioni La Nuova Italia.
Desinan, C. (1997). *Orientamenti di educazione interculturale*. Franco Angeli.
Deterding, S., Dixon, D., Khaled, R., & Nacke, L. (2011). From game design elements to gamefulness: Defining "gamification." In *Proceedings of the 15th International Academic MindTrek Conference* (pp. 9–15).
Di Lucca, L., & Masiero, G. (2005). La lingua materna. In G. Pallotti & Associazione Interculturale Polo Interetnico (Eds.), *Imparare e insegnare l'italiano come seconda lingua: Un progetto di formazione per insegnanti e operatori*. Bonacci Editore.
Dörnyei, Z. (2001). *Motivational strategies in the language classroom*. Cambridge University Press. doi.org/10.1017/CBO9780511667343
Dressler, R. (2010). "There is no space for being German": Portraits of willing and reluctant heritage language learners of German. *Heritage Language Journal, 7*(2), 162–182. doi.org/10.46538/hlj.7.2.2

Driever, S. L., & Bagheri, N. (2020). Heritage languages and bilingualism in the United States. In *Handbook of the changing world language map* (pp. 1047–1068). Springer.

Dubey, A. D. (2020). The resurgence of cyber racism during the COVID-19 pandemic and its aftereffects: Analysis of sentiments and emotions in tweets. *JMIR Public Health and Surveillance, 6*(4), e19833. doi.org/10.2196/19833

Duff, P. (2008). Language socialization, participation and identity: Ethnographic approaches. In N. H. Hornberger (Ed.), *Encyclopedia of language and education* (pp. 2120–2132). Springer. doi.org/10.1007/978-0-387-30424-3_65

Dumoulin, C., Thériault, P., Duval, J., & Tremblay, I. (2013). Rapprocher l'école primaire et les familles par de nouvelles pratiques de communication [New communication practices to bring primary school and families together]. *La recherche en éducation, 9*(1), 4–18.

Dutro, E., Kazemi, E., & Balf, R. (2005). The aftermath of "you're only half": Multiracial identities in the literacy classroom. *Language Arts, 83*(2), 96–106. doi.org/10.58680/la20054448

Eaton, J., & Turin, M. (2022). Heritage languages and language as heritage: The language of heritage in Canada and beyond. *International Journal of Heritage Studies, 28*(7), 787–802.

Écoles suisses à l'étranger. (n.d.). *Écoles suisses à l'étranger [Swiss schools abroad]*. educationsuisse.ch/fr/ecoles-etranger

Education Suisse – Schweizerschulen im Ausland. (2023). educationsuisse.ch/de

Edwards, J. (1994). *Multilingualism*. Routledge.

Ee, J. (2016). Exploring Korean dual language immersion programs in the United States: Parents' reasons for enrolling their children. *International Journal of Bilingual Education and Bilingualism, 21*(6), 690–709. doi.org/10.1080/13670050.2016.1208144

ElHawari, R. (2021). *Teaching Arabic as a heritage language*. Routledge.

Ellis, C. (2007). Telling secrets, revealing lives: Relational ethics in research with intimate others. *Qualitative Inquiry, 13*(1), 3–29. doi.org/10.1177/1077800406294947

Elsie, R., & Gross, J. (2009). *Albanian dialects.* dialects.albanianlanguage.net

Emilsson Peskova, R. (2021). *School experience of plurilingual children: A multiple case study from Iceland* (Doctoral dissertation, University of Iceland). opinvisindi.is/handle/20.500.11815/2648

Emilsson Peskova, R., & Ragnarsdóttir, H. (2016). Strengthening linguistic bridges between home and school: Experiences of immigrant children and parents in Iceland. In P. P. Trifonas & T. Aravossitas (Eds.), *International handbook of heritage language education research and pedagogy* (pp. 561–576). Springer International Publishing. doi.org/10.1007/978-3-319-38893-9_29-1

Emilsson Peskova, R., Lindholm, A., Ahlholm, M., Vold, E. T., Gunnþórsdóttir, H., Slotte, A., & Esmann Busch, S. (2023). Second language and mother tongue education for immigrant children in Nordic educational policies: Search for a common Nordic dimension. *Nordic Studies in Education, 43*(2), 128–144. doi.org/10.23865/nse.v43.3982

Jennings-Winterle, F., & Lima-Hernandes, M. C. (Orgs.). (2015). *Português como língua de herança: A filosofia do começo, meio e fim* (pp. 28–55). BeM.

Epstein, J. L. (2011). *School, family and community partnerships: Preparing educators and improving schools.* Westview Press.

Et-Bozkurt, T., & Yağmur, K. (2022). Family language policy among second- and third-generation Turkish parents in Melbourne, Australia. *Journal of Multilingual and Multicultural Development, 43*(9), 821–832.

European Agency for Special Needs and Inclusive Education. (2017). *Education for all in Iceland: External audit of the Icelandic system for inclusive education.* stjornarradid.is/media/menntamalaraduneyti-media/media/frettatengt2016/Final-report_External-Audit-of-the-Icelandic-System-for-Inclusive-Education.pdf

European Union: Council of the European Union. (2000). *EU Charter of Fundamental Rights. Official Journal of the European Communities, 2000/C 364/01.* europarl.europa.eu/charter/pdf/text_en.pdf

Femia, N. (2021). Experiences and desires of adolescent heritage language speakers: A biographical study of attitudes towards, and investment in multilingualism (master's thesis, Stockholm University, Department of Swedish Language and Multilingualism). urn.kb.se/resolve?urn=urn:nbn:se:su:diva-201227

Ferguson, C. (1959). Diglossia. *Word, 15*(2), 325–340.

Ferreira, T., & Melo-Pfeifer, S. (2015). Desenvolvimento da competência plurilingue: Quebrar o habitus monolingue em manuais de língua. In M. H. Araújo e Sá & A. Pinho (Dirs.), *Intercompreensão em contexto educativo: Resultados da investigação* (pp. 133–156). Universidade de Aveiro.

Ferroni, R. (2010). L'eco della lingua materna. *EL.LE*, Supplemento, June issue.

Fillmore, L. W. (2000). Loss of family languages: Should educators be concerned? *Theory into Practice, 39*(4), 203–210. doi.org/10.1207/s15430421tip3904_3

Fisher, S., Reynolds, J. L., Hsu, W., Barnes, J., & Tyler, K. (2014). Examining multiracial youth in context: Ethnic identity development and mental health outcomes. *Journal of Youth and Adolescence, 43*(10), 1688–1699. doi.org/10.1007/s10964-014-0163-2

Fishman, J. A. (2001). 300-plus years of heritage language in the United States. In J. K. Peyton, D. A. Ranard, & S. McGinnis (Eds.), *Heritage languages in America: Preserving a national resource* (pp. 81–97). Center for Applied Linguistics.

Fishman, J. (1985). *The rise and fall of the ethnic revival*. Mouton de Gruyter.

Fishman, J. A. (1991). *Reversing language shift: Theoretical and empirical foundations of assistance to threatened languages*. Multilingual Matters.

Fishman, J. A. (1966). *Language loyalty in the United States*. Mouton.

Flores, C. M. M. (2015). Understanding heritage language acquisition: Some contributions from the research on heritage speakers of European Portuguese. *Lingua, 164*(B), 251–265. doi.org/10.1016/j.lingua.2014.09.008

Flores, N. (2013). The unexamined relationship between neoliberalism and plurilingualism: A cautionary tale. *TESOL Quarterly, 47*(3), 500–520.

Flores, N., & Schissel, J. L. (2014). Dynamic bilingualism and equitable language education policy in the United States. *TESOL Quarterly, 48*(3), 575–600.

Floridi, L., & Cowls, J. (2019). A unified framework of five principles for AI in society. *Harvard Data Science Review, 1*(1).

Fogg, B. (2009). A behavior model for persuasive design. In *Proceedings of the 4th International Conference on Persuasive Technology*.

FOHLC Europe. (2022). hlenet.org/fohlc-europe

Foley, L., & Piper, N. (2020). *COVID-19 and women migrant workers: Impacts and implications*. International Organization for Migration. publications.iom.int/system/files/pdf/covid19-and-women.pdf

Fong, E., & Shibuya, K. (2005). Multiethnic cities in North America. *Annual Review of Sociology, 31*, 285–304. doi.org/10.1146/annurev.soc.31.041304.122246

Fowler, S. (2022). Motivating speaking in the world language classroom and beyond. *NECTFL Review, 89*, 95–102.

France Diplomatie. (2023a). *La communauté française à l'étranger en chiffres.* diplomatie.gouv.fr/fr/services-aux-francais/l-action-consulaire-missions-chiffres-cles/la-communaute-francaise-a-l-etranger-en-chiffres/

France Diplomatie. (2023b). *Fil d'Ariane.* fildariane.diplomatie.gouv.fr/fildariane-internet/accueil

Freire, P. (2016). *A pedagogia do oprimido.* Paz e Terra.

Fryer, L. K., & Bovee, H. N. (2016). Supporting students' motivation through interest-driven learning. *Educational Psychology Review, 28*(4), 759–779.

Fu, S. (2024). Tracing the history: Language education policy and emergent bilingual learners in the United States. *GATESOL Journal, 33*(1), 18–27.

Gambhir, S., & Gambhir, V. (2014). Critical and less commonly taught languages: The journey of Hindi in the United States. In T. G. Wiley, J. K. Peyton, D. Christian, S. C. K. Moore, & N. Liu (Eds.), *Handbook of heritage, community, and Native American languages in the United States: Research, policy, and educational practice* (p. 175). Routledge. doi.org/10.4324/9780203122419

Gándara, P. (2015). Is there really a labor market advantage to being bilingual in the U.S.? *ETS Research Report Series, 2015*(2), 1–17.

Gándara, P., & Escamilla, K. (2017). Bilingual education in the United States. In O. García, A. M. Y. Lin, & S. May (Eds.), *Bilingual and multilingual education* (pp. 439–452). Springer.

Gándara, P., & Mordechay, K. (2017). Demographic change and the new (and not so new) challenges for Latino education. *The Educational Forum, 81*(2), 148–159.

Garcez, P., & Schlatter, M. (2017). Professores-autores-formadores: Princípios e experiências para a formação de profissionais de educação linguística. In E. Matheus & J. R. A. Tonelli (Eds.), *Diálogos (im)pertinentes entre formação de professores e aprendizagem de línguas* (pp. 13–36). Bluch.

García, O., & Yip, J. (2015). Introduction: Translanguaging—Practice briefs for educators. *Theory, Research, and Action in Urban Education, 4*(1).

García, O. (2009). *Bilingual education in the 21st century: A global perspective.* Wiley-Blackwell.

García, O. (2015). Translanguaging and abecedarios ilegales. In T. M. Kalmar (Ed.), *Illegal alphabets and adult biliteracy: Latino migrants crossing the linguistic border* (pp. 131–136). Routledge.

García, O., & Kleifgen, J. A. (2018). *Educating emergent bilinguals: Policies, programs, and practices for English learners* (2nd ed.). Teachers College Press.

García, O., & Kleyn, T. (Eds.). (2016). *Translanguaging with multilingual students: Learning from classroom moments.* Routledge.

García, O., & Lin, A. M. (2021). Translanguaging and bilingual education. In O. García, A. Lin, & S. May (Eds.), *Bilingual and multilingual education* (pp. 117–130). Springer.

García, O., & Otheguy, R. (2021). Conceptualizing translanguaging theory/practice juntos. In CUNY–NYSIEB (Eds.), *Translanguaging and transformative teaching for emergent bilingual students: Lessons from the CUNY–NYSIEB Project* (pp. 3–24). Routledge.

García, O., & Seltzer, K. (2016). The translanguaging current in language education. In B. Kindenberg (Ed.), *Flerspråkighet som resurs [Multilingualism as a resource]* (pp. 19–30). Liber.

García, O., & Wei, L. (2014). *Translanguaging: Language, bilingualism, and education.* Palgrave Macmillan.

García, O., & Wei, L. (2018). Translanguaging. In C. Chapelle (Ed.), *The encyclopedia of applied linguistics.* Wiley. doi.org/10.1002/9781405198431.wbeal1488

Gee, J. P. (2017). *Teaching, learning, literacy in our high-risk high-tech world.* Teachers College Press.

Ghorayeb, D. Z. (2022). *La vie en français aux États-Unis: Exploring identity and language shifts from a geographic territory to an imaginary homeland* [Doctoral dissertation, University of Maryland, Baltimore County]. *ProQuest Dissertations & Theses Global.*

Ginsberg, R. (2017). Finding comfort in the discomfort of being multiracial: Lessons from my schooling. *Multicultural Perspectives, 19*(2), 103–108. doi.org/10.1080/15210960.2017.1301097

Giordano, J. (2015). *Birds of passage: An Italian immigrant coming of age story.* Harvard Square Editions.

Gist, C., Jackson, I., Nightengale-Lee, B., & Allen, K. (2019). Culturally responsive pedagogy in teacher education. In *Oxford research encyclopedia of education.* Oxford University Press.

Gjinari, J. (1988). *Dialektologjia shqiptare [Albanian dialectology].* Akademia e Shkencave të Shqipërisë.

Global Seal of Biliteracy. (2023). *Global Seal of Biliteracy.* theglobalseal.com/international-landing

Goldring, L., & Krishnamurti, S. (2007). *Organizing the transnational: Labour, politics, and social change.* University of British Columbia Press.

Gollifer, S., Gunnþórsdóttir, H., & Emilsson Peskova, R. (2024). "We can do much more and better": Understanding gatekeepers' perspectives on students' linguistic human rights. *Human Rights Education Review, 7*(1), 26–48. doi.org/10.7577/hrer.5306

Gonçalves, M. L. (2017). Espaços (in)formais de desenvolvimento profissional docente: O ensino de português no estrangeiro. In A. Souza & C. Lira (Orgs.), *O POLH na Europa – II Simpósio Europeu sobre o Ensino do Português como Língua de Herança* (pp. 80–125). J. N. Paquet.

Gonçalves, M. L. (2019). Quando lá e cá se entrecruzam: Professores de LH, profissionais em trânsito. *Lincool, 3*, 41–53.

Grillo, M. C., & Gessinger, R. M. (2008). Constituição da identidade profissional, saberes docentes e prática reflexiva. In M. C. Grillo, A. L. de Freitas, R. M. Gessinger, & V. M. Lima (Orgs.), *A gestão da aula universitária na PUCRS* (pp. 35–42). EdiPUCRS.

Gruntová, B. (2018). *Familles plurilingues: Transmission et apprentissage des langues et des cultures. La diaspora tchèque en France, en Russie et en Croatie* [Doctoral dissertation]. Université Sorbonne Paris Cité.

Guo, S. (2013). Immigrants as active citizens: Exploring the volunteering experience of Chinese immigrants in Vancouver. *Globalisation, Societies and Education, 12*(1), 51–70.

Gutiérrez, K. D. (2008). Developing a socio-critical literacy in the third space. *Reading Research Quarterly, 43*(2), 148–164.

Gutiérrez, K. D., Baquedano-López, P., & Tejeda, C. (1999). Rethinking diversity: The third space and the politics of language. *International Journal of Bilingual Education and Bilingualism, 3*(1), 8–34.

Guzula, X., McKinney, C., & Tyler, R. (2016). Languaging-for-learning: Legitimising translanguaging and enabling multimodal practices in third spaces. *Southern African Linguistics and Applied Language Studies, 34*(3), 211–226.

Hagstofa Íslands [Statistics Iceland]. (2023). statice.is

Hall, S. (2006). *A identidade cultural na pós-modernidade* (11th ed., T. T. da Silva & G. L. Louro, Trans.). DP&A.

Harris, H. L. (2014). A national survey of school counselors' perceptions of multiracial students. *Professional School Counseling, 17*(1), 1–19.

Hatoss, A. (2013). *Displacement, language maintenance and identity: Sudanese refugees in Australia. Impact: Studies in language and society* (Vol. 34). John Benjamins. doi.org/10.1075/impact.34

Hattie, J., & Timperley, H. (2007). The power of feedback. *Review of Educational Research, 77*(1), 81–112.

Haynes, E. (2010). What is language loss? *Heritage Briefs*. Center for Applied Linguistics.

He, A. W. (2010). The heart of heritage language education: Fostering learner identity. *Annual Review of Applied Linguistics, 30*, 66–82.

Heineke, A. J., & Davin, K. J. (2018). The Seal of Biliteracy: Successes and challenges to implementation across contexts. *Foreign Language Annals, 51*(2), 275–289.

Heineke, A. J., & Davin, K. J. (2020). Prioritizing multilingualism in U.S. schools: States' policy journeys to enact the Seal of Biliteracy. *Educational Policy, 34*(4), 619–643.

Heineke, A. J., & Davin, K. J. (2021). Implementing the Seal of Biliteracy: A multiple case study of six high-awarding districts. *Modern Language Journal, 105*(2), 395–411.

Hélot, C. (2007). *Du bilinguisme en famille au plurilinguisme à l'école*. L'Harmattan.

Helps, L., Silvius, R., & Gibson, R. (2021). Vulnerable, inequitable, and precarious: Impacts of COVID-19 on newcomers, immigrants, and migrant workers in rural Canada. *Journal of Rural and Community Development, 16*(4). journals.brandonu.ca/jrcd/article/view/2102

Hendricks, C. C. (2017). *Improving schools through action research: A reflective practice approach* (4th ed.). Pearson.

Heugh, K., Prinsloo, C., Makgamatha, M., Diedericks, G., & Winnaar, L. (2017). Multilingualism(s) and system-wide assessment: A southern perspective. *Language and Education, 31*(3), 197–216. doi.org/10.1080/09500782.2016.1261894

Hillman, S. (2019). "I'm a heritage speaker of the Damascene dialect of Arabic": Negotiating the identity label of Arabic heritage language learner. *Heritage Language Journal, 16*(3), 296–317. doi.org/10.46538/hlj.16.3.2

Hong, J. (2018). The origins and construction of Korean America: Immigration before 1965. In R. M. Joo & S. S.-H. Lee (Eds.), *A companion to Korean-American studies* (pp. 3–20). BRILL. doi.org/10.1163/9789004335332_002

Hoover-Dempsey, K. V., & Sandler, H. M. (1995). Parental involvement in children's education: Why does it make a difference? *Teachers College Record, 95*(1), 310–331.

Hornberger, N. H. (2008). Multilingual language policies and the continua of biliteracy: An ecological approach. In J. Cummins & N.

H. Hornberger (Eds.), *Encyclopedia of language and education* (pp. 159–170). Springer.

Hornberger, N. H., & Wang, S. C. (2008). Who are our heritage language learners? Identity and biliteracy in heritage language education in the United States. In D. Brinton, O. Kagan, & S. Bauckus (Eds.), *Heritage language education: A new field emerging* (pp. 3–35). Routledge.

Hornberger, N., & Swinehart, K. F. (2012). Not just situaciones de la vida: Professionalism and indigenous language revitalization in the Andes. *International Multilingual Research Journal, 6*, 35–49.

Hou, F., Schimmele, C., & Stick, M. (2023). Changing demographics of racialized people in Canada. *Statistics Canada.* doi.org/10.25318/36280001202300800001-eng

Howard, T. C. (2021). Culturally responsive pedagogy. In *Transforming multicultural education policy and practice* (p. 137). Teachers College Press.

Hsu, T. (2019). Chow mein kampf. In A. Garrod, R. Kilkenny, & C. Gomez (Eds.), *Mixed: Multiracial college students tell their life stories* (pp. 125–138). Cornell University Press. doi.org/10.7591/9780801469169-011

Hughes, P., & MacNaughton, G. (2000). Consensus, dissensus or community: The politics of parent involvement in early childhood education. *Contemporary Issues in Early Childhood, 1*(3), 241–258.

Hurh, W. M. (1998). *The Korean Americans.* Bloomsbury Publishing.

Hyllested, A., & Joseph, B. D. (2022). Albanian. In T. Olander (Ed.), *The Indo-European language family* (pp. 223–245). Cambridge University Press.

Ibrahim, Z., & Allam, J. (2006). Arabic learners and heritage students redefined: Present and future. In K. Wahba, Z. Taha, & L. England (Eds.), *Handbook for Arabic language teaching professionals in the 21st century* (1st ed., pp. 437–446). Routledge.

Indiana University. (n.d.). *Global Classroom Initiative.* global.iu.edu/education/internationalization/classroom/index.html

IU Newsroom. (2024). IU Arabic Debate Team ranks first in nation. *IU News.* news.iu.edu

Ivanova, O. (2019). "My child is a perfect bilingual": Cognition, emotions, and affectivity in heritage language transmission. *Languages, 4*(2). doi.org/10.3390/languages4020044

Jaumont, F. (2022). *Conversations on bilingualism.* CALEC / TBR Books.

Jennings-Winterle, F., & Bittens, C. (2015). O começo do começo: A promoção do vínculo afetivo e o desenvolvimento emocional e cognitivo pela língua de herança. In F. Jennings-Winterle & M. C. Lima-Hernandes (Orgs.), *Português como língua de herança: A filosofia do começo, meio e fim* (pp. 58–79). BEM.

Jennings-Winterle, F. (2020). Quem são as educadoras brasileiras de PLH e quais são suas perspectivas. In S. Melo-Pfeifer & M. L. da Silva Gonçalves (Orgs.), *Português língua de herança e formação de professores*. LIDEL.

Jennings-Winterle, F. (2023). *Didática de línguas de herança: Contribuições a partir de estudos e práticas de língua portuguesa. Conceitos e fundamentos* (Vol. 1). Plurall by BeM.

Jennings-Winterle, F., & Lima-Hernandes, M. C. (2015). *Português como língua de herança: A filosofia do começo, meio e fim*. Brasil em Mente.

Jeon, M. (2007). Language ideologies and bilingual education: A Korean-American perspective. *Language Awareness, 16*(2), 114–130. doi.org/10.2167/la369.0

Jeon, M. (2008). Korean heritage language maintenance and language ideology. *Heritage Language Journal, 6*(2), 206–223.

Jo, M. H. (1999). *Korean immigrants and the challenge of adjustment*. Bloomsbury Publishing.

Johnson, D. W., & Johnson, R. T. (2009). An educational psychology success story: Social interdependence theory and cooperative learning. *Educational Researcher, 38*(5), 365–379.

Johnston-Guerrero, M., & Pecero, V. (2016). Exploring race, culture, and family in the identities of mixed-heritage students. *Journal of Student Affairs Research and Practice, 53*(3), 281–293. doi.org/10.1080/19496591.2016.1165109

Jones, K., & Smith, L. (2024). *Generative AI in the heritage language classroom*. UCLA Press.

Jones, P., & Smith, A. (2024). User satisfaction and personalization in adaptive AI learning systems. *Computers & Education Research Quarterly, 48*(2), 102–118.

Jónshús. (2023). *Jónshús – Iceland's Culture House*. jonshus.dk/icelands-culture-house/jonhus/

Jung, J.-D. (1991). *A study of Korean immigrants in America, 1872–present* [Master's thesis, San Jose State University].

Kang, H.-S. (2013a). Korean American college students' language practices and identity positioning: "Not Korean, but not American."

Journal of Language, Identity, and Education, 12(4), 248–261. doi.org/10.1080/15348458.2013.818473

Kang, H.-S. (2013b). Korean-immigrant parents' support of their American-born children's development and maintenance of the home language. *Early Childhood Education Journal, 41*, 431–438. doi.org/10.1007/s10643-012-0566-1

Kang, H.-S. (2015). Korean families in America: Their family language policies and home-language maintenance. *Bilingual Research Journal, 38*(3), 275–291. doi.org/10.1080/15235882.2015.1092002

Kara, S., & Schmitt, S. (2020). Il valore delle lingue. *Internazionale, 1368*, 23 July.

Katz, G. (2020). Mind genomics: Understanding preferences and decision-making through experimental designs. *Journal of Behavioral Studies, 16(2), 45–62.*

Kelleher, A. (2010). What is a heritage language? *Heritage Briefs.* Center for Applied Linguistics, 3, 1–4. cal.org/

Kerfoot, C., & Bello-Nonjengele, B. O. (2014). Game changers? Multilingual learners in a Cape Town primary school. *Applied Linguistics, 37*(4), 1–24. doi.org/10.1093/applin/amu044

Khaled, A., & Anderson, J. (2024a). Textart, identity and the creative process: A case study with Arabic heritage language learners. *International Journal of Bilingual Education and Bilingualism, 27*(1), 113–130. doi.org/10.1080/13670050.2022.2158721

Khaled, A., & Anderson, J. (2024b). Towards alternative spaces of engagement: Exploring the potential of text-based visual art in Arabic heritage language classrooms. *International Journal of Bilingual Education and Bilingualism*, 1–17. doi.org/10.1080/13670050.2022.2158721

Khudayberdievich, K. S. (2024). Ethnocultural identity in the context of globalization. *EPRA International Journal of Research and Development, 9*(5).

Kim, J.-I. (2017). Immigrant adolescents investing in Korean heritage language: Exploring motivation, identities, and capital. *Canadian Modern Language Review, 73*(2), 183–207. doi.org/10.3138/cmlr.3334

Kim, S. Y. (2009). Heritage language fluency, ethnic identity, and school. National Institutes of Health.

Kim, Y., & Lee, H. (2018). Storytelling in second language acquisition: A review of research. *Language Teaching, 51*(4), 536–552.

King, A. R. (2008). Student perspectives on multiracial identity. *New Directions for Student Services, 2008*(123), 33–41.

doi.org/10.1002/ss.284

King, K. A., Fogle, L., & Logan-Terry, A. (2008). Family language policy. *Linguistics and Language Compass, 2*(5), 907–922. doi.org/10.1111/j.1749-818X.2008.00076.x

Kircher, R. (2024). Linguistic discrimination of heritage-language-speaking children: Why does it happen and how can parents tackle it? *Babylonia Journal of Language Education, 3*, 42–45. doi.org/10.55393/babylonia.v3i.431

Kondo-Brown, K. (2010). Curriculum development for advancing heritage language competence: Recent research, current practices, and a future agenda. *Annual Review of Applied Linguistics, 30*, 24–41. doi.org/10.1017/S0267190510000012

Kono, N., & McGinnis, S. (2001). Heritage languages and higher education: Challenges, issues, and needs. In J. K. Peyton, D. A. Ranard, & S. McGinnis (Eds.), *Heritage languages in America: Preserving a national resource*. Delta Systems.

Kramsch, C. (2013). *Culture in foreign language teaching and learning*. Oxford University Press.

Krashen, S. (2000). Bilingual education, the acquisition of English, and the retention and loss of Spanish. In A. Roca (Ed.), *Research on Spanish in the United States: Linguistic issues and challenges* (pp. 432–444). Cascadilla Press.

Krause, L. S., & Prinsloo, M. (2016). Translanguaging in a township primary school: Policy and practice. *Southern African Linguistics and Applied Language Studies, 34*(4), 347–357. doi.org/10.2989/16073614.2016.1261039

Krulatz, A., Christison, M., Lorenz, E., & Seviç, Y. (2021). The impact of teacher professional development on teacher cognition and multilingual teaching practices. *International Journal of Multilingualism*, 1–17. doi.org/10.1080/14790718.2022.2107648

Kwon, J. (2017). Immigrant mothers' beliefs and transnational strategies for their children's heritage language maintenance. *Language and Education, 31*(6), 495–508. doi.org/10.1080/09500782.2017.1349137

Labrianidis, L., & Hatziprokopiou, P. (2005). Albanian return migration: Migrants tend to return to their country of origin after all. In R. King, N. Mai, & S. Schwandner-Sievers (Eds.), *The new Albanian migration* (pp. 93–117). Sussex Academic Press.

Laleko, O. (2023). The roadmap of heritage language research in North America. In *Needed research in North American dialects* (Vol. 108, Issue 1, pp. 95–114). Duke University Press.

Lamb, T. (2020). Supplementary schools as spaces of hope for a more inclusive world: Challenging exclusion and social injustice in multilingual London. *Journal of Linguistics and Language Teaching, 11*(2), 99–127.

Landis, D., Bennett, J., & Bennett, M. (Eds.). (2004). *Handbook of intercultural training* (pp. 166–184).

Lane, T. (2013). The development of a happa. In A. Garrod, R. Kilkenny, & C. Gomez (Eds.), *Mixed: Multiracial college students tell their life stories* (p. 86). Cornell University Press.

Lannutti, V. (2014). *Identità sospese tra due culture: Formazione identitarie e dinamiche familiari delle seconde generazioni nelle Marche.* Franco Angeli.

Lannutti, V. (2016). La formazione identitaria delle seconde generazioni. *La Critica Sociologica, 198*(2).

Lanza, E., & Curdt-Christiansen, X. L. (Eds.). (2018). Multilingual family language management: Efforts, measures and choices. *Multilingua: Journal of Cross-Cultural and Interlanguage Communication, 37*(2).

Lanza, E. (1997). *Language mixing in infant bilingualism: A sociolinguistic perspective.* Oxford University Press.

Lao, R., & Lee, J. S. (2009). Heritage language maintenance and use among 1.5-generation Khmer college students. *Journal of Southeast Asian American Education & Advancement, 4.* jsaaea.coehd.utsa.edu/index.php/JSAAEA/article/view/50/59

Lave, J., & Wenger, E. (1991). *Situated learning: Legitimate peripheral participation.* Cambridge University Press. doi.org/10.1017/CBO9780511815355

Lee, G. L., & Gupta, A. (2020). Raising children to speak their heritage language in the USA: Roles of Korean parents. *Journal of Language Teaching and Research, 11*(4), 521–531. doi.org/10.17507/jltr.1104.01

Lee, J. S. (2002). The Korean language in America: The role of cultural identity in heritage language learning. *Language, Culture and Curriculum, 15*(2), 117–133.

Lee, J. S., & Shin, S. J. (2008). Korean heritage language education in the United States: The current state, opportunities, and possibilities. *Heritage Language Journal, 6*(2), 1–20.

Lee, J. S., & Wright, W. E. (2014). The rediscovery of heritage and community language education in the United States. *Review of Research in Education, 38*(1), 137–165. doi.org/10.3102/0091732X13507546

Lee, S. S.-H. (2018). After the watershed: Korean migration since 1965. In R. M. Joo & S. S.-H. Lee (Eds.), *A companion to Korean American studies* (pp. 21–46). BRILL. doi.org/10.1163/9789004335332_003

Lee, S., & Bang, Y. S. (2011). Listening to teacher lore: The challenges and resources of Korean heritage language teachers. *Teaching and Teacher Education, 27*(2), 387–394. doi.org/10.1016/j.tate.2010.09.008

Leeman, J. (2015). Heritage language education and identity in the United States. *Annual Review of Applied Linguistics, 35*, 100–119.

Levitt, P. (2010). Transnationalism. In K. Knott & S. McLoughlin (Eds.), *Diasporas: Concepts, intersections, identities* (pp. 39–44). Zed Books.

Li, W. (2011). Moment analysis and translanguaging space: Discursive construction of identities by multilingual Chinese youth in Britain. *Journal of Pragmatics, 43*(5), 1222–1235. doi.org/10.1016/j.pragma.2010.07.035

Liang, F. (2018). Parental perceptions toward and practices of heritage language maintenance: Focusing on the United States and Canada. *International Journal of Language Studies, 12*(2), 65–86.

Lico, A. L. (2015). Family and community in the teaching–learning process of Portuguese as a heritage language: From beginning to end [Família e comunidade no processo de ensino-aprendizagem de PLH: Do começo ao fim]. In F. Jennings-Winterle & M. C. Lima-Fernandes (Eds.), *Portuguese as a heritage language: The philosophy of beginning, middle, and end.* (pp. 214–226). BEM.

Lico, A. L. C. (2011). Ensino do português como língua de herança: Prática e fundamentos. *Revista SIPLE, 2*(1), 22–33. assiple.org/revista-siple

Lico, A. L. C., & Pires, L. F. (2022). Caminhos para manter viva a conexão dos adolescentes com sua língua e cultura de herança. In M. L. O. Alvarez, J. A. Ferraz, R. Albuquerque, & C. Moisés (Orgs.), *Bilinguismo e línguas de herança: Construindo pontes e diálogos entre línguas–culturas.* Pontes.

Lico, A. L. C., & Silva, G. V. (2021). Associações comunitárias. In A. Pilati & N. Viana (Orgs.), *Panorama da contribuição do Brasil para a difusão do português* (pp. 41–50). FUNAG – Fundação Alexandre de Gusmão. funag.gov.br/biblioteca-nova/produto/1-1162

Lindholm-Leary, K. J. (2001). *Dual language education.* Multilingual Matters.

Liu, N., Musica, A., Koscak, S., Vinogradova, P., & López, J. (2011). Challenges and needs of community-based heritage language programs and how they are assessed. *Heritage Briefs Collection.* cal.org/resource-center/resource-archive/heritage-briefs

Lo Bianco, J., & Peyton, J.K. (Eds.) (2013, Winter). Vitality of heritage languages in the United States. Special issue of the Heritage Language Journal, 10(3). *Heritage Language Journal* Volume 10 Issue 3 (2013) (brill.com) researchgate.net/publication/284165876

Lo Bianco, J., Liddicoat, A. J., & Crozet, C. (Eds.). (1999). *Striving for the third place: Intercultural competence through language education.* Australian National Languages and Literacy Institute.

LoBianco, M. (2022). A Cadillac in Briatico. In S. J. Sacco & A. De Marco (Eds.), *Calabrian voices: Diaspora stories from the younger generations* (pp. 108–122). Rubbettino.

Loi sur les écoles suisses à l'étranger (LESE, 21 March 2014). fedlex.admin.ch/eli/cc/2014/771/fr

Looyestyn, J., Kernot, J., Boshoff, K., Ryan, J., Edney, S., & Maher, C. (2017). Does gamification increase engagement with online programs? *Journal of Medical Internet Research, 19*(3), e70.

Ludanyi, R. (2014). German as a heritage language in the United States. In T. Wiley, J. K. Peyton, D. Christian, S. C. K. Moore, & N. Liu (Eds.), *Handbook of heritage, community, and Native American languages in the United States: Research, policy, and educational practice* (pp. 229–232). Routledge.

Lueder, D. C. (2011). *Involving hard-to-reach parents: Creating family/school partnerships.* Rowman & Littlefield Education.

Madrid, D. L., Cañas, M., & Ortega-Medina, M. (2007). Effects of team competition versus team cooperation in classwide peer tutoring. *Journal of Educational Research, 100*(3), 155–160.

Maggio, J., Soenens, M., & Marchesi, J. (Producers). (2020). *Birds of passage: The Italian Americans* [Documentary]. THIRTEEN. pbs.org/show/italian-americans/

Makalela, L. (2015). Translanguaging as a vehicle for epistemic access: Cases for reading comprehension and multilingual interactions. *Per Linguam, 31*(1), 15–29. dx.doi.org/10.5785/31-1-628

Makoe, P. (2018). Translanguaging in a monoglot context: Children mobilising and (re)positioning their multilingual repertoires as resources for learning. In G. Mazzaferro (Ed.), *Translanguaging as everyday practice* (Multilingual Education, Vol. 28, pp. 13–30). Springer.

Malone, M. E., Peyton, J. K., & Kim, K. (2014). Assessment of heritage language learners: Issues and directions. In T. G. Wiley, J. K. Peyton,

D. Christian, S. C. K. Moore, & N. Liu (Eds.), *Handbook of heritage, community, and Native American languages in the United States: Research, policy, and educational practice* (pp. 352–354). Routledge. doi.org/10.4324/9780203122419

Marashi, H., & Dibah, P. (2013). The comparative effect of using competitive and cooperative learning on the oral proficiency of Iranian introvert and extrovert EFL learners. *Journal of Language Teaching and Research, 4*(3), 545–556. doi.org/10.4304/jltr.4.3.545-556

Martinez, S. (2023). AI and cultural integration in reviving endangered languages. *ArXiv Linguistic Studies.*

Martinez, S., & Lee, H. (2024). Speech genomics applications for language learning. *ResearchGate Academic Press.*

Marvasti, A., & Tanner, S. (2020). Interviews with individuals. In D. Beach et al. (Eds.), *Handbook of qualitative research in education* (pp. 329–337). Edward Elgar. doi.org/10.4337/9781788977159.00039

May, S. (2013). *The multilingual turn: Implications for SLA, TESOL, and bilingual education.* Routledge.

Mbirimi-Hungwe, V. (2016). Translanguaging as a strategy for group work: Summary writing as a measure for reading comprehension among university students. *Southern African Linguistics and Applied Language Studies, 34*(3), 241–249. doi.org/10.2989/16073614.2016.1250352

McKinney, C., & Tyler, R. (2024). (Trans)languaging-for-learning: A perspective from the South. *Reading & Writing, 15*(1), a508. doi.org/10.4102/rw.v15i1.508

Means, B., Petersen, R., & Baker, E. (2014). *Learning online: What research tells us about whether, when, and how.* Routledge.

Megale, A. (2019). O conceito de repertório linguístico e sua implicação no ensino de PLH. *Lincool, 3*, 15–22.

Melo-Pfeifer, S. (2019). O que podem a "Toranja", os "Anfíbios" e os "Todo-o-Terreno" explicar acerca da LH? Reflexões acerca da didática do Português Língua de Herança. *Lincool, 3.*

Menken, K., & Sánchez, M. T. (2019). Translanguaging in English-only schools: From pedagogy to stance in the disruption of monolingual policies and practices. *TESOL Quarterly, 53*(3), 741–767. doi.org/10.1002/tesq.513

Menken, K., & Solorza, C. (2014). No child left bilingual: Accountability and the elimination of bilingual education programs in New York City schools. *Educational Policy, 28*(1), 96–125.

Mignolo, W. (2011). *The darker side of Western modernity: Global futures, decolonial options.* Duke University Press.
Min, P. G. (2000). Korean Americans' language use. In S. L. McKay & S. L. C. Wong (Eds.), *New immigrants in the United States: Readings for second language educators* (pp. 306–332). Cambridge University Press.
Min, P. G. (2011). The immigration of Koreans to the United States: A review of 45-year (1965–2009) trends. *Development and Society, 40*(2), 195–223. doi.org/10.2307/deveandsoci.40.2.195
Mingol, I. C. (2013). "Philosophical Perspectives on Caring Citizenship." *Peace Review* 253: 406–13.
Ministère de l'Éducation nationale et de la jeunesse. (2023a). *Les établissements scolaires d'enseignement français à l'étranger.* education.gouv.fr/les-etablissements-scolaires-d-enseignement-francais-l-etranger-8312
Ministère de l'Éducation nationale et de la jeunesse. (2023b). *Conseil d'orientation interministériel de l'enseignement français à l'étranger.* education.gouv.fr/conseil-d-orientation-interministeriel-de-l-enseignement-francais-l-etranger-378647
Ministerstvo školství, mládeže a tělovýchovy České republiky [Ministry of Education, Youth and Sports]. (2021). *Rámcový vzdělávací program pro základní vzdělávání* [Framework curriculum for compulsory education]. edu.cz/rvp-ramcove-vzdelavaci-programy/ramcovy-vzdelavaci-program-pro-zakladni-vzdelavani-rvp-zv/
Ministerstvo školství, mládeže a tělovýchovy. (2023). msmt.cz
Ministerstvo zahraničních věcí České republiky [Ministry of Foreign Affairs of the Czech Republic]. (2023). mzv.cz
Ministry of Education, Science and Culture. (2014). *The Icelandic national curriculum guide for compulsory schools – With subject areas.* government.is/library/01-Ministries/Ministry-of-Education/Curriculum/adalnrsk_greinask_ens_2014.pdf
Mister, B. (2023). The impact of heritage language on children's sense of belonging and connection to cultural heritage. LinkedIn.
Mkhize, D., & Balfour, R. (2017). Language rights in education in South Africa. *South African Journal of Higher Education, 31*(6), 133–150. dx.doi.org/10.20853/31.6.1633
Modern Language Association. (2021). Enrollments in Languages Other Than English in United States Institutions of Higher Education.
Molefe, E. (2022). Multilingualism in South African classrooms: Pedagogical practices and learner engagement. *Language and Education, 36*(5), 448–462.

Montrul, S. (2012). Is the heritage language like a second language? *EUROSLA Yearbook, 12*, 1–29.

Montrul, S. (2015). *The acquisition of heritage languages.* Cambridge University Press.

Montrul, S. (2016). *The acquisition of heritage languages.* Cambridge University Press.

Montrul, S., & Polinsky, M. (2021). *The Cambridge handbook of heritage languages and linguistics.* Cambridge University Press.

Morina, M. (2025). *Albanian heritage language learning in Canada: Understanding language maintenance and identity development among second-generation immigrants* (Doctoral dissertation, University of Calgary). University of Calgary Library. dx.doi.org/10.11575/PRISM/50278

Moreno-Fernández, F., & Lamas, Ó. (2023). Heritage languages and socialization: An introduction. *Journal of World Languages, 9*(1), 1–14. doi.org/10.1515/jwl-2022-0051

Moroni, A. (2015). Português como língua de herança: O começo de um movimento. In F. Jennings-Winterle & M. C. Lima-Hernandes (Orgs.), *Português como língua de herança: A filosofia do começo, meio e fim* (pp. 28–55). BeM.

Moroni, A. (2017). *Português como língua de herança na Catalunha: Representações sobre identificação, proficiência e afetividade* [Doctoral dissertation, Universidade Estadual de Campinas & Universitat de Barcelona]. Repositório da Unicamp. repositorio.unicamp.br/handle/REPOSIP/325381

Moskowitz, H. (2022). *A new science is born: Mind genomics.* Springer.

Moskowitz, H. R. (2022). *Mind genomics: The new science of everyday decisions.* Springer.

Motlhaka, H. A., & Makalela, L. (2016). Translanguaging in an academic writing class: Implications for a dialogic pedagogy. *Southern African Linguistics and Applied Language Studies, 34*(3), 251–260. doi.org/10.2989/16073614.2016.1250356

Mullis, I., Von Davier, M., Foy, P., Fishbein, B., Reynolds, K., & Wry, E. (2023). *PIRLS 2021 international results in reading.* TIMSS & PIRLS International Study Center. doi.org/10.6017/lse.tpisc.tr2103.kb5342

Müllner, J. (2021). K transformaci vzdělávacích soustav a evaluačních systémů na přelomu tisíciletí [On the transformation of educational and assessment systems at the turn of the millennium]. *Historia Scholastica: International Review for History of Education, 7*(2), 119–138.

Museus, S. D., Sariñana, S. A. L., Yee, A. L., & Robinson, T. E. (2016). A qualitative analysis of multiracial students' experiences with prejudice and discrimination in college. *Journal of College Student Development, 57*(6), 680–697. doi.org/10.1353/csd.2016.0068

Nadal, K. L., Sriken, J., Davidoff, K. C., Wong, Y., & McLean, K. (2013). Microaggressions within families: Experiences of multiracial people. *Family Relations, 62*(1), 190–201. doi.org/10.1111/j.1741-3729.2012.00752.x

National Heritage Language Resource Center. (2019). *Data on the demographics of presenters and participants in the NHLRC Heritage Language Research Institute (2010, 2014–2018).* NHLRC institutional archives.

New York State Education Department. (2019). *Blueprint for English language learner success.* nysed.gov/bilingual-ed/blueprint-english-language-learner-success

Nigris, E. (2015). *Pedagogia e didattica interculturale: Culture, contesti, linguaggi.* Pearson.

Norton, B. (2000). *Identity and language learning: Gender, ethnicity and educational change.* Pearson Education.

Norton, B. (2013). *Identity and language learning: Extending the conversation* (2nd ed.). Multilingual Matters.

Norton, B., & Davin, R. (2015). Identity, language learning, and critical pedagogies in digital times.

O'Brien, D. (2019). We aren't that different. In A. Garrod, R. Kilkenny, & C. Gomez (Eds.), *Mixed: Multiracial college students tell their life stories.* 147–157. Cornell University Press. doi.org/10.7591/9780801469169-013

O'Reilly, M., & Dogra, N. (2017). *Interviewing children and young people for research.* SAGE.

Obolensky, N. (2014). *Complex adaptive leadership: Embracing paradox and uncertainty.* Gower.

OECD. (2020). *What is the impact of the COVID-19 pandemic on immigrants and their children?* read.oecd-ilibrary.org/view/?ref=137_137245-8saheqv0k3&title=What-is-the-impact-of-the-COVID-19-pandemic-on-immigrants-and-their-children%3F

OECD. (2023). *PISA 2022 results (Volume I): The state of learning and equity in education.* OECD Publishing. doi.org/10.1787/53f23881-en

OECD. (2024). Greece. oecd-ilibrary.org/sites/7678fb89-en/index.html?itemId=/content/component/7678fb89-en

Office fédéral de la statistique. (2022). *Effectif des Suisses de l'étranger selon le pays ou le territoire de résidence, la circonscription consulaire, le droit de cité, le sexe et l'âge, 2016–2022.* bfs.admin.ch/bfs/fr/home/statistiques/population/migration-integration/suisses-etranger.assetdetail.24310292.html

Office for National Statistics. (2022). *Language, England and Wales: Census 2021.*

Office of the Secretary-General of the European Schools. (2023). *European schools locations.* eursc.eu/en/European-Schools/locations

Oh, J. S., & Fuligni, A. J. (2010). The role of heritage language development in the ethnic identity and family relationships of adolescents from immigrant backgrounds. *Social Development, 19*(1), 202–220.

Ólafsdóttir, S., Birgisdóttir, F., Ragnarsdóttir, H., & Skúlason, S. (2017). Íslenskur orðaforði og lesskilningur nemenda með íslensku sem annað mál: Tengsl við móðurmálskennslu [Icelandic vocabulary and reading comprehension of students with Icelandic as a second language: Connections with mother tongue instruction]. *Glæður, 27,* 35–51.

Otheguy, R., García, O., & Reid, W. (2015). Clarifying translanguaging and deconstructing named languages: A perspective from linguistics. *Applied Linguistics Review, 6*(3), 281–307. doi.org/10.1515/applirev-2015-0014

Ovando, C. J. (2003). Bilingual education in the United States: Historical development and current issues. *Bilingual Research Journal, 27*(1), 1–24.

Oyěwùmí, O. (1997). *The invention of women: Making an African sense of Western gender discourses.* University of Minnesota Press.

Ozturk, M. A., & Debelak, C. (2008). Academic competitions as tools for differentiation in middle school. *Gifted Child Today, 31*(3), 47–53. doi.org/10.4219/gct-2008-785

Pahl, K., & Kelly, S. (2005). Family literacy as a third space between home and school: Some case studies of practice. *Literacy, 39*(2), 91–96.

Pahl, K., & Rowsell, J. (2012). *Literacy and education: Understanding the new literacy studies in the classroom.* SAGE.

Pajares, F. (1996). Self-efficacy beliefs in academic settings. *Review of Educational Research, 66,* 543–587.

Palmer, D. K., Mateus, S. G., Martínez, R. A., & Henderson, K. (2014). Framing the debate on language separation: Toward a vision for translanguaging pedagogies in the dual language classroom. *Modern Language Journal, 98*(3), 757–772.

Paltridge, B. (2015). Language, identity, and communities of practice. In D. N. Djenar et al. (Eds.), *Language and identity across modes of communication*. De Gruyter.

Papi, M., & Hiver, P. (2020). Language learning motivation as a complex dynamic system: A global perspective of truth, control, and value. *Modern Language Journal, 104*(1), 209–232. doi.org/10.1111/modl.12624

Park, E. (2018). In search of the "Korean part": Reinforcing cultural boundaries in a Korean language school. *Anthropology & Education Quarterly, 49*(3), 279–295. doi.org/10.1111/aeq.12255

Park, M. Y., & Choi, L. J. (2022). Study abroad, heritage language learning, and identity: A study of a mixed-heritage learner of Korean. *Critical Inquiry in Language Studies, 19*(3), 286–306. doi.org/10.1080/15427587.2022.2086552

Park, M. Y., & Chung, K. (2023). Identity and heritage language learning: A case study of two mixed-heritage Korean university students in New Zealand. *Multilingua, 42*(2), 285–307. doi.org/10.1515/multi-2022-0044

Park, M., & Yun, J. (2017). Personalized learning analytics in online language education. *Educational Technology & Society, 20*(3), 211–223.

Park, S. M., & Sarkar, M. (2007). Parents' attitudes toward heritage language maintenance for their children and their efforts to help their children maintain the heritage language: A case study of Korean-Canadian immigrants. *Language, Culture and Curriculum, 20*(3), 223–235.

Patrikakou, E. N., Weissberg, R. P., Redding, S., & Walberg, H. J. (2005). *School–family partnerships for children's success*. Teachers College Press.

Patte, K. A., Gohari, M. R., & Leatherdale, S. T. (2021). Does school connectedness differ by student ethnicity? A latent class analysis among Canadian youth. *Multicultural Education Review, 13*(1), 64–84. doi.org/10.1080/2005615X.2021.1890310

Paulovicova, N., McCabe, M., & Emilsson Peskova, R. (2023). Transformations of diasporic heritage identities in Canada during the COVID-19 pandemic: From land-based communities to language-based global cyberspora. *History, Culture, and Heritage, 2*, 199–208 (AHM Conference 2023: Diasporic Heritage and Identity, Amsterdam). aup-online.com/content/papers/10.5117/978904856222/AHM.2023.022

Paulovicova, N., McCabe, M., & Emilsson Peskova, R. (2022). How heritage language schools offered grassroots community support through the pandemic. *The Conversation.* theconversation.com/how-heritage-language-schools-offered-grassroots-community-support-through-the-pandemic-177704

Pavlenko, A. (2006). Emotions and multilingualism: An integrated perspective. In *Emotions and multilingualism* (pp. 227–246). Cambridge University Press.

Pavlenko, A. (2012). Multilingualism and emotions. In M. Martin-Jones, A. Blackledge, & A. Creese (Eds.), *The Routledge handbook of multilingualism* (pp. 454–469). Routledge.

Pereira, M. (2020). O ensino de português como língua pluricêntrica: Perspectivas e desafios em um contexto de herança. In A. Souza & M. L. O. Alvarez (Orgs.), *Português como língua de herança: Uma disciplina que se estabelece* (pp. 21–45). Pontes.

Perkins, D. F., Davenport, K. E., Morgan, N. R., Aronson, K. R., Bleser, J. A., McCarthy, K. J., Vogt, D., Finley, E. P., Copeland, L. A., & Gilman, C. L. (2023). The influence of employment program components upon job attainment during a time of identity and career transition. *International Journal for Educational and Vocational Guidance, 23*(3), 695–717.

Perlin, R. (2024). *Language city: The fight to preserve endangered mother tongues in New York.* Atlantic Monthly Press.

Perrenoud, P. A. (2002). *Prática reflexiva no ofício de professor: Profissionalização e razão pedagógica.* ARTMED.

Peyton, J. K., Ranard, D. A., & McGinnis, S. (Eds.). (2001). *Heritage languages in America: Preserving a national resource.* Delta Systems & Center for Applied Linguistics.

Piccardo, E. (2013). Plurilingualism and curriculum design: Toward a synergic vision. *TESOL Quarterly, 47*(3), 600–614. doi.org/10.1002/tesq.110

Pimienta, D. (2021). Internet and linguistic diversity: The cybergeography of languages with the largest number of speakers. *LinguaPax Review 9: Language Technologies and Language Diversity,* 9–38. linguapax.org/wp-content/uploads/2022/02/LinguapaxReview9-2021-low.pdf

Pinho, A. S., Gonçalves, L., Andrade, A. I., & Araújo e Sá, M. H. (2011). Engaging with diversity in teacher language awareness: Teachers' thinking, enacting and transformation. In S. Breidbach, D. Elsner, & A. Young (Eds.), *Language awareness in teacher education:*

Cultural-political and socio-educational dimensions (pp. 41–61). Peter Lang.

Pope, A. (2024). Migration can work for all: A plan for replacing a broken global system. *Foreign Affairs, 103*(1).

Porter, L., et al. (2023). *Bilingual education and America's future: Evidence and pathways.* eScholarship.

Portera, A. (2019). Dal multiculturalismo all'educazione e alle competenze (realmente) interculturali. *Educazione Interculturale. Teorie, Ricerche, Pratiche, 17*(2).

Portes, A., & Rumbaut, R. G. (2001). *Legacies: The story of the immigrant second generation.* University of California Press.

Portes, A., & Rumbaut, R. G. (2014). *Immigrant America: A portrait* (4th ed.). University of California Press.

Pozzi, S. (2014). Trasmissione della lingua, integrazione e identità nelle famiglie immigrate. In M. V. Calvi, I. Bajini, & M. Bonomi (Eds.), *Lingue migranti e nuovi paesaggi.* Edizioni Universitarie di Lettere Economia Diritto.

Probyn, M. (2015). Pedagogical translanguaging: Bridging discourses in South African science classrooms. *Language and Education, 29*(3), 218–234. doi.org/10.1080/09500782.2014.994525

Probyn, M. (2019). Pedagogical translanguaging and the construction of science knowledge in a multilingual South African classroom: Challenging monoglossic/post-colonial orthodoxies. *Classroom Discourse, 10*(3–4), 216–236. doi.org/10.1080/19463014.2019.1628792

Project 1907. (2022). *Another year: Anti-Asian racism across Canada two years into COVID-19 pandemic.* ccncsj.ca/wp-content/uploads/2022/03/Anti-Asian-Racism-Across-Canada-Two-Years-Into-The-Pandemic_March-2022.pdf

Pshigusa, E. (2024). Equity/heritage and globalized human capital discourses in Ohio's Seal of Biliteracy policy, promotional materials, and stakeholder perceptions. *Foreign Language Annals, 57*(3), 593–611.

Ramezanzadeh, A.-M. (2015). *Exploring GCSE Arabic: An analysis of heritage and non-heritage language learner performance* (Master's thesis). University of Oxford.

Ramezanzadeh, A.-M. (2016). One size fits all? An analysis of heritage and non-heritage language learner performance in GCSE Arabic.

Roger, A., & Vinot, D. (2019). *Skills management: New applications, new questions.* John Wiley & Sons.

Rohlf, K. (2023, January 30). Birds of passage: Making sense of Italian ancestors who made multiple trips in and out of America. *New York Genealogical and Biographical Society*. newyorkfamilyhistory.org/blog/birds-passage-making-sense-italian-ancestors-who-made-multiple-trips-and-out-america

Rothman, J. (2009). Understanding the nature and outcomes of early bilingualism: Romance languages as heritage languages. *International Journal of Bilingualism, 13*(2), 155–163. doi.org/10.1177/1367006909339814

Ruiz, R. (1984). Orientations in language planning. *NABE Journal, 8*(2), 15–34.

Sacco, S. J. (2019). *Growing up Calabrese and other stories: A memoir*. DaSh Factor.

Sacco, S. J. (2024). Vedova bianca. In D. Candeloro, F. Di Pietro, & A. Angiuli Weiss (Eds.), *Italian women in Chicago* (pp. 17–21).

Sacco, S. J., & De Marco, A. (Eds.). (2022). *Calabrian voices: Diaspora stories from the younger generations*. Rubbettino.

Schader, B. (2015). *Principes et contextes. Matériel pour l'enseignement de la langue et de la culture d'origine* [Principles and contexts. Materials for the teaching of heritage language and culture]. Centre IPE, Haute école pédagogique de Zurich / University of Zürich.

Schaffer, M. (2005). Bound to Africa: The Mandinka legacy in the New World. *History in Africa: A Journal of Method, 32*, 321–369. jstor.org/stable/20065748

Scheckle, E. (2022). Mediating meaning in book talk: Reading clubs as third spaces. *Per Linguam: A Journal of Language Learning, 38*(1), 27–43.

Schiefer, D., & van der Noll, J. (2017). The essentials of social cohesion: A literature review. *Social Indicators Research, 132*(2), 579–603. doi.org/10.1007/s11205-016-1314-5

Schoeman, J. C., Geertsema, S., Le Roux, M., & Pottas, L. (2023). The effect of pedagogical translanguaging on Foundation Phase classrooms in a South African private school. *Journal of Language, Identity & Education*, 1–18.

Schröder-Sura, A., Noguerol, A., & Molinié, M. (2012). *Le CARAP – Un Cadre de Référence pour les Approches plurielles des langues et des cultures: Compétences et ressources*. Conseil de l'Europe.

Schwartz, A. M. (2001). Preparing teachers to work with heritage language learners. In J. K. Peyton, D. A. Ranard, & S. McGinnis (Eds.), *Heritage languages in America: Preserving a national resource*

(Language in Education: Theory and Practice). Delta Systems Company Inc.

Seals, C. (2017). Positive and negative identity practices in heritage language education. *International Journal of Multilingualism, 15*(4), 329–348. doi.org/10.1080/14790718.2017.1306065

Seals, C. A., & Peyton, J. K. (2017). Heritage language education: Valuing the languages, literacies, and cultural competencies of immigrant youth. *Current Issues in Language Planning, 18*(1), 87–101. doi.org/10.1080/14664208.2016.1168690

Seals, C. A., & Shah, S. (2018). Heritage language policies around the world: Mapping an emerging field. *Current Issues in Language Planning, 19*(1), 1–7.

Seltzer, K., & García, O. (2020). Broadening the view: Taking up a translanguaging pedagogy with all language-minoritized students. In *Envisioning TESOL through a translanguaging lens: Global perspectives* (pp. 23–42).

Seo, Y. (2022). Becoming and belonging: Ethnic identity development of young children through language socialization. *Heritage Language Journal, 19*, 1–30.

Service de la recherche en éducation de Genève. (2023). *[Publications and reports]*.

Service Public. (2023). *Simulateur : Scolarité d'un enfant français à l'étranger*. service-public.fr/particuliers/vosdroits/F1898

Shibata, S. (2000). Opening a Japanese Saturday school in a small town in the United States: Community collaboration to teach Japanese as a heritage language. *Bilingual Research Journal, 24*(4), 465–474.

Shin, S. J. (2004). *Developing in two languages: Korean children in America*. Multilingual Matters.

Shin, S. J. (2013). Transforming culture and identity: Transnational adoptive families and heritage language learning. *Language, Culture and Curriculum, 26*(2), 161–178. doi.org/10.1080/07908318.2013.809095

Shin, S. J. (2014). Language learning as culture keeping: Family language policies of transnational adoptive parents. *International Multilingual Research Journal, 8*(3), 189–207. doi.org/10.1080/19313152.2014.911052

Shin, S. J., & Lee, J. S. (2013). Expanding capacity, opportunity, and desire to learn Korean as a heritage language. *Heritage Language Journal, 10*(3), 357–366. doi.org/10.46538/hlj.10.3.7

Shohamy, E. (2006). *Language policy: Hidden agendas and new approaches*. Routledge.

Showstack, R., Pascual y Cabo, D., & Vergara Wilson, D. (2024). *Language ideologies and linguistic identity in heritage language learning*. Routledge.

Shute, V. J., & Zapata-Rivera, D. (2012). Adaptive educational systems. In W. J. van der Linden & C. A. Pashley (Eds.), *Elements of adaptive testing* (pp. 129–154). Springer.

Sierens, S., & Van Avermaet, P. (2014). Language diversity in education: Evolving from multilingual education to functional multilingual learning. *European Journal of Applied Linguistics, 2*(1), 1–23. doi.org/10.1515/eujal-2014-0001

Sikes, C. L., & Piñón, L. (2024). *The path to a stronger state seal of biliteracy: Advancing Texas student success through bilingualism and biliteracy* (IDRA Policy Brief). Intercultural Development Research Association.

Silva, G. V., & Da Costa, E. V. (2020). What do teachers want? Professional development opportunities for instructors of Portuguese as a heritage language. In S. Melo-Pfeifer & M. L. S. Gonçalves (Orgs.), *Português língua de herança e formação de professores* (pp. 41–62). Lidel.

Silva, G. V. (2016). Nem nativo nem estrangeiro: O português como língua de herança. *New Routes, 59*, 28–30. disal.com.br/newR/

Simkin, J. (2020). *Italian immigration*. Spartacus Educational. spartacus-educational.com/USAEitaly.htm

Skerrett, A. (2013). *Bilingual teaching and learning in primary schools*. Routledge.

Školský zákon [Education Act] 561/2004 Sb. (Czech Republic). zakony.centrum.cz/skolsky-zakon/cast-3-hlava-1-paragraf-38

Smith, T., Jones, R., Abu-Khalid, S., & Lee, H. (2023). The science of mind genomics and its application. *MedCrave Scientific Publishing*.

Soliman, R., & Khalil, S. (2022). The teaching of Arabic as a community language in the UK. *International Journal of Bilingual Education and Bilingualism, 27*(9), 1246–1257. doi.org/10.1080/13670050.2022.2063686

Song, D. S., Ahmed, A., Gilkes Borr, T., & Antonio, A. L. (2022). Multiracials' membership and identification practices on campus: A boundary-work approach. *Race, Ethnicity and Education*, Advance online publication, 1–21. doi.org/10.1080/13613324.2022.2114510

Song, K. (2016). "Okay, I will say in Korean and then in American": Translanguaging practices in bilingual homes. *Journal of Early Childhood Literacy, 16*(1), 84–106. doi.org/10.1177/1468798414566705

Song, M., & Liebler, C. (2022). What motivates mixed heritage people to assert their ancestries? *Genealogy, 6*(3), 61. doi.org/10.3390/genealogy6030061

Spaull, N. (2023). *Background report for the 2030 Reading Panel.* groundup.org.za/media/uploads/documents/embargoed_2023_reading_panel_background_report_7_feb_2023.pdf

Statista. (2023). *Population totale de la France de 1950 à 2023.* fr.statista.com/statistiques/471946/population-totale-france/

Statistický informační systém Ministerstva školství, mládeže a tělovýchovy. (2023). *Ročenka školství* [Education yearbook]. statis.msmt.cz/rocenka/rocenka.asp

Statistics Canada. (2016). *Census profile: Canada.*

Statistics Canada. (2021). *Generation status: Canadian-born children of immigrants.* www12.statcan.gc.ca/nhs-enm/2011/as-sa/99-010-x/99-010-x2011003_2-eng.cfm

Statistics Iceland. (2023). *Inhabitants.* statice.is/statistics/population/inhabitants/

Su, C.-H., & Cheng, C.-H. (2015). A mobile gamification learning system for improving the learning motivation and achievements. *Computers & Education, 88*, 48–58.

Svensson, P. (2004). *Dispelling the myth of the real in educational technology.* Paper presented at the Open University, Milton Keynes, UK.

Szoszkiewicz, L. (2017). Linguistic human rights in education. *Przegląd Prawniczy Uniwersytetu im. Adam Mickiewicza, 7*, 105–118. doi.org/10.14746/ppuam.2017.7.07

Taylor, L. (2008). Looking north: Exploring multiracial experiences in a Canadian context. *New Directions for Student Services, 2008*(123), 83–91. doi.org/10.1002/ss.289

Þjóðskrá [Registers Iceland]. (2023). skra.is/english/

Thomas, W. P., & Collier, V. P. (2012). *Dual language education for a transformed world.* Dual Language Education of New Mexico.

Thornberg, R., & Charmaz, K. (2014). Grounded theory and theoretical coding. In *The SAGE handbook of qualitative data analysis* (pp. 153–169).

Tollefson, J. W. (2013). *Language policies in education: Critical issues.* Routledge.

Tomlinson, C. A. (2017). *How to differentiate instruction in academically diverse classrooms* (3rd ed.). ASCD.

Topping, K., Duran, D., & Van Keer, H. (2015). *Using peer tutoring to improve reading skills* (0 ed.). Routledge. doi.org/10.4324/9781315731032

Trentman, E. (2015). Arabic heritage learners abroad: Language use and identity negotiation. *Al-'Arabiyya, 48,* 141–156. Georgetown University Press.

Tronto, J. C. (2013). *Caring Democracy: Markets, Equality and Justice.* NYU Press.

Trump, D. J. (2025, March 1). Executive Order 14224: Declaring English as the official language of the United States. *Federal Register, 90*(45), 11363–11365. federalregister.gov/d/2025-04224

Tungohan, E. (2023). *Care activism: Migrant domestic workers, movement-building and communities of care.* University of Illinois Press.

Tyler, R. (2023). *Translanguaging, coloniality, and decolonial cracks: Bilingual science learning in South Africa.* Multilingual Matters.

UN General Assembly. (1989). *Convention on the Rights of the Child.* United Nations, Treaty Series, 1577(3). refworld.org/docid/3ae6b38f0.html

UNESCO. (1996). *World Conference on Linguistic Rights: Barcelona Declaration.* unesdoc.unesco.org/ark:/48223/pf0000104267

UNESCO. (2003). *Language vitality and endangerment.* UNESCO Publications. unesdoc.unesco.org/ark:/48223/pf0000183699

UNESCO. (2021). *World report on endangered languages.* United Nations Educational, Scientific and Cultural Organization.

United Nations. (2020). *Population Division.* un.org/development/desa/pd/content/international-migration-1

United Nations. (1948). *Universal Declaration of Human Rights.* un.org/en/about-us/universal-declaration-of-human-rights

U.S. Census Bureau, *The Foreign-Born Population in the United States: 2022* ACSBR-019, April 2024.

U.S. Census Bureau. (2021). *Languages spoken at home: 2021 American Community Survey.* census.gov/data.html

U.S. Census Report. (2019). *2019 U.S. population estimates continue to show the nation's growth is slowing.*

U.S. Department of State. (2025). *Non-Governmental Organizations NGOs in the United States.*

Usher, A., & Kober, N. (2012). *Student motivation: An overlooked piece of school reform.* files.eric.ed.gov/fulltext/ED532666.pdf

Val, A., & Vinogradova, P. (2010). What is the identity of a heritage language speaker? *Heritage Briefs.* Center for Applied Linguistics.

Valdés, G. (2000). The teaching of heritage languages: An introduction for Slavic-teaching professionals. In O. Kagan & B. Rifkin (Eds.), *The learning and teaching of Slavic languages and cultures* (1st ed., pp. 375–403). Slavica Publishers.

Valdés, G. (2001). Heritage language students: Profiles and possibilities. In J. K. Peyton, D. A. Ranard, & S. McGinnis (Eds.), *Heritage languages in America: Preserving a national resource. Language in Education: Theory and Practice* (pp. 37–77). Delta Systems Company Inc.

Valdés, G. (2005). Bilingualism, heritage language learners, and SLA research: Opportunities lost or seized? *The Modern Language Journal, 89*(3), 410–426.

Van Deusen-Scholl, N. (2003). Toward a definition of heritage language: Sociopolitical and pedagogical considerations. *Journal of Language, Identity & Education, 2*(3), 211–230. doi.org/10.1207/s15327701jlie0203_4

VanLehn, K. (2011). The relative effectiveness of human tutoring, intelligent tutoring systems, and other tutoring systems. *Educational Psychologist, 46*(4), 197–221.

Vasquez, C. (2020). *Critical literacies in the classroom: Teaching and learning through the lens of social justice.* Routledge.

Vehabovic, N. (2020). Stories as life performances: Humanizing research as honoring, respecting, listening to, and learning with children, youth, and families from refugee backgrounds. *Multiculturalism Perspectives, 22*(4), 210–219.

Velásquez, I. (2019). *Household perspectives on minority language maintenance and loss.* Multilingual Matters.

Vollmer, H. (2010). Lingua(e) delle altre discipline. *Italiano LinguaDue,* (1).

Vygotskij, L. S. (1990). *Pensiero e linguaggio* (L. Mecacci, Ed.). Laterza.

Vygotsky, L. S. (1978). *Mind in society: The development of higher psychological processes.* Harvard University Press.

Výzkumné projekty Čeští krajané [Research Projects Czech Compatriots]. (2023). cestikrajane.cz

Wallace, K. R. (2004). Situating multiethnic identity: Contributions of discourse theory to the study of mixed heritage students. *Journal of Language, Identity, and Education, 3*(3), 195–213. doi.org/10.1207/s15327701jlie0303_2

Wang, S. C. (2024, November 6). Looking at the components of learning in community-based heritage language schools. *Community-based Heritage Language Coalition Webinar.*

Wang, X. (2015). *Maintaining three languages: The teenage years* (Parents' and Teachers' Guides Book 22). Channel View Publications. multilingual-matters.com/page/detail/Maintaining-Three-Languages/?k=9781783094479

Wang, Y. (2023). Speaking Chinese or no breakfast: Emotional challenges and experiences confronting Chinese immigrant families in heritage language maintenance. *The International Journal of Bilingualism, 27*(2), 232–250. doi.org/10.1177/13670069221126043

Warschauer, M. (2000). The changing global economy and the future of English teaching. *TESOL Quarterly, 34*(3), 511–535.

Wenger, E., McDermott, A. R., & Snyder, W. (2002). *Cultivating communities of practice: A guide to managing knowledge.* Harvard Business School Press.

Wernicke, M. (2022). "I'm trilingual—so what?" Official French/English bilingualism, race, and French language teachers' linguistic identities in Canada. *Canadian Modern Language Review, 78*(4), 344–362.

Wild, L., Emoekabu, D., & Graham, R. (2022). *Teaching of Arabic in U.K. schools: Research report.*

Wilder, S. (2014). Effects of parental involvement on academic achievement: A meta-synthesis. *Educational Review, 66*(3), 377–397. doi.org/10.1080/00131911.2013.780009

Wiley, T. G. (2001). On defining heritage languages and their speakers. In J. K. Peyton, D. A. Ranard, & S. McGinnis (Eds.), *Heritage languages in America: Preserving a national resource. Language in Education: Theory and Practice* (p. 29). Delta Systems Company Inc.

Wiley, T. G., & García, O. (2016). Language policy and planning in language education: Legacies, consequences, and possibilities in the United States. *The Modern Language Journal, 36*, 48–63.

Wiley, T. G., & Valdés, G. (2000). Editors' introduction: Heritage language instruction in the United States: A time for renewal. *Bilingual Research Journal, 24*(4). doi.org/10.1080/15235882.2000.10162770

Wiley, T. G., & Wright, W. E. (2004). Against the undertow: Language minority education policy and politics in the "age of accountability." *Educational Policy, 18*(1), 142–168.

Wiley, T. W., Peyton, J. K., Christian, D., Moore, S. C., & Liu, N. (Eds.). (2014). *Handbook of heritage, community, and Native American languages in the United States: Research, educational practice, and policy.* Routledge.

Woodley, X. M., & Lockard, M. (2016). Womanism and snowball sampling: Engaging marginalized populations in holistic research. *The Qualitative Report, 21*(2), 321–329. doi.org/10.46743/2160-3715/2016.2198

Woolf, B. P. (2010). *Building intelligent interactive tutors: Student-centered strategies for revolutionizing e-learning.* Morgan Kaufmann.

Yazan, B., & Ali, N. L. (2019). Pedagogical translanguaging in bilingual classrooms: An introduction. *International Journal of Bilingual Education and Bilingualism, 22*(2), 157–162. doi.org/10.1080/17501229.2019.1579219

Yip, J., & García, O. (2015). Translanguaging: Practice briefs for educators. *Theory, Research, and Action in Urban Education, 4*(1).

Yu, S. C. (2015). The relationships among heritage language proficiency, ethnic identity, and self-esteem. *FIRE: Forum for International Research in Education, 2*(2), 57–71.

Zhou, Y., & Liu, Y. (2022). Theorizing the dynamics of heritage language identity development: A narrative inquiry of the life histories of three Chinese heritage speakers. *Language and Education, 37*(3), 383–400. doi.org/10.1080/09500782.2022.2068351

Zimmerman, B. J., & Schunk, D. H. (2011). *Handbook of self-regulation of learning and performance.* Routledge.

About TBR Books

TBR Books is a program of the Center for the Advancement of Languages, Education, and Communities. We publish researchers and practitioners seeking to engage diverse communities on education, languages, cultural history, and social initiatives. We translate our books into various languages to further expand our impact.

BOOKS IN ENGLISH

Myths and Facts about Multilingualism by J. Franck, F. Faloppa, T. Marinis.
Mosaic of Tongues: Multilingual Learning for the Arabic-speaking World by C. Allaf, F. Jaumont, and S. Tahla Jebril
A Bilingual Revolution for Africa by A.C. Hager M'Boua, F. Jaumont
Bilingual Children: Families, Education, Development by Ellen Bialystok
The Heart of an Artichoke by Linda Ashour and Claire Lerognon
French All Around Us by Kathleen Stein-Smith and Fabrice Jaumont
Navigating Dual Immersion: by Valerie Sun
Conversations on Bilingualism by Fabrice Jaumont
The Hummingbird Project by Vickie Frémont
One Good Question by Rhonda Broussard
Can We Agree to Disagree? by Sabine Landolt and Agathe Laurent
Salsa Dancing in Gym Shoes by T. Oberg de la Garza and A. Lavigne
Beyond Gibraltar; The Other Shore; Mamma in her Village by M. Lorch
The Clarks of Willsborough Point by Darcey Hale
The English Patchwork by Pedro Tozzi and Giovanna de Lima

Peshtigo 1871 by Charles Mercier
The Word of the Month by Ben Lévy, Jim Sheppard, Andrew Arnon
Two Centuries of French Education in New York by Jane Flatau Ross
The Bilingual Revolution by Fabrice Jaumont

BOOKS FOR CHILDREN (available in several languages)

The Adventures of Zenzi and the Talking Bird by Fadzai Gwaradzimba
Biscotte and The New Kid by K. Cohen-Dicker and A. Angeles
Lapin is Hungry by Tania & Olivier Czajka
Uniquely You! by Bertrand Tchoumi
Franglais Soup e by Adrienne Mei
Morgan; Rainbows, Masks, and Ice Cream by Deana Sobel Lederman
Korean Super New Years with Grandma by Mary Kim, Eunjoo Feaster
Math for All by Mark Hansen
Rose Alone by Sheila Decosse
Uncle Steve's Country Home; The Blue Dress; The Good, the Ugly, and the Great by Teboho Moja
Immunity Fun!; Respiratory Fun!; Digestive Fun! By D. Stewart-McMeel
Marimba by C. Hélot, P. Velasco, A. Kojton

Our books, such as paperbacks and e-books, are available on our website and in all major online bookstores. Some of our books have been translated into over twenty languages. For a listing of all books published by TBR Books, information on our series, or our submission guidelines for authors, visit our website at:

www.calec.org

About CALEC

The Center for the Advancement of Languages, Education, and Communities (CALEC) is a nonprofit organization that promotes multilingualism, empowers multilingual families, and fosters cross-cultural understanding. The Center's mission aligns with the United Nations' Sustainable Development Goals. Our mission is to establish language as a critical life skill by developing and implementing bilingual education programs, promoting diversity, reducing inequality, and helping to provide quality education. Our programs seek to protect world cultural heritage and support teachers, authors, and families by providing the knowledge and resources to create vibrant multilingual communities.

The specific objectives and purpose of our organization are:

- To develop and implement education programs that promote multilingualism and cross-cultural understanding, and establish an inclusive and equitable quality education, including internship and leadership training. [SDG # 4, Quality Education]
- To publish and distribute resources, including research papers, books, and case studies that seek to empower and promote the social, economic, and political inclusion of all, focusing on language education and cultural diversity, equity, and inclusion. [SDG # 10, Reduced Inequalities]
- To help build sustainable cities and communities and support teachers, authors, researchers, and families in advancing multilingualism and cross-cultural understanding through collaborative tools for linguistic communities. [SDG # 11, Sustainable Cities and Communities]

- To foster solid global partnerships and cooperation, mobilize resources across borders, participate in events and activities that promote language education through knowledge sharing and coaching, empower parents and teachers, and build multilingual societies. [SDG # 17, Partnerships for the Goals]

SOME GOOD REASONS TO SUPPORT US

Your donation helps:

- Develop our publishing and translation activities so that more languages are represented.
- Provide access to our online book platform to daycare centers, schools, and cultural centers in underserved areas.
- Support local and sustainable action in favor of education and multilingualism.
- Implement projects that advance dual-language education.
- Organize workshops for parents, conferences with large audiences, meet-the-author chats, and talks with experts in multilingualism.

DONATE ONLINE

For all your questions, contact our team by email at contact@calec.org or donate online on our website:

www.calec.org

www.ingramcontent.com/pod-product-compliance
Lightning Source LLC
Chambersburg PA
CBHW031843220426
43663CB00006B/480